INDIAN ANGLES

Sri Rāga, c. 1595. From *The Yorck Project: 10.000 Meisterwerke der Malerei.*

INDIAN ANGLES

ENGLISH VERSE IN COLONIAL INDIA FROM JONES TO TAGORE

Mary Ellis Gibson

Ohio University Press

Athens

Ohio University Press, Athens, Ohio 45701
www.ohioswallow.com

Printed in the United States of America
Ohio University Press books are printed on acid-free paper ∞ ™

First paperback printed in 2023
Paperback ISBN: 978-0-8214-2521-3

Library of Congress Cataloging-in-Publication Data

Gibson, Mary Ellis, 1952–
Indian angles : English verse in colonial India from Jones to Tagore / Mary Ellis Gibson.
p. cm.
Includes bibliographical references and index.
ISBN 978-0-8214-1941-0 (hardcover : alk. paper) — ISBN 978-0-8214-4358-3 (electronic)
1. Anglo-Indian poetry—History and criticism. 2. Indic poetry (English)—History and criticism. 3. India—In literature. 4. Colonies in literature. I. Title.
PR9490.4.G53 2011
821.009'954—dc22

2010053693

for Sanjukta Dasgupta and Elizabeth K. Helsinger

CONTENTS

ILLUSTRATIONS

ACKNOWLEDGMENTS

A book long in the making gathers many debts. Many institutions and colleagues, my long-suffering family, and my friends here and in India have encouraged my work and made it a pleasure.

My debts to scholars whom I do not know or have only met briefly, I acknowledge as often as I can in the chapters that follow. I want to express here my gratitude to several scholars who are pioneering new ways of understanding English language literature in India. I owe more than I can acknowledge to Priya Joshi, Rimi Chatterjee, Ghulam Murshid, and especially Rosinka Chaudhuri, whose wonderful edition of Derozio appeared just as I was revising my work and whose monograph and essays had already guided my thinking.

Without substantial material support at crucial times, I would not have been able to research this book, and for this I am grateful to my home institution, the University of North Carolina at Greensboro, which provided travel funding and research assignments on more than one occasion. I am especially grateful to Anne Wallace, chair of the English Department and fellow scholar of nineteenth-century literature, to Timothy Johnston, dean of the College of Arts and Sciences, and to former provost Edward Uprichard for their willingness to support an extended research assignment. Another form of support, no less important, came from Carole Lindsey-Potter, whose exemplary patience, energy, and creativity allowed me to continue work on this project even during my administrative assignment as director of the Women's and Gender Studies Program.

For the financial assistance that made this research possible, I am grateful to the Fulbright Commission, and for assistance in India, to the wonderful staff at the U.S. Educational Foundation office in Kolkata, including Sunrit Mullick and Shevanti Narayan. They did much to make my stay in Kolkata pleasant and to connect me with scholars in Kolkata and North Bengal.

I received crucial support from the National Endowment for the Humanities, whose research fellowship allowed me to complete this project. At the National Humanities Center, help went well beyond the financial. The John Sawyer Fellowship at the Humanities Center had more impact on this project than any other form of assistance I have received, for the center provided exactly the kind of cross-disciplinary exchange that fed my thinking—and it fed me in body and spirit as well. The staff of the NHC and its director, Geoffrey Harpham, created an atmosphere of congenial exchange and intellectual excitement. I am grateful to Kent Mullikin for being master of arrangements and raconteur par excellence; to Lois Whittington for providing photocopying, scheduling, and encouragement to enable a year-long seminar; to Pat

Shreiber and James Getkin for keeping me fit and wonderfully fed; to Joel Elliott for technical support; to Marie Brubaker; to Marianne Wason for teaching me to create effective PowerPoint presentations; to Sarah Payne for biscuit baking; and to all the staff for much good conversation.

My colleagues at the center influenced this work in more ways than I can say. Amelie Rorty, Judith Farquhar, Kate Flint, Roger Gilbert, Alexandra Wettlaufer, John Wilkinson, Terry Smith, and Maud Ellman provided ideas, argument, lunch companionship, and personal encouragement. To the members of the Master Languages and Vernaculars Seminar, I am especially grateful. Nigel Smith and Timothy Kircher provided organizational energy, and they and other members of the seminar (Catherine Chin, Su Fang Ng, Stephen Rupp, Alison Keith, David Samuelson) profoundly shaped my thinking on matters of language, culture, and power. In addition, Tim and Nigel read a very long first chapter, and Alison Keith helped me to untangle Propertius and other matters of Latin translation. I extend a thousand thanks to them all. And finally, I cannot express adequate thanks to Elizabeth Helsinger, a fellow at the center but much more to me—both my mentor and my example over many years and at last, for a year, a colleague.

Nor could this book have been made without ongoing assistance from many librarians. The librarians at the National Humanities Center were indispensable to this project: Eliza Robertson provided important ideas and database assistance, Jean Houston provided books of all sorts, and Josiah Drewery managed to find in distant libraries obscure texts in languages he did not read. To the librarians at the University of North Carolina, Greensboro, I am equally grateful—they supplied books from storage and remained patient when the dog ate the ones made with horsehair glue. To Gaylor Callahan, head of Interlibrary Loan, and to Nancy Fogarty, head emerita of the Reference Department, I owe a major debt. In Kolkata, I am grateful to M. Mukherjee of reader services at the National Library, who saved me from despair. I am also grateful to Fr. Dr. Felix Raj, director of the Goethals Library, St. Xavier's College, Kolkata, and to the staff of the library, especially former head of staff Warren Brown, who provided kind assistance and searched the collection in aid of my project. Similarly, the staff of the Carey Library, Serampore, allowed me access to their valuable collection of English language books and pamphlets. The staff of the Asian and African Studies Reading Room of the British Library were unfailingly helpful; to all of them I am grateful, as I am to special collections librarians at the Bodleian Library, Oxford, and at Harvard University, the University of Virginia, the University of Delaware, the University of North Carolina, and Duke University.

For research assistance, I thank Thera Webb, fine poet and patient bibliographer; Charles Orzech, who can find anything on the Web; and, in Kolkata, Hena Basu of Basu Research and Documentation Services, who provided me with invaluable aid of all sorts. Julia Kimmel was of invaluable assistance at the end of this project, as was Hao Nguyen.

All writing is a group effort, and that is true of this project more than most. For editing an early draft of the initial chapter, I am grateful to Karen Carroll of the National Humanities Center. For reading a tangled draft of the last, I am indebted to Richard Alan Schwartz, who cut to the heart of the matter. For getting me through the last stages of this project, I am deeply grateful to my writing group. Karen Kilcup, Hepsibah Roskelly, and Karen Weyler brought their great love of poetry, their historical acumen, and their incisive editing skills to my prose. They gave me deadlines, and they read sections of my manuscript when they were overwhelmed with work.

The editors at Ohio University Press have made this book a better one from the beginning. David Sanders, former director of the press, had faith in the project and encouraged me to undertake both volumes, monograph and anthology, at once. Nancy Basmajian, managing editor, and copyeditor Sally Bennett have provided a level of editorial oversight beyond my best hope, sharpening the prose, correcting my errors, and attending to the details of a lovely design by Beth Pratt.

I also thank my colleagues in Kolkata, especially Jharna Sanyal, who made my affiliation with Calcutta University particularly delightful. I thank as well Geraldine Forbes, colleague extraordinaire, and I remember, with sadness and gratitude, the late Lucinda Peach, my Fulbright companion in 2004. To Mousumi Mukherjee, I owe what I know of Bangla and how to direct a cab driver in Kolkata; I am vastly appreciative of her help in myriad ways during my stay in Kolkata and for the hospitality of her family.

This book began with Paul Courtright of Emory University, who got me started. Years ago he shared poems by Horace Hayman Williams and introduced me to the Orientalist-Anglicist debates in nineteenth-century Calcutta—though I am sure he has forgotten this. I owe deep thanks to Tony Stewart, who picked up the baton from Paul and has encouraged me in so many ways—translating, correcting my pronunciation, laughing me out of my errors (or, at least, as many as possible), sharing his love for poetry, and sharing his friends in Kolkata. His help has been enabling in endless ways; the errors remaining are my own. And to our mutual friends in Kolkata—Ajoy and Trina Roy and to the late Anna Roy, to Rukshana and Nasheed Moiz and the late Jaweed Moiz—I owe many happy hours, much laughter, delicious jazz and biryani.

Finally, I thank Sanjukta Dasgupta, professor of English and now dean at Calcutta University: the best of landladies, the best of colleagues, the best of friends. She argued with me about mother tongues, took me to poetry readings, fed me, introduced me to many fine colleagues and students, and rescued me from a thousand difficulties. To her and to Anjan Dasgupta I am most grateful.

To my husband, Charles Orzech—fine historian, incisive theorist, enthusiastic traveling companion, and general encourager—and to my daughter, Emily Orzech, who paints across cultures and loves to travel and argue ideas, I owe so much. They have tolerated my obsessions, supported my work, and cheered me on. In too many ways to count, they have made this a better book.

A NOTE ON NAMES

Aside from the acknowledgments and mentions of contemporary cities (for which I follow current usage), I have followed the nineteenth-century convention in naming Indian cities. Thus, instead of using the names Kolkata, Mumbai, and Chennai, I refer—as the poets I discuss do—to Calcutta, Bombay, and Madras, respectively.

In referring to persons with Indian names, I have followed the conventions of Anglicization they adopted, so rather than Torulata Datta or Rabindranath Thakur, I use Toru Dutt and Rabindranath Tagore. Similarly, though Roy (Rammohun Roy) can be transliterated as Ray and Ghosh (Kasiprasad Ghosh) as Ghose, I follow these writers' own practices. A more complex case is Michael Madhusudan Datta, who at the end of his life preferred Datta to Dutt. His translator Clinton Seely follows his wishes and always transliterates his name as Datta; because I am discussing primarily his early English work, published under the name Dutt, I use the poet's earlier transliteration.

Many writers in Bengal share surnames—for example, Toru, Aru, Omesh Chunder, Girish Chunder, and Michael Madhusudan Dutt—and they are conventionally referred to by given name as well as surname. I follow this practice for writers with Indian names. When discussing writers with European names, however, I follow the common scholarly practice of referring to them by surname. For example, I speak of Toru when referring to Toru Dutt but to Carshore when speaking of Mary Seyers Carshore.

A second issue of transliteration—the use of diacritics—arises with respect to words from Indian languages. When I quote texts directly, I always reproduce diacritics, if any, as given in the text. When I refer to terms now commonly used as English words (e.g., *sati*), I follow common English practice, omitting the diacritics.

INTRODUCTION

The Asiatic Society, Kolkata. A toxic blend of coal dust and diesel exhaust streaks the façade with grime. The concrete of the new wing, once a soft yellow, now is dimmed. Mold, ever the enemy, creeps from around drainpipes. Inside, an old mahogany staircase ascends past dusty paintings. The eighteenth-century fathers of the society line the stairs, their white linen and their pale skin yellow with age.

I have come to sue for admission, bearing letters with university and government seals, hoping that official papers of one bureaucracy will be found acceptable by another. I am a little worried, as one must be about any bureaucratic encounter.

But the person at the desk in reader services is polite, even friendly. Once he has enquired about my project, he becomes enthusiastic.

"Ah, English language poetry," he says. "Coleridge. 'Oh Lady we receive but what we give . . . and in our lives alone doth nature live.'"

And I, "Ours her wedding garment, ours her shroud."

And he, "In Xanadu did Kublai Khan a stately pleasure dome decree."

"Where Alf the sacred river ran," I say.

And we finish together, "down to the sunless sea."

I get my reader's pass. But despite the clerk's enthusiasm, the Asiatic Society was designed for a different project than mine. The catalog yields plentiful poems—in manuscript, on paper and on palm leaves, in printed editions of classical works, in Sanskrit and Persian, Bangla and Oriya—but no unread volumes of English language Indian poetry.

In one sense, though, I have already found what I need: that appreciation of English poetry I have encountered everywhere, among strangers, friends, and colleagues who studied in Indian English-medium schools. Such encounters have punctuated my experience over the past twenty years, leading me to wonder: Why would a young man in Pune be ordered by his father to write a thesis on Marathi poetry rather than on Shelley? And why did he choose Shelley in the first place? Why did the junior official at the police station in Kolkata delight in reciting Wordsworth to me? And the immigration clerk in Mumbai? How did the poems they loved persist as part of a cultural repertoire for so many years? More broadly, I came to ask how poets and readers in India created, perpetuated, and challenged a canon of English language poetry.

This book aims to answer these questions. My project combines historical and theoretical reflection, adding to the canon of English language poetry written outside of Great Britain and at the same time critiquing that canon. In the years since Indian independence, scholars have collected and anthologized poems by important nineteenth-century poets writing English language verse in India. But this scholarship includes, with one exception, only those poems written by poets born in India of Indian parents. The exception, Henry Louis Vivian Derozio, is claimed as the "father" of Indian English poetry—as the first Indian poet to write in English—despite the fact that his mother was born in Hampshire and his father's parents were of Portuguese and Indian extraction. Derozio called himself an "East Indian," and those who admired him called him, after his early death, "the Indian Keats." It is ironic—but absolutely right—that a poet of complex political views and of complex ethnic, religious, and familial identifications should be thought of as the paterfamilias of Indian English poetry.

I argue here that all poets writing in English in India worked necessarily in a web of affiliation and rupture, identifications and disidentifications. They inhabited polyglot locations. They defined themselves within, against, and across canonical understandings that included much of the British poetic canon, classical European and modern European poetry, and classical and contemporary poetry in the languages of the subcontinent. Writing English language poetry in India is, at best, an uneasy undertaking—and was so from its beginning, both for poets we understand now as "Indian" and for those totally forgotten poets we might now understand as "British." I use scare quotes here to emphasize that the meanings of nation are always in the making. For the writers I discuss here, whether they were born in India of Irish Catholic parents (Mary Carshore) or schooled in England from the age of ten (Manmohan Ghose), what it meant to be Indian or British or something else was always at issue, never a given. I want to hold in abeyance for the moment—insofar as possible—the taken-for-granted categories of nationalism to look afresh, often for the first time in decades, at poets who made English verse in colonial India. If we were to look only at the current canon of "Indian English poets," who are, in any case, scarcely known to North American readers, we would be missing at least half the conversation that shaped their practices. Conversely, if we were to follow the lead of an old anthology, *Poets of John Company,* in focusing only on poets associated with the East India Company, we would ignore both Indian poets and the considerable number of British women who wrote poetry on the subcontinent in the long nineteenth century. My aim here is to bring back into conversation all those who were, in fact, parties to literary exchanges in this period.

Scholars of Indian English have shaped the canon of English language verse to the contours of nationalism. Constructing a canon in this way, however, renders *invisible* poets who are not claimed as Indian. It renders *illegible* many nuances of poetic form and influence shaping the texts of those poets who are claimed as Indian. Scholars in India and very recently in the United States and in Britain are beginning to rethink these canonical boundaries and the nationalist discourses that necessarily shaped earlier critical writing. In particular, Rosinka Chaudhuri and the scholars whose work is represented in Arvind Mehrotra's *Illustrated History of Indian Literature in English* have begun to critique the nationalist and linguistic assumptions that shaped and at the same time delegitimated

English language poetry written in India. Building on their work, I double the scope of English language poetry in India to re-create the mutually constitutive history of British and Indian poets working on the subcontinent in the nineteenth century.

The very awkwardness of the phrase "English language poetry" points to significant historical and critical issues, and I retain it here to clarify and to navigate the vexed territory marked by such phrases as "Indian English poetry" and "Indo-Anglian" and "Anglo-Indian poetry." The first two phrases conventionally designate poets that include H. L. V. Derozio, Toru Dutt, and Rabindranath Tagore and exclude Sir William Jones and Rudyard Kipling. The third has an ambivalent history. "Anglo-Indian poetry" could be understood in two contradictory ways. Before independence, it would have designated poems written by British people in India; postindependence, it typically indicates poetry in English either by Indian writers or by those who in some circumstances were called "Eurasians." As a result of this confusion, the category "Indo-Anglian" was sometimes—and awkwardly—used as a marker for English language poetry written in India, excluding poetry written by the British. I want to talk here about poetry written in the English language in India, hence I use the seemingly redundant phrase "English language poetry."

Describing the family backgrounds of the poets themselves is equally awkward. Some of the poets I discuss here, beginning with Derozio, would once have been described as "Eurasian." I prefer here to use either the name current among the community in 1820s Calcutta, "East Indian," or simply—if wordily—to refer to persons of mixed ethnicity. No category is ever innocent of its past or free of the ideology of its own construction. My ostensibly neutral "English language poetry" entails its own polemic, its own claims and disclaimers. Through its very pleonasm, I want to drive a wedge between the nationalist claims of "English" and its denotative linguistic claim, between adjective and noun. I hope in this way to make possible a new understanding of the canon, and here, too, I refer to the notion of canon in its most capacious sense—as poems known and discussed, whatever judgments might further be made about their political efficacy or aesthetic value.

I claim that poetry written in colonial situations can tell us as much as or even more than novels can about figuration, multilingual literacies, and histories of nation and nationalism. In making this claim, I seek to redress what I believe has been a disproportionate emphasis on fiction in the study of colonial, postcolonial, and transnational literatures. From the beginning, poetry was the most important belletristic English form in India. Writing English language poetry, being educated in British poetic tradition, and translating poetry from various Asian and European languages into English were central to the development of Indian English. Taking fiction as the primary form of both colonial and postcolonial Indian English writing obscures the contours of the literary canon as it was experienced by writers in the nineteenth century and as it is often still experienced by Indian poets and novelists. This study (and the anthology that accompanies it—*Anglophone Poetry in Colonial India, 1780–1913*) recovers and makes available carefully edited texts; it provides a new historical approach to understanding poems written in English in nineteenth-century India; and it argues for an understanding of a canon that takes nationalism as a subject of inquiry rather than a criterion for selection.

The canon of English language poetry in India was in the twentieth century constructed almost entirely on nationalist lines. Poems written by persons identified as "Indian" were read in the context of each other but only incidentally in relationship to poems written by persons identified as "British." This practice was both useful and problematic. It led to such anthologies as Eunice de Souza's recent *Early Indian Poetry in English* and to Sisir Kumar Das's magisterial history of Indian English literature, published by the Sahitya Akademi. Under the categories of "Indian English," Anglo-Indian, or Indo-Anglian poetry, many poets have been discovered, discussed, and defended from the wider charge—a common feature of linguistic nationalism in India—that no good poetry can be written in English on the subcontinent. Yet despite the critique of linguistic nationalism that is implicit in any defense of poets such as Derozio and Toru Dutt, this poetic canon was itself built on a nationalist foundation. The result is a curious dehistoricization effacing the contestation and conversation that in fact created English language literary culture in India.

Like the scholars I implicitly critique, I too argue for the importance of nationalisms in reading any number of poems, but with the caveat that twentieth-century postcolonial nationalism makes some poets and some poems legible while rendering others mute, uninteresting, or obscure. Attaining an Archimedean point from which to leverage nationalist presuppositions would be impossible: my intention here is to survey the complexities of their construction and to render visible a wide swath of English language poetry, its literary and linguistic contexts, its formal claims, its place in the social formation.

Even the idea of "English language" in the phrase "English language poetry in India" contains more ambiguity than at first meets the eye, for there was a reasonably significant infusion of Scots poetry and, to a lesser extent, of Irish sentiment into the construction of Indian English. I share the premise of Elleke Boehmer and Katie Trumpener that globalization must be understood not only as a late twentieth-century development but also as a phenomenon of the late eighteenth and early nineteenth centuries, a time when metropolis and colonial peripheries were constituted also by transperipheral relationships—among, for example, London, Calcutta, the American colonies, Edinburgh, and Dublin. Trumpener is primarily concerned with bardic nationalism as it played out in Scotland and Ireland and to some extent in North America; building on her work, I show how the tropes of bardic nationalism, integral to linguistic and cultural identities marked as Scottish and Irish and recuperated in a depoliticized way by the English, were reprised in nineteenth-century India. The distinctions between the peripheries of internal colonialism and the metropole were important to writers of English language poetry in colonial India. That one might identify with Scots bards or, later, with Irish nationalists meant that British domination had internal fissures and that British, Indian, and East Indian writers responded to these differences.

It is true that when military action was at issue in India, the common identity of "Britishness" overcame the ideological divisions of English internal colonialism; but in political appointments, in what we might call cultural activity, and sometimes in political activity, such differences mattered. Take, for example, John Leyden, who came to India to make his fortune when he found that a career in the Scottish church was impossible. Born a "peasant," as one of his biographers puts it, he was (like his contemporary Thomas Carlyle) a product of Scots education and his own intellectual ambition.[1] Leyden aspired to rival the great linguist Sir William Jones in classical and oriental learning and might have done so had he not died in 1811, at age thirty-six. Just before he boarded the *Hugh Inglis* bound for Madras, Leyden published his long poem, *Scenes of Infancy, Descriptive of Teviotdale.* The last section of this poem places Leyden's emigration in a context of enclosures and enforced peasant displacement: the poet identifies with the Scots of his generation who have left their homes, whether to farm in North America or to fight in the Scottish regiments. He identifies too with the "sons of Erin" in the wake of the Act of Union (1801), which followed the bloody rebellion of 1798, and he makes common cause with the Cherokees of North America, who have been turned out of their land in the process of enclosure by some of these same Scots and Irish settlers:

> Long may the Creek, the Cherokee, retain
> The desert woodlands of his old domain,
> Ere Teviot's sons, far from their homes beguiled
> Expel their wattled wigwams from the wild!
> For ah! not yet the social virtues fly,
> That wont to blossom in our northern sky,
> And, in the peasant's free-born soul, produce,
> The patriot glow of Wallace and of Bruce;
> . . . .
> Not yet our swains, their former virtues lost,
> In dismal exile roam from coast to coast;
> But soon, too soon, if lordly wealth prevail,
> The healthy cottage shall desert the dale,
> The active peasants trust their hardy prime
> To other skies, and seek a kinder clime.
>
> (*Poems*, 200–201)

Leyden's *Scenes of Infancy*, written in English rather than in Scots, followed his work assisting Walter Scott collect materials for the *Minstrelsy of the Scottish Border. Scenes of Infancy* at once captured and resisted the long-term economic and cultural consequences of the Scottish Act of Union (1707). And it drew the lines connecting the Scots diaspora with the fate of those inhabiting the reaches of empire.

Leyden found that it was a long road from a cottage in the Borders even to the drawing rooms of Edinburgh, much less to the shores of India. When he was promoted from his post in Madras to a better one in Calcutta, Leyden experienced yet another sort of displacement. Upon arriving in Calcutta in 1805, he was given friendly advice by his fellow Scot, General Sir John Malcolm, who later recounted this exchange: "I was most solicitous regarding his reception in the society of the Indian capital. 'I entreat you, my dear friend,' I said to him the day he landed, 'to be careful of the impression you make on entering this community; for God's sake, learn a little English, and be silent upon literary subjects except among literary men.' 'Learn English!' he exclaimed—'no, never; it was trying to learn that language that spoilt my Scotch.'"[2] Though Leyden learned to write "proper" English (he, unlike Burns, was persuaded that his best poetry was written in English rather than Scots), he considered his *speech* too precious to lose. Leyden's stubborn insistence on his "Scotch" makes clear that even the "English language" in the Indian context comprised competing dialects and identifications. From Teviotdale to Calcutta, from Edinburgh to Madras, from Cherokee lands to the Scottish Borders, highlands, and islands, the transperipheral was as important as the metropole/colony exchange in making the cultural space of English poetry.

As is obvious in Leyden's experience, the English language in India consisted of multiple regional and class dialects, and these dialects were in turn situated in a thoroughly multilingual space. Though few people on the subcontinent were even literate, those who wrote English language poetry operated among multiple classical languages (Persian, Arabic, Greek, Latin, and sometimes Sanskrit) and vernaculars (Hindustani and Bangla principally, though also in South Indian languages). In entering this multilingual space, poets choosing to write in English had widely different access to language depending on their place of birth, education, religion, gender, and social class or caste. Religion, class, and gender were crucial markers of access to literacy, to belletristic writing, and to participation in constructions of nation and nationalism. In the chapters that follow, I attend to these differences as I delineate the material and social contours that shaped the scene of writing.

Moving among the multiple vernaculars, not to mention classical languages, at play on the subcontinent and moving within and outside of discourses of nation, poets were sometimes tempted to claim a kind of valorizing indigeneity for a particular vernacular or dialect—whether that vernacular be identified, for example, as Scottish or as Bengali. And yet, as Sheldon Pollock has argued, recourse to ideas of the indigenous (for example, to the "mother tongue") functions as a powerful illusion: "No form of culture can therefore ever be 'indigenous'; that term, it bears repeating, is only the name we give to what exhausts our capacity for historicization. When taken as anything more than this, the idea inhibits our perceiving that all cultures participate in what are ultimately global networks of begging, borrowing, and stealing, imitating and emulating—all the while constructing themselves precisely by sublating this history and affirming a specious autogenesis. . . . From this processual perspective culture becomes . . . a freeze frame in a film taken for the whole story" (*Language*, 539). Pollock defines cultures as sites for "reprocessing cultural goods that are always already someone else's" (539). A processual perspective, moreover, suggests a corrective to a singular reliance on spatial metaphors in the historiography of empire.

It is tempting, as I have done above, to think of the multilingual dimensions of empire in spatial metaphors—in terms of center/periphery and transperipheral spaces—but another crucial way of thinking these differential connections is temporal. Patrick Williams argues, following Elleke Boehmer and Ernst Bloch, that global interconnections were also marked by "simultaneous uncontemporaneities" (31). This notion of fissures within what we take to be contemporaneous phenomena allows us to think of the empire as a heterogeneous space—heterogeneous as to technologies of publishing and distribution, as to reception and reading practices, as to language itself.

To capture both temporal and spatial heterogeneity, I move among three registers here: the material histories of uneven development; the geocultural history of the transperipheral; and the psychic history of what Homi Bhabha calls "unhomeliness" (*Location*, 13). These theoretical strands are drawn through each chapter, though with differing emphases. With respect to the histories of uneven development, I am particularly interested in the technologies of publishing and distribution and the development of cultural institutions, including English medium schools and libraries. A focus on the geocultural histories of imperial space brings into view institutions of literary sociality, including the differential reception of English language poetry in Indian and metropolitan periodicals. Finally, a focus on the psychic history of "unhomeliness" allows me to trace the differentials suggested in experiences of displacement, marginalization, and migration and in gendered access to culture. In all these registers, I attend to the consequences for literary conventions, tropes, and formal choices. I ask, for example, what conventions were available to poets writing in India, what forms or tropes were dominant, what other languages or dialects could be evoked through the medium of English language verse, and whether or how these elements of English poetics shifted over time and in their "simultaneous uncontemporaneity" from one social location to another.

Fundamental to this argument is the assumption that poetry is crucial to an understanding of the development of English language culture in India. In colonial India at least through about 1860, poetry was the most important form of English language belletristic writing. As I show in more detail in subsequent chapters, from the eighteenth century onward, English language newspapers printed much more poetry than fiction, and printers in the presidencies—Madras, Bombay, and especially Calcutta—brought out various volumes of verse. The publishing of English language verse began in Calcutta, though authors were also eager to print collections in Britain that were then imported to India. Graham Shaw shows that practical items and government regulations, not surprisingly, formed the preponderance of books printed in Calcutta before 1800, but he notes that the majority of belletristic volumes were "collections of very mediocre poetry" or plays (*Printing*, 19). Such titles as *The Oriental Masonic Muse* (1791), *The Oriental Asylum for Fugitive Pieces* (1788), *The Oriental Miscellany* (collecting "airs of Hindoostan"), and Sir William Jones's translation of *Śakuntalā* indicate the variety of this early publishing.[3] Fiction was often imported but seldom locally produced, at least before the 1860s.

More important for my purposes than its relatively strong place in the world of colonial publishing is the nature of poetry itself. Although all literary forms—novel, story, novella, verse—exist only through convention, formal verse makes still greater claims than fiction on an understanding of convention, operating through meter and rhyme even at the level of lexical choice and syntax. And of course verse genres (epic, elegy, and ballad) and verse forms (ballad stanza, Spenserian stanza, sonnet, and blank verse) have particular histories through which these conventions and poetic practices are transmitted. The result, I believe, is that poetry can be thought of as a kind of pressure cooker for historical and ideological contradictions. I claim here not only that poetry has been understudied and largely untheorized in colonial and postcolonial scholarship but that poetry provides an important site for investigating the cultural contradictions of empire. The pressure of poetic convention makes especially evident the rifts and fissures within the colonial scene of writing. Finally, I argue, poetry is crucial to our understanding of the colonial scene precisely because it is, of all genres, the one most fully understood through writers' and readers' repertoires.

Here I borrow Tracy Davis's extremely useful definition of repertoire, which she has developed to account for the ways an audience finds innovation or invention intelligible. Davis argues that repertoire can be thought of as mutual knowledge and accretions of practice through which, in her case, theatrical performances are made legible. In a recent lecture, she defined repertoire as the "multiple, circulating recombinative discourses of intelligibility that habituate audiences to understand performative tropes, recognizing and incorporating the unfamiliar."[4] Repertoire, then, is not simply the accumulation of texts (songs, roles, and so forth) to which a performer has access; rather, it can be understood as an accretion of possibilities made through reiteration, revision, and citation.

In the chapters that follow, a central concern is precisely this process of reiteration, revision, and citation. Indeed, I argue that reiteration entails revision. For example, when the trope of exile, much favored by early nineteenth-century British poets writing in India, is repeated by Michael Madhusudan Dutt at midcentury, it is radically revised, almost reversed. The teenaged poet living in Calcutta who sighed "for Albion's distant shore" did not long for a family he had lost. Rather, he manufactured a family he was loath to leave. A more subtle kind of reiteration and revision is evident in Kasiprasad Ghosh's metrical experiments, which turn such forms as Spenserian stanza to his own purposes. And a complex web of citations in their most literal sense is constructed in hundreds of orientalist footnotes attached to hundreds of poems during this period.

The processes of repetition, citation, and revision are key to the development of English language poetry in India, but the divisions within the colonial scene of writing and the divisions between the colony and the metropole often rendered poems illegible or differently legible to audiences in India and in Britain. The repertoire of colonial

English language poetics was built from the intersection of British, classical and vernacular European, and classical and vernacular Indian canons. In this heteroglot and often ambilingual scene of writing, legibility was a moving target. As a result, poets in India surrounded their verse with an extraordinary number of paratexts: footnotes, endnotes, glosses, prefaces, and dedications. This can be understood generally as the poets' attempts to establish the forms of knowledge from which repertoire is built. These paratexts both deflect and invite criticism, both justify the poetic undertaking and excuse its failings. Paratexts are put to a variety of uses in these poems; they create ironies, they apologize, they rhetorically situate poets and readers. But often they also point to poets' insecurities about the very audience that the notion of shared repertoire necessarily takes for granted. Who exactly was the audience for this verse? Where was the audience located? Would the poet be judged by virtue of his attempt to write English poetry in the first place? Would she be judged by her distance from the metropole?

This introduction is, along with the acknowledgments, my own paratext, my place to make my excuses as the poets I discuss often do, to say what this study does not do, as well as what it does. Much like some of those writers whom I describe, I am limited by my linguistic competence (in my case, modern European languages and Latin). Different books could—and should—be written by scholars fluent in Bangla, Hindi and Urdu, Persian and Sanskrit; still another focus might emerge from the nexus of English and South Indian languages. In one sense, this book is only part of a story, steeped as it is in the British poetic tradition and attempting as it does to account for the importance of that tradition in the making of Indian English verse. A different but significantly overlapping story might be told from the perspectives of bhakti poetry, Bengali and other vernacular verse, and classical verse, especially Sanskrit, Persian, and Arabic poetry as understood in north India in the eighteenth and nineteenth centuries. I bow toward these traditions, as I understand them through translation, in discussing poets to whom such traditions were important.

A second dimension of this study that requires some explanation is its focus largely in Bengal. The simplest reason for this focus is that books are endless and life is short. But more pertinent to my argument is the fact that Calcutta was the administrative capital of British India in this period, and as a consequence, English language publishing flourished in the city from an early period. I have attended to poetry from other locations both here and in the accompanying anthology, but nevertheless most of the poets I discuss were either persons of British parentage or mixed ethnicity who lived part of their lives in Bengal (as well as in other areas of India and South Asia) or were children of Bengali parents who lived part of their lives in Bengal (as well as in Europe or other parts of India). Much—though by no means all—of the historical detail that I bring to bear on the sociology of the book, the history of publishing and reception focuses on Calcutta. This focus enables a fine-grained understanding of the linguistic, educational, and economic conditions that subtended the creation of English language verse, and it allows me to focus attention on English language periodicals in the period.

Moreover, because Calcutta was the administrative capital of the East India Company and then of the British government in India, a considerable amount of historical data is available about topics ranging from sanitation to the collection of Sanskrit manuscripts. This kind of historical detail allows me to yoke broader social concerns to the close reading of poetic texts. At the same time, I have at various points briefly summarized for readers new to these materials larger trends and significant historical events.

THE CHAPTERS THAT follow examine the rise and expansion of English language poetics in India, beginning in the late eighteenth century and ending around 1913, the year Rabindranath Tagore won the Nobel Prize in Literature. Although I trace the larger historical shifts that mark this period—from the invention of orientalist poetics by Sir William Jones and others to the intertwined influences of fin-de-siècle decadence and nationalism in the poems of Sarojini Naidu—my goal is not a cultural history in the broad sense. Rather than creating a sweeping narrative history of English language poetry in India, in which individual poems and even poets would be subsumed to a single paradigm, I want instead to suggest ways of reading these poems by attending to their recalcitrance and contradictions and by bringing these contradictions to bear on our taken-for-granted binaries (colonizer/colonized, colony/metropole, British/Indian). I want also to emphasize that, despite unequal power differentials, persons from multiple backgrounds and from different social locations created among themselves a new repertoire of performative tropes and what Davis calls "recombinative discourses." Hence, each chapter that follows brings together poets from differing backgrounds, and in all but the first, each chapter reads together British and Indian (or "East Indian") poets. In some cases, these readings uncover literary friendships: for example, H. L. V. Derozio and Emma Roberts. In other cases, they juxtapose poems through a common interpretative strategy: for example, in my reading of poetic tropes and forms in the poems of Kasiprasad Ghosh, Michael Madhusudan Dutt, and Mary Carshore. Each chapter returns to a series of common threads—or interpretative strategies—that ground my argument. Each chapter forms part of an implicit argument that the canon of English language poetry in India cannot be fully understood through a retrospective nationalist reading. And in each chapter, I bring to light poets who shared a cultural space but whose connections have not been understood, and I analyze poems that are unknown or scarcely legible to most readers of colonial and postcolonial literature.

The first section of this study, chapters 1 and 2, examines the origins of English language poetry in India and its dominant tropes. Chapter 1 addresses issues of language and education, the classical and the vernacular, and the place of orientalist learning at the foundation in India of English language literature. It focuses on Sir William Jones, a radical Whig, the dominant force in Indian orientalism and the founder of the linguistic argument for the common origin of Indo-European languages. I pair Jones with two other British poets: Sir John Horsford, who left his Oxford fellowship for reasons unknown to enlist in the Indian army; and the anonymous Anna Maria, a young woman who was deeply influenced by the "Della Cruscan" poets of late eighteenth-century London. These three poets represent different kinds of access to poetic tradition and different orientations to the metropole. Anna Maria longed to make a mark in London; Jones, having already established himself, longed to gather as much knowledge in India as he possibly could and imagined his audience globally to include Europe and North America as well as India; Horsford, happily ensconced with his Indian partner and a family of East Indian children, gave little thought to the metropole.

Chapter 2 examines the dominant tropes of English language verse as they emerged in a terrain marked by ideological and cultural divisions among the colonizers—many of whom were of Scottish, Welsh, or Irish origins. The tropes of bardic nationalism were exported from Britain's "internal colonies" to India, but they were realized in the specific terrain of local political debates (about sati and the condition of women, for example), even as these debates also shaped British thinking about India. The two poets I focus on in chapter 2 are the East Indian writer H. L. V. Derozio and his friend Emma Roberts, the first British woman to make her living as a journalist in India. Roberts's work in turn influenced the orientalist poems of her colleague Letitia Landon, who was one of the most popular British poets of this period. Derozio is still something of a hero in Calcutta, where his birthday is celebrated annually by students of Presidency College. I read together their poems on Indian "scenes"—ruins and graveyards particularly—to argue that writing empire entailed remaking both the sublime and the picturesque. And I read their Oriental tales as they were imbricated in political controversy in the colony and the metropole.

Although chapters 1 and 2 also attend to the material conditions of book production and consumption, the second section of this study looks in much greater detail at English language publishing in India in the first half of the nineteenth century. In chapter 3, I discuss periodical publishing, the importation of English books, patterns of book ownership, the development of libraries, and formal and informal educational curricula. I focus primarily on Bengal, with some attention to publishing and distribution of English language literature in the other presidencies, and in light of these developments I discuss a group of poets who moved in and out of Calcutta in midcentury. Central to this chapter is the impresario of English verse in nineteenth-century India, David Lester Richardson, whose multifarious roles as editor, reviewer, teacher, poet, and publisher of annuals placed him at the center of canon formation and literary taste-making. Richardson's anthology of British poetry, published at the request of Thomas Babington Macaulay and the Calcutta Schoolbook Society, could be thought of as the English language canon in India in the shape of a doorstop: it contained a bookshelf in a single volume. I contrast Richardson with two poets, T. W. Smyth and Henry Page, who are more obscure. Smyth and Page were friends of Derozio's; from a radical position informed by Baptist views and perhaps by complexities of race and ethnicity, they were highly critical of mid-Victorian empire and allied themselves to

Derozio's memory in attempting to imagine English as a crucial language in an Indian "land of poesy."

In chapter 4, I turn my attention from the material circumstances of publishing and reception to the poetic repertoire itself. I examine in detail the poems of Kasiprasad Ghosh, who described himself as the first Hindu poet writing in English; Michael Madhusudan Dutt, a student of Richardson's who wrote much English juvenilia but is best known as the outstanding Bangla poet at midcentury; and Mary Seyers Carshore, the daughter of Irish parents, who lived all her life in India, dying in the uprising of 1857 at Jhansi. I compare these three very different poets to trace the layered mimicry of colonial poetics, arguing that both mimicry in Bhabha's sense of recalcitrant mimesis and imitation in the more usual sense of repetition and citation are key to understanding the development of the colonial repertoire. I focus especially on the choice of verse forms and the ways these forms shift through repetition and citation.

Chapters 5 and 6 form the last section of this study, situated after the Sepoy Rebellion of 1857. Chapter 5 addresses the role of religion and the drama of exile in the making of Indian English poetry. As Bruce King has pointed out in *Modern Indian Poetry in English,* many of the Indian poets writing in English in the nineteenth century were Christian or came from Christian families or, like Tagore, came from the unorthodox Brahmo Samaj. As I argue with respect to Derozio in chapter 2 and Madhusudan Dutt in chapter 4, deconversion or religious conversion was perhaps even more important in India than in Britain, throwing a writer into a highly contradictory social space. In chapter 5, we can see the impact of this contradiction in the men of the Dutt family, whose conversion and whose identification with the British administration profoundly shaped their verse, and in the work of Toru Dutt—the most distinguished poet of the family, whose work was triangulated by English, French, and Bengali vernacular poetry and finally by Sanskrit poetics. I contrast Toru Dutt with Mary Eliza Leslie, who like Toru found her experience as a poet profoundly shaped by her family's religious affiliation. As the daughter and granddaughter of Baptist missionaries, Leslie wrote as much missionary literature and devotional verse as secular poetry. These two poets, both interested in formal experimentation, nevertheless represent very different situations, with the elder, Mary Leslie, constrained by religious ideology and the younger, Toru Dutt, claiming a cosmopolitan and multilingual space within the confines of a circumscribed domesticity.

My final chapter is shaped by recent theories of cosmopolitanism; it examines the new situation at the fin de siècle in which Indian writers moved much more freely in Europe and America than they had before. I show how conventions and discourses of late nineteenth-century aestheticism and the discourses of empire and nationalism uneasily intersected. Cross-cultural friendships coupled with international travel and residence abroad shaped poets' reception in London and their reputations at home. Here I focus on three pairs of friends, all of whom shared space in the literary world of fin-de-siècle London: Manmohan Ghose published poems in London and established an abiding and crucial friendship with Laurence Binyon, who became keeper of Oriental Prints and Drawings at the British Museum and introduced East Asian art to the British public; Sarojini Naidu (later the first woman president of the Indian Congress Party, a feminist, and a friend of Gandhi's, Nehru's, and Jinnah's) was as a very young woman befriended by Arthur Symons, a leading Decadent poet; and finally Rabindranath Tagore (the first Indian to win the Nobel Prize in Literature), who in part owed his European fame to his friendships in London with the painter William Rothenstein and the poets W. B. Yeats and Ezra Pound. London hospitality brought together strangers, but as Jacques Derrida and Seyla Benhabib have argued, *hospis* (host) and *hostes* (enemy) have common roots.[5] The lyrics of Manmohan, Sarojini, and Rabindranath can be read as extended meditations on, even theorizations of, the unhomeliness implied in the double valence of hospitality. An epilogue retraces these steps in a satiric mode, returning through poems by Rabindranath and Kipling to the figure of the "griffin," the callow youth who represents all the uneasiness of colonial encounter.

FRIENDSHIP, POETRY, CONVENTIONS, canons, languages, commerce. Few were foolish enough to imagine making a living by writing English language verse in India—but many negotiated the straits between belles lettres and commerce, for poems functioned as a form of social currency. Few understood this function of verse as well as John Leyden, who frankly said that languages—if not poetry itself—might enable his political and material success. His "Ode to an Indian Gold Coin," written at the beginning of the nineteenth century, was much anthologized over the next hundred years. It established a trope of exile yet, in its own contradictions, was proleptical of unhomeliness yet to come. In the metonym of the gold coin, the poet addressed his ambition, his need for material success—the deepest motive for empire:

> Slave of the dark and dirty mine!
> What vanity has brought thee here?
> How can I love to see thee shine
> So bright, whom I have bought so dear?—
> . . . .
> By Cherical's dark wandering streams,
> Where cane-tufts shadow all the wild,
> Sweet visions haunt my waking dreams
> Of Teviot loved while still a child,
> Of castled rocks stupendous piled
> By Esk or Eden's classic wave,
> Where loves of youth and friendships smiled,
> Uncursed by thee, vile yellow slave!
>
> (*Poems*, 312)

At this point Leyden, suffering a liver complaint, might well have seen in himself a "vile yellow slave," his face matched to that imprinted on the guinea he sought. The poet's valediction curses the vehicle of his own curse: "Vile slave, thy yellow dross I scorn, / Go mix thee with thy kindred clay!"[6]

The Scottish poet abroad saw himself transformed in the mirror of gold through the medium of English language verse. In the long nineteenth century, as English language poets negotiated differentials of power, money, gender, and language, many of them were, like Leyden, forced to consider what might count as "kindred clay."

PART ONE

Languages, Tropes, and Landscape in the Beginnings of English Language Poetry

Old Fort Playhouse and Holwell's Monument, Calcutta, by William Daniell. Aquatint, 1786.

ONE

Contact Poetics in Eighteenth-Century Calcutta

Sir William Jones, Sir John Horsford, and Anna Maria

To what shall I compare my literary pursuits in India? Suppose Greek literature to be known in modern Greece only, and there to be in the hands of priests and philosophers; and suppose them to be still worshippers of Jupiter and Apollo; suppose Greece to have been conquered successively by Goths, Huns, Vandals, Tartars and lastly by the English; then suppose a court of judicature to be established by the British parliament, at Athens, and an inquisitive Englishman to be one of the judges; suppose him to learn Greek there, which none of the countrymen knew and to read Homer, Pindar, Plato, which no other Europeans had even heard of. Such am I in this country; substituting Sanscript for Greek, and the *Brahmans* for the priests of *Jupiter* and Vālmic, Vyāsa and Cālidāsa for Homer, Plato and Pindar.

—Sir William Jones to George John Spencer, August 23, 1787

Adieu to INDIA's fertile Plains,
Where *Brahma's* holy Doctrine reigns;
Whose virt'ous Principles still bind
The *Hindoo's* meek untainted Mind;
Far other Scenes my Thoughts employ,
Source of Anguish, Hope and Joy;
I hasten to my NATIVE SHORE,
Where *Art* and *Science* blend their Lore:
There *Learning* keeps her chosen Seat—
A million Vot'ries at her Feet,
Ambitious of the LAUREL BOUGH,
To wind about their honor'd Brow.
Yet ere I go—a grateful Pain
Involves the Muse's parting Strain.

—*The Poems of Anna Maria*, 1793

GANGA, for him, with drooping head appears,
For him ev'n holy Pundits shed their tears!
CRISHNA for him wail'd MATRA's groves among,

> And his romantic grot with cypress hung;
> Alive!—we prais'd the path sublime he trod,—
> Dead!—LEARNING HAILS HIM AS HER DEMI-GOD!
>
> —Sir John Horsford, "Literary Characteristicks of the Most Distinguished Members of the Asiatic Society, 1799"

On September 25, 1783, two days after his thirty-seventh birthday, William Jones, recently knighted, disembarked from the *Crocodile* at Calcutta's Chandpal Ghat. Within weeks he had recommenced his studies of Persian, Arabic, and Hindustani, taken up a position as judge on the Supreme Court of Judicature, founded the Asiatic Society, and purchased a suitable house on the banks of the Hooghly at Garden Reach. Over the next twelve years, he did more than any other single person to invent English language poetry in India. By the time of his death in 1794, it seemed only natural that he was hailed as learning's "demi-god."[1]

When Jones arrived in Calcutta, the metropolitan area was home to half a million people, half the population of London. Like London, the city was an important port, stretched along the banks of a river. Like London, it had impressive private homes and equally impressive slums, lovely gardens and open drains. As the Scots poet James Atkinson put it a generation later, Calcutta had its "tombs / And dazzling splendors, towering peerlessly," yet "bitters too" under "attractive seeming" (*City,* 6). A center of credit, commerce, and trade both internal and external, Calcutta was already the first city of empire. Atkinson called it the City of Palaces, a name that stuck, but not a name that would have impressed a man of William Jones's republican turn of mind. Instead of aspiring to palaces, Jones had modeled himself upon Cicero and hoped to combine learning, letters, and law to create a life of civic virtue. He saw his legal researches as a step toward creating a civic society within, and against, the trajectory of empire. Yet poetry was his first love, what Wordsworth was to call at century's end "the breath and finer spirit of all knowledge."[2] Jones took far more seriously than Wordsworth the fundamental importance of knowledge to poetry, perhaps because he defined knowledge comparatively and with reference to multiple languages. Although he did not live, as he had hoped, to cultivate poetry in retirement, we might compare Jones's intellectual though not his religious disposition to Milton's.

Jones's impact on European letters, particularly the impact of his translations of *Śankuntalā,* the *Hitopadesha,* and the *Laws of Manu,* has been clear at least since Raymond Schwab's *Oriental Renaissance,* published more than half a century ago. His impact on British romantic poetry has been widely recognized.[3] But his place in the beginnings of English language poetry in India has been largely ignored. I begin this study accordingly with Jones and with his contemporaries, to lay a foundation for understanding the complex intertexual relationships between English language poetry written in India and the reception of Indic studies in Britain and Europe.

Jones forms the center of a triptych in this chapter, placed between two other writers both more typical of their times and less influential. With Jones there began a dialectic in which European and Indian writings developed multiple intertextual connections. However Jones has fared among postcolonial theorists and historians, scholars agree that he was both an exemplary figure and sui generis. He was at once an eclectic genius and a systematic thinker, a jurist and an artist, and a man whose insatiable curiosity allowed him to feel more awe than condescension toward the cultures he encountered in eighteenth-century Calcutta. Jones's poems written in India reveal the complex decisions faced by poets who write at the intersections of cultures and languages. Because he was unusually gifted as a linguist and unusually open-minded as a human being, Jones's texts reveal tensions and contradictions that other poets ignored, elided, or dismissed but that necessarily shaped their poetics.

Flanking Jones in my triptych are two other poets of fewer gifts and therefore perhaps more representative than William Jones of the typical range of English language belles lettres on the subcontinent in the late eighteenth century. Of these two, one was anonymous and is still unidentified; the other was an officer in the East India Company's army. Several years after Jones's arrival in Calcutta, "Anna Maria" bade the city farewell, hoping to achieve literary fame in London. Her verse represents an Anglo-Indian desire for metropolitan literary success that was to become still more powerful in years to come, and it also indicates how quickly—and how slowly—poetic news moved within the ambit of empire. Anna Maria was painfully attuned to the latest literary developments in London, and hers was a poetry of literary sociality rather than intellectual adventure. Her slim volume of verse allows us to measure the social uses of art even within a culture whose main concerns were undoubtedly martial and commercial. The other figure I discuss here is John Horsford, who died a major general in the Bengal Army and a Knight Commander of the Order of the Bath. Horsford's checkered early career had taken him from an Oxford fellowship to enlistment as a private under the pseudonym John Rover in 1772.[4] By 1800, though, he was a highly commended officer who had published two volumes of verse. His *Poems in Three Parts* brought together facing-page English translations of his friend William Jones's Latin poems, a versified history of the Asiatic Society that began with the paean to Jones in my epigraph, and a series titled "Miscellaneous Poems."

Taken together, these three poets—Sir William Jones, Anna Maria, and Sir John Horsford—represent the dominant poetic trends in late eighteenth-century British India. The early world of English language belles lettres in India was defined against and also outside of metropolitan culture. It was necessarily multilingual and often learned. It was enamored of translation. It took for granted that literary pursuits were an important form of sociality. And its lifeblood was poetry.

Polyglossia and Poetry

In choosing these three poets, I am concerned here primarily with late eighteenth-century Bengal, for this relatively narrow focus will allow us to understand in some detail how material and linguistic conditions in India were given shape in literary networks, tropes, and conventions. As they moved into northern India, British poets entered a complex linguistic contact zone, where various vernaculars and classical languages were put to varied use by differing segments of the population. Literacy, though certainly not common from a demographic perspective, was for those who *were* literate very often a matter of multiple literacies occasioned by shifting dynamics of the classical and the vernacular.

These multiple literacies can best be understood as a kind of cosmopolitan polyglossia. As they shaped efforts to create an English language literary culture, polyglot writers multiplied paratextual and intertextual elements in English literary texts. Pseudonyms, subscribers' lists, footnotes, epigraphs, dedications, and illustrations functioned as a kind of literary liminality, a space where poets tried to make meaning in light of new languages and new circumstances.

These two notions—cosmopolitan polyglossia and paratextual liminality—shape my argument here, for both emphasize boundaries, borders, the porous space made by differences of language, class, economic power, education, gender, and religion. What I mean by cosmopolitan polyglossia will become clear in my discussion of the vernacular and of Sir William Jones's Latin poetry, but first I provide, briefly, a more general frame.

The liminal nature of English language literary culture in Bengal, particularly in Calcutta, was a function of complex demography.[5] Although the English language in eighteenth-century India was far from powerless, it was nevertheless a minority language. Precisely ascertaining the demographic makeup of Calcutta in the eighteenth century is difficult, though we do have good figures for the city proper (not the metropolitan area) for the late 1830s based on the house tax. I reproduce the table from Tithi Bhattacharya's "World of Learning: The Material Culture of Education and Class in Nineteenth-Century Bengal" (185):

English	3,138	Western Hindus	17,333
Euro-Asians	4,746	Bengali Hindus	120,318
Portuguese	3,181	Moguls	527
French	160	Parsees	40
Chinese	362	Arabs	351
Armenians	636	Mugs	683
Jews	307	Madrasees	55
Western Muslims	13,677	Native Christians	49
Bengali Muslims	45,067	Low Castes	19,054
			228,714[6]

One can assume different numbers but roughly similar proportions of residents in Calcutta at the turn of the nineteenth century. If we think about this population in terms of language, we can readily imagine a social space brimming with a mixture of Bengali, what we would now call Hindi/Urdu (then known as Hindustani), Chinese,

French, Portuguese, Arabic, Persian, Burmese, Armenian, and Tamil,[7] as well as the possible languages spoken by Parsis and Jews or read by those classically trained in Sanskrit or Hebrew, Greek or Latin—or various dialects of all these languages.

As I argue with respect to bardic nationalisms in the next chapter, even the "English" of Bengal in this period was a vivid mixture of dialects. I estimate that at least a third of the so-called native speakers of English spoke Irish or Lowland or Highland Scots dialects. If we include enlisted men as well as officers in this mix of what Bhattacharya calls "English" residents, then dialects would have varied significantly by social class as well as region of origin. Of the non-European residents of Calcutta who learned English, one can infer that their learning, too, was various, reflecting the dialects of their teachers. Indeed, judging from the names of schoolmasters in the city, many of those who taught English to nonnative speakers were Scottish.[8] To imagine the "sound" of English in Calcutta in this period accurately is to imagine the language not of Oxbridge but of Burns.

In a polyglot environment distant from the metropolitan center of English language publishing, poets struggled to establish new poetic repertoires and to make their work legible to colonial and metropolitan readers. Their paratextual strategies are particularly revealing. I follow Gérard Genette's definition of paratexts, though with a focus not just on the typology of the paratext but on its cultural work in particular historical circumstances. Genette defines paratexts synchronically, but he emphasizes their transtextual, liminal nature, an emphasis that suggests the importance of a diachronic reading as well.

Both Richard Macksey's foreword to *Paratexts* and Genette's introduction emphasize the function of the paratext as the "threshold of interpretation."[9] In an essay in *Poetique,* Genette speaks of the paratext as "this fringe at the unsettled limits that enclose with a pragmatic halo the literary work" (*Paratexts,* xvii). As Genette describes it in his introduction to the volume, a paratext is a "'vestibule' that offers the world at large the possibility of either stepping inside or turning back. It is an 'undefined zone' between the inside and the outside, a zone without any hard and fast boundary on either the inward side . . . or the outward side . . . an edge, or, as Philippe Lejeune put it, 'a fringe of the printed text which in reality controls one's whole reading of the text'" (1–2).

At the conclusion of his study—after creating a typology of dedications, inscriptions, epigraphs, prefaces, notes, and so on—Genette finds a second metaphor, one especially apt to my purposes. He cautions that we not over-read the paratext, replacing a fiction of the closed text with a fetish of the paratext, for the paratext, he declares, is "only an assistant": "And if the text without its paratext is sometimes like an elephant without a mahout, a power disabled, the paratext without its text is a mahout without an elephant" (410).

On the thresholds between languages—in the liminal polyglossic space of multiple languages—in late eighteenth-century India, we may imagine multiple mahouts, multiple elephants, each beast responding, however imperfectly, to a different set of commands. The poems themselves, never completely perspicuous on their own, require a significant paratextual apparatus in order to appear, let alone to do social work, in their new environment.

The poets I discuss in this chapter—and in the chapters that follow—attempted to create an audience and an authorial self in a polyglossic space. As we see in their differing approaches to text and paratext, their elephants and their mahouts, Jones, Anna Maria, and Horsford were differently situated with respect to language, power, and social milieu. Each functioned in a different personal or professional context, and each had a different repertoire of languages upon which to draw.

For all their differences, however, we can see in William Jones, the anonymous Anna Maria, and John Horsford that India provided an opportunity for self-invention. Unlike many of their British-born successors in later generations, none of these three poets exploits the trope of "exile." For each of them, the reinvention of self and poetry across space and time made for a continuing sense of possibility, though it necessarily involved alienation from the local context as well as from a former sense of self. Even Anna Maria (the only one of the three who may have left Calcutta and returned "home") could not depart without "a grateful Pain" that measured her transformation in India. Poetic and personal self-invention were accompanied by and even created through a sense of cultural discovery. For Jones and Horsford, such cultural translation threatened to overwhelm, if not the poet, then the poem itself.

For all three poets, paratexts reflected the literal and metaphorical necessities of cultural and literary translation.[10] The cultural exchanges and translations represented in their collections of verse were necessarily grounded in material exchanges. Books were made within the possibilities of available technology. In eighteenth-century India, distribution of English language texts was both a cultural challenge and a means of solidifying networks of literary and cultural sociality.

The Context of Early English Language Publishing in Bengal

Although type, ink, and paper were expensive in eighteenth-century Calcutta, as in India more generally, printed books and periodicals were key to social life.[11] Reading, writing, play-going, and scholarship were central to maintaining sociality among educated East India Company employees, both military and civilian, and among other Europeans and people of mixed European and Indian descent. Educated Britons, moreover, sought through literary exchanges to maintain links to Britain and among themselves, despite both frequent travel and slow foreign mails. In Calcutta, and to some extent in other towns and cities, they created new institutions of sociality—from the St. Andrews Society to the Masons, from theatre (amateur and semiprofessional) to the literary tea table, from newspaper reading to the military book club.[12] All this activity of reading, writing, manuscript circulation, and printing was merely a ripple on larger economic and military currents; yet for those who were dependent on uncertain mails for news from home, found themselves with stretches of leisure, felt isolated in the mofussil (or countryside), or lived between cultures, literary interactions were highly valued.

A surprising array of books was readily available in Calcutta. Graham Shaw, in his indispensable history of printing to 1800, describes the development and importance of private circulating libraries: during the last two decades of the century, two such establishments were operating at any one time in Calcutta. When the stock of the Calcutta Circulating Library was sold in 1800, the collection was advertised at more than 3,500 volumes (Shaw, *Printing*, 22).

A survey of the *Calcutta Chronicle* and the *India Gazette* from 1788 through 1790 reveals the ready availability of books for sale or loan. These papers routinely advertised commodities newly arrived from Britain; such advertisements appeared alongside notices of bankruptcy sales, advertisements for employment, announcements of tutoring and schools, sales of horses and carriages, and anything else one might want. Books featured prominently. The *Chronicle and General Advertiser* of August 21, 1788, for example, displayed a long list of books newly arrived in the *Phoenix* and available at "Mr. Yeats's New Commission Ware-house"; among them, all "handsomely Bound and Gilt," were numerous novels—*Count Fathom, Peregrine Pickle, Humphrey Clinker*—but also Voltaire's *History*, Johnson's *Rambler*, *The Muse's Mirror: A Collection of Poems*, Thomson's *Works*, Smollet's *Plays and Poems*, various travelogues, and political publications on the impeachment of Warren Hastings, the former governor-general, who was then enduring the long prosecution led by Edmund Burke in the House of Commons. In the same week, the *India Gazette* advertised incoming "goods from the first Houses in London" consisting of claret and hock, elegant glassware, cheeses, floor cloths, shoes and books, perfumery, and so forth. Immediately below this tempting list, the reader was promised by the Calcutta Circulating Library a "very considerable addition of books" for loan and "a very valuable collecion [*sic*] for sale." The proprietors claimed to "flatter themselves" that "the above will be found one of the most valuable collections of Books ever brought to this Country, being a particular Commission sent to Europe by them, and chiefly selected by several Gentlemen of the first literary Character in this Country" (*India Gazette*, August 16, 1790).[13] The *Gazette* advertised in the same number an additional fine collection of books received at the warehouse of Davidson and Maxwell. Adjacent to such advertisements, one might find poetic riddles and enigmas in Persian and English and occasional poems addressed to local inamorata by anonymous gentlemen.

The patrons of these subscription libraries, booksellers, and warehouses were doubtless among those who figured as subscribers to volumes of locally published verse. Subscribers' lists appended to books of poetry in the period indicate the importance of book circulation among army officers, company officials, and private circulating libraries. Like their eighteenth-century British counterparts, but well into the nineteenth century, Calcutta poets depended for financing on the subscription form, which enabled local printers to meet their expenses even if it did little for the financial position of the author. In 1793, Anna Maria managed to pre-sell 195 copies of her small volume of poems, no doubt enabling the printers, Thomson and Ferris, and perhaps the poet as well to at least break even or make a profit. The sixty-eight pages of text were priced at "one gold mohur." Five years earlier, W. H. Bird had advertised "A Collection of the best Songs of this Country," for which he solicited subscriptions at "only two gold mohurs"—"the Expences attending the Publication not being like to amount to so large as sum as Mr. Bird at first imagined" (*Calcutta Chronicle,* August 21, 1788).[14] Bird, incidentally, was also in the business of organizing subscriptions for concert series, no doubt appealing to many of the same subscribers he sought for his book. The two volumes of John Horsford's *Poems in Three Parts* published in 1800 were, like Anna Maria's volume, advertised at one gold mohur, though Horsford's text was more than double the length of Anna Maria's. Like Anna Maria, Horsford managed to acquire substantial subscribers' lists, pre-selling 170 copies of *A Collection of Poems, Written in the East Indies* (Calcutta, 1797) and 196 copies of *Poems in Three Parts* (Calcutta, 1800). A similar calculation of costs is clear in Sir William Jones's correspondence relative to the *Asiatick Researches* and in the calculations of Francis Gladwin, who edited the *Asiatick Miscellany.*[15]

If we estimate the European population of Calcutta at between three thousand and four thousand in 1790, we see that poets managed to attract as subscribers a substantial proportion of the population literate in English.[16] One must imagine, too, that each subscribed volume was available to multiple readers. These numbers alone attest to the importance of belletristic publishing in fostering social as well as intellectual ties. Volumes of belles lettres also served more easily than musical culture as a portable mode of cultural exchange and a readily available means of intellectual and emotional diversion.

The printed volume of verse and the miscellaneous periodical, then, had an importance for those who valued intellectual pursuits out of any easily measured proportion to their quality. Perhaps the most interesting, if unusual, example of this dedication to belles lettres in a multilingual context comes from George Addison, who as a very young man became an indigo planter in rural Bengal. Born at Calcutta in 1792, Addison was educated in England and returned to Bengal around 1807; by the time he was nineteen, he was attempting to manage an upcountry plantation. This endeavor was no more successful than, as we shall see, was a similar effort by Henry Derozio at about the same time. Addison, like Derozio, fortified himself against business angst with literary and intellectual diversion. His correspondence attests to the importance of sharing books, by personal exchange and by post. Away from the centers of publishing in Calcutta (let alone London), he even went so far as to create his own magazine—persuading employees on the plantation to copy by hand the magazine he produced in manuscript. The *Moofussil Magazine* ran to six issues beginning in June 1811—a decade and more after the texts I am primarily concerned with here. But Addison's efforts indicate the persistence of belles lettres as an arena for creating community.

The author, a relation of the famous Joseph Addison, commenced his "publishing" venture much in the spirit of eighteenth-century satire, even self-satire. The second issue of the magazine includes a gratifying letter to the editor saying that the *Moofussil* has made "a great noise in our little world; some say it is good; others hope the following numbers may equal the first, others again are of the opinion it will shortly die a natural death, for want of a little scandal, or go off in an apoplectic fit." "For my own part," the letter writer says, "I trust it will live to a good old age . . . diffusing around the social circle of Moorshidabad, and its neighbourhood, mirth and good humour, combined with information and amusement."[17] Shortly after his magazine endeavor, Addison moved on to different and probably more congenial employment, as private secretary to Stamford Raffles, then governor of Java, where Addison died in about 1814. His biographer, prefacing a volume of Addison's writings published posthumously in London, attested to the young man's abilities: "[H]is correspondence with friends he valued, on literary topics, and very varied subjects, evinces a playfulness of fancy, delicacy of feeling, and soundness of judgment, remarkable in one so young;—in a word, he was master of six languages—a first-rate mathematician, an admitted classic, a firm and zealous friend."[18] The *Moofussil Magazine* mixed information and amusement including travelogues, poems, essays, and numerous translations from Persian, Greek, Latin, Italian, and French.

Addison's letters, like the magazine itself, make it clear that literary exchanges between Calcutta and towns of the mofussil were a crucial vehicle for sociality. The importance of this network is confirmed by subscribers' lists, which show significant overlap among those purchasing various volumes of verse, as well as by diaries, newspaper columns, memoirs, and travelogues of the period.[19]

Paper was expensive, type hard to come by, and the certainty of the post less than adequate. Nonetheless, belletristic publishing, particularly poems and translations, created cosmopolitan social and intellectual space first for British and European inhabitants of the subcontinent and within a few years for English-educated Indians and "East Indians." Addison avoided the issue of printing by recourse to the scribal traditions that underwrote the majority of literary production on the subcontinent. In the presidencies (Madras, Calcutta, and Bombay), particularly in and near Calcutta, the late eighteenth century saw the invention of types for Indian languages and the printing of books and newspapers designed to compete with, if not supplant, British articles. Addison's hand-copied magazine was, thus, a residual form for English but, in the larger Indian context, not an unusual way of transmitting literary texts.

Graham Shaw has created an exhaustive picture of the challenges attendant on printing in the eighteenth century that makes clear why even in 1811 an upcountry planter would have hired copyists in lieu of printing. Shaw describes in detail the difficulty of acquiring materials and creating fonts. He outlines the rapid turnover of printers and proprietors, the sorrows of proofreading, and the labor of achieving accurate texts. Putting together records from newspapers and many archival sources, he identified for Calcutta more than 350 works published predominantly or in significant part in English in the period between 1777 and 1800 and categorized them by subject. It is interesting, given the fact that the company and its army were entirely engaged in commercial projects and military strategy, that belletristic and cultural matters actually bulked large. On the basis of Shaw's analysis, I have simplified the picture to highlight the relative number of volumes published in each arena:[20]

Utilitarian and political publications:	
[registers, government publications, and military regulations	100]
almanacs and calendars	81
useful subjects (arithmetic, travel, maps, medicine, economics)	70
Indian and European affairs, politics	24
Total:	175
Cultural publications:	
Translations from Persian and Sanskrit historical works	14
Translations from Persian and Sanskrit poetry, prose, and drama	10
Religion, music, and artworks	15
Creative literature in English, mostly poetry	22
Total:	61
Volumes of periodicals (both cultural and utilitarian)	12

If we except government publications, registers, and regulations, the largest single category of works printed for the general reader was almanacs and calendars. These eminently practical items contained tide tables, commodities prices, and shipping information for their mercantile clientele, yet they also were a form of cultural translation, for they provided a collation of the three calendars in which their readers operated: the Gregorian calendar, the Muslim Hijri calendar (specifying the dates and times for prayers and holy days according to the lunar calendar), and the Bangla calendar (a solar calendar, put into place by Akbar in 1584). In this sense, even almanacs, not unlike belletristic texts, represented contact zones, an arena of multiple languages and cultural systems. Newspapers and periodicals functioned similarly, bringing together bits and pieces of all the types of publications then available and reprinting or pirating materials from European periodicals.

Like George Addison, authors, editors, and printers moved among languages and cultural systems, operated in complex and sometimes contradictory temporalities, and reinvented themselves accordingly. In doing so, they also reinvented English language poetry.

Classical and Vernacular Languages at the Origins of Indian English Poetry

English language poetry in India was born in a world of polite letters that, like its counterparts in Britain and America, included groups and coteries connected by location, learning, gender, or shared interests. It was built on differences of class, social and religious position, gender, colonial and economic domination, and divergent political views. For those who might imagine composing poetry in English, divergent access to a variety of languages created divergent possibilities. When we measure the aesthetic, formal, and thematic variety that characterized English language verse in eighteenth-century India, we can understand it as a vernacular poetry in the contexts of orientalist scholarship, European classical learning, and a multilingual spoken and written culture.

I evoke the tortured concept of the vernacular to emphasize not an essence but a set of relationships: the concept of the vernacular like the notion of Asia or, especially, of the Orient is always relative. To describe a language as a vernacular is to concede that it has no stable definition and to emphasize the simple fact that all spoken languages are always in flux. This destabilization of the very notion of language is precisely what is useful for thinking about English language literary writing in India. Obviously, all living languages are always changing as they draw upon multiple sources of contact, but I would argue that there are periods of linguistic change when such contacts take on special intensity.

India between about 1760 and 1860 provides such a period of intense multilingual contact and English vernacular invention. These cultural exchanges are documented most strikingly in the work of poets from the British Isles (or born in India of first-generation parents) in the first half of the period and by Indian or so-called Eurasian poets in the second half.

Now to argue that English served as one among several vernacular languages in this period is to beg the question of what constitutes the "vernacular." It would seem that English language poetry can be vernacular only to those to whom English is "native"; the *Concise Oxford Dictionary of Linguistics* describes the vernacular as "native to a given community, as opposed to a learned or other second language . . . thence generally of languages that are not standardized . . . of forms used locally or characteristic of non-dominant groups or classes."[21] By this definition, in India English has a curious status, which was even more complex in the eighteenth century than in the present. Then as now it functioned as vernacular vis-à-vis learned languages, but at the same time it was a language spoken by a dominant group or class.[22]

The very imprecision—the tangle—of defining the vernacular is what makes it useful for thinking about English language poetry in India. For the male poets I discuss in this chapter, English is a "vernacular" both in the sense of "native" language and in the sense of its opposition to classical or learned languages, including Latin,

Persian, and often Arabic, Sanskrit, Greek, and Hebrew.[23] It is also one vernacular in the context of others—primarily Hindustani (or Hindi/Urdu, the lingua franca of North India in this period), Bangla, Italian, and French. At the same time, these men of letters and East India Company employees relied for both professional and scholarly reasons on often-unacknowledged male collaborators (Indian "pandits" and "maulvis"). For the pandits, such English as they acquired was one of several languages both vernacular and learned. Though we can presume their direct and indirect contributions, for example, to William Jones's English hymns to Indian deities and to his Sanskrit translations, I have found no evidence that there was verse composed in English solely by Indian pandits or maulvis in the eighteenth century.[24]

For most British women, English served as a vernacular in contradistinction to classical learning of all sorts, both European and oriental. In the multilingual arena of eighteenth-century India, English would have functioned for British women in the context of whatever Bangla and Hindi/Urdu they might have learned in addition to other modern European languages. Anna Maria, interestingly, unlike most of her female counterparts in this period, seems to have been at least reasonably well acquainted with Latin. There is no evidence that she was learned in any Asian or oriental classical language, but her identification with the "Della Cruscan" poets of late eighteenth-century Florence and London argues for knowledge of modern European languages, presumably French and Italian. Emma Roberts and Mary Carshore, whom I discuss in later chapters, seem to have learned no classical languages, though Carshore would have been acquainted with the Latin mass.

The instability of these terms—English language poetry, European and oriental languages, classical and vernacular, native versus other second languages, dominant versus nondominant languages—allows us to chart the tangled territory in India that gave rise both to poetry in English and to the continuing critical controversies it raises. Who speaks what language or mixture of languages to whom and on what occasions? Although speech is not properly my subject here, as I am interested in pursuing the growth of belletristic *writing* in English, clearly the multilingual nature of the Indian scene necessarily inflected written practices. Indeed, we might follow the lead of Braj Kachru, who describes twentieth-century Indian English not only as a vernacular but also as a contact language (*Indianization*, 1–26). If Indian English in the twentieth century remains a contact language, linguistic contact in the eighteenth century was formative and powerful along multiple vectors.

English language poetry in the eighteenth century not only reflected the creation of a new social space for belles lettres but also served as a contact zone where disparate cultures, ideas, and material realities met. Within this definition, a contact language must be understood as, like other social spaces, a scene of uneven development and disparate practices. Different writers are differently open to and able to work from a position of comfort with multiplicity. Education, expectation, social milieu, religious values, and family and professional obligations and constraints make any individual writer's position more or less closed or open, that is, make any particular individual more or less able to inhabit the contradictions of contact and thus to make successful art from it.[25]

Arguably, William Jones's poetry had such a significant impact in Europe because of all the British-born poets of eighteenth-century India he was the most curious as well as the most intellectually and linguistically talented. It was precisely the movement between the vernacular and the classical, the movement among languages in the contact zone, the re-creation of English as a contact language that inspired him. Jones saw himself as a person to whom the responsibility of contact, of translation both literal and figurative, and thus of cultural mediation was entrusted by historical circumstance.[26] On the banks of the Hooghly, he imagined himself to be making discoveries as important as those made by the humanists who encountered classical learning in the early modern period. But more, it was as if the world of classical Greece were a living civilization. As he wrote to his friend Richard Johnson about the *Mahābhārata,* its heroes appeared to him, now that he could read Sanskrit, "greater in [his] eyes than Agamemnon, and Ajax, and Achilles appeared, when [he] first read the *Iliad*" (*Letters,* 2:652). It should be no surprise, then, that Jones's original verses—hymns to Indian deities—were mistaken by many readers for translations. To push the point further, one could say that Jones's impact on late eighteenth-century Europe and on English-speaking India was analogous to, if much greater than, Salman Rushdie's impact on the novel two hundred years later—and for similar reasons. Within radically different linguistic and literary contexts, each could be said to have reinvented the English vernacular as a contact language for literary purposes.[27]

Sir William Jones and the Re-creation of Classical Poetics

We could see Addison's *Moofussil Magazine* as typifying the possible discourses of contact, while Jones's original poetry both defined and exceeded the usual practices of "contact" poetry. Addison brought together genres that indicated the complexities of contact, including the learned translation, translations among modern European languages, occasional verse and jeux d'esprit, and lyric poems arising from the writer's efforts to invent himself within a multilingual and diverse cultural arena. While Sir William Jones's poetry written in India connects all these strands, at its best it blends them in a way that had profound effects on his peers in India and on subsequent poems in both India and Europe. At the core of his influence was a ready movement among multiple classical languages and vernaculars.

Jones's influence of course extended well beyond his poetry, for he was not only multilingual but also a polymath in many arenas, each informing the others. Born to a Welsh father who was a distinguished mathematician and to a gifted mother who was the daughter of a cabinetmaker, Jones had to make his own way in the world, for his father died when Jones was three years old. Demonstrating great precocity, Jones won a scholarship to Harrow at seven. At Harrow and later at University College, Oxford, he distinguished himself in the study of languages—Latin, Greek, Hebrew, Arabic, and Persian. During the vacations, he studied Italian, Spanish, and Portuguese. He supplemented scholarship funds by tutoring George John Spencer, Lord Althrop, a post that provided him a lifelong friendship, an entrée to the great Whig families of England, and access to one of its finest libraries. After graduating from Oxford, he studied for the bar and served first on the Oxford circuit and then on the Welsh circuit. Although his major poems are oriental translations and original compositions based on Hindu subjects, Jones studied the Welsh harp, joined the Cymmrodorion Society (for the promotion of Welsh literature, science, and the arts), and became sympathetic to Welsh claims to identity. His sympathy with Welsh poets and peasants was of a piece with his republican views and his defense of the American Revolution. During his British legal career, he was a warm defender of the American cause, becoming friends with Arthur Lee, John Adams, and, in Paris, Benjamin Franklin. When he began to despair of an Indian appointment, he contemplated practicing law in Delaware.

Although Jones was a freethinker in religion and a republican in politics, he longed for a legal appointment to the East India Company in Bengal, believing that he might there indulge his love for languages—and botany, numismatics, and music—while acquiring financial independence. After various politically motivated delays and a dozen years on the Welsh circuit, Jones was appointed judge in Calcutta and was able finally to marry Anna Maria Shipley, daughter of the bishop of Llandaff and St. Aspah and sister of William Davies Shipley. William Shipley, like Jones, was known for his radical politics and indeed was prosecuted for seditious libel after he distributed an anonymous pamphlet written by Jones, an attack on aristocratic privilege and argument for parliamentary reform. Jones left for Bengal as the libel proceedings were pending. In India, Jones experienced the contradictions implicit in his position: "That the middle-class British, with their respect for the extension of liberty in their own country, should have to realize power in India by operating a despotism was a situation fraught with ideological tensions, especially for a radical Whig."[28] Jones's major work in India was designed to legitimate British rule through the collection and codification (in English translation) of Hindu and Muslim law—a work so monumental that Jones left it unfinished upon his sudden death in 1794.

To English letters and scholarship, William Jones made a different but perhaps still more important contribution. Within six months of arriving in Calcutta, he had founded the Asiatic Society and had delivered his "Third Discourse," in which he proposed the familial relationship of Sanskrit, Greek, and Latin as the offspring of a common Indo-European language. With this hypothesis, Jones virtually invented historical comparative linguistics, and his assertion of the common ancestry of North Indian and European languages suggested kinship among the speakers of those languages. Coupled with his linguistic investigations were botanical and musicological projects, in which, as his biographer Michael Franklin argues, Jones combined European systems of knowledge with those of his Indian teachers.

As we will see in the texture of Jones's English language poems, these influences converged, creating a new and cosmopolitan discourse that in its very novelty demanded much of poet and audience alike. Contact poetics, the intermingling of knowledges and of classical and vernacular traditions, is never a simple matter. The most easily legible signs of this "contact poetics" are Jones's paratexts—the titles, headnotes, footnotes, and illustrations that created the possibility of writing across cultural and linguistic divides.

Though it was a jeu d'esprit, paratexts and multiple literacies combined in one of the first poems Jones wrote in India. In their first summer, in 1784, Jones and his wife hired a boat for a trip up the Ganges, intending to conclude their journey at Benares, where Jones was hoping to inspect Sanskrit manuscripts. Suffering from a fever, he was forced to curtail his plans, and he wrote in August in Bihar a brief ballad. "Plassey-Plain" could be taken as a lighthearted but accurate description of Jones's position as a poet. This little poem in quatrains evokes the mock heroic and the mock epic, even as it re-creates the field of conquest as a field of literary contact. The poem also undoes the trope of the evening walk, long familiar to readers of eighteenth-century verse:

'Tis not of Jâfer, nor of Clive,
　　On Plassey's glorious field I sing;
'Tis of the best good girl alive,
　　Which most will deem a prettier thing.

The Sun, in gaudy palanqueen
　　Curtain'd with purple, fring'd with gold,
Firing no more heav'n's vault serene,
　　Retir'd to sup with Ganges old.

When Anna, to her bard long dear,
　　(Who lov'd not Anna on the banks
Of Elwy swift, or Testa clear?)
　　Tripp'd thro' the palm grove's verdant ranks.

(*Works*, 2:503)

From this beginning, the poet recounts Anna's evening stroll, innocent as she is of the dangers surrounding her. Various animals attempt to warn her of her peril, but she is as yet ignorant of their languages. Her only, but effective, shield is her virtue.

"Plassey-Plain" has the slenderest paratexts of any of Jones's Indian English poems—merely two footnotes and a headnote, reading "A Ballad, Addressed to Lady Jones, by her Husband. Aug. 3, 1784." Jones's friend, John Shore, Lord Teignmouth, first published "Plassey-Plain" in his *Memoirs of the Life, Writings, and Correspondence of Sir William Jones* and appended a further parenthetical headnote, a note to the poet's note: "Lady Jones having been exposed to some danger in an evening walk over the plains of Plassey,

Sir William almost immediately wrote the following stanzas." Jones (or perhaps Lady Jones, who edited his work) had also appended further annotation, for the dateline provided below the title was accompanied by an editorial reminder to the reader (though "it can scarcely be necessary") that Plassey Plain was the scene of Lord Clive's victory over Siraj-Ud-Daulah upon his betrayal by Mir Jafar. Through a mock heroic (itself an intertextual form), through introductory paratexts, and through multiple literary allusions, Jones recuperates tragedy (the Mughal nawab's defeat at the hands of the British) or comedy (Clive's successful conquest) in a scene of linguistic misunderstanding.

Anna's bard, not quite a Welsh bard but rather a cosmopolitan one, has loved her on the bank of the Elway (in Wales) as on the bank of the Testa, or Teesta (on the border of West Bengal). Lady Jones is said to resemble Edmund Spenser's Una, protected by her virtue, but like Spenser's Redcrosse knight, William is missing in action while the damsel suffers distress. Though it would be wrong to make too much of the Spenserian allusions in a mock heroic ballad, Spenser surely provides a fit starting point for reflection on poetry in a contact zone. Jones's poem seeks to remake a former field of battle under a more benign construction of contact. Heroics are avoided in favor of the domestic (or mock heroic). A happy ending is guaranteed.

Though it had been a generation since Clive's victory and though the East India Company was supposed to be firmly in command, Plassey Plain in this poem is still ringed with dangers. Like Una, Anna Maria should be saved from more violent beasts by the helpful animals she encounters, but she is in worse straits than Una: not only is her knight absent but also, given the language barriers, Anna Maria cannot understand her would-be protectors:

> Wild perroquets first silence broke,
>   Eager of dangers near to prate;
> But they in English never spoke,
>   And she began her moors of late.
>
> Next, patient dromedaries stalk'd,
>   And wish'd her speech to understand;
> But Arabic was all they talk'd;—
>   Oh, had her Arab been at hand!
>
> A serpent dire, of size minute,
>   With necklace brown, and freckled side,
> Then hasten'd from her path to shoot,
>   And o'er the narrow causey glide.
>
> Three elephants, to warn her, call
>   But they no western tongue could speak;
> Tho' once, at Philobiblian stall,
>   Fame says, a brother jabber'd Greek.[29]

Unlike the famous linguist to whom she is married, Anna Maria is missing the classical languages—Arabic, Greek, and whatever other learned language these elephants have chosen (Persian? Sanskrit?). She might hope, instead, to understand the birds' warning, since the parakeets speak a local vernacular—"moors," or Hindustani. Being but lately arrived, however, she has yet to master it. For Anna Maria and for the poet's probable domestic reader, the poem seams together conflicting frames of reference. If we cannot manage either "moors" or classical learning, perhaps we will catch the poet's allusions to Spenser and to John Gay's fable "The Elephant and the Bookseller," which itself alludes to Pliny the Elder.

On Plassey Plain the scene of writing becomes a scene of translation. The very animals speak a polyglot mixture of learned and vernacular tongues. Ideally, the damsel in distress would be adept at polyglossic code switching among them. The elephants, alas, "no western tongue could speak."

In his next jeu d'esprit, Jones employs the mahout as well as the elephant. He turns to paratextual strategies to navigate a similar linguistic contact zone. His comic poem "The Enchanted Fruit; or, The Hindu Wife: An Antediluvian Tale Written in the Province of Bahar (1784)" was first published in a privately printed edition in Calcutta in the same year.[30] It subsequently appeared in the *Asiatick Miscellany* in 1785 and was reprinted in London two years later. In 1792, it appeared again in London with various of Jones's hymns in the edition of the *Miscellany* that collected pieces from the Calcutta editions of 1785 and 1786. The poem was next included in Jones's *Collected Works* (1807) and then in Michael Franklin's modern edition, *Selected Poetical and Prose Works.*

The first appearance of "The Enchanted Fruit" in pamphlet form in 1784 includes no footnotes, but the subsequent editions are heavily larded with them, perhaps reflecting the difference between what Jones expected from a small audience of friends in Bengal as opposed to a larger audience, including a metropolitan one. In short, for readers abroad (and possibly in Calcutta as well), Jones's jeu d'esprit required explanation, which in the first printed copies he deemed unnecessary.[31] The paratextual apparatus on some pages dominates the textual. Franklin's edition includes all of Jones's notes and adds more than twenty additional ones for the benefit of modern readers. With Jones's own version, and still more with Franklin's, we are perhaps in the same position as readers of *The Dunciad,* negotiating through an entire palimpsest of commentary.

Certainly "The Enchanted Fruit," like "Plassey-Plain," has a Scriblerian tinge, as it mingles the learned and the mock heroic. Jones instructs—via translation, via literary allusion, and via scholarly citation—but his goal is chiefly to delight:

> 'O Lovely age,* by *Brahmens* fam'd
> 'Pure *Setye Yug*** in *Sanscrit* nam'd!
> 'Delightful! Not for cups of *gold,*
> 'Or wives *a thousand centuries* old;
> 'Or men, degenerate now and small,

'Then *one and twenty cubits* tall:
'Not that plump *cows* full udders bore,
'And bowls with *holy curd**** ran o'er;
'Not that, by Deities defended
'*Fish, Boar, Snake, Lion,***** heav'n-descended,
'Learn'd *Pendits,* now grown sticks and clods,
'Redde fast the *Nagry of the Gods******
'And laymen, faithful to *Narayn*******
'Believ'd in *Brahmá*'s mystick strain;********
'Not that all Subjects spoke plain truth,
'While *Rajas* cherish'd eld and youth,
'No—yet delightful times! because
'*Nature* then reign'd, and *Nature's laws;*
'When females of the softest kind
'Were unaffected, unconfin'd;
'And this grand rule from none was hidden;*********
'WHAT PLEASESTH, HATH NO LOW FORBIDDEN.'

(*Selected,* 81, lines 1–22)

Jones quotes and translates Tasso in his jesting assertion that the golden age, like the age of Tasso's pastoral *Aminta,* is one of delight—no law then had been passed against pleasures. Anything that pleases, unless legally sanctioned, is to be enjoyed. Tasso's pastoral land, Jones implies, is to be found on the banks of the Ganges. What is more, in this splendid time, learned pandits could simply breeze through their Sanskrit. The intertextual play here brings together Tasso with the *Purāṇas* and probably even Hesiod. I have used asterisks to indicate Jones's notes, rather than following his complex set of symbols. Obviously, this poem published early in his time in India is both playful and, in Martin Priestman's words, "encrusted" with references (51). The European pastoral is equated with the "Setye Yug," or Satya Age, the age of truth, and the poem evokes the late eighteenth-century debate about monogamy and prefigures Erasmus Darwin's treatment of plants by "using Linnaeus' account of plant reproduction to point out the variety of sexual combinations available to plants and hence, by implication, to humans" (Priestman, 76).[32]

In the next stanza, this golden age is characterized anew, when "swarthy nymphs of Hindustan" answer the poet. It is not pastoral plenty or the genius of pandits, they say, that marked the golden age; rather, the golden age was delightful, for then "ONE BUXOM DAME MIGHT WED FIVE MEN." With this preface—a mock heroic and pastoral rendition of the "golden age"—Jones inaugurates the story of Draupadī and the five Pāṇḍava brothers (to whom she is married). In the *Mahābhārata* story, one of the Pāṇḍavas has shot from its tree a brahmin's fruit—to restore the fruit and avert the brahmin's curse, all five brothers and their wife-in-common must confess their sins.

Each brother, in turn, does so, expressing regret for martial or other manly excesses. Draupadī comes last and by confessing her relatively innocent dalliance with her Sanskrit pandit restores the fruit. The epilogue sees the poet address British wives, wishing that they like Draupadī could replace Eve's apple on its parent tree. Britannia at last comes to the defense of British wives, vanquishing the demon Scandal and making a gesture to defuse the possible domestic implications of Jones's tale.

Along the way to Draupadī's amusing "confession," Jones delights in cataloging the flora of India, in addition to joking about its fauna. Both varieties of discourse produce their own serious or comic annotations. Beginning with fauna, Jones jokes about polyandry, first citing in his note "Mr. Bogle," who contributed a study of Tibetan polyandry to the *Philosophical Transactions,* and then alluding to Linnaeus as a "learned northern Brahmen":

> Thus Botanists, with eyes acute
> To see prolifick dust minute,
> Taught by their learned northern *Brahmen**
> To class by *pistil* and by *stamen,*
> Produce from nature's rich dominion
> Flow'rs *Polyandrian Monogynian,*
> Where embryon blossoms, fruits and leaves
> *Twenty* prepare, and One receives.
>
> (*Selected,* 83, lines 65–72)

Jones's note reads "Linnaeus," and indeed there is something quite wonderful about thinking of Linnaeus as a "northern Brahmin," not to mention the Hudibrastic amusement of rhyming Brahmen/stamen, and dominion/polyandrian/monygian. Jones goes on to enact the Linnaean project, but with a difference.[33]

Rather than simply assimilating the flora of India to the Linnaean model (as he and Anna Maria did in their botanizing projects), Jones assimilates Linnaeus to the Indian context and provides a catalog of flora in terms of Indian terminology along with numerous footnotes for the edification of his British readers and amusement of his Anglophone Indian readers:

> Light-pinion'd gales, to charm the sense,
> Their odorif'rous breath dispense;
> From *Béla's** pearl'd, or pointed, bloom,
> And *Málty* rich, they steal perfume:
> There honey-scented *Singarhár,*
> And *Júhy,* like a rising star,
> Strong *Chempá,* darted by *Cámdew,*
> And *Mulsery* of pale hue,

*Cayora,*** which the *Ranies* wear
In tangles of their silken hair,
Round*** *Bábul*-flow'rs, and *Gualchein*
Dyed like the shell of Beauty's queen,
Sweet *Mindy***** press'd for crimson stains,
And sacred *Tulsy,****** pride of plains,
With *Séwty,* small unblushing rose,
Their odours mix, their tints disclose,
And, as a gemm'd tiara, bright,
Paint the fresh branches with delight.

(84–85, lines 107–24)

Jones's paratext, his notes (indicated as before by asterisks), can be summarized as follows: *Béla, Málty, Singarhár,* and *Júhy* refer to varieties of jasmine; Jones glosses *Cayora* as "Indian spikenard," and the *Bábul* as the mimosa or true gum acacia; *Mindy* he says is "called Albhinná by the Arabs," and *Tulsy* (holy basil) is glossed as "of the kind called Ocymum." Now, Jones presumes or imagines that his audience will have no trouble with *Chempá* and *Mulsery,* or even with *Mindy* or *Tulsy,* as his notes for these plants are scarcely explanatory. Nor does he help his audience out with *Cámdew* (or Camdeo, as he elsewhere transliterates the name). Thus Franklin, Jones's modern editor, finds himself cross-referencing Jones's other works—his "Hymn to Camdeo" and "Botanical Observations." Even with Jones's own paratext—and assisted by Franklin—the reader who is not a Linnaean Brahmin may be hard pressed to make sense of the references.

One can only speculate that Jones created both text and paratext for his own amusement—and perhaps for the learned amusement of the other members of the Asiatic Society or for his friend Joseph Banks, the eminent botanist and president of the Royal Society. We might think of "The Enchanted Fruit" as Jones's own Banksian botanical exercise: the famous Draupadī becomes a "five-mal'd single-femal'd flower." Jones's Eve manages to restore the apple to its place, to right the world, and to amuse the reader—at least, the reader who has a Banksian knowledge of botany.

Jones's poem itself represents a novel and unusual literacy—after all, Draupadī's encounter with a learned Brahmin is what gives rise to her need for confession.[34] Like an Indian Héloïse, she finds female (and classical) literacy not without its temptations. Reading exotic flora, like reading the Sanskrit text, may be fraught with temptation. But ultimately, the tree of knowledge and the tree of life in this Indian garden are one. Unlike Héloïse, Draupadī inhabits a golden age, where there is no distinction between knowledge and pleasure.

As Garland Cannon notes, the paratext here threatens, despite the poem's thematic, to overwhelm the text. In Cannon's view, "the poem lacks verve and drama, partly because of Jones's scholarship. Trying to convey local color across the vast cultural and linguistic gap, he extensively transliterates Sanskrit words for foods, geography, and aspects of Hinduism." Cannon characterizes the footnotes as "obtrusive" and argues that the apparatus of notes and transliteration make the poem "fail as an Anglo-Indian romance based lightly on an Indian plot" (*Life*, 218). Nonetheless, this poem along with several other early translations and invented tales contributed to the romantic penchant for Indian materials and for footnotes guaranteeing both their exoticism and their authenticity.

The encrusted nature of these poems is a testimony to the larger work of cultural translation, which in this case is also a work of transliteration. As Priestman argues, Jones found himself between cultures, engaging Indian religions with an open mind; at the same time, his project of knowledge was part of the effort to "confirm British power as ruling the colonized society from the inside, and as it were on its own behalf" (53). But the nature of Jones's freethinking meant an unusual kind of sympathy with Indian thought and poetry, even as the poet had to compartmentalize his dislike for political tyranny and monarchism of all sorts. The difficulties, then, of cultural and linguistic translation make for seams showing, for awkwardness in the production and reception of Jones's poetry.

Jones's Hymns to Indian Deities: Paratext as Argument

Neither of his mock heroic poems was central to Jones's powerful impact on European poetry. Rather, his hymns to Indian deities and his translation of Kālidāsa's *Śakuntalā* had the more profound impact on European letters. Jones's first hymn, "A Hymn to Camdeo," was composed in 1784, before he learned Sanskrit; it was based on his reading of Persian translations of Sanskrit texts. As Franklin details in his helpful introduction to the hymn, the poem was first read to the Asiatic Society and subsequently published in London (1784) in *A Discourse on the Institution of a Society*, along with Jones's "First Charge to the Grand Jury." The title page to the first London edition announced, misleadingly, that the hymn was "translated from the Hindu into Persian, and from the Persian into English" (quoted in Franklin, *Selected*, 98). This gave rise to the British misapprehension that the poem was indeed a translation, a misapprehension not clarified when the poem was reprinted in the *Asiatic Miscellany* (1785) and in the *Annual Register* (London, 1784–85). In 1796, two years after the author's death, the *Monthly Review* finally clarified the provenance of Jones's hymns (Franklin, 98).

Jones's hymns, taken singly, had less European impact than the translation of *Śakuntalā*, but as a group they made a mark. Their impact came both despite and because of their difficulties. Garland Cannon has aptly described the poems' difficulties for European readers:

> Jones partly evokes the sensuous, delicate Indian atmosphere by transliterating place-names and other proper nouns. Though usually phonetically accurate, these strange words constitute stumbling blocks that are one reason

> why even his hymns to Narayana and Kama are not fine English poetry. This is the familiar problem of his learning. Having experimented with intrusive footnotes in 'The Enchanted Fruit,' he scrupulously avoids them in the hymns and burdens his Arguments with a bewildering array of information. Some contemporary periodicals omitted these little scholarly essays, leaving the reader without an explanation of the names. Sometimes Jones had added a stanza simply to present more epithets, thereby making his subject culturally remote for most Western readers. But if the hymns are not poetry of the highest order, they are nonetheless aflame with enthusiasm and knowledge. (*Life*, 237)

Despite his doubts, Cannon still considers Jones's hymns the greatest English odes between Gray and Wordsworth. And perhaps for the reader of modernist poetry or, for that matter, of Blake or Milton or Shelley, Jones's burden of learning is not quite so daunting as Cannon would suggest. Moreover, one might argue the reverse: the very quality of unfamiliarity, the orientalizing of English, was the primary attraction of these poems. With Jones's hymns, as with Ezra Pound's *Cantos* much later, the attraction of the poetry is, in no small part, its opacity.

A closer look at the hymns makes clear that the nature of English as a contact language is precisely what troubles Cannon—and troubled the poet. While the paratext in the form of notes threatens to overwhelm "The Enchanted Fruit," in the hymns the prefatory prose "argument" serves as paratext; in many instances, these arguments are as substantial as the verse. In nearly every prefatory argument, the poet engages in and then draws back from explanation, both inviting and repelling the English language reader, whom he clearly imagines to be only dimly acquainted with his materials. In this respect, though the poems are original compositions, they function both as a seam of cultural contact and as a species of cultural, if not textual, translation.

Virtually all of the prefatory materials demonstrate the poet's uneasy compromise between fluidity and legibility. In the second hymn, "To Náráyena," Jones begins the argument by claiming, "A complete introduction to the following Ode would be no less than a full comment on the VAYDS and PURÁNS of the HINDUS, the remains of *Egyptian* and *Persian* Theology, and the tenets of the *Ionick* and *Italick* Schools; but this is not the place for so vast a disquisition" (*Selected*, 106). In the miniature disquisition that does follow, the poet connects the Hindu notion of maya to ancient and modern European notions that all bodies and their qualities "exist only so far as they are *perceived*"; he goes on to draw comparisons among Platonic, Egyptian, and Indian philosophical ideas of divine essence.

Jones makes similar moves in the paratexts to other hymns. He claims in the "Hymn to Sereswaty" that "full discussion of so copious a subject" as Indian music "would require a separate dissertation; but here it will be sufficient to say, that almost every allusion and every epithet in the Poem, as well as the names, are selected from approved treatises, either originally *Persian* or translated from the *Sanscrit,* which contain as lively a display of genius, as human imagination ever exhibited" (*Selected,* 115). Similarly, he commences the argument prefacing the more accessible "Hymn to Gangá" by acknowledging, "This poem would be rather obscure without geographical notes; but a short introductory explanation will supply the place of them, and give less interruption to the reader" (124). He goes on for about a thousand words of prefatory geographical commentary. Similarly, the "Hymn to Indra" commences with an argument acknowledging, "So many allusions to Hindu Mythology occur in the following Ode, that it would be scarce intelligible without an explanatory introduction, which on every account and on all occasions, appears preferable to notes in the margin" (134).

The argument prefacing the "Hymn to Súrya" concludes, "After this explanation the Hymn will have few or no difficulties, especially if the reader has perused and studied the *Bhagavadgítá,* with which our literature has been lately enriched, and the fine episode from the *Mahábhárat,* on the production of the *Amrita,* which seems to be almost wholly astronomical, but abounds with poetical beauties. Let the following description of the demon *Ráhu,* decapitated by *Náráyan,* be compared with similar passages in *Hesiod* and *Milton*" (145). Jones brings the argument to a close with a transliterated passage from the *Mahābhārata,* evidently hoping that his readers, who cannot be assumed to know Sanskrit, will be charmed by the rhyme and rhythm they can draw from the verses:

> tach ch'hailasringapratiman dánavasya sirò mahat
> chacraḉh'hinnam c'hamutpatya nenáditi bhayancaram,
> tat cabandham pepátásya visp'hurad dharanítalè
> sapervatavanadwípán daityasyácampayanmahím.
>
> (145)

This passage from the *Mahābhārata* is probably the account of the beheading of Rāhu. Wendy Doniger translates it this way: "The great head of the demon, which was like the peak of a mountain, fell to the earth as it was cut off by the discus, and it shook the earth. The severed head rose up to the sky, roaring terribly, but the headless torso of the demon fell and split open the surface of the earth, causing a tremor throughout the earth with its mountains, forests, and islands" (278). Just how even the learned reader of English is to compare Jones's untranslated but transliterated passage to Hesiod and Milton is unclear, though with a translation one can readily see the allusion to the fall of Satan. Jones's comparisons to Hesiod and Milton, not to mention the numerous Miltonic echoes in the hymns, indicates that the poet envisions at least some of his audience as speaking or at least exploring all the languages, both classical and vernacular, available in the polyglot culture that was late eighteenth-century India.

Whatever their linguistic and cultural difficulties, as Michael Franklin shows, the hymns had a significant impact on such nineteenth-century poems as *Prometheus*

Unbound and "The Rime of the Ancient Mariner." The "Hymn to Sereswaty," for example, appears to have influenced both poems, shaping the musical allegory of the Spirits of the Hours in Act IV of Shelley's *Prometheus Unbound* (Franklin, *Selected*, 117n29).

As it is a poem itself about poetry and music, the "Hymn to Sereswaty" provides an unusually good example of the linguistic and cross-cultural challenges Jones faced in trying to create a poetry adequate to experiences of Indian poetry and art. Though Jones eschewed notes, Franklin creates more than forty notes of his own for a poem of only 169 lines. Franklin's notes have at least as many words as the poem and are crucial to a modern reader's understanding—as they would have been, had they been available, to the eighteenth-century reader.

The "Hymn to Sereswaty" celebrates the divinity in her role as the goddess of "Musick and Rhetorick," as Jones puts it. In the prefatory argument, Jones compares "Sereswaty" to "Minerva Musica" in Greece and Italy, who "invented the flute, and presided over literature." The "Hymn to Sereswaty" does not simply allude to Persian and Sanskrit treatises on music and to the complex system of classical ragas, however; it also is based on Indian paintings for music (*rāgamālā* paintings), which would have been unknown to many in Jones's audience. Jones knew such paintings through those collected by his friend Richard Johnson, who was attached to the East India Company's Board of Revenue when Jones arrived in Calcutta. Johnson was a Persianist and a student of Indian music and (according to Cannon) was invited to dine with the Joneses twice weekly shortly after the poet arrived in Calcutta.[35] He was also an art collector, and the fine collection of *rāgamālā* miniatures he acquired is now in the British Library (see the Johnson Collection, India Office Prints and Drawings).

Harold Powers has provided one of the clearest and most succinct descriptions of the *rāgamālā*, a genre that flourished in northern and western India and in the Deccan from the sixteenth to the nineteenth centuries:

> A *rāgamālā*—'garland of *rāgas*'—in this context is a uniform set of miniature paintings each of which shows one or more individuals in some kind of standardized human and/or natural environment. An individual *rāga* painting (*rāga-citrā*) can depict an easily identifiable situation or relationship, or its central figure or figures may be striking a characteristic pose, or they may be accompanied by one or more easily recognizable emblematic props. Each painting is supposed to be the visual counterpart of a named Indian melodic type, a *rāga* (Hindusthani *rāg*); the feminine form *rāgiṇi* (Hindusthani *rāgani* or *rāgini*) is a term with the same musical sense that is used only in this context. There also exist poetic stanzas describing the situations depicted in these vignettes, both in Sanskrit and in Hindi vernaculars, and latterly in Persian. Often not only the name of a *rāga* but also a descriptive verse appears on a painting, or on its reverse. (473)

Jones's friend Johnson was actively collecting such paintings and acquired one of the most famous albums still extant. These albums of paintings were made in sets, and according to Powers "in the commonest structural systems there is a standard number of six male *rāgas* each of which is accompanied by the same fixed number of female *rāgiṇis,* usually five." Powers calls these collections "set structures" and describes the commonest one as a "36 + 6 x (1 *rāga* = 5 *rāgiṇis*)" (476). Johnson's album followed this thirty-six painting structure, and each painting was inscribed with verses from the Hindi translation of the *Sangita-darpana.* This Hindi volume (a manual of instrumental music, singing, and dancing) was, according to Toby Falk and Mildred Archer, based on a Sanskrit work of the same title written by Damodara.[36]

Jones worked from a translation of the *Sangita-darpana* and from various Sanskrit sources to write his essay "On the Musical Modes of the Hindus." In this essay, begun in 1784 and revised many times over the next decade, Jones praised the Indian artists' way of linking music with "poetical fables"; such work, he believed, equaled or surpassed the "inventive talents of the Greeks." He argued that "the fancy of Shakspeare and the pencil of Albano might have been finely employed in giving speech and form to this assemblage of aerial beings, who people the fairy-land of Indian imagination; nor have the Hindu poets and painters lost the advantages, with which so beautiful a subject presented them" (*Works,* 4:193). Indeed, Jones argues that the descriptions of the musical modes and "a metrical tract on musick ascribed to the God Náred himself" demonstrate that the Sanskrit language is "equal to Italian in softness and elegance" (4:194).

In the summer of 1785, Jones promised Richard Johnson a copy of his "Hymn to Sereswaty" (see *Selected,* 113), and he acknowledged Johnson's and his friend John Hay's collections of *rāgamālā* paintings as "wonderfully diversified." He was evidently inspired by these works, for he fantasizes in "On the Musical Modes" about a lovely but costly book that might be made from a collection of Indian Sanskrit poems and treatises on music. Such a book would combine "the old melodies of So'ma applied to the songs of Jayade'va, embellished with descriptions of all the modes accurately translated, and with Mr. Hay's Ragamala delineated and engraved by the scholars of Cipriani and Bartolozzi" (*Works,* 4:194).

The paintings on which Jones based his hymn—Johnson's and Hay's collections of miniatures—followed the system of associations of particular *ragas* or musical modes with seasons, times of day, and particular deities. In the argument to the "Hymn to Sereswaty," Jones briefly and confusingly describes this system. Jones writes that the various modes of the *ragas* are "elegantly formed on the variations of the Indian year," seasons, and times of day. As Jones puts it in his treatise on Indian music, each *raga* is "a Genius or Demigod, wedded to five Ráginis or Nymphs, and father of eight little Genii" (quoted in Franklin, *Selected,* 118n53). Thus, each *raga* is associated with what Johnson called a "singular personification" and with a particular iconography (for iconography, see Falk and Archer).

Following this theory of music and painting, Jones's hymn nevertheless begins in a relatively accessible way even for the Anglophone reader unfamiliar with his subject, for the poet's argument has provided a key to all the allusions of the first stanza. In the "argument," he writes that Sereswaty is the "subordinate power" of Brahma, "which may justly be termed *creative*" (*Selected*, 114):

> Sweet grace of BREHMA's bed!
> Thou, when thy glorious lord
> Bade airy nothing breathe and bless his pow'r,
> Satst with illumin'd head,
> And in sublime accord,
> Sev'n sprightly notes, to hail th' auspicious hour,
> Ledst from their secret bow'r:
> They drank the air; they came
> With many a sparkling glance,
> And knit the mazy dance,
> Like yon bright orbs, that gird the solar flame,
> Now parted, now combin'd,
> Clear as thy speech and various as thy mind.
>
> (116, lines 1–13)

Jones deliberately echoes Shakespeare's Theseus (who declares that art gives to "airy nothing" a "local habitation and a name") but in a diction raised to a Miltonic level, as appropriate to the Pindaric ode. Indeed, Jones has likely taken a page from Gray's Pindaric odes as well as from Tasso's, for the "Hymn to Sereswaty" can be understood as Jones's version of or reply to Gray's "Progress of Poetry." Like Gray, Jones too has recourse to the paratext. Gray began his ode with a passage from Pindar in the Greek and with the declaration that he was "advised even by his Friends to subjoin some few explanatory Notes; but had too much respect for the understanding of his Readers to take that liberty."[37] Like Jones, who subsumed his notes in his argument, Gray initially eschewed but then came to rely on interpretive explanation.

Jones commences, then, with material that would have made sense to his Anglophone reader, for Sereswaty (that is, Sarasvatī) is explained in the argument. The procession of *rāgas* and *rāgiṇis* that follows this first stanza no doubt posed a more significant challenge. As the goddess leads forth the *rāgas,* each of these demigods, like a new planet, brings a musical mode to life. The hymn proceeds through the *rāgas,* in thirteen stanzas of thirteen lines; each stanza varies line lengths according to a repeated formula.

In the tenth stanza, Jones comes to the Srīrāga, the fifth of the *rāgas,* accompanied by his five *rāgiṇis.* Jones's description of Srīrāga in the hymn attempts to capture the spirit of a passage he quoted in "On the Musical Modes":

Lílá viháréna vanántarálé
Chinvan prasúnáni vadhú faháya,
Viláfi vésódita dvya múrtih
Srírága ésha prat'hitah prit'hivyám.

(*Works,* 4:194)

Jones translates these lines: "The demigod Srírága, famed over all this earth, sweetly sports with his nymphs, gathering fresh blossoms in the bosom of yon grove; and his divine lineaments are distinguished through his graceful vesture" (4:194). The tenth stanza of the hymn attempts something of the Sanskrit text's play:

Sing loud, ye lucid spheres;
Ye gales, more briskly play,
And wake with harmony the drooping meads:
The cooler season cheers
Each bird, that panting lay,
And Siry bland his dancing bevy leads
Hymning celestial deeds:
Marvá with robes like fire,
Vasant whose hair perfumes
With musk its rich-eyed plumes.
Ásávery, whom list'ning asps admire,
Dhenásry, flow'r of glades,
And *Málsry,* whom the branching *Amra* shades.

(*Selected,* 118)

Franklin glosses this stanza liberally, but Jones was content to allow his European readers to glimpse unexplained an exotic procession of *rāgiṇis* (Srīrāga's dancing bevy). Srīrāga's *rāgiṇis* would have been as foreign to European readers as the flora Jones described in "The Enchanted Fruit." Indeed, we could think of this stanza as a kind of poetic and linguistic cornucopia, one that might evoke one set of understandings from Jones's friend Richard Johnson but quite another from British readers in the metropole, for whom it would have been an exotic litany.

The last stanza of the "Hymn to Sereswaty" anticipates the hymn next in composition, "A Hymn to Gangá." Like the beginning of the "Hymn to Gangá," the last stanza of the "Hymn to Sereswaty" deliberately creates a web of "oriental" allusions. Here the names of Sarasvatī are multiplied, and the goddess takes the form of the river that bears her name.

These are thy wond'rous arts;
Queen of the flowering speech,
Thence Sereswaty nam'd and Vány bright!

Oh, joy of mortal hearts,
Thy mystic wisdom teach;
Expand thy leaves, and, with ethereal light,
Spangle the veil of night.
If LEPIT please thee more,
Or BRÁHMY, awful name,
Dread BRÁHMY's aid we claim,
And thirst, VÁCDÉVY, for thy balmy lore
Drawn from that rubied cave,
Where meek-ey'd pilgrims hail the triple wave.

(*Selected*, 122, lines 157–68)

In the argument, Jones has informed us that the "triple wave" alludes to the "confluence" of the "Gangá and the Yamná, which the Sereswaty, another sacred river, is supposed to join underground" (115).[38] The allusions are buttressed not only by this paratext but also by the bibliographical code, as the poet demarcates the epithets of Sereswaty with small caps. A reader of Sanskrit would have no trouble with the goddess's alternative names: "Vány," or Mahāvāni (transcendent word); "Vácdévy," or Vakdevī (goddess of speech); and Bráhmy, or Brahmi (wife or *shakti* of Brahma). As is evident in Horsford's translation of Jones's Latin version of Sappho, Jones here no doubt recognized the practice common to Greek and Sanskrit poetry of invoking deities by their many names—the poet seeks the epithets that will please the deity most.

But of course virtually all of Jones's European readers (and most of his Anglophone readers in India) would have known no Sanskrit, and the litany of names in the "Hymn to Sereswaty" would have been vocatory rather than allusive. Indeed, the poem's final stanza echoes the invocatory tone of the poem's beginning even as it functions as an astonishing testimonial to Jones's deist approach to religious questions. Though he considered himself a Christian, it was of the most broad-minded sort; given his absolute dedication to learning and to poetry, one must take this invocation to "queen of flowing speech" still more seriously than one might understand Milton's invocation of "Urania."[39]

It should be no surprise that the conclusion of the "Hymn to Sereswaty" leads to the Miltonic commencement of the "Hymn to Gangá." In this next hymn, Jones describes the maternal spirit of the sacred river in a Miltonic simile:

As when an eagle, child of light,
On *Cambala*'s unmeasur'd height,
By *Pótala*, the pontiff's throne rever'd,
O'er her eyry proudly rear'd
Sits brooding, and her plumage vast expands,
Thus GANGÁ o'er her cherished lands

. . . .

Throws wide her fost'ring arms, and on her banks divine
See temples, groves, and glitt'ring tow'rs, that in her crystal shine.

(*Selected*, 127, lines 5–10, 12–13)

As the poet says in the argument to this hymn, his stanza form is "partly borrowed from Gray." The substitution of a final line of fourteen syllables expresses "the long and solemn march of the great Asiatick rivers" (126). Jones proceeds here by matching meanings—the Dalai Lama becomes the Buddhist "pontiff," the deity/spirit of the Ganges becomes the holy spirit creating the world from the waters. Accompanying the "Hymn to Gangá" is an illustration of the maternal spirit of the river, walking upon the water with a lotus in either hand, appearing in a kind of framed medallion and subtended by a garlanded plaque with her name in devanagari script.

As in similar medallions accompanying the other hymns, the visual here performs an orientalist function. The top of the medallion is matched by a devanagari equivalent below it, and the figure could easily be read by European audiences unfamiliar with Indian art—not as iconographical but as exotic. At the same time, the crudeness of the engravings, especially in contrast to the elegance of the *rāgamālā* paintings Jones knew, is antithetical to the seriousness of the hymns and to the claims, made both in the arguments and in the poetic texts, for the sublimity of the deities addressed.

Paratext and intertexts as well as linguistic and bibliographical codes tell overlapping, but sometimes contradictory, stories. From the allusions and mock heroic of "Plassey-Plain" to the copious footnotes of "The Enchanted Fruit" to the arguments accompanying the hymns, the seams between text and paratext and between bibliographical and linguistic codes are often evident: sometimes deliberately so, sometimes inadvertently. But these conjunctures reveal the necessities of English poetry entering a new geography where it functions, differentially depending upon its audience, as a contact vernacular.

Sir John Horsford: Led Astray by Poetry

A different but related situation obtains in the case of Sir John Horsford. Horsford was a great admirer of Jones and was certainly his friend, if not an intimate. Both men were learned, though Horsford was so in a narrower range, as reflected in his general attitudes, ethical disposition, and education. We might view Horsford's two collections of poetry as exemplifying a different course of learning from Jones's and a different approach to the seams between vernacular and classic, European and Indian cultures. They reflect, as well, the habitus of a soldier, for Horsford spent his entire adult life in the Bengal Artillery. With Jones, Horsford shared an education but not a profession. Horsford was a Fellow of St. John's College, Oxford, during the same period when Jones was a Fellow of University College.

Evidently he shared Jones's love of the Greek and Latin classics, if not his broad study in Persian and Sanskrit.

The paratexts and the intertexts of Horsford's poetry bespeak unease with the cultural, social, and linguistic geographies in which he functioned. In 1800, Horsford reprinted a collection of poems he had published three years earlier as "J.—H.—." Whereas the first edition had been titled *A Collection of Poems Written in the East Indies, with Miscellaneous Remarks on Real Life*, the later volume added two additional sections and was titled *Poems in Three Parts*. This long volume was printed in Calcutta by Thomas Hollingbery at the Hircarrah Press. The first of these new sections comprised a facing-page translation of Sir William Jones's Latin verse; the second was a versified history of the Asiatic Society. Part three reprinted the poetry, but not the prose essays, of the earlier volume.

Though he aspired to poetic fame and assembled an impressive list of subscribers for his first volume of verse, Horsford was at best a workmanly poet. We have only scant biographical details, but clearly he wished to become a poet from an early age, and his poetic ambitions in some way complicated his professional future. The *Oxford Dictionary of National Biography* notes that Horsford abruptly gave up his Oxford fellowship in 1771 and enlisted in the army of the East India Company under the assumed name John Rover. Probably Horsford was seeking to avoid taking holy orders, the "profession for which his friends intended him," as the *DNB* elegantly puts it. Legend has it that his identity was discovered, or confirmed, by his commanding colonel when Horsford corrected an error in a Greek tag in the colonel's correspondence.[40] This anecdote, however apocryphal, encapsulates the realities of class, education, and profession then shaping the army. No enlisted man would have been expected to know Greek; few would have been truly literate in English. Horsford, a.k.a. John Rover, would obviously have been a gentleman masquerading beneath his station. Obviously, too, India was scarcely distant enough for a young man with a genteel upbringing to escape his past. However, his six years as an enlisted soldier clearly led to Horsford's success as an officer; he died as a major general (with honors including Knight Commander of the Order of the Bath), after serving thirty-nine years as an officer in the Bengal Artillery. His first book of poems, published in 1796 in Calcutta, is dedicated to "the officers of the Indian army on the Bengal Establishment," and many of these officers appear in the list of subscribers.

It is not surprising, given his professional circumstances, that Horsford's poetry is suffused with a kind of nationalism and patriotism foreign to Jones's much more resolutely comparative thought. At the heart of Horsford's poetry, moreover, is a profound ambivalence about verse itself. The paratext of the poem standing first in the 1796 volume displays a recurrent theme—that the poet has been, more or less, led astray by imaginative pursuits. He voices his admiration for his poetic hero William Hayley, "Learning's brightest son," but in a footnote the poet confesses that in his youth in Britain, he had been led astray in the process of pursuing this poet, presumably across the Continent: "The Author of this volume, struck with the beauty of his [Hayley's] writings, conceived an enthusiastic desire of having a sight of so great a man; and left his country with that sole intention, but was disappointed;—Mr. Hayley being abroad.—This extraordinary journey among strangers, led him into innumerable extravagant irregularities, which hastened his ruin, as being then too young to guard against the allurements of folly; it also drew on him the frowns of maternal displeasure" (*Collection*, 3). It is little wonder, then, that Horsford concluded his first volume with prose musings, including advice to his younger brother and a counsel against reading novels. These short prose pieces stand as paratexts or, put simply, appendixes to the poems. Their claim to engage "real life" manifests a profound, if illusory, contest between "real" and literary life.

Other paratexts in Horsford's first volume also threaten to take over from the poetic texts, for virtually every poem has a proem in the form of a dedication, a descriptive title, or a brief paragraph describing the occasions of its writing. Some also have explanatory footnotes. Typical are the ode celebrating Lord Cornwallis's arrival in India and "The Prospect, written during the late war with Tippoo, Inscribed to ———, 1790." "The Prospect" aims to describe not a pleasant rural scene, the typical focus of a prospect poem, but rather a happy imperial future. Jones makes a somewhat similar ideological move in his "Hymn to Gangá" where he imagines Britain bringing benign law to India. But Horsford, unlike Jones, celebrates conquest directly. The "prospect" is equally the field of battle and the future of empire:

> Soon shall oppression lift her stubborn head,
> And ruthless Tyrants number with the dead,
> And 'venging War, which new erects his crest,
> Restore Hindostan to primaeval rest;
> Then shall fair Freedom bless the happy land,
> And Science flourish 'neath her genial hand,
> Peace know no foe, the Arts meet no controul,
> But British knowledge warm the Indian soul.
>
> (*Collection*, 24–25)

Horsford imagines "Enlightened" Europe witnessing a "free" and yet "dependently allied" India. His imperial prospect is populated by fallen heroes and living victors, free arts and letters, and flourishing science and soulful Indians.

Horsford navigates his own prospects through fulsome dedications and patriotic encomiums, yet the volume betrays its divided mind in the next poem, written during the Mysore wars: "Epistle to Sir William Jones, Written to Him during the Late War with Tippoo, 1790." In this verse epistle, Horsford celebrates Jones's learning, his hymns to Indian deities, his support of the orphans' asylum and other good causes, and, enviously, his Persian learning. Listing the most famous Persian poets, Horsford declares, "Their daring works to justly understand, / I'd give thy wealth, O golden Samercand!" (30). Reflections on learning and poetry lead him to conclude by rejecting the very war he has celebrated only pages earlier:

> To us what joy can jarring armies yield,
> Or levell'd cities, or th' ensanguin'd field,
> Or sack'd Pagodas, or the plunder'd fanes,
> Or Indians gasping on their native plains,
> Or pillag'd wealth from Hyder's lov'd abodes,
> Or ransack'd ornaments from idol gods?
> The spoils of war no real joys can give,
> 'Tis Poesy's soothing voice that makes us live.
> With her I left my home in hapless hour,
> And felt of diff'rent climes th' unequal pow'r:
> With her thro' either tropic have I gone,
> And burned beneath an equinoctial sun;
> Refin'd Europa's fatal pomp she's shewn;
> And Afric's sooty race to me made known.
> With her I rov'd the sunny wilds among,
> When brown-hair'd Ganga only heard my song;
> Retir'd to contemplate at her command,
> With your immortal tablets in my hand.
> Th' enthusiast I, of that enchanting art,
> Which charms and steals away the human heart.
>
> (31–32)

Thus, a poem that begins with the evocation of war ends by turning to the "human heart."

Perhaps one might argue, along the lines of Mary Louise Pratt, that these verses are a perfect exhibition of the anti-conquest, the ostensible rejection of conquest disguised as praise for learning. Though Horsford pursues that strategy elsewhere, especially in his verse history of the Asiatic Society, here the straightforward look at the spoils and the suffering of war ("Indians gasping on their native plains") manifests instead a profound contradiction. An analogous contradiction shapes the second volume of Horsford's verse; in "The Art of Living in India," the conflict is not between poetry and war but between the poet's love for his biracial daughter and the casual racism of young British men, who court the pleasures of India only to scorn the children born of their liaisons.[41]

The second volume of Horsford's verse (1800) repays reading, not only for the satire in "The Art of Living in India" but also as an enactment of the linguistic complexity of late eighteenth-century India. The paratexts and intertexts in this volume create a dense web; they guide the prospective reader in a maze of allusions, citations, and translations. In the first section of *Poems in Three Parts,* Horsford translates Jones's Latin versions of poems originally written in classical Chinese, Persian, and Arabic. This section also includes translations of Jones's Latin versions of a friend's poem, a poem that was first written in English and subsequently translated by Jones into Greek. Horsford also translates Jones's original Latin compositions and his Latin imitations of Sappho. The headnotes to each poem provide a polyglot paratext with a vengeance. Jones's and Horsford's project as a whole reflects Jones's evident view that as an inflected language Latin might serve as a kind of linguistic bridge between Persian or Arabic and English.

Two examples will suffice to give the flavor of Horsford's effort. They reveal the challenge the soldier-poet faced in re-creating in English his friend's elegant Latin meters. Just as he had hoped for a glimpse of Hayley in his youth, so too as a middle-aged man Horsford provides a glimpse of Jones by printing Jones's Latin and his own translations on facing pages. Horsford's "A Persian Ode (The Approach of Spring)" was initially translated by Jones into Latin "from the celebrated poet dewan hafez [*sic*]." Obviously, Horsford's Persian learning has not caught up with his ambition, as oddly he (or the printer) uses the word *dewan* in the Persian sense indicating an official title rather than with the appropriate Persian meaning: "collected works." Hāfiz was not a "dewan" in the Mughal sense of chief financial minister; rather, a divan (or *dewan*) here indicates a collection of short poems. The paratext may lead the unsuspecting reader into a wrong turn; reading blindly here, one could easily get the elephant by the tail.

The paratexts and intertexts created by reprinting Jones's Latin translations of oriental languages on facing pages with Horsford's English versions evoked at least two kinds of readers and reading. Horsford's English versions of Jones's translations are evidently intended in part to reach readers who lack classical education. Yet the Latin itself is multiply intertextual and hence would be best appreciated by competent classicists. These multiple paths are especially obvious in the English translation "Approach of Spring." Here Horsford transforms Jones's Latin tercets into English couplets:

> Now is the Season, Roses gay,
> Light purple-ținctur'd blooms display;
> When Sires thus jovial youths invite,
> To the fair gardens of delight.
> "Time will your sprightliness destroy,
> Then give the present hours to joy.
> Assemble all!—convivial join!
> The sacred carpet* sell for wine!
> And while you feel the fanning breeze,
> Which whispers through the waving trees,
> Pray that beside you may be laid
> Some playful laughter loving maid."
>
> (*Poems in Three Parts,* 1:5)

Horsford annotates "the sacred carpet" as that "upon which the Mahomedans prostrate themselves at the time of prayers" (1:5). His lines translate Jones's Latin:

Jam rosa purpureum caput explicat. Adsit, amici,
Suavis voluptatum cohors:
Sic monuêre senes.
Nunc laeti sumus; at citiús laeta avolat aetas,
Quin sacra mutemus meor
Stragula nectareo.
Dulcè gemit zephyrus: ridentem mitte puellam,
Quam molli in amplexu tenens
Pocula laeta bibam.

(*Poems in Three Parts,* 1:4)

Surely the concision of the Latin, as well as its metrical and acoustic density, is what appealed to Jones as the apt equivalent of the Persian. For the classically attuned reader, these texts evoke numerous intertexts, particularly Catullus's lyric:

Ille mi par esse deo videtur,
Ille, se fas est, superare divos,
qui sedens adversus identitidem te
spectat et audit
dulce ridentem

(Catullus, 51.1–5)

[He seems to me to be equal to a god, he, if it may be,
seems to surpass the very gods, who sitting opposite
you again and again gazes at you and hears you sweetly
laughing.]

So Jones's bilingual play, taking the Persian into the Latin, translating Hāfiz while echoing Catullus's famous "dulce ridentem," becomes in Horsford's translation part of a trilingual intertext.

Something is necessarily lost in translation, but one might argue at least for Jones's Latin that something is also gained. Horsford's second translation of Jones's Latin version of Hāfiz, "GO, Boy! and bring a copious bowl, / Whose sides are purpled o'er," transforms Jones's three-line stanza into quatrains. This stanza form creates difficulties for meter and syntax. Certainly Jones was aware of such problems, for he had made his own translation of Hāfiz into English quatrains. In often choosing Latin as his target language, Jones had found one way out of the difficulties presented by the Persian ghazal. Latin, Jones believed, provided a mediating language between the classical Persian source and the modern vernacular.

Jones's single attempt to replicate the form of the Persian ghazal was his "An Ode of Jami," which he printed in landscape fashion to replicate the nature of the ghazal stanza. Compare Jones's Latin and Horsford's English quoted above with Jones's English version of a poem in similar form:

How sweet the gale of morning breathes! Sweet news of my *delight* he brings;
News, that the rose will soon approach the tuneful bird of *night,* he brings.
Soon will a thousand parted souls be led, his captives, through the sky,
Since tidings, which in every heart must ardent flames *excite,* he brings.
Late near my charmer's flowing robe he pass'd, and kiss'd the fragrant hem;
Thence, odour to the rosebud's veil, and jasmine's mantle *white,* he brings.

(*Works,* 2:583)

Here, but not in the Latin, Jones captured the complex repetition of the ghazal couplet, in which two rhymes (or more technically, the *radif,* or refrain, and the *quafia,* or monorhyme) weave through the verse and the verses themselves are joined by the skill of the poet who can vary syntax so as to ring the changes on this double schema. The Latin versions of Hāfiz create a similar degree of complexity, but through allusion to Latin intertexts—texts that Jones's most gifted readers would have known by heart.

Horsford's English translation of Jones's Latin translation of Hāfiz presents the Persian original through a glass darkly. As in many translations of Hāfiz, the reader truly is as blind as the poor men confronted with the proverbial elephant. The English translation of Jones's Latin necessarily misses the complexity that Horsford himself could barely have glimpsed without significant study of Persian.

A poem more easily accessible to classically educated English gentlemen would have been Jones's Latin version of Sappho's hymn to Aphrodite. Jones's Latin version of these famous lines begins wonderfully, addressing Venus under the sign of love's treachery:

Perfido ridens Erycina vultu,
Seu Joci mater, tenerique Amoris,
Seu Paphi regina potens, Cyprique
Laetior audis

(Horsford, *Poems in Three Parts,* 24)

O Erycina, thou whose face
Deceives with such beguiling grace!
O parent of the Smiles and Loves!
Supreme of Paphos' blissful groves!
Of joyous Cyprus!—O appear
And graciously thy votary hear!

(translated in Horsford, *Poems in Three Parts,* 25)

Again, Jones's Latin version of the Greek provides the Greek original with numerous classical Latin intertexts, particularly Horace's *Odes*, Book 1.2.[42] Jones also echoes Ovid's *Amores* and Catullus, as Sappho evokes Aphrodite's sparrows.

Horsford's version of Jones, however, provides a different classical intertext. Horsford prefaces his translation of Jones's Sappho with an elaborate note, replacing Jones's intertexts with his own complexities. Horsford substitutes Cicero for Ovid, Horace, and Catullus, perhaps to disarm the vernacular reader of Sappho. The paratext, once again, overwhelms the text:

> When such a Master as our Author has imitated such an exalted Poetess as Sappho, much may be expected in the following translation. If the reader is disappointed, let him recollect how difficult the task is to transfuse into English the sentiments of the melting Lesbian (a Lady whose soul was made up of Poetry and Love!) and them sentiments refined by so chaste, so universal and so polite a scholar as the immortal William Jones—a man for erudition, eloquence, and purity of life, equal to the illustrious Cicero! (*Poems in Three Parts,* 25)

Certainly Jones modeled himself on Cicero, desiring to be as eloquent and as statesmanlike, as above corruption, as he believed his model to be. But clearly, Horsford is made most uneasy by the task of translating Jones's translations of the "melting Lesbian." Perhaps because he chose Latin rather than English as his target language or perhaps because of his general religious disposition, Jones appears to have been undisturbed. Sappho's demand of Aphrodite, her entreaty, her "maddened heart," all these Jones is willing to capture in Latin verse. Horsford found himself uncomfortable with the task.

In his original poetry, Horsford sought to create the audience by which he wished to be appreciated, but his situation bred more anxiety than assurance. The many fulsome dedications of his poems, the occasional nature of the verse and its recurrent address to his superiors, and his footnotes are part of his larger effort to establish a context for belles lettres among officers and East India Company servants in Calcutta and the Bengal Presidency. Many of these company servants and officers would have shared his education in the Greek and Latin classics; a very few would more closely have approximated Jones's learning in Persian and Arabic, if not Sanskrit.

Whereas Jones aspired to a republic of letters (despite the contradictions implicit in his employment) and envisioned himself in the tradition of Benjamin Franklin and Arthur Lee uniting learning and law to literary endeavor, Horsford was by necessity inclined to imagine the realm of learning as a function of arms. The distinction between the republic of letters and the realm of belles lettres reflects the scope of political as well as aesthetic differences that persisted at least through about 1810 among English speakers in north India. Moreover, the role of learning, not yet reducible to a conflict between Orientalists and Anglicists, might best be captured in Horsford's couplet "Now warriours burn, each man of letters warms, / And all the Arts shall prosper like our Arms.[43] Like Horsford, Jones celebrated "martial grace," particularly in the "Hymn to Gangá," but the hymn's conclusion makes clear that Jones believed, however idealistically, that wealth, joy, and peace depended upon the preservation of Indian law. Horsford was more confident in martial means to a Ciceronean ideal.

Both men attempted to create a new kind of verse on the banks of the Hooghly. For Horsford, India presented the prospect of "British knowledge" warming the Indian soul. For Jones, the opposite held true. India offered for him the prospect of classical "Asian" learning invigorating a European and, for that matter, an American republic of letters to come. There is little indication that Horsford ever sought an audience beyond India or, after his enlistment, seriously aspired to poetic fame. Indeed, he seems to have anticipated living happily with his children in India and gives no indication of any plan to return to England. We cannot know all the circumstances that led to his original departure from England. We only know that he died of heart failure at age fifty-six while still on active duty. His spirited defense of his children and evident love for them make his contemplation of a retirement "at home" unlikely. When Horsford reinvented himself, first as John Rover and then as a rising military man and father, he defined home anew as well.

Sir William Jones, unlike Horsford, had already made his reputation as a poet before going out to India, and his letters show that he viewed poetry as his great love but one that had to take second place to his duty—in this case, his legal researches and his position as a judge. As we have seen, though, Jones hoped that both his earlier work and the original poems and translations he made in India would spark a new awakening, a renaissance in a European literary tradition that needed fresh ideas. The metropole was defined for Jones, not always positively, against equally important cultural centers abroad. The new republic in America and the learning available to him in India and in Persia provided a scale against which Jones judged both the politics and the poetry of London. The third poet I treat here, Anna Maria, had perhaps the most anxious relationship to her audience, an anxiety occasioned not only by her gender but also by her distance from London, which remained for her the literary epicenter.

Sensibility and Learning: Anna Maria and the Della Cruscans

Classical learning and vernacular ease, sensibility and reflection each had a place in the poems of Jones and Horsford and in the lives of their presumed audience. But the proportions of learning to sensibility varied by the circumstances of the participants in the Indian world of English belles lettres. The early period of English language poetry in India had, to my knowledge, no Indian participants and very few British women.

A signal exception was the anonymous "Anna Maria," who like Horsford assembled a large group of subscribers for the volume she published. The most important paratextual element of her single volume of verse, and the key to its cultural meanings, was the author's pseudonym.

Anna Maria clearly named herself for the poetry phenomenon that swept the London newspapers in the late 1780s. Her volume of verse, published in 1793, relied on newspaper publication, bringing together poems previously printed in the *Asiatic Mirror* and the *Calcutta Morning Post.* In her newspaper publications as well as in her choice of pseudonym, Anna Maria connected her work to the London scene, where Robert Merry as "Della Crusca" and Mrs. Hannah Cowley as "Anna Matilda" conducted a sensational poetic affair in the pages of the *Oracle* and the *World*—two "low-brow periodical organs" (McGann, 83). "Della Crusca" had allied himself, by defending the vernacular, to the language of Petrarch and Boccaccio. His "low-brow" vernacular was for Anna Maria a chosen medium.

The Della Cruscan phenomenon, as Judith Pascoe has shown, became all the rage between 1785 and 1790. It began in the summer of 1785 when Hester Thrale Piozzi, Robert Merry, Bertie Greatheed, and William Parson published in Florence their collection of convivial poetry, *The Florence Miscellany.*[44] It took a turn toward serious popularity when "Merry, on returning to England in 1787, adopted the sobriquet 'Della Crusca' and published 'The Adieu and Recall to Love' in the *World*" (Pascoe, 68). This poem provoked Hannah Cowley's response under the name Anna Matilda and began an exchange lasting two years that culminated in a staged "adieu" between the virtual lovers (subsequent to their actual, but productively delayed, meeting). As Pascoe argues, Della Cruscan verse was an "odd mixture of the general and the sensually specific" (73). It was verse in costume, verse as melodrama, verse made of and in the moment. The Della Crusca–Anna Matilda exchange, besides significantly boosting newspaper circulation, licensed many women poets, including Mary Robinson, who became "Laura Maria" and "Julia." Other women became "Charlotte," "Emma," and "Ariadne." These women, at a remove from Merry's Italian countryside, were, Pascoe says, "in several regards, Della Cruscans manquées" (Pascoe, 69). If these English poets were at a remove from the sensational epicenter of Della Cruscan poetics, Anna Maria of Calcutta was at a still greater disadvantage.

The paratexts and intertexts of Anna Maria's verse measure her distance in space and time from London. Like the Della Cruscans, she tags each poem with a date and usually with a location. For her, as for the Della Cruscans in London, datelines were crucial to creating a sense of immediacy, the poem made in the moment. As Jerome McGann has argued, Della Cruscan verse is both occasional and presentist in several senses—it does not so much describe the present as enact it (80–83). Jones and even Horsford could look toward a *longue durée,* classical worlds made alive in the present through analogous new creation or through translation from learned languages. Anna Maria's verse, in contrast, heightens a sense of fleetingness—the reaches of empire seem expanded because of anxiety about the global experience of time. Paradoxically, rather than making the world seem smaller, the temporal gap between London and Calcutta, experienced as an inability to create poetry in the metropolitan moment, for Anna Maria made the distance between the cities yet greater.

Anna Maria's datelines mark both the presentism of the Della Cruscans and the poet's colonial consciousness of time and space. According to her "datelines," Anna Maria was in London in 1790 and in Calcutta for some months between March and November 1793. All but two of the poems are given a date and place, as if Anna Maria, like her predecessor Anna Matilda, were writing from the moment. Della Crusca published his "Adieu and Recall to Love" on June 29, 1787, and Anna Matilda's reply appeared on July 10; his response reached its readers on July 31, and Anna Matilda penned her response to him that morning and published it on August 4 (see Cowley and others, *The British Album*). Anna Maria imagines a similar compression of time, but she is multiply distanced from the conversation. Her earliest poem was, according to its dateline, composed in London in 1790, presumably before the poet's departure for India. The last dated poem, "Adieu to India," is labeled "Gardens, November 24, 1793." All the rest are datelined either from Calcutta or from "Gardens" (that is, Garden Reach, the suburb along the river where Sir William and Anna Maria Jones also lived).

But who was this "Anna Maria"? Why was she behind the curve of this London sensation? What can we know or conjecture about her social placement? What anxieties or pleasures generated the paratexts and intertextual elements of her poetry?

Paula Feldman repeats the conjecture of Graham Shaw, who in *Printing in Calcutta* adduces evidence that the anonymous poet "Anna Maria" may have been Anna Maria Shipley Jones, wife of Sir William Jones. Shaw's evidence for this identification is the coincidence in first name and place of residence of the poet and Lady Jones and the coincidence in probable dates when the two "Anna Marias'" departed for England. Despite the attractions of this identification and despite the tiny number of British women in Bengal in the 1790s, there are numerous reasons to believe that Anna Maria was not Lady Jones but a different person. In the first place, the pseudonym "Anna Maria" is very likely a bow to Anna Matilda of London fame; the poet also could conceivably bow to Anna Maria Jones and perhaps even to Anna Maria Hastings, who had left India a few years earlier.

I conjecture that the poet was female, as she lists more female subscribers than any other poet publishing in Calcutta in the late eighteenth and early nineteenth centuries. Among her subscribers was Lady Jones. Sir William also purchased a copy of the volume, as did his friend John Shore, the death of whose children is commemorated by Anna Maria in an elegiac poem. It seems improbable that Anna Maria Jones, were she the author, would have listed herself and her husband as subscribers to a volume of her own composition. Moreover, there is no evidence from William Jones's correspondence that his wife wrote verse. In his many letters, Jones frequently speaks of "A. M.," but only to record her health, her botanizing, and her frequent letter writing. He never mentions any other form of writing, either memoir or poetry, and considering his passion for verse it would have been an odd omission. Finally, Anna Maria datelines her rather lugubrious "Ode to Suicide" from London in 1790, when Lady Jones resided not in London but in India. Given the Della Cruscan penchant for representing the immediate occasion and location of each poem, this notation of date and place of composition is unlikely to have been fictionalized.

If we assume, then, that we cannot yet positively identify Anna Maria the poet, what can we deduce about her social position, education, and sense of the Anglo-Indian poet's situation?

We are forced to rely on internal clues. First is the matter of tone. Not only was Anna Maria distanced from the London literary world, but she also seems to have aspired toward literary recognition in a way that had implications for her understanding of her social status. The paratexts she supplies to her volume bespeak both social and poetic aspiration. Her dedication, for example, reads in full,

> The flattering Approbation with which some of the following poems were received, on their Appearance in the Asiatic Mirror and Calcutta Morning Post, induced the Authoress to arrange and publish Them, with Additions.—Anna Maria is impressed with the most grateful Pleasure for the very distinguished Patronage she has been honored with; and regrets, that her ill State of Health, for some Time past, has prevented her from making the Book more extensive and complete.—Proud of the Encomiums bestowed on the Efforts of her Muse, Anna Maria will ever be zealous to merit the applause of a polished People,—to whom these Poems are most respectfully dedicated.

In short, Anna Maria thanked her subscribers for their support and asserted the value and the taste of her Calcutta audience. Her aspiration is further indicated in the quotation from James Thompson's "Summer" that provides an epigraph on the volume's title page: poetry, in Thompson's words, is the "Treasure" of mankind, their "highest Honour, and their truest Joy."

Anna Maria thus hoped to equal both the presumed aesthetic expectations and the social status of her patrons. One wonders, nonetheless, how secure she was economically or socially. Her volume of verse may have been published in the hope of defraying the expenses of a return home. Ten of the seventeen poems were written between September 13 and November 24, 1793, and the volume was published in the same year, presumably in late November or December. Whatever her financial motives, Anna Maria probably wished not only for local fame but also to make a splash in London.

Sadly the poet's aspirations—certainly her poetic aspirations, and probably her social aspirations—were unequal to her means. She experienced India, not like Jones as proximity to new kinds of learning and not like Horsford as access to a new name and new life, but as estrangement from the metropole. This estrangement was at once limiting and productive. It led Anna Maria to hope for new materials, new images, and new subject matter. In her "Invocation to the Muse," she aspires to "Virgin Images," whose novelty would be guaranteed by the novelty of her place in India:

> At Eve on Hougly's winding Side,
> Attentive to the ripling [*sic*] Tide;
> I trace the Moon serenely bright,
> Pass in full Pomp the splendid Night;
> Or mark th' elusive silv'ry Beam,
> Flash faintly o'er the sapphire Stream;
> Enraptur'd with the Scene around,
> Methinks I tread on fairy Ground.
>
> (27)

Admittedly, this fairy ground is scarcely grounded, being even more fully fanciful than Jones's Plassey Plain. But it allows Anna Maria to claim that she unites the flowers of Ida with the beauties, however vague they be, of India. "Virgin Images" are at once novel and pure; they might deflect the readers' expectation of Della Cruscan sensuality while at the same time claiming oriental opulence.

The poet's anxiety—though occasioned by the distance between India and Europe, Ida and Calcutta—is not elided but increased in the two poems Anna Maria penned in honor of Della Crusca himself. Their paratexts reveal the awkwardness of writing presentist verse at a temporal and geographical remove. The two Della Crusca poems enact an unintended comedy, for the first responds to the false report of Della Crusca's death. Anna Maria wrote an ode to Della Crusca's memory, only to discover five months later that the poet was still alive. The first ode, the headnote tells us, "was written on the information, that the elegant and admired Author, had paid the last Debt of Nature" (23). Rather than omitting the first ode, the volume retains it, along with another that the poet wrote, correcting the record, so to speak. The second ode is introduced thus: "The Propriety of the following Ode to Della Crusca, it is presumed, will be readily admitted.—An Elegiac Poem to that distinguished Writer's Memory was written in consequence of the Intelligence of his Death, and is inserted in Page 23:—Anna Maria has the pleasure of knowing Mr. Merry still lives" (46). This second ode echoes Anna Matilda's verses to Della Crusca, for it claims that Anna Maria, like Anna Matilda, has been inspired by Della Crusca with a "wild Delirium" (45, line 3). But Anna Maria's poem differs from both Della Crusca's and Anna Matilda's verse in its classical aspirations.

Della Crusca and Anna Matilda wished to display their wit more than their learning. Their melodramatic courtship was seasoned with a liberal soupçon of self-consciousness, polish, and panache. When Della Crusca declared his despair at his distance from Anna Matilda, when he lamented that he could not "catch a ray of bliss—a glimpse of Heaven," when he took on the pose of the longing lover, he aptly concluded that his "proudest boast was but an idle song" ("To Anna Matilda," *British Album*, 1:32). In a similar vein, Della Crusca followed his lines "To Werther" with "Ode to Folly":

> So shall I love you, ever-changing!
> And what is most ador'd to-day,
> From system still to system ranging,
> To-morrow shall be thrown away,
> And in the never-settled round,
> A glorious vacancy be found.
>
> (*British Album*, 1:18)

Anna Maria is more serious, though she too attempts Della Cruscan polish. She begs Della Crusca to fire her muse "with wild Ambition" and "bid the burning Thought to Fame aspire" (*Poems*, 47). The "Ode, Inscribed to Della Crusca," begins with a request that the poet conduct her through "the hallow'd Glade, / Where Learning's mould'ring Sons are laid" (47). Anna Maria invokes Virgil, Sappho, and Petrarch and equates her hero with them. She wishes to "Derive from Thee the lucid Ray, / That dignifies the modern Lay." But should that not be possible, she will be left, not with Della Crusca's brilliant sun, but with an Indian moon:

> Or, I will stray by Night's pale Orb;
> Whose Beams the lesser Lights absorb:
> Where India's God in secret roves,
> Through the rich consecrated Groves;
> Where Brahma pours his pious Pray'r,
> To the religious, list'ning Air;
> And from the Fervor of his Lays,
> I'll weave a Wreath of magic Praise;
> Shall circle round thy crescent Brows,
> *Proud Token of far distant Vows!*—
> And should'st *Thou* e'er my hapless Verse peruse,
> Pause on the Line, and own the simple Muse;
> Say, that in Regions far from laurel'd Fame,
> Maria wept o'er Della Crusca's Name;
>
> (47–48)

Thus Anna Maria, in her "hapless Verse," calls upon both classical poets and Indian deities, perhaps thinking the while of Jones's "Hymn to Náráyena." Though Anna Maria's "Brahma" rather improbably seems to invoke himself, Maria's previous lament for Della Crusca grounds her quest for fame and guarantees a kind of sincerity, however premature and mistaken her cause for sorrow.

Like the Della Cruscans in the metropole but estranged by time and distance, Anna Maria engages in a kind of passionate make-believe. Her virtual reality—Della Crusca's death—is transformed into virtuous reality. Like her muse and hero, Anna Maria engages in a poetic correspondence between "*a Shadow and a Shade*" (Della Crusca, "To Anna Matilda," *British Album,* 1:100).[45]

Anna Maria's final verse, "Adieu to India," attempts to bridge the distances, spatial and temporal, that have constituted her poetics. Unlike Jones, who defined the sources of learning broadly, and unlike Horsford, whose classical education allowed him to appropriate Jones's learning for his own poetics, Anna Maria traces the source of learning to Europe even as she identifies with India. The paratext for Anna Maria's "Adieu" creates a marvelous ambiguity. She takes her epigraph from Ovid's *Heroides,* the "Oenone Paride": "Quam vix sustinuit dicere Lingua—'vale!'" [Your tongue was scarcely able to utter a last farewell.][46] It is unclear here whether the poet adopts the persona of Oenone, who in this epistle laments the desertion of Paris, or whether the poet herself, like Paris, is deserting Calcutta, her own Oenone. The longer Ovidian passage in Oenone's voice is translated this way: "You clasped your arms round my neck, more closely than the curling vines embrace the towering elm. How did your companions smile, when you complained of the unfriendly winds! They favored; but love detained you. How often at parting did you repeat the ardent kisses; while your tongue was scarcely able to utter a last farewell!"[47]

Like Paris caught between Oenone and the promise of Helen, Anna Maria is caught between the anticipated blandishments of Britain and the real support and affection she has received in Calcutta:

> I hasten to my native shore,
> Where Art and Science blend their Lore;
> There Learning keeps her chosen Seat—
> A million Vot'ries at her Feet,
> Ambitious of the Laurel Bough,
> To wind about their honor'd Brow.
> Yet ere I go—a grateful Pain
> Involves the Muse's parting Strain;
> The sad Regret my Mind imbues,
> And fills with Grief—my last Adieus!
> For I have felt the subtle Praise,

That cheer'd the Minstrel's doubtful Lays;
That fed the infant lambent Flame,
And bade me hope for future Fame.

("Adieu to India," *Poems*, 67)

So Anna Maria makes her bow to Calcutta. She might well have claimed, like Ovid's Oenone, "me miseram, quod amor not est medicabilis herbes defecior predens artis ab arte mea" [miserable me—that love has no medicinal herb! Skilled in an art, I am failed by my own art!]. At the end of this poem, Anna Maria made her farewell. The paratext—the dateline—reads, "Gardens, November 24, 1793. Finis." Finis in print became finis indeed, for after this volume we hear no more from Anna Maria.

Learning, Arts, and Artifice

In my story of Anna Maria, Sir William Jones, and Sir John Horsford, text and paratext—elephant and mahout—have perhaps changed places. But like the blind men seeking to understand the elephant by focusing on its appendages, we can learn at least something from these paratexts that is otherwise difficult to know, namely, how poetic consciousness was formed in a polyglossic arena of cultural contact.

Sir William Jones, Sir John Horsford, and Anna Maria represent the possibilities for English language poetry in late eighteenth-century North India. The distances between Britain and India—both spatial and temporal—had differing meanings for each of them, as each defined differently the arenas of learning, poetics, and power. For all three poets, these differences were negotiated through text, intertext, and paratext. Webs of cross-cultural explanation were woven in their paratexts: their dedications, epigraphs, datelines, footnotes, and headnotes. To establish a new repertoire in India, they called up multiple worlds of learning and social intercourse through a polyglot mixture of tongues, forms, repetitions, and citations.

Through these means, both allusive and sometimes elusive, Jones negotiated the republic of letters, Horsford the realm of belles lettres and learning, and Anna Maria the more popular world of newspaper publication. Anna Maria hoped, vainly, for London fame. Jones longed for a bucolic retirement in rural England reached via Shiraz and Philadelphia. John Horsford appears to have imagined retirement on half pay with his half-Indian children in Calcutta. As far as we know, none of them ended their lives as anticipated: Anna Maria apparently departed from Calcutta to be heard from no more; Sir John Horsford died of heart failure in his fifties while still on active duty; and Sir William Jones died suddenly of a liver infection only weeks after putting his beloved wife on board a ship for England, his dream of reuniting with her in Ciceronean retirement unfulfilled.

A similar abrupt ending awaited two of the most significant poets in the next generation. Although in the next century the constraints on political and religious thought increased, Emma Roberts and H. L. V. Derozio continued to create a new idiom for English verse in north India. Operating within the controversies raised by evangelicalism and utilitarianism, Roberts and Derozio made English verses by calling upon the poetics of a radical romanticism.

Ruins near the Taj Mahal, Agra. Engraving after sketchbook of Robert Elliott, *Fisher's Drawing Room Scrap-Book* (London: Fisher, Son, and Jackson, 1833).

TWO

Bards and Sybils

Landscape, Gender, and the Culture of Dispute in the Poems of H. L. V. Derozio and Emma Roberts

—They sat them on the ground: each glowing face
Was but the mirror of the mind within;
And when they spake, the universal din
Of storms would have been silent to have heard
. . . . many a plan
For spreading wide the ties that fasten man
Even to his slighted brotherhood they formed.—
What is the fire with which such breasts are warmed?

—H. L. V. Derozio, "Philosophical Utopia,
A Fragment," *Bengal Annual,* 1831

No brutal warfare mars the solitude
Where, in his marble shroud, the Moslem rests.
Scene of majestic beauty! lingering still
The rapt eye gazes on thy mantling woods,
The fortlike tomb that crowns yon beacon hill
And the swift rush of Ganges' sounding floods.
Thoughts of a distant home, a foreign grave
With augurs sad upon the feelings press,
Sighing we leave the pious and the brave,
The alien warrior to his loneliness!

—Emma Roberts, "The Tomb of the Faithful,"
Oriental Scenes, Dramatic Sketches and Tales

Sir William Jones, Sir John Horsford, and Anna Maria variously inhabited the polyglot linguistic territory of northern India at the end of the eighteenth century. In the next generation, the tropes they introduced to English language poetry were filtered through British poets such as Robert Southey, Letitia Landon, Lord Byron, and Thomas Moore and displayed their longevity and their propensity to be remade across time and geo-cultural terrain. The two poets on whom I focus here reinterpreted, reiterated, and recast the tropes of European, particularly British (English, Scottish, Irish), poetics. Each of them was placed, personally and politically, athwart the seemingly clear divide between colonizer and colonized. Each negotiated complex identifications and disidentifications with European and British forms of power as they attempted to extend or to reiterate the repertoire of English language verse. Like their predecessors in the late eighteenth century, both Derozio and Roberts developed these negotiations through paratexts, their prefaces, epigraphs, and footnotes providing complex glosses on the scene of writing. Still more than eighteenth-century poets they were attracted by the romantic development of bardic claims, yet their gendered and ethnic identities provided difficult access to bardic nationalisms.

Henry Louis Vivian Derozio and Emma Roberts were friends and colleagues, both poets, both journalists. Derozio, known as the "father" of Indian writing in English and the first Indian poet writing in English, is sometimes also called the "Indian Keats." But these appellations beg a number of questions about Derozio's identity and affiliations. Emma Roberts is remembered, if at all, chiefly as the author of *Scenes and Characteristics of Hindostan,* a three-volume travel account that went into multiple editions in the London of the 1830s and remained an important point of reference through a considerable part of the century. Derozio's and Roberts's poems speak to each other both directly and implicitly as they address the political and the picturesque. Their poems arose from the meeting point of British poetics and the culture of Bengal in the 1820s and 1830s, where, as Rosinka Chaudhuri puts it, "everything seemed open to dispute and charged with value" (*Gentlemen,* 33). Derozio and Roberts can be placed firmly within this culture of dispute, with their understandings of the poet's role, authority, and audience, having been shaped by education and gender.

Gendered and Ethnic Identities in a Culture of Dispute

Both Derozio and Roberts operated in India partly outside and partly within the structures of power. The former—in ethnic identity, language, and religion—was neither wholly British nor, from some points of view, wholly Indian. The latter, by virtue of her gender and her lack of independent income and classical education, came from a social location in which full access to political power or poetic authority was likewise problematic.

Born in 1791 in London to a military family of Welsh origins, Roberts set out for India in 1828 with her sister Laura and her sister's husband, Robert McNaghten, a captain in the Bengal Army. She lived with them at Agra, Cawnpore, and Etawah, until her sister's death in 1830, when she moved to Calcutta, where she remained for some time.[1] Her only volume of verse, *Oriental Scenes, Dramatic Sketches and Tales,* had just been published in Calcutta (seen through the press by her friend Derozio).[2] Roberts republished the revised collection of poems in London in 1832. She sold essayistic accounts of her travels to British and Indian periodicals and later collected many of these essays under the title

Scenes and Characteristics of Hindostan (first edition, 1835, three volumes). A second travel book, *The East India Voyager; or, Ten Minutes Advice to the Outward Bound* (London, 1839), provided practical suggestions for prospective British travelers. A third, *Notes of an Overland Journey through France and Egypt to Bombay,* appeared posthumously in 1841. Roberts appears to have been a canny businesswoman, for she managed to support herself throughout her adult life—recycling her periodical publications in book form, editing two different newspapers in India, and acquiring more than 350 subscribers in north India for her book of verse. Her estate at her death amounted to 860 pounds.[3]

Between 1832 and 1839, Roberts returned to London, where for some time she shared lodgings with the poet Letitia Landon, already famous for highly emotional and effusive poems published in British newspapers and annuals. Landon was to appropriate Roberts's knowledge and connections in editing the wildly popular *Fisher's Drawing Room Scrap-Book,* a literary annual for which Landon's poems served as verse illustrations to the engraved "text." After Landon's marriage to the British governor of Cape Coast Castle, West Africa, and her scandalous death there—by accidental overdose according to the inquest—Roberts edited her posthumous volume of verse and furnished a memoir. Thus, Roberts's greatest metropolitan influence as a poet was through a largely undocumented collaboration with Landon. For reasons we cannot fully know—probably both economic and personal—Roberts returned to India in 1839. In Bombay, she became editor of a new newspaper, the *United Services Gazette.* She died in 1840 at the home of friends in Pune.

Henry Louis Vivian Derozio was considerably younger than Roberts but known to all as precocious. He published his first book of verse three years before Roberts did. Born in 1809, he died of cholera in 1831, at the age of twenty-two. But in his short career, Derozio wrote reams of verse, worked for a time in the business that employed his father in Calcutta, assisted his uncle on an indigo plantation, took a teaching position at Hindu College (the best English-medium school in Bengal), and was later fired for corrupting the minds of his students. The poet had studied with David Drummond, the freethinking Scots master of Dhurmatola Academy in Calcutta, and was imbued with the philosophy of the Scottish Enlightenment and the radicalism of Thomas Paine. The master of Hindu College—another Scotsman, David Hare (who had come to India a political radical, with a working-class background as a watchmaker)—hired Derozio as a teacher. Hare was soon unable to defend his young teacher from the ire of scandalized Hindu parents who believed that Derozio had led their children into freethinking, atheism, and contempt for custom. As the *Oriental Magazine* put it, "the native managers of the College were alarmed at the progress which some of the pupils were making by actually cutting their way through ham and beef and wading to liberalism through tumblers of beer" (quoted in Mukhopadhyay, vii). In the last months of his life, Derozio engaged full time in political journalism, founding and editing a newspaper, the *East Indian.* In her fine recent edition and study of the poet, Rosinka Chaudhuri details Derozio's numerous contributions, in prose and verse, to Calcutta periodicals.

We might parallel Derozio's multifarious identities with Roberts's peripatetic existence. Derozio's paternal grandfather, initially a Catholic of Portuguese and Indian ancestry, joined the Baptist Church as an adult. He was described in the St. John's Baptismal Register as "a Native Protestant" and in the *Bengal Directory* of 1795 as a "Portuguese Merchant and Agent in Calcutta." Derozio's father, Francis, grew up in an atmosphere of evangelical piety. His mother, Sophia, probably also a Baptist, was from Hampshire. After her death, his father was married a second time, to Anna Maria Rivers, another Englishwoman, who by all accounts quickly won the affection of her new family (Mukhopadhyay, 471–75).

We can presume that Derozio grew up speaking English and Bangla, and clearly he expanded his command of languages significantly in a short time. He likely learned French from his stepmother, who after his death advertised a school offering instruction in French and other subjects to young ladies (Mukhopadhyay, 454). Derozio studied Latin and seems to have educated himself in Italian as well.[4] His poems include Persian epigraphs, indicating at least some acquaintance with Persian.

Certainly Derozio's British friends—including Henry Meredith Parker, a talented poet and musician and member of the Bengal Civil Service—were trained in Hindustani and Persian and possibly in other languages, and Chaudhuri reports Derozio as having been a fixture at Parker's dinner table. Parker had been at Haileybury College in Hertfordshire in the first decade of the college's existence. Founded in 1806 to train civil servants for the East India Company, it offered Sanskrit instruction as well as other languages, but in one year Parker is unlikely to have done more than commence his work in Hindustani and Persian, which provided the languages curriculum for the majority of students at that time.[5] Like Parker, Derozio's Indian and "East Indian" friends from Drummond's academy, many of his Hindu friends, and his British friends educated there and elsewhere would also have been multilingual. Derozio's strong friendships across various communities attest to the heteroglot atmosphere of Calcutta.

Drummond's academy, like Haileybury and Fort William College in Calcutta, provided English-medium instruction but offered a range of classical and modern languages in addition to practical subjects. At least as important as its language offerings was the social and intellectual climate of Drummond's school. As Chaudhuri points out, it nurtured "Indian, Eurasian, and European children [boys] in the same classes without any distinction made on the basis of race or class, a fleeting pedagogical moment that would be consigned to history very quickly in a few years time" (*Derozio*, 1). She quotes David Drummond's speech to his pupils in 1821, in which he said to them, "[I]n you we have an omnipotent confutation of that impious doctrine which would make colour the test of intellect. That blasphemy is now leaving the world; and man over all the earth begun to be considered solely as the child of circumstances" (1). Moreover, Drummond was both a poet and a strong supporter of the skeptical thought of the Scottish Enlightenment, a spirit Chaudhuri describes being transmitted to Derozio and his friends as a "trenchant zeal for reform, radicalism, and the spirit of enquiry" (liii). Derozio's poetry reflects Drummond's influence and the intellectual current among his friends.

Another Scot, Alexander Duff, characterized Derozio and his circle as fortifying their discussion with quotations from Robertson and Gibbon, Adam Smith and Bentham, Newton and Davy, Hume and Paine, and from Locke, Reid, Stewart, and Brown—the whole enlivened by passages from Byron, Scott, and Burns (614–15). Though Duff was appalled at religious skepticism, he described the climate that ensued when Derozio came to teach at the Hindu College as nothing short of electrifying. There arose numerous debating and discussion societies, and according to Duff, "the most striking feature in the whole was the freedom with which all the subjects were discussed" (614). Indeed, the culture of dispute—of religious, political, intellectual, and social dispute, both in political action and the columns of newspapers and in belletristic texts—is what engaged Derozio and Roberts.

The poets' social locations, their reading, their horizons of expectation about life's possibilities, their community or lack of community, and the metaphors and memories that shaped their understandings of poetic tradition can in no way be reduced to any simple counters of identity or to noncontradictory homologies. In the Bengal of the 1820s, Derozio and Roberts engaged in a society that, despite significant divisions along lines of religion, economic power, caste, class, and to some extent race, was also home to multiple personal connections among the literate elites. As Chaudhuri has argued, prior to 1857 imperial values "had not yet formed rigid barriers between the races, and there was prevalent at this time an equality among upper-class members of all communities that was to be gradually eroded" (*Gentlemen*, 30). Chaudhuri rightly argues for the importance of a "cosmopolitan entrepreneurial quality of the East India Company rule in early nineteenth-century Calcutta" (32). Certainly the intellectual, political, and religious differences that created this cosmopolitan culture existed in equal measure (if in different flavors) among the elites of different backgrounds.

Bengal, especially Calcutta, in the 1820s was home to a polyglot mix of persons with markedly different religious, political, and social positions. That it also included political divisions crisscrossing other divisions is clear, for example, in the case of the "Academic Association" formed by Derozio, his students at the Hindu College, and his friends. According to their critic Alexander Duff these young men engaged in speculation antithetical both to Duff's Calvinist beliefs and to the orthodoxy of the very Indians whom Duff wished to convert. The association, which functioned much like an Oxford or Cambridge debating society, might well have been modeled on the Dialectic Society at Edinburgh University. Political and religious freethinking was rife. In the Scottish minister's jaundiced view, the young were corrupted equally by Hume's essays and Paine's *Age of Reason:* "With copies of the latter, in particular, they were abundantly supplied. . . . It was some wretched bookseller in the United States of America, who,—basely taking advantage of the reported infidel leanings of a new race of men in the East, and apparently regarding no God but his silver dollars,—dispatched to Calcutta a cargo of that most malignant and pestiferous of all anti-Christian publications" (Duff, 616). In addition, Duff lamented the ready availability of Thomas Paine's collected works, including *Rights of Man.* The young men of Calcutta were endangered—as, ironically, both the missionizing Duff and the conservative parents of Derozio's Hindu students could agree. While the Hindu parents of Derozio's young students feared that he was leading them away from their religious traditions and—hence—toward Christianity by way of Humean skepticism, Duff was horrified by his conviction that radical reform in all matters, including religious ones, would be the inevitable result of Derozio's thought.

Roberts and Derozio, publishing in Calcutta in the 1820s, were thus engaged in an arena where, far from having a single hegemonic view, Europeans were divided in their opinions and Indians (a word that, like "Europeans," is itself a marker for multiple meanings) were equally divided. In the 1820s and 1830s, indeed, we can measure British differences by the gap between Duff and Drummond—and that only among the Scots. These differences were played out in English language newspapers, as *John Bull* aired major disagreements on multiple political and ideological fronts with such newspapers as the *India Gazette* and Derozio's paper.

It is beyond my purview here to attempt to summarize the intellectual climate in Bengal. Recent historiographical controversy, while laying to rest the problematic label "Bengal Renaissance," has nonetheless made clear that this was a period of extraordinary intellectual ferment, one that Tapan Raychaudhury encourages us to regard as a moment of cultural encounter—analytically distinct from but certainly overlapping with colonial encounter. By this, Raychaudhury means to adduce the complexity of the ongoing engagement of educated Bengalis with European ideas and ideas from their own culture. Though in the historiographical debates on the Bengal Renaissance, as in nineteenth-century reactions to Derozio and his peers, the most extreme positions sometimes seem to read the Bengali *badhralok* (educated middle classes) as merely aping European thought and ways, even a skeptical observer such as Alexander Duff had to admit that something more profound was occurring:

> Indeed, the boldness and fearlessness with which they canvassed the established opinions and practices of their countrymen, and the daring hardihood with which they assailed the sentiments of some of the greatest masters in the republic of letters, whether European or Asiatic, I seldom have seen equalled, and never surpassed, in that happy land, the very touch of whose soil is freedom [Britain]. It was an exhibition which could not fail to impress with astonishment the mind of a stranger, who had been accustomed to regard a Hindu as the very personification of superstitious credulity, and blind unthinking submissiveness to the dictation of a domineering priesthood. (616)

Though some rightly enough saw Duff himself as a missionary of a domineering priesthood—as his own narrative makes clear—even Duff seems to have shared a sense of intellectual excitement, at some risk to his previous prejudices.

Derozio and his friends were participating in wider currents of thought, comparing the "greatest masters in the republic of letters, whether European or Asiatic." In this sense, they continued the reforming efforts of Rammohun Roy and anticipated those of Ishwar Chandra Vidyasagar. Though one would need to disagree with Romesh Chunder Dutt's observation in 1877 that traditional beliefs and ways were supplanted in Bengali literature and culture by Western ideas, still his summary of European influences that mattered to young educated men in Bengal is cogent: "The independence of America, the French revolution, the war of Italian independence, the teachings of history, the vigour and freedom of English literature and English thought, the great effort of the French intellect of the 18th century, the results of German labor in the field of philology and ancient history, Positivism, Utilitarianism, Darwinism,—all these have influenced and shaped the intellect of modern Bengal" (*Literature,* 166).

Evidently what might be construed as exciting intellectual ferment can equally be understood as contradiction, both intellectual and material. Intellectually, such contradictions can be measured by the presence at this moment in Calcutta of reformist members of the Brahmo Samaj, alongside those Hindus who vigorously opposed Brahmo causes (such as the abolition of sati and the diffusion of education); the presence of David Hare, the freethinking head of the Hindu College, and Alexander Duff, who vigorously opposed Hare's religious views; the presence of Derozio's friends Horace Hayman Wilson (an orientalist in Jones's tradition) and the utilitarian Anglicists (of whom Thomas Babington Macaulay has become the synecdochic representative). In material terms, the agency trading houses in Calcutta in the late 1820s began to suffer seriously from the global economic downturn and their own patterns of speculation; employment and income became precarious, even for the educated, and especially for those—all educated European women and most educated Indian men—who could not rely on government or military posts.

That Derozio and Roberts, neither of whom had a long career as a poet, had to manage at once the precarious finances entailed by their social positions and the intellectual contradictions of their milieu is not surprising. Their poems contain these efforts in a fairly unresolved way. The elements of their milieu—its social, political, gendered, raced, and linguistic differences—appear mingled and unresolved; their poems are more like conglomerate than metamorphic rock.

For these complex mixtures and the mediations of orientalist poetics, personal friendships, and dislocations, notions of diaspora or hybridity can provide only a wavering theoretical compass. Though in some measure Roberts could be thought of as a diasporic poet and Derozio as a poet of complex or even hybrid identity, conceptualizing their positions with reference to their multiple social locations can be helpful. The two poets shared both a British literary tradition and a position of relative economic uncertainty, as both had to make a living by their pens. They operated in a world of multiple meanings, loyalties, identifications, and disidentifications. Each negotiated these complexities differently within the literary terms established by British romanticism and by orientalist poetics as it developed after Sir William Jones (owing, in part, to the impact of Jones's work).

In the wake of Thomas Moore, Thomas Campbell, Walter Scott, and Byron, Derozio negotiated a political and poetic identity by assuming the position of the national bard—or by attempting to. But if this essential element of an imagined identity, or imagined community, was problematic enough for poets such as Moore, for Derozio it was still more difficult to imagine a nation for which he might be the bard. The vision of the past that might provide a basis for the bard's speech was riven not with subtle but with obvious contradiction, for reclaiming India's past, a central part of the orientalist project, had been envisioned by many writers in English through communal or religious terms (this foundation of "nation" is especially clear in the British historiography of Hindu and Muslim conflict and identity, which generally casts the British as freeing India from a Muslim power, conceived as foreign). Such religious and communal definitions of nation were problematic to someone of multiple religious and ethnic identities—someone, moreover, who found freethinking and skepticism to lie at the foundation of his own worldview. I read Derozio's poems under the sign of this problematic bardic claim.

Emma Roberts's position was both analogous to and significantly different from Derozio's. As a journalist and as a female poet working within, necessarily, the conventions of the poetess and working her way, literally, out of the typical position of the dependent middle-class European woman in the company's India, Roberts too takes British romantic poetics as her starting point; but she cannot constitute herself as a national bard. If such an undertaking was a strain for Derozio, for Roberts it was out of the question. Like Sir William Jones, Roberts came from a Welsh background but spent most of her life in England. In Cawnpore, she certainly did not imagine herself taking up the "harp of her country"—whether that country be Britain, England, Wales, or India. Such bardic attempts were in fact being made in a place and a language that were, as far as I can tell, completely inaccessible to Roberts; as a babe in arms, she could hardly have joined Edward Williams's Welsh *eisteddfod,* or bardic competition, in 1792. Distanced in time and space and disqualified by gender, Roberts needed a different point of entry to the poem.

Rather than the bard, Roberts might have chosen the role of sybil, a figure she does not employ directly but one that undergirds the practice of the poetess, or the "improvisatrice," as Roberts's friend Letitia Landon called her. Roberts was too like Derozio, however—too skeptical, too ironic—to strike a sybilline stance more than intermittently. She was perhaps even too old (her Indian poems were published when she was in her mid thirties) to throw herself fully into the poetic fit that is characteristic of Landon's early poems. Indeed, Roberts's poems partook of and perhaps influenced a different aspect of Landon's more mature work, the ironic juxtaposition of text and paratext and the uneasiness of what I will call poetic ventriloquism.[6] For Roberts, then, the landscape figures the weight of contradiction. Rather than establishing a continuity of "nature" and the poetic self, as would be claimed, for example, in Wordworth's "Tintern Abbey" or Coleridge's conversation poems, Roberts consistently presents landscape as scene. The imagination of the scene (and its reimagining in the poem) provides evidence of dislocation and violence and the conviction of a mortality that cannot be recuperated in any transcendental claim. For Roberts, not only is the speaking voice in the poem, the lyric "I," unstable, but so too is the meaning of landscape. The lovely landscape does not tell a univocal tale, for the picturesque often turns violent or becomes a horizon of mortality. The sublime—even the gothic—lurks just over the horizon with no promised recuperation into the domestic or the picturesque. Derozio's poems share these difficulties as well, given the historical layers and complex identifications suggested in any attempt by an East Indian poet to meditate on Indian ruins.

Even as they put the landscape to differing uses, Roberts and Derozio also used the genre of the Oriental tale to address either directly or indirectly current political controversies. The nature of education, women's position in society, and the practice of sati were particularly salient issues for both poets, and at the end of his life Derozio was also much concerned with the political position of the "East Asian" community, which was laboring under new political and economic disadvantages.

Derozio and the Constructions of Bardic Nationalism

While Roberts tried on a variety of poetic personae in her poems from the late 1820s and early 1830s, Derozio rang the changes on the trope of the bard. Though his career was too short to allow a great deal of development, still his early poetry adopts the bardic posture in a broadly generic way, whereas his later poetry is more likely to take up the bardic position with a more explicit political agenda.

The sixteen-year-old Derozio began the year 1825 by publishing poems under the apt pseudonym "Juvenis" in the *India Gazette,* which was then edited by his friend and mentor the Scotsman John Grant. Among his first efforts was an effusion called "The Poet's Grave," which argues that any child of nature must pay tribute to the spirit of the bard buried therein:

> The hand that swept the lyre is cold,
> The heart that wrought the song is still,
> The mournful tale of life is told,
> And left beyond an awful thrill.—
> What tho' the heart has ceased to beat,

What tho' unstrung's the lyre sublime?—
The bard's soft numbers shall defeat
The rudest shocks of wasting time.

(*Derozio*, 16)

Clearly indebted to Letitia Landon for his depiction of the dying bard, the young poet is most interested in the opportunity to claim poetry as his own fate: "who would not die / With him such honors vast to share?" (*Derozio*, 16). The lyre is not unstrung by the force of history, the passage of national or communal time, but only by the forces of nature and perhaps by the wild devotion of the poet to his art. "The Broken Harp," published some three months later, makes a similar move, directing its emotion, as Chaudhuri observes, not toward the nation but to "individual grief" (*Derozio*, 22). The Byronesque or Landonesque "feeling heart" thus quickly becomes the focus of Derozio's poem. Although the broken harp has seen "ruin and destruction," the causes of this neglect are never described, and, lacking specificity, the scene was easily recycled in "The Bard's Last Song," which Derozio published in June.

Moreover, in these poems the bardic stance begins to take on a particularly Scottish tinge as Derozio continues to adapt it—no wonder, given the importance of Campbell, Burns, and James Macpherson's Ossian poems in popularizing the notion of the bard. The territory of bardic nationalism as Derozio inherited it from his Scottish friends and from his reading was deeply invested in a version of the Enlightenment project that, as Katie Trumpener puts it, was "at once actively involved in the project of modernization, visibly anxious about its consequences for traditional culture, and, thanks to the self-scrutiny of sentimentalism, intensely sensitive to its own ambivalent feelings" (31).

The three poems I have discussed so far, along with several conventional love lyrics, were clearly practice pieces; by the end of 1825, Derozio had moved from naïve imitative and conventional verse to more self-conscious—and therefore more interesting—imitative verse. On the day after Christmas, he published the beginning of a long satirical poem, imitative at once of Byron's *Don Juan* and of the many satiric poems, starting with Quiz's *Qui Hi* (1816), that had lampooned young British cadets and writers in India. Derozio's "Don Juanics" runs to fifty-four stanzas of *ottava rima* in best Byronic style; his verse demonstrates a greater command of rhythm, rhyme, and meter—both serious and playful—than he had before managed, and it betrays a serious if playful immersion in British poetic controversies. Coupled with a turn toward more political subjects, particularly the current war between Greek nationalists and the Ottoman Empire (where Byron's influence is also apparent), the poems of late 1825 are clearly the ground on which Derozio was to become a bard in search of a nation.

The youthful hero and narrator of "Don Juanics," like his namesake, moves from sentimentality to irony and back. The instability of his position as bard, as an East Indian, and as a poet of the modern commercial world is made clear in the multiplicity of the intertexts he evokes, from Byron's long poems to Walter Scott's famous lines in the "Lay of the Last Minstrel" to Anglo-Indian satire. A few stanzas taken from the beginning of Derozio's canto contain these difficulties in small and need to be quoted in their entirety, for Derozio has caught Byron's tricks of enjambment, subordination, and the parenthetical aside:

III
'Twas then that Juan thought (for think we will
When the blank soul has nothing else to do)
On fleeted days, but blooming freshly still,
Nourished betimes with pure celestial dew;
And unforgotten forms his bosom fill,
While memory holds their image to his view:—
Such thoughts will come, wherever we may roam,
And one will always point to *Home, sweet Home!*

IV
Where breathes the soulless clay that will not turn
While leaving home, to gaze upon the shore?
Beats there a heart that will not bleed nor burn
To part with all it ne'er may welcome more?
The bosom that can feel, may justly spurn
Such selfish monsters, till their day is o'er:
Then what will all their pride avail?—they must
Rot unremember'd in their kindred dust.

V
Even I (though India is my native land)
Can picture to my mind a parting scene;
The lonely maiden weeping on the strand
For all that is and all that once had been,
Then gently waving her up-lifted hand,
As glides the ship o'er waters vast and deep
One last, long, lingering look she takes—and then
"Heaven guard thee, love! and may we meet again!"

(*Derozio*, 34)

The poem continues in the same way for another two stanzas until the poet brings us up short: "But I am wandering.—We left Juan thinking;— / His thoughts were somewhat similar to mine, / Each after other in oblivion sinking" (35). These lines in turn preface the poet's praise of wine, "a cure for sorrow in the flowing bowl."

The young poet is caught between Byron and Scott, between Britain and India, between an Indian version of Byron's hock and soda water and Hāfiz's overflowing bowl. Moreover, Derozio echoes the most famous lines in Scott's wildly popular "Lay of the Last Minstrel,"

> Breathes there the man, with soul so dead,
> Who never to himself hath said,
>   This is my own, my native land!
> Whose heart has ne'er within him burn'd
> As home his footsteps he hath turn'd,
>   From wandering on a foreign strand!
>
> (Scott, 161)

"Beats there a heart that will not bleed?" the poet asks. But this echo is just Juan's rather-too-saccharine daydream, a blank mind's remembrance of a pretty girl. As for the narrator, he claims firsthand knowledge of the pleasures of drink. For him, the pleasures of exilic melancholy are merely a put-on: "Even I (though India is my native land) / Can picture to my mind a parting scene" (*Derozio*, 34). This might be translated as "even I, born and bred here, have known so many Scotsmen in Calcutta who tell stories about their native shores that I can make one up to match them."

For Derozio, departure from home is not much of an impetus to patriotism; rather, the notion of leaving *India* is measured in equal parts by opportunity and apprehension. At this point, or certainly by August 1826, Derozio's brother was in Edinburgh, where he had been sent to pursue a medical education. The poet addressed him in verses titled "To My Brother in Scotland." The sorrow of parting is quite real to the poet, not mediated through tropes of exile but rather prefaced by a prose treatise on Indian education, in which he laments the "backward state" of education in India and thus defends the practice of sending children abroad. The issues, as Derozio brings them forward, are germane to the instabilities of patriotic sentiment invoked through Scott's intertext as well as to Derozio's later work as editor of the *East Indian.* Derozio is working through what it means virtually to lose a brother and, simultaneously, what it might mean to be a national bard.

In the prose piece that precedes "To My Brother," Derozio is quite critical of "our *East Indian Community.*" He chides his fellows for their lack of unanimity, though addressing them in the third person: "Let them unite, let them bring themselves together, form associations and societies, learn the sentiments of each other, find out their own value, and ascertain what they are capable of effecting, then, and not till then, will they be able to improve their condition" (*Derozio,* 88). The patriotic sentiments of Scott's bard are understood by Derozio in the context of pressing political and social claims. The poet declares, "I was born in India, and have been bred here; I am proud to acknowledge my country, and to do my best in her service, but even love of country shall not hinder me from expressing what I believe to be right. I have a brother in Scotland, where he is to study a profession which here he could never learn:

Would it not have been injustice to have detained him here, and then to say to him at a future period, 'you might have been doing well in the world, but you were educated in India from a patriotic motive?'" (*Derozio*, 89). The nuances of his situation are clear in "To My Brother" where the poet thinks of his brother not as exiled but as hopeful, while he—the elder—feels apprehensive. Dismissing his fears he sends his blessing toward Scotland, exhorting his brother to be of good cheer:

> Still be thy heart, fair, light, and gay,
>   And gladness in thine every tone;
> Nor dream thou once far o'er the sea
>   That hearts are aching here for thee.
>
> Then, o'er the boundless watery waste
>   To that far land where now thou art,
> Be many a blessing borne to thee
>   By guardian seraphs of the heart!
>
> (*Derozio*, 90)

In 1825–26, Derozio tried on, tried out, the potential meanings of patriotism, still breathing in his poetry the sentiments of the heart but investigating more complexly in his prose and satiric verse the role and status of the bard.

When he came to reprint "To My Brother in Scotland" in his first collection of poems, it immediately preceded "Here's a Health to Thee, Lassie," a direct imitation of Scottish verse, echoing both Burns and probably Derozio's teacher David Drummond (who was well known for a fine song, "The Bonnie Lass o' Levenside").[7] Derozio's Scottish pastiche (like the poem to his brother) is a song about separation, though of a purely conventional sort, and it is followed by "Ode from the Persian of Hafiz, freely translated." Even "Here's a Health to Thee, Lassie," however much it echoes Scottish verse, ends with a sentiment at least as derivative of Hāfiz as of Burns. The speaker exclaims, "Come hither, boy! fill up my bowl," for when wine wakens the soul the "draught's indeed divine" (*Derozio*, 110). Thus, Derozio addresses the issues of nation, exile, and nationalism through multiple identifications—Persian, Scottish, Indian, and (as he bows to Byron, Landon, Shelley, and Keats) English.

It is no wonder, then, that the last gasp of the "Don Juanics" is an envoi, invoking Byron, taking a swipe at Southey, and implicitly claiming future laurels for Derozio's bardic self:

> "Go boldly forth my artless verse" I'd say,
>   But mighty Byron said so long ago—
> I beg the Laureate's pardon—(for *his* lay
>   Was sung before the noble bard of woe

Bid his wild strain, in these words, live its day)
I would not snatch the laurel from his brow

(*Derozio*, 49)

The harp, the laurel, the relationship of patriotism to poetic glory—all these elements came to shape his efforts when Derozio collected many of these poems, though not the "Don Juanics," in his two volumes of verse.

Derozio's first collection, *Poems*, appeared in 1827, when the poet was but eighteen years old. The paratextual elements framing the verse create a transperipheral frame. India and the poet himself are placed in a web of identifications; they are of a piece with earlier Scottish, Welsh, and Irish claims to distinctive culture and national heritage. As Trumpener argues, writers from the internal colonies of Great Britain at the end of the eighteenth century conceived "a new national literary history under the sign of the bard, a figure who represents the resistance of vernacular oral traditions to the historical pressures of English imperialism and whose performance brings the voices of the past into the sites of the present. . . . Bardic nationalism insists on the rich fullness of national knowledge, on the anchoring of discursive traditions in landscape, in a way of life, in custom. The English, in comparison, have only borrowed words" (33–34).

Such a view was at once natural and problematic for the young Derozio: if the English had only "borrowed words," Derozio's situation was still more vexed than theirs. Hence, like his predecessors, he relied on paratextual elements to buttress his poetic claims. Derozio began his first volume with three major elements: an epigraph, a dedication, and a preface. The epigraph he took from Thomas Moore's "To the Harp of Erin":

If the pulse of the patriot, soldier, or lover
Have throbbed at our lay, 'twas thy glory alone;
It was but as the wind passing heedlessly over,
And all the wild sweetness I waked was thy own.

Derozio dedicated his volume to John Grant, a Scotsman who was then editor of the *India Gazette* and had published many of these efforts in his newspaper. In his preface, Derozio put himself forward as one "born, and educated in India" who at the age of eighteen "venture[d] to present himself as a candidate for poetic fame." He went on to claim, accurately, that "the publication of a work of this nature in India [was] not a frequent occurrence" (Preface, *Poems*).

His entirely Indian education is the center of Derozio's self-presentation; his name, which appears on the title page, counts for the rest. Indeed, in reviewing Derozio's book in the *India Gazette*, Grant begins by arguing that the poet's work is "highly creditable to the author, and, we may add, to the rising class to which he belongs"; Grant refers to Derozio's youth and concludes by strongly recommending the "volume to all who would encourage the aspirations of Eastern genius, or who feel interested in the advance of Eastern literature" (Chaudhuri, *Derozio*, 389–90).[8] Thus Grant underscores Derozio's paratextual identification as patriot and bard, even though the concept of the "East" remains unspecified.

Grant may have imagined Derozio becoming something like the Walter Scott of the "East," subsuming cultural nationalism in a wider imperial project (see Trumpener, 246). But Trumpener notes that Scott and Moore could as easily be taken to represent different approaches to the politics of poetry. Even in settler colonies such as Canada, Scott's accommodation to empire (which, after all, was the project of generations of Scotsmen like Grant himself) could be problematized by Scottish or Irish resistance to English domination and the Act of Union. It is not Scott who appears in Derozio's first reference to the bard but the Irish Tom Moore, whom Derozio certainly recognized not only for his poetry but also for his friendship with Byron. Moore and Byron present the possibility, at least, of a more radical nationalism than Scott's, though in Derozio's case we might call it protonationalism.

The first poem of Derozio's initial collection of verse, his famous "The Harp of India," itself functions almost paratextually. Unlike subsequent poems in the volume, it appears unpaginated and with a special wingding between the poem's title and the text.[9] In "The Harp of India," Derozio begins his book of verse with a quatrain of questions. The harp is an enigma, a mute monument, an instrument only in potential but not yet in practice:

> Why hang'st thou lonely on yon withered bough?
> Unstrung, forever, must thou there remain?
> Thy music once was sweet—who hears it now?
> Why doth the breeze sigh over thee in vain?—
> Silence hath bound thee with her fatal chain;
> Neglected, mute, and desolate art thou,
> Like ruined monument on desert plain!—
>
> (*Poems*, 1)

For a Calcutta poet to take up a desolate harp and recapture its ancient music is a tall order. The bardic harp (which by implication resembles an Aeolian harp as well) is silent, its strings turned to chains. The poet must become the agent of transformation. But this raises obvious difficulties: What ancient music is to be evoked in memory? Irish music like Moore's? Scottish music like the last minstrel's? Indian music? If so, which music? How does the poet construct nation in this context?[10]

"The Harp of India" enacts a poetics of cancellation. Each element of the past—music and monuments and, in the second half of the poem, earlier bards, flowers, and the wreaths woven for them by fame—is evoked only to be negated. Earlier poets and audiences are now in their graves, Derozio writes:

> O! many a hand more worthy far than mine
> Once thy harmonious chords to sweetness gave,

And many a wreath for them did Fame entwine
Of flowers still blooming on the minstrel's grave:
Those hands are cold—but if thy notes divine
May be by mortal wakened once again,
Harp of my country, let me strike the strain.

(1)

The harp, the breeze, the monuments and memorials of earlier grandeur, the music of the past, all are made present only to be made absent. The self-canceling dimension of Derozio's poem, which he found implicit in Moore's evocation of Irish harpers, arises from the complexity of the poet's situation as a person of multiple identities and identifications, from the impossibility of writing a national poetry for a nation that can only be imagined in some futurity, and from the extreme tensions already visible in the biblical progenitor of the bardic trope.

Derozio shares the source lying behind Moore and all the other eighteenth- and nineteenth-century poets who evoked the harp hung upon the willow; he evokes the lament of the psalmist remembering the Babylonian captivity. The poet does not entirely take up the psalmist's stance, but it nevertheless remains crucial. Though "The Harp of India" has an immediate ancestor in Moore, Derozio would certainly have known Psalm 137, for his father (and probably his mother and stepmother) was a devout Baptist. I quote Psalm 137 in the King James version, the one Derozio would have known:

> By the rivers of Babylon, there we sat down, yea, we wept, when we remembered Zion.
>
> We hanged our harps upon the willows in the midst thereof.
>
> For there they that had carried us away captive required of us a song; and they that wasted us required of us mirth, saying, Sing us one of the songs of Zion.
>
> How shall we sing the Lord's song in a strange land?

The psalm famously concludes with the exile's vow of revenge against the captors who brought him into exile: "Happy shall he be, that taketh and dasheth thy little ones against the stones."

Given this violent intertext and the evocation of exile, where does Derozio fit? As a person born in India of Indian, Portuguese, and English ancestry, he can hardly think of himself as an exile from England. Instead, the bardic harp creates an allusion to a kind of internal exile, one in which the poet's culture is reduced to a desert he must attempt to restore. Clearly Derozio had some reason to configure the British as Babylonian captors or, in the language of eighteenth-century European radicalism, as "tyrants." Some of his Baptist friends (as I suggest in the next chapter) and David Hare differed on religious matters but shared anti-imperialist attitudes, which were partially based in their class position and in the traditions of radical Protestantism. Hare was an atheist watchmaker; his missionary compatriot William Carey, a shoemaker. For widely divergent reasons, both were more or less levelers, sharing a distrust of class privilege. Neither advocated violence, but both argued for standards of political judgment based on moral principle rather than mercantile advantage. Derozio's bardic trope was constructed also in the company of men such as David Drummond and John Grant who professed a Scottish identity but also, having no intention of returning to Scotland, were permanent expatriates.

Derozio's communal or national identification, then, was fraught. Though he grew up speaking English and attended English-medium schools, this did not necessarily lead to an identification with British interests. To the contrary, the shift in the position of "East Indians" in early nineteenth-century Calcutta made any such identification particularly precarious. "East Indians," the community that shared Derozio's background, were laboring under new disadvantages in the 1820s. The government had forbidden their appointments in the civil service; the economy of Bengal was struggling in the wake of an economic downturn, which shortly led to a collapse of major trading houses; a new class of educated Indians taught by Derozio, among others, was competing for employment with East Indians; and the indigo business—a chief export through 1800—had fallen on hard times.[11]

A poet beginning in this context, a poet seeking a nation for which he might become the bard, required an elision of differences among Hindu, Muslim, and East Indian communities. For whom, then, was the poet to play the harp? And why a harp rather than a traditional Indian instrument? It is little wonder that Derozio's poem, almost but not quite a sonnet, comes to rest on a final rhyme, the word *strain*. Indeed, this rhyme pervades the poem from the second line: *remain, vain, chain, plain, again, strain*. The poet must strain, and the trope itself must be strained, stretched, and curiously displaced to construct a poem proleptical of national unity.[12]

Southwest view of the Fakir's Rock in the River Ganges, near Sultanganj, by Thomas Daniell. Pencil and wash drawing, October 1788.

Derozio reprises the trope of the harp hung upon the willow at the beginning of his second volume of verse, *The Fakeer of Jungheera, a Metrical Tale; and Other Poems,* published in 1828, only a year after the first. Here, again, the initial poem in the volume stands as a kind of preface. In this instance, the poem is untitled, appearing almost as an epigraph. It follows the volume's dedication to Derozio's friend the orientalist Horace Hayman Wilson, who was in the Bengal Medical Service and served as secretary to the Asiatic Society. A poet as well as a translator of Sanskrit, Wilson would defend Derozio to the managers of Hindu College in the controversy that led to dismissal in 1831. Wilson would have been one of those poets who brought "from out the ages that have rolled / A few small fragments of those wrecks sublime." He thus carried the role that Derozio wishes to claim for himself in his introductory poem:

> Well—let me dive into the depths of time,
> And bring from out the ages that have rolled
> A few small fragments of those wrecks sublime,
> Which human eye may never more behold;
> And let the guerdon of my labour be
> My fallen country! one kind wish for thee!
>
> (*Fakeer*)

Yet the poet's desire for wrecked sublimity is highly problematic, falling as it does into the orientalist notion that the glories of eastern cultures are all in the past.

Derozio gives this historiography a twist by suggesting in his initial poem that India has been pinioned like an eagle in chains. Implicitly, the eagle, until recently, could soar on its own. The passive voice creating the metaphor, however, allows the poet to avoid assigning responsibility for this sad state of affairs. Of India, the poet asks, "where is that glory, where that reverence now?"

> Thy eagle pinion is chained down at last,
> And groveling in the lowly dust art thou:
> Thy minstrel hath no wreath to weave for thee
> Save the sad story of thy misery!—
>
> (*Fakeer*)

The eagle enchained, owing much to Byron and Shelley, becomes the metaphorical representation of India. But the figure is unstable, inasmuch as the eagle can function as a figure for poetry, as in Shelley's verse, or as a metonymy for Napoleon, as in *Childe Harold's Pilgrimage.*

These introductory lyrics, both of them variations on the sonnet, are reprised in two different keys in Derozio's volumes. Their political dimensions are amplified in a series of poems on Greek themes obviously inspired by the Greek War of

Independence from the Ottoman Empire (1821–29) as well as by Derozio's classical reading. A second reprise of the bardic theme takes the poet back to the personal concerns of such poems as "The Poet's Grave."

Indeed, the conflict between the Greeks and the Ottomans becomes Derozio's stalking horse for issues of nation, civil liberties, and freedom in the volume of 1827. But, as Rosinka Chaudhuri has argued in "An Ideology of Indianness," this configuration is problematic in the Indian context, because the discourse of Greek freedom was often couched as a resistance to Muslim tyranny. Though his prose clearly indicates an interest in combating communal differences, the common British historiographical move that configured Hindus as oppressed by Muslims dovetails in an unfortunate way with the radical potential of the Greek revolution. Derozio's first volume includes numerous poems on the Greek war and on Greek topics: "Greece," "The Greeks at Marathon," "The Grecian Sire and Son," "Address to the Greeks," "Phyle," and a poem related in its concerns with freedom but clearly inspired by the abolition movement, "Freedom to the Slave." Thomas Campbell, Byron, Henry Bulwer (*An Autumn in Greece*), and the "Hellenic Chronicle of Missolonghi" furnish epigraphs and headnotes for the poems.

When Derozio turns his attention to the poet's career, these larger claims about freedom and tyranny are figured in the register of the psyche. He takes a more personal than political view of the poet and freedom in his poems on Tasso and Sappho (published in *Poems*, 1827). Ignoring the possibility that Tasso was mad, Derozio laments that Tasso's spirit "in a prison pined." The result: "Upon a cypress bough thy harp was hung, / Silent, neglected, mournful, and unstrung!" But Derozio can now crown Tasso's tomb with "everlasting bloom" (*Derozio*, 142–43). Sappho provides a different figuration of the poet. Derozio takes his epigraph to "Sappho" from *Don Juan* and, like Byron and Landon, figures Sappho as a poet of unrequited love: "Hers was melodious mourning; like the dew / Her bright tears fell, for madness made her weep" (*Derozio*, 164). The bard's position, implicated in these poems, was made still more obvious in the "Song of the Hindoostanee Minstrel" (published in *Poems*, 1827). Here Derozio conflates the European and Indian traditions (exactly what he might mean by a "Hindoostanee" minstrel is unclear). The speaker's metaphorical horizon is clearly Muslim, and his praise of his "fair Cashmerian girl" includes the usual allusions to the pearls of Oman and the roses of Basra. But in contrast to the local schema of the Greek poems and "The Harp of India," the "Hindoostanee minstrel" is rendered homeless in this poem. He tells his beloved,

> Nay weep not, love! thou shouldst not weep,
> The world is all our home;
> Life's watch together we shall keep,
> We'll love where'er we roam.
>
> Like birds from land to land we'll range,
>
> (*Derozio*, 161–62)

The minstrel promises that he and his beloved will play the "sweet sitar," but the instability of this premise is made obvious by Derozio's footnote clearly aimed at both a London and a local audience and playing on the knowledge, or lack of it, of both. He glosses *sitar:* "A musical instrument. It does not justify the application of the epithet given to it in the text, as it is not remarkably *sweet*" (*Derozio,* 162). Thus the "Hindoostanee" minstrel is at once local and homeless, the singer of a nation (if only a nation yet to be) and the singer of love.

In his two volumes of verse, then, Derozio experimented with the various potential meanings in the trope of the bardic harp—exile, lost love, the revival of a lost national authenticity. For Derozio, the harp hung upon the cypress or the willow (the sitar played on the wing) bespoke a complex poetic geography. Emma Roberts shared this complex territory, but from a very different starting point. Their cooperation and collaboration attests to the heterogeneity of their geographical, gendered, and linguistic situations.

Emma Roberts: Poet as Landscape Artist

Derozio and Emma Roberts shared a common passion for landscape, though Roberts was in no position to claim a bardic stance or to propose reviving a lost authenticity. While Derozio diffidently sought the laurel crown or at least the bard's reward, Roberts made more modest claims in *Oriental Scenes.* The scenic poem, the poem as landscape, for Roberts, can be understood as a mode made possible by the imagined stability of British conquest. But even this apparent stability is belied by the contradictions both among Roberts's poems and within the poems' conflicted voices.

The first edition of *Oriental Scenes* was published in Calcutta in 1830, seen through the press by Derozio while Roberts was living at Agra with her sister. A second substantially different edition appeared in 1832 in London. While the first edition bore a dedication to Lady Bentinck, wife of the then governor-general, and included an impressive list of subscribers in Calcutta and beyond, the second edition was dedicated to Roberts's friend Letitia Landon, who was by then not only a wildly popular poet but also an important editor of London literary annuals. In both editions, Roberts, like Derozio, shaped the paratext to her advantage. Like Derozio she apologized for intruding her work upon the public, but like him she also mingled assertion with apology. Where Derozio sought literary fame, Roberts claimed a place as an artist of the poetic scene.

Even Roberts's title promised the picturesque and the diverting: scenes, sketches, and tales. The tilt toward the picturesque is even clearer in the London edition than in the Calcutta edition, no doubt reflecting Roberts's estimation of the London market. Whereas the Calcutta edition was titled *Oriental Scenes, Dramatic Sketches and Tales,* the London edition was simply *Oriental Scenes, Sketches and Tales.* Moreover, the London edition added ten poems that had not appeared earlier and eliminated all poems from the earlier edition that did not treat Indian themes.[13] Here Roberts was obviously attempting to market her volume as an analog to collections of engravings. The preface to the London edition also eliminated mention of Derozio, who would have been virtually unknown to Roberts's London audience and would have had no role in the revised version.

In the preface to the 1832 edition of *Oriental Scenes,* Roberts highlights her wish to provide the reader with mental pictures. The temptation to "illustrate scenes and incidents, which during my travels in India, struck me as being particularly interesting and picturesque, was irresistible," she says. "The Poems written merely with a view to amuse an idle hour, or to fill a niche in a periodical, have swelled into a volume; and in giving them to the world in their present form, I am not without a hope that they will convey some portion of the gratification to my readers, which I myself experienced while wandering over the sunny provinces of Hindoostan" (viii).

In promising these delightful views of "sunny Hindoostan," Roberts was drawing on the continued popularity in Britain and India of actual engravings and aquatints. Conceiving the poems as scenes and sketches, she, like Derozio, implicitly acknowledged the importance of word and image.[14] Thomas and William Daniell had published numerous volumes of engravings and aquatints from their travels in India between March 1795 and 1816, beginning with *Oriental Scenery: Twenty-four Views in Hindoostan.* The influence of the Daniells' aquatints was not limited to print media but extended as well to china design, wallpaper, and even architecture.[15] Moreover, their aquatints of Indian scenes were followed by similar volumes resulting from their travels around the periphery of the British Isles, including *A Voyage Round the North and North-West Coast of Scotland, and the Adjacent Islands: With a Series of Views, Illustrative of Their Character and Most Prominent Features* (1820). Plates from the Daniells' Indian work appeared anew in London shortly after Roberts's London volume of verse and simultaneously with her travel book, *Scenes and Characteristics of Hindoostan* (1835). The Daniells' work formed the illustrations for the *Oriental Annual,* edited in 1833 through 1840 by William Daniell and Hobart Cauntor, and later by Cauntor and others. The aquatints were equally popular in Calcutta, where even in the late twentieth century they retained a central role in the picturesque delineation of the historical city.[16]

As the continuing popularity of the Daniells' work indicates, Roberts was in the thick of a new kind of publishing, made possible by improvements in engraving and printing. She and her friend and housemate Landon were deeply involved with the creation of literary annuals and with the publishers H. Fisher and R. Fisher, who specialized both in annuals and in high-end collections of engravings; in short, they published what we now think of as coffee-table books. Fisher published *Views in India, China and on the Shores of the Red Sea* in 1835 with text written by Roberts; Landon recycled many of these plates in *Fisher's Drawing Room Scrap-Book,* writing poems to illustrate the prints.

But Roberts's involvement with the annuals—and with the picturesque qualities they implied—was already significant before most of her poems on Indian subjects were conceived. *The Poetess Archive* lists ten poems published by Roberts in London literary annuals between 1826 and 1834, including poems in *The Literary Souvenir, The Amulet,* and *The Bijou.*[17] The annuals formed her sense of the picturesque and the poetic quite as much as orientalist poetry did. As in the work of the Daniells, so too in the poetry of the annuals, the proper subjects for landscape were defined transperipherally—Cornwall, the Highlands and islands of Scotland, and the reaches of empire were subject to more than a fair share of pictorial and poetic illustration. In this way, editors capitalized at once on the popularity of engravings and on the popularity of oriental subjects in the poetry of Moore, Southey, and Byron. In poetry, as in printmaking, landscape served as a medium of exchange, or in W. J. T. Mitchell's formulation, as a "frame and what a frame contains, both a real place and its simulacrum, both a package and the commodity inside the package" (5). Mitchell argues that while landscape as a medium is found in all cultures, it is also "a particular historical formation associated with European imperialism" (5). The trope of exile is intimately bound up with and in its particular formation enabled by and through the medium of landscape.

In shaping her volume toward the picturesque or scenic landscape, then, Roberts was well aware of commercial possibilities. "Scenic" engravings and the poems illustrative of them were commodities sold by subscription in Calcutta; moreover, through the annuals, poems were sold via association with engravings or aquatints in metropole and colony alike. Although as a commodified object the poem or the engraving serves to replicate the relationships of nation and imperial possession, within the poem or the engraving itself these relationships may be unstable.

In Roberts's actual practice of poetry, landscape, which assumes a stable relationship between viewer and prospect, by its very excess provides its own undoing. Roberts's numerous poems about graves provide particularly good examples of this instability. Landscape, in Mitchell's words, provided within the empire an "unbounded 'prospect' of endless appropriation and conquest," but a landscape including graves serves as an affective limit of appropriation. As Mitchell puts it, "empires have a way of coming to an end, leaving behind their landscapes as relics and ruins" (18–19). When the poet meditates on the grave, a relic or ruin may be both world historical and intensely personal.

To examine this process at work, I turn to three of Roberts's poems: "Indian Graves," "The Moosalmaun's Grave," and "The Taaje Mahal." "Indian Graves" appeared in *Oriental Scenes* with a very long prose note lamenting the condition of Christian graves in India. While a few Christian graves, Roberts says, "stand alone in picturesque spots," they are more generally crowded together in "small enclosures of consecrated ground." But the Christian ground is in no way picturesque or even "soothing" to the spirits of the living, for "few Europeans can view without horror the crowded but neglected cemetery in which they may expect to find a grave. Choked up with weeds, the resort of carrion birds and loathsome beasts, and rarely visited, except upon those melancholy occasions in which another exile is deposited

. . . they present the most dismal *memento mori* imaginable" (1832, 196). Roberts finds a much more comforting prospect among graves of Indians, which are often "well-frequented" or even inhabited.

In "Indian Graves," the poet paints a lovely scene of Indian graves and an appalling scene of European ones. She freely alternates quatrains and couplets of iambic tetrameter, almost as if the two kinds of graves are to be given two different and disconcerting musical voices. The poem begins with a "prospect," of sunset "on India's plains." In this tropical paradise, "rich odorous" scents, gemlike birds, and the lights of mosques and Hindu temples mingle to create repose for the eye. The cool of evening allows the traveler who has been "pent" in a riverboat to walk on the shore; the traveler who has avoided the heat in a "sultry tent" can explore a broad expanse. Thus, the poem moves from what would seem to have been a particular view—a person's view—to a general view seen by no single individual, and back to the particular. Finally, forty lines into the poem, a particularized lyric "I" or eye emerges:

> Whene'er through copse and flowery glade
> In the cool evening air I've strayed,
> However bright and richly fraught
>   The varied scene before me spread,
> My wandering footsteps still have sought
>   The quiet mansions of the dead,
> The scattered graves where Moslems lie
>   Enshrined within their massy tombs
> Beneath some tall tree's canopy,
>   Which mantles o'er their sacred homes,
> And not those crowded charnels, where
> A sickening taint infects the air.
> And o'er each dark and loathsome grave
> Earth's rankest weeds delight to wave
>
> (1832, 115–16)

Though the lyric speaker declines to walk among the charnels of the Europeans, the poem visits them, cataloguing the jackals and vultures that unearth the bones of the departed. In such scenes,

> How many thoughts oppress the heart,
>   Where early doomed, an exiled band
> From their paternal homes apart
>   Lie buried in a heathen land,
> Unwept, unhonoured, and unknown,
>
> (116)

In contrast to the European, the unnamed deceased Muslim lies in "some romantic chosen spot." Whether it be in the "palace-tomb of Agra's plains" or in a "small Musjeed's lowly porch," true believers (later, it turns out, both Hindu and Muslim believers) make offerings of lights and flowers. This venerated and romantic grave, the poet declares, is the kind of resting place she envies. If she must die in India, she asks for "a sepulchre remote / From human haunts, some forest cell" (118). In such a lovely place—described at length—the wind will tell a "melancholy tale," the story of "the exile lost / To all that hope's bright augurs gave," an exile who found only "One sad sole boon, a lonely grave" (119).

Before she dilates on this final and fourth scene in "Indian Graves," the poet provides a third scene: nearly twenty lines descriptive of a rural grave in a nameless British place. The rural British grave is thoroughly overdetermined; it is at once the package and the commodity. The sheer conventionality of its description defies any attempt to invest it with a longed-for but absent reality. The exclamatory "Oh!" and the bathos of the rhyme only emphasize the factitiousness of the sentiment for a lost homeland:

> Oh! since beyond the western wave
> I may not hope to find a grave,
> Nor yield my weary spirit up,
> Where springs the glittering butter cup,
> And daisies led their silvery shrouds,
> And violet mourn in purple clouds
>
> (118)

Roberts goes on in this vein through the seasons and bird songs—moss, holly berries, larks, sheep-bells, and "bubbling brooklets" all complete. So despite the poem's title, "Indian Graves," the poem offers multiple layered landscapes: a Muslim shrine; a deserted European cemetery in India; a rural British cemetery; and the lone grave or "tangled solitude" hoped for by the lost exile.

"Indian Graves" attempts something more complex but ultimately achieves something more reductive and transparently ideological than "The Moosulmaun's Grave." In the latter poem, Roberts celebrates the kindness of donors who have built gardens and tanks (bathing places) on the grounds of "the pious Moslem's lowly tomb." The poet shares the gratitude of those who find shelter and refreshment in its precincts. She describes the scene and then generalizes it to all India, in the process describing both Hindu and Muslim shrines and the "blessed work of charity—a tree / Planted for love of human-kind" or a mosque or temple's "o'ershading canopy." All can make "the heart with holy feelings swell" (*Oriental Scenes* [1832], 73). Implicitly, the praise of Indian tombs creates a critique of Christianity in India; far from being barbarous heathens, Indians are shown to build monuments and shrines, not for glory alone but as acts of piety and kindness to strangers. In contrast to "The Moosulmaun's Grave,"

"Indian Graves" is a fraught and unstable poem; for rural Britain, however lamented, seems less deeply felt than the landscapes of "The Moosulmaun's Grave."

"The Taaje Mahal" addresses the most famous mausoleum in India, and necessarily it does so at once in the register of the psyche and in the register of history. The Taj Mahal, unlike the nameless Muslim's grave, is no "lowly tomb." The building's fame burdens the poet with the weight of describing a scene both familiar and obligatory. Like the Daniells, who found that they needed to add a view of the Taj Mahal to later editions of their Indian aquatints, Roberts too had to oblige the reader with what was already the most famous of Indian scenes. Surprisingly—in a daring and not very successful move—she commences the poem as a dramatic lyric spoken to his dying wife by the monument's builder, the emperor Shāh Jāhan. The emperor laments Mumtaz's death and predicts that her tomb will awe future generations. As in "The Rajah's Obsequies," Roberts creates a dramatic speaker. In "The Rajah's Obsequies," as I will argue shortly, the rajah's wives take prophetic roles, whereas here in "The Taaje Mahal," the husband prophesies history to come. Shāh Jāhan predicts that "pilgrims . . . from many a distant clime" will "gaze upon the work sublime" and pay homage to his beloved's "sainted clay" (*Oriental Scenes* [1832], 32–33). But at this point the poem is interrupted with a row of asterisks, and the second half of the poem becomes a pastiche of the poet speaker's omniscient voice and the imagined voice of a stranger—the predicted pilgrim. The stranger with rapt and "dazzled eye" repeats "A tale of love's idolatry" to his "throbbing heart" (34).

In "The Taaje Mahal," it is certainly not clear that the poet speaker herself (if we can ascribe gender to her) has the same reaction to the Taj as the pilgrim from a distant clime whose thoughts she imagines. Instead, this pilgrim could be said to ventriloquize empire in describing the replacement of the Mughal empire by the British one:

> The warriors of the western world
> The red cross banner have unfurled.
> Mingled with mosques and minarets,
> O'er Christian spires the sun's beam sets,
> And strangers from a foreign strand
> Rule unopposed the conquered land.
>
> (36)

Yet despite this record of successive conquest, the speaker says, the mausoleum is "untouched by time, unscathed by war": "Of precious marbles richly blent / Shines the imperial monument" (36). To the imagined stranger, the pilgrim from a distant clime, the Taj seems almost a dream, an "evanescent pageantry" (37). Finally, the poem ends with the usual moralizing in the poet speaker's voice—the Taj remains a record of strong affection enduring beyond the grave.

In "The Taaje Mahal," Roberts ventriloquizes empire twice—first in the voice of Shāh Jāhan and then in the voices of the poet speaker and the western stranger whom she imagines. The "western" visitors through whom the landscape is made visible in the poem cannot but be diminished by the scene they view. The tomb and its environs become the landscape of empire; and as empires are always shadowed by their own ruin, built upon the ruins of others, the assertion that the "warriors of the western world" rule unopposed seems less predictive than provisional.

The landscapes of death in Roberts's poems are always inflected by larger political and social contexts. The contrast is clear if we compare Roberts's treatment of the Taj with Maria Nugent's. Lady Nugent included two poems in her travel diary, *A Journal of the Year 1811 till the Year 1815, Including a Voyage to and Residence in India* (London, 1839, two volumes). The first was a poignant farewell to three of her children (all under the age of ten), whom she left behind to accompany her husband to India. The second poem was the obligatory meditation on the Taj Mahal. Maria Nugent's view of the Taj is wholly a matter of Christian moralizing, which, given her evangelical leanings, is not surprising. The Taj becomes a monument to wedded bliss and the hope of heaven and Shāh Jāhan the singlemindedly faithful husband—never mind his two additional wives or the various other women at his court. The jewels of the Taj are moralized, ending finally with the emerald, which points

> to regions far beyond the sky,
> Regions of peace, the mansions of the blest—
> For Hope is e'er arrayed in brightest green,
> All nature too in Hope's attire is seen!
>
> (1:364)

So, empire aside, Lady Nugent imagines for Shāh Jāhan and Mumtaz a reward of eternal joy. From her evangelical perspective, the Muslim emperor and his bride are translated from a very Christian looking marriage to a very Christian looking heaven.

The Taj, then, is for both Maria Nugent and Emma Roberts a mirror for ideology; but interestingly Roberts brings to bear a skeptical turn of mind, one that destabilizes even her attempt at voicing imperial sentiments. This instability is in part the function of the grave itself, which creates the limit of the imperial landscape whether as a sublime sight—monument or ruin—or as a gothic and horrifying romantic landscape of death and decay.

In *The Tropics and the Traveling Gaze,* David Arnold calls the sorts of scenes Roberts depicts "deathscapes," and he traces their importance throughout nineteenth-century British travel accounts, including Roberts's. He calls Roberts a "connoisseur of graveyards" (51). Arnold acknowledges Roberts's personal sense of loss, in the death of her sister, but also points to the ways Roberts's *Scenes and Characteristics of Hindostan* responded to the conventions of the time and exploited the grave for "literary effect"

(51). As Arnold points out, Roberts's prose reflects the shocking quality of sudden death and the need for immediate burial in a tropical climate. He argues, moreover, that because European women as well as men attended funerals (unlike in England), the traumatic effect of such rites was redoubled, and doubled again by the "tragedy of dying abroad" (52). Although Roberts furthers the tropes of the deathscape that were common to other Europeans writing in India, even within the literary conventions entailed in the foreign grave she brings to bear a more detailed and historicized understanding of these conventions than a poet on the order of Maria Nugent.

It is precisely this historicization, however, that can wreck the poem, its conflicting agendas unresolved. Even Roberts's living landscapes devolve into a kind of incoherence. "Stanzas Written in a Pavilion of the Rambaugh," for example, ends with an explicit evocation of a wreck, a rent picture. We might think of the poem itself as a landscape painted on a canvas already torn and scarcely mended. The poem, descriptive of the gardens in Agra, lovingly details the beauties of these gardens but asserts that nonetheless the "lonely exile pants for home" (*Oriental Scenes* [1832], 110). Immediately, though, the poem shows that at "home" such a person would have looked at landscape painting and longed for India.

The seduction of landscape painting draws the traveler to India, in imagination or in the flesh. Roberts evokes the painter as a necromancer:

> How oft, when gazing on some fairy spot,
> Wrought by the painter's necromantic skill,
> Bedecked with temple, palace, bower and grot,
> The gushing fountain, and the silvery rill,
> The soul has languished for some angel's wings,
> To waft it swiftly on the willing breeze,
> And scarcely could repress its murmurings,
> That his own earth possessed not scenes like these.
> Here is the blest reality—not even
> In the bright wonders of the summer skies,
> Are lovelier forms or purer splendours given
>
> (111)

After numerous lines celebrating the extraordinary beauty of the gardens, the poem takes a final turn:

> But all is foreign—'mid the dazzling glare,
> The pensive gazer would rejoice to see
> The gorgeous pageant melt away in air,
> While on its wrecks arose the old oak tree.
> The soft green sward with daisies spangled o'er,

The brawling stream by rustic arches spanned,
The jasmine trailing round the cottage door,
The humblest village of his native land.

(III)

The Rambaugh gardens become a pageant of clouds, which are wrecked only to be transformed into a British rural cot. The cot here figures as a place so stylized that it cannot be thought ever to have existed. The poem's final turn—"But all is foreign"—is itself a kind of wreck.

"Stanzas Written in a Pavilion" begins with a prospect viewed and described from a stable position; then the historical spectacle of succeeding conquest by the Mughals, the Jats, and the British destabilizes the prospect and calls up the notion of exile; next the exiled, presumably British, person is shown to have longed for precisely this exile, having been lured to India through the painter's necromancy; and finally the very scene at the beginning of the poem is re-entered through painterly mediation once again, only to be wrecked on an imagined image of an English oak.

In "Stanzas Written in a Pavilion," as in "The Taaje Mahal," the landscape is not only a wreck of history but is wrecked by the implicit gendering of the gaze. The "exile" longs for the painted scenes of India because "his own earth" does not possess such scenes; this same exile longs for the humble villages of "his native land." The "exile" is presumably the same male and British citizen who is said in "The Taaje Mahal" to rule unopposed in India. The poet, however, seems to remain conscious that she is neither a citizen nor a ruler. Can she then be said to be an exile? The contradictions of the poems ask, but do not answer, this question.

Precisely because Roberts has a modicum of skepticism about religion, empire, British claims to superiority, and the gendered relationships of power among the British, Muslim, and Hindu inhabitants of India and because she at the same time exploits the poem as commodity, her "oriental scenes" are indeed wrecked pageants. The political potential of this poetry is at once developed and curtailed, particularly when she moves from landscape to narrative. Whereas Derozio struggles to find a song and a country suited to the bardic harp, Roberts struggles to stabilize a landscape long enough to make a poem of it. But since the landscape cannot, for her, be understood as nation and since the grave cannot be understood as home, landscape itself becomes flying clouds or sea-wrack.

Derozio's poem on the Rajmahal provides an interesting contrast to Roberts's landscape poems. In "The Ruins of Rajmahal," Derozio wants, like Roberts, to paint a landscape scene in words, to meditate on a ruin. But he quickly acknowledges how factitious the emotion elicited by ruins can be:

I would not have the day return
That saw these wrecks in all their pride—

As he who weeps o'er Beauty's urn
Feels what he felt not by her side.

(*Derozio*, 140)

The poet goes on to describe the graffiti defacing the remains of the famous palace built by Shah Shuja (in 1639), and this description in turn leads him into Roberts-like reflections on the ruin, despite his earlier intention to the contrary. Quickly, the poet calls himself back to the cold realities of the present:

These thoughts, like clouds, have gather'd o'er me—
Enough of them—a wreck's before me:
Three marble columns still are there,
That Desolation fail'd t'impair,

(141)

Finally the poet turns again, allowing himself to take this "wreck" as his theme, for "My native land" is that which Shah Shuja once commanded, and despite the fall of the Mughals, "she" will retain her spirit as long as rivers and mountains remain.

Finally, the "Ruins of Rajmahal" allows itself to become the proleptical citizen's celebration of nature as a guarantor of nation. The nation, or landscape, is feminized, and the poet becomes her male admirer. Such an effort, however, is not without its potential violence. The poet bids farewell to the ruin in a last stanza, perhaps alluding subtly to the fire that consumed the place in 1740, killing seventy-five women of Shah Shuja's harem. And he likens the ruin both to a "rose-bud" in the wilderness and finally, in her wrecked condition, to "a woman in her widowhood" (142).

Though Derozio does not detail the history of the stone palace at Rajmahal, one should note that Shah Shuja was the second son of Shāh Jāhan and Mumtaz and was appointed by his father as the ruler of Bengal and eventually of Orissa and Kuch Bihar. A man of great culture and learning, he contested with his brothers for power after the death of Shāh Jāhan and eventually fled to Arrakan, where he and all his family were, after some months, brutally murdered by the rulers. That the stone palace of Rajmahal stands a widowed wreck in Derozio's poem, then, is little wonder.

The metaphor of marital grief glances back at Shāh Jāhan and forward to Derozio's treatment of sati in the title poem of his next volume, *The Fakeer of Jungheera*. "The Ruins of Rajmahal" moralizes landscape in spite of itself and ultimately takes a political turn. For both Derozio and Roberts, the widow figures larger political questions. The proximate topical referent is sati, but the political horizon is considerably wider.

Sati: The Pyre as Political Plot

In writing about India, a burning widow is never only a burning widow. She necessarily entails an entire politics, including religious politics. Given that the controversy over sati (suttee) was always and from the beginning an international controversy, English language poems about sati are never only about India. In the 1820s, the sati controversy was a constant source of contention, letters to the editor, and literary labors, so it is not surprising that both Roberts and Derozio foregrounded the issue in putting together their collections of poetry.

Both of Derozio's volumes of verse began with the same pattern, an invocation followed by a poem celebrating a dying wife or widow. Derozio's *Poems* (1827) featured "The Harp of India," followed by "The Maniac Widow." In his second volume (1828), Derozio's long title poem, "The Fakeer of Jungheera," followed directly after his initial invocation of the bardic harp. "The Fakeer" begins with a sati and ends with a woman's death over the corpse of her lover. Similarly, Roberts began her *Oriental Scenes* with "A Scene in the Doab," a concatenation of the tropes of Hindu barbarism—child sacrifice and "the frantic shrieks of widowed brides" (1830, 3; 1832, 26). Moreover, the longest and most substantial poem in the first section of Roberts's volume, "The Rajah's Obsequies," provides a detailed depiction of sati that owes much more to Derozio's poem than to any actual event. "The Rajah's Obsequies" deliberately triangulates British, Indian, and Anglo-Indian political concerns. Derozio's "Fakeer" likewise responds in a complex way to political exigencies even as it is structurally and topically closely allied to the orientalist narrative poem.

In "The Fakeer of Jungheera," Derozio creates a long narrative poem with lyric interludes to tell a story of star-crossed lovers. Nuleeni, a Hindu girl, has been married off to a husband who subsequently dies. The poem begins as she is to commit sati on her husband's funeral pyre. This she is willing to do, but not out of pious love for her departed husband—rather, she is motivated by despair at never seeing again the lover whom she has lost. At the last moment, her lover, a Muslim robber-bridegroom, sends his men to the rescue, and she is plucked from the burning. Here Derozio echoes the multiple tales of rescue from the pyre—including the famous tale that Job Charnock, the founder of Calcutta, rescued his wife in a similar way. Nuleeni is whisked away to the rocks of Jungheera, where her beloved has masqueraded as a *fakeer* (fakir). The robber-bridegroom reveals himself and declares that he will worship Nuleeni instead of Allah. Despite their happiness, Nuleeni's father is granted his petition for vengeance by Shah Shuja, the builder of Rajmahal, who sends a troop of soldiers. In the ensuing battle, the robber-bridegroom dies upon the field of battle, and Nuleeni, sitting by his corpse, becomes one with him in death:

> The morning dawned—upon that sun-steeped plain
> What saw the peasant?—Steed and rider slain—
> But chief his eye was daunted by a form
> So bold, in life it might have ruled a storm—
> And fondly ivying round it were the arms
> Of a fair woman, whose all-powerful charms

Even death had failed to conquer. . .
. . . .
. . . . but they who thought
That life was tenanting her breast, and sought
Some answer from her heart to hush the doubt,
Found that its eloquence had all burned out.—

(*Derozio*, 227)

So Nuleeni, at first rescued from sati on the pyre of a husband whom she does not love, is in the end united in death with her Muslim lover. The poetic text conjures Nuleeni's death as the consequence of love:

Aye—break the chain of slumber from the mind
And watch the wreck that vision leaves behind—
Then mark the spirit in its solitude,
Its scorn, and torture, and despairing mood.

(227)

The poet delineates the daring rescue of Nuleeni, but she is saved only to perish—presumably of a broken heart—in the arms of her beloved, the satiation of romantic and fated love. Nuleeni's eloquence is "all burned out."

Derozio's footnotes tell a different but related tale, and they provide a commentary on Indian religious practices and social organization. But social commentary and romance are uneasy companions in "The Fakeer." While the poem creates a sensational story and displays the beauty of its heroine, the notes have quite a different tone. In the notes, Derozio provisionally defends sati, but on the ground that women in India are "wholly occupied in the drudgeries of domestic life, and in administering to the common comforts of their husbands with all the servility of hirelings. Such is their state in the miserable capacities of daughters and wives; but doubly degrading and tenfold more unhappy is their situation as widows" (230). In this long note, Derozio quotes an article in the *Indian Magazine,* and as Chaudhuri argues, while he is on the one hand "unabashedly against the misery of women, on the other he is firmly against banning the rite" (*Derozio,* 285). Derozio argues that under these circumstances, banning sati would be intolerant for, as Chaudhuri puts it, "reform should come from within . . . and education will achieve reform; what needs to be reformed above all is the deplorable condition of women in India" (286). In espousing this view, Derozio agreed at least in general principles with the two great reformers of nineteenth-century Bengal: his contemporary Rammohun Roy and, in the next generation, Ishwar Chandra Vidyasagar, who believed that the position of women in India needed serious improvement.

Not until his poem "On the Abolition of Suttee" was published in 1829, however, did Derozio take an unambiguous position—after the fact—on the actual ban against the practice of immolating widows. This ban, passed after decades of agitation by Roy and by evangelical Christians and their utilitarian allies, was made law under William Bentinck in 1829. The controversy and the ban caused a backlash among conservative Hindus, but the ban is celebrated by Derozio in a poem that feels more like an official occasional poem than like his early lyrics. While praising Bentinck, Derozio concludes "On the Abolition of Suttee" with a more general restatement of principles, a prophetic vision of "a rising spirit speaking peace to man" (*Derozio,* 288).

In contrast to his unambiguous praise of Bentinck in "On the Abolition of Suttee," Derozio's notes to "The Fakeer" are more nuanced. They present a detailed eyewitness account of a sati (interestingly, of a woman who was given every chance to change her mind and refused to do so) but also an acknowledgment that the poet has romanticized Nuleeni's sati: "I have taken license with the fact which thus assumes a romantic character" (*Derozio,* 232). In this romanticization, Nuleeni is the ivy to her lover's fallen oak. If her lover, then, becomes metonymically the country itself, he is also an outlaw (suggesting that the country under imperial sway is itself an outlaw, beyond law). Thus, the woman whose initial sati is deplored remains merely the ivy, the dependent of the state and not its prop.

In "The Fakeer," the gender and nationalist politics of the poetic text cannot be read coherently against the paratext. The assertion of Enlightenment principles of liberty, citizenship, and rights comes in Derozio's footnotes, where the practice of sati is described as a spectacle that must excite "in the spectator a melancholy reflection upon the tyranny of superstition and priest-craft" (*Derozio,* 229). But the romantic demise of the "ivying" woman and the outlaw oak about whom she twines suggests the gendered and national limits of the Enlightenment discourse of rights. The romance of fated love cannot fit neatly in its radical political frame. If Roberts's picturesque poems are torn canvases, unable to sustain pictorial illusion, so too, analogously, does Derozio's Oriental tale exceed its bounds, its narrative breaking the bounds of the political discourse that, paratextually, attempts to circumscribe it.

A similar awkwardness attends Roberts's poem "The Rajah's Obsequies." I would argue that this awkwardness had to be deliberate, for Roberts took the trope of sati from Derozio and borrowed liberally from his notes. Text and paratext—and the contradictions between them in Roberts's poem—owed a great deal to Derozio's practice. Roberts's notes to "The Rajah's Obsequies" echo Derozio's in several particulars. Derozio wished to debunk what he called the "mistaken opinion" that self-immolation was an "act of unparalleled magnanimity and devotion" (*Derozio,* 229). Most satis, he argued, made a reasoned judgment that immediate death was more to be wished than protracted suffering. Roberts makes a similar point, arguing that any woman sufficiently high-spirited would readily exchange a life of drudgery and penance for "the brief though keen pangs she must suffer in her passage to the grave" (*Oriental Scenes* [1832], 178). "The women of India," Roberts goes on to say, "will derive little benefit from the abolition of the rite, unless it be followed by the settlement of some specified portion of the property of the deceased upon his widow" (178). In the first edition of the poem, Roberts's footnotes are shorter but make more explicit her debt to Derozio: "Mr. Derozio, in his very beautiful and truly Oriental Poem, 'The Fakeer of Jungheera,' has taken advantage of the license to depart from the beaten track, universally allowed, and has placed a highly poetical and spirited effusion, relating to things of far diviner nature than the transmigrations of the soul into the bodies of animals, in the lips of his heroine. I have followed his example by varying the parting address of Mitala from that of her sister victim, but can make no pretensions to the eloquence and harmony of Mr. Derozio's verse" (1830, 257–58). With Derozio's poem for a precedent, then, Roberts too uses the "Oriental Poem" as a means of talking about liberty, tyranny, and priestcraft. But for Roberts, unlike Derozio, the political horizon is more European than Indian, and the contradictions within the poem and between the poem and paratext are correspondingly different.

Whereas Derozio's "Fakeer" becomes incoherent when political discourse in the paratext is contradicted by the romantic conventions of the "Oriental Poem," Roberts's poem founders on a different contradiction. In "The Rajah's Obsequies," Roberts's heroine predicts a succession of imperial conquests (culminating in the British conquest of India); the poem presents such conquests as history's revenge for the Hindu oppression of women. To read pure British imperial triumphalism into the poem's historiography is difficult, however, for Roberts's British audience would have understood the poem in the context of current debates over married women's property.

I have space here only briefly to summarize the complex history of the sati controversy and its relationship to British internal concerns. As Andrea Major has shown, in the metropolitan context "the increased British concern with the nature of Hindu women's inheritance as a cause of sati takes on added significance, reflecting as it does contemporary domestic tensions between widows' rights and concerns about the alienation of property. It is hardly surprising that sati should be increasingly represented as the ultimate solution to the problem of widows' property rights by a British society that was in the throes of renegotiating its own inheritance laws."[18] The first phase of this renegotiation culminated in the Dower Act of 1833, passed only months after the second and expanded edition of "The Rajah's Obsequies."

According to Susan Staves, the Dower Act of 1833, though apparently clarifying widows' rights to shares of real and personal property, actually had the effect of institutionalizing the already diminished value of married women's claims to jointure at the death of their husbands. As Henry Horwitz succinctly puts it in assessing Staves's research, by 1830 the value of dower

> had been steadily and gravely undercut by economic, social and legal changes including the increasing recourse to agreements for widow's "jointure" made between the families of the marrying couple. Hence, the legislation of 1833 constitutes but the final episode in a story whose overall theme is

> the persisting strength, despite otherwise major changes in material circumstances and in ideas and values, of "the deeper structures of male domination" (p. 35)—structures in which men (both fathers vis-à-vis their married daughters and husbands vis-à-vis their wives) are concerned that widows have enough to survive at a level appropriate to their social standing, but not sufficient to exercise the power that comes with a significant aggregation of property, a role to be confined to males. (237)

Following Major, Horwitz, and Staves, then, we can see Roberts's poem as engaging current political controversy both in the empire and in the metropole even as it furthers the conventions of the orientalist romance.

For Roberts—who took care of her widowed mother until the mother's death and who for reasons at least partly financial accompanied her married sister to India—the issues of widows' and daughters' inheritance was real and personal. Not surprisingly, Roberts's narrative poem concerning widows is just as "rent," that is, just as torn or bifurcated, as her lyrics of landscape.

Indeed, "The Rajah's Obsequies" begins with a landscape, but it turns out to be an illusory one. The poem commences with a vivid appreciation of the beauties of Benares and the kindness of the Brahmins toward all creatures. But the poem turns, next, on the irony that kindness to living things does not extend to widows: "In fierce and torturing pangs expires, / Untimely doomed, the shrinking bride." The division in the poem's narrative mirrors the double quality of the landscape, for the deceased rajah has two wives, one the very type of wifely devotion and the other "an offended goddess." Each wife speaks in turn. The younger wife (parenthetically said to be the better loved) is characterized as a bird, a spirit, a gentle divinity. She is eager for her fate, which will be the end of a short but happy life. She declares, "Yes, to my thrice blessed hands 'tis given / To ope the saffron gates of heaven" (*Oriental Scenes* [1832], 55). She will then become a "Peri bird," a sparkling fish, a star, and finally a heavenly being. "Saint-like" she gives herself to the flames.

Not so the elder bride, Mitala. She, rather, revolts "at the sacrifice," declaring,

> Think not, accursed priests, that I will lend
> My sanction to these most unholy rites;
> And though yon funeral pile I may ascend,
> It is not that your stern command affrights
> My lofty soul—it is because these hands
> Are all too weak to break my sex's bands.
>
> I, from my earliest infancy, have bowed
> A helpless slave to lordly man's control,
> No hope of liberty, no choice allowed,

Unheeded all the struggles of my soul;
Compelled by brutal force to link my fate
With one who best deserved my scorn and hate.

(58)

Mitala has no pity for the rajah. She says over his corpse, "The tyrant sleeps death's last and endless sleep" (59). She refuses to become a beggar, "despised, and desolate," but could she fight she would withstand the cruel custom of sati and "uphold the right / Of woman to share of gold and gems, / Sceptres and sway, and regal diadems" (59). Thus Mitala forwards the discourse of liberty, in the same terms as in Derozio's notes to "The Fakeer." Slavery, tyranny, and priestcraft all stand against Mitala's vision of liberty. The ivying woman of "The Fakeer" also returns but here is consigned to death by burning. The reader is left to reconcile the two.

A still more disturbing turn comes with Mitala's prophecy. In the tradition of the last prophetic words of the sati, the younger bride has predicted her husband's ascent to heaven and her own less direct but still happy ascent. Mitala, in contrast, historicizes her vision. She predicts nothing for herself, but in the vein of Roberts's stanzas on the Rajmahal, she foresees the conquest of India:

Oh craven race
Not long shall this fair land endure your sway;
Shame and defeat, and capture and disgrace
Await the closing of a blood-stained day;
I see, I see the thickly gathering bands
Crowding in conquering ranks from distant lands!

The Persian Satrap and the Tartar Khan
The temples of your gods shall overthrow,
And all the hundred thrones of Hindoostan
Before the west's pale warrior shall bow,
Crouching where'er the banners of the brave,
The silver crescent, and the red cross, wave!

(60)

Neatly avoiding the "red cross" of this last line, Roberts explains the stanza in a note: "This prediction relates to the outrages perpetrated by Aurungzebe, mentioned in a foregoing note" (178). Thus Mitala predicts vengeance, and the poet leaves us to read both the Mughal empire and the East India Company's conquests in India as a recompense for female suffering. The Enlightenment discourse of religious, civil, or personal liberties finds its realization where? It hovers uncertainly in Roberts's historicization; it hovers uncertainly in her notes; and it hovers, at least as weakly as the younger wife's flight, somewhere between the protofeminist discourses of the early nineteenth century and the imperialist claims of the metropole.

If Roberts can claim to be a sybil through the prophecies of the sati, she never makes such claims in her own person. Perhaps the fate of the British Empire lies beyond her ken. Certainly it lay beyond the dominant taste of the market. Derozio's claims to bardic nationalism were only slightly less vexed than Roberts's prophetic widows, though the politics that underlay his bardic claims were more coherent than Roberts's. For both poets, establishing a position from which to speak—establishing an identity for the lyric speaker, for the narrator of romance, or for the painter of poetic landscape—was a shifting and difficult matter of identification and disidentification. In 1830, a British woman was not a citizen; an East Indian was neither Portuguese nor Hindu, neither Muslim nor British. The British—English, Scottish, Irish, Welsh—poetic tradition was necessarily stretched, or "strained," to accommodate their songs.

PART TWO

The Institutions of Colonial Mimesis, 1830–57

David Lester Richardson. By Colesworthy Grant, from *Lithographic Sketches of the Public Characters of Calcutta, 1838–1850* (Calcutta: W. Thacker and Co., St. Andrew's Library, n.d.)

THREE

Books, Reading, and the Profession of Letters

David Lester Richardson and the Construction of a British Canon in India

In 1824 an unknown poet, signing himself D.L.R., published a most unoriental effusion in a new London newspaper, the *Oriental Herald.* Evidently the editor needed to fill an empty half page, for the poet had much ambition and little to say. For no appreciable reason—other than the general popularity of the bardic trope in the wake of Tom Moore and Walter Scott—D.L.R. produced "The Warrior's Farewell to the Family Bard." His third, and concluding, stanza sounded a patriotic note:

Then oh! subdue those notes of pain,—
Strike the inspiring string again;
For strains of woe, like maiden's sigh,
Or magic of her tearful eye,
Too oft the secret spell impart
That melts the sternest warrior's heart.
Then hush, oh! hush those notes of pain,
Wake the stirring song again!
Wilder let the wild lay flow,
Kindling with the kindling glow,—
Raise the British battle-cry
"Freedom,—Death,—or Victory!"[1]

The location of D.L.R.'s family "hall" is mercifully unspecified, as is any possible historic occasion that might have provoked such martial sentiments. But we *can* specify who the poet was, the details of his career, and the reasons he might have written this poem. His story touches a generation of poets writing in English in India, for D.L.R. became a fixture of English language literary publishing and education in mid-nineteenth-century India.

D.L.R. was David Lester Richardson (1801–1865), who was born in London and lived most of his adult life in India. Richardson published several volumes of verse and a treatise on gardening but was more important as an editor of newspapers, literary annuals, and a famous school anthology of British poetry. His career exemplifies the historical developments in commerce, books, and reading that enabled an English language literary tradition to take such firm root in India. He became an impresario of letters in nineteenth-century India and, by extension, an important arbiter of the English language poetic canon.

In the first half of the nineteenth century, readers experienced a print explosion on the subcontinent, which was paralleled and augmented by the growth of institutions that shaped reading and reading habits. Libraries and English-medium schools, clubs, and voluntary associations formed both social and institutional connections in the world of belles lettres. From small groups of readers and writers, supported—if at all—by patronage, from a group who initially read and wrote within the conventions of orientalist poetics or metropolitan publishing, the English language literary scene broadened and also commodified. Though literary verse in English—in contrast to vernacular oral poetry—remained very much a minority affair, the participants in the literary scene and their productions become much more varied than in the late eighteenth century.

By 1840, the participants in Indian English language belles lettres found themselves in a new world of print where vernacular Indian languages, classical European languages, and modern European languages competed with orientalist learning. The government had shifted from a policy of classical education in Persian and Sanskrit to a policy of English-medium and vernacular education, as infamously encapsulated in Thomas Babington Macaulay's minute on Indian education (1835). In this shift, official policy was catching up with actual practice, the importance on the ground of private or religious vernacular and English-medium schools. Moreover, the purpose, style, audience, success, and meanings of poetry were up for grabs in India, as in Britain. What was the purpose of poetry? Who would read it? What would be the next big thing after the deaths of Byron, Keats, Shelley, Hemans, Scott, Coleridge, and Landon, the poets who formed the pantheon of English-speaking India in the early decades of the nineteenth century? The trope of the bard, the Oriental tale, the hudibrastic satire, and the traveler's encounter with a ruin: each of these poetic forms, popular between 1780 and 1830, threatened to devolve into bathos or cliché. Poets from different social locations had widely different understandings of the British role in India. Forming a canon of English language verse was, consequently, a contested and complex endeavor.

To see how an English language poetic canon was formed in India, the way it was differentially shared by poets from various social, ethnic, religious, and political locations, one must first understand exactly what constituted the institutions and practices of literary culture in this period. Developments in these arenas—periodicals, bookselling, libraries, book consumption, and education—are necessarily treated succinctly here, but they are crucial to our understanding of what exactly provided the literary and material contexts for working poets. In India as in Britain, participation in the world of belles lettres was shaped by class, gender, and education, but with the added issues of place of birth and childhood and of ethnic/religious/racial identity. Differential access to print, for readers and for poets, was a matter of crucial import, both materially and ideologically.

Anxious about homegrown English verse, conservative commentators deplored the role of English language poetry (and some of its nonelite practitioners), though other critics viewed English language literary culture more optimistically. Whatever the anxieties of those in charge of—or commenting on—schooling, both formal and informal curricula shaped English language verse in India. The poems of Richardson and his friend Henry Meredith Parker reflect and even satirize the very world of print they helped to create. The process of seeking new opportunities to get into print for himself and others is evident in Richardson's checkered career and in the contrasting example of his friend Parker, who rose in the civil service to a place on the Board of Customs, Salt, and Opium. Parker and Richardson by turns helped others to bridge differences of race or education to publish poetry, though in the end they policed these boundaries. Richardson, more than any other poet I have discussed thus far—with the possible exception of Anna Maria—was also painfully conscious of his role, or lack of it, in the metropolitan world of British letters. His career reveals the challenges of becoming "a man of letters" in nineteenth-century Calcutta.

The Expanding World of Letters

In his history of the Bengali book in this period, Mofakhkhar Hussain Khan begins by paraphrasing the Sanskrit sloka that Nathaniel Brassey Halhed had chosen to preface the first printed grammar of the Bangla language: "When it is beyond the power of Indra to keep track of the fathomless ocean of words, how is it possible for a human being?"[2] The task of telling the story of print culture in nineteenth-century India is easier than Indra's but daunting enough for human beings. I take on only one part of this task here, limiting myself to English language literary culture. Whereas Khan's invaluable work details the history of Bangla printing and bookmaking, I concentrate here on English language printing, publishing, and circulation of texts.

But it is important to remember that the Indian ecumene in the nineteenth century, as Khan and C. A. Bayly have shown in detail, involved an immensely lively and vibrant literary culture, much of it not confined to print but circulated in manuscripts, letters, and placards, as well as oral forms. Moreover, the work of Khan, Bayly, and others should stand as a reminder that English language print formed only a subset of Indian print cultures in the first half of the nineteenth century and that this period also saw the rapid increase of Bangla print materials and a significant increase in printed materials in Hindu and Urdu and eventually in Tamil and other South Indian languages.[3] Nonetheless, between the time Sir William Jones edited the *Asiatic Researches* (beginning in 1784) and the mid-nineteenth century, readers in India experienced a print and reading explosion in English as well as in Indian languages. This explosion was made possible by increased English language literacy and by technological and educational changes. Although the number of speakers and readers of English remained small as a subset of the larger population (as it still does), the print explosion for fully literate people was certainly analogous in its rapidity and significance to the rise of the Internet in the late twentieth century.[4]

While in the broadest terms my generalizations about English language publishing apply to all three presidencies—Calcutta, Madras, and Bombay—I focus here, for the most part, on Calcutta and Bengal. As the capital of British India as well as a presidency capital, Calcutta and its environs supported more presses and periodicals in English than any other city in the subcontinent; hence the data for Calcutta is fuller than for other cities. Clearly, Calcutta took the lead in shaping English language literary culture in this period, but its residents often defined their own cultures against metropolitan success, whether the metropole was London or Edinburgh—or, later, Paris. As I argue in the next chapter, the metropolitan/colonial axis usually (but not always) mattered less to poets who were born and lived in India than it did to expatriate poets. At the same time, the world of letters, defined from a Calcutta center, also continued to engage the transperipheral dynamics of bardic nationalism.

In Calcutta, where publishing of all kinds proceeded apace, a "Calcutta School" of English verse could be parodied by 1822. This amusing take on Anglo-Indian poetics highlights not only the coherence of the English language literary scene but also the possibility that something new might be required. Many newspapers at this period had a poet's corner (or page) that published occasional verse, acrostics, translations, and serious original poems. The *India Gazette* gave poets and belletristic writers not a corner but a swath of the front page. Anonymous satirists took full advantage.

One such writer had no trouble identifying Calcutta verse. On August 5, 1822, we find the twenty-ninth column written by a satirist calling himself "The Proser." The Proser, or "M.," provides a sketch of his friend, one Rory Bombshell—an artillery officer—who is seized by the muse when his gardener's mule eats his prize thistle. Rory tells his friend M. that his attempt to grow a huge thistle has indeed given "birth to reflections, the nature of which, as a Scotchman and a man earning his bread by the sweat of his brow, must be immediately apprehended by you." Alert to both the popular poems of Scottish patriotism and the numerous imitations and translations of Hāfiz, Rory opines that no Persian gardener could be more enraged at finding his rosebeds plundered than he has been, for "what are all the roses of Damascus compared to my Thistle?" And he goes on, with provoking modesty, to declare,

> My effusion will not, I am assured, bear a comparison with even the ordinary productions of the Calcutta School, and both in point of elegance, of diction, harmony of numbers, or the happy introduction of pathetic

interjections, must be considered by all Savants to be immeasurably deficient and inferior to the common run of fugitive pieces inserted in our Indian prints. Indeed, having a desire to write only what I understand, and understand always what I write, I have not, since my emancipation from school, been in the habit of making verses, either sense or nonsense.

After a bit more in this vein, the poem appears under the title "Stanzas by Rory Bombshell, Esq., Fireworker."

Two stanzas from the midst of this verse satire give its flavor—and betray the satirist's conviction that his audience will recognize a well-worn conceit when they see one. Rory Bombshell addresses the lost thistle thus:

How oft, oh how oft, while thy stern crest surveying
    As it martially waved the sun flowers among,
Has my heart still its fond strong attachment betraying
    For my dear native Scotland sighed sorely and long.

How oft, too, when sunk in poetical dreamings
    My reason was wont her frail seat to desert,
Have thy apropos prickles recalled me from seemings
    To parade, post the guards, or put on a clean shirt.[5]

Here Roby Bombshell could be called, if not the Byron, then at least the Thomas Hood of Calcutta, his satire made possible by ubiquitous tropes he knows his audience will find familiar. The exile's thistle, the Persian ghazal, the Byronic satire, the "pathetic interjection," all are exploded. Yet the parody also serves to demonstrate the longevity and cultural salience of things parodied.

The Calcutta school was of course shifting even as it was parodied or even because it could be so easily parodied. What kind of poetic canon, what tropes and genres might have cultural power? These were continuing questions, answered in the next three decades in newspapers, annuals, books, and school curricula.

Poetry in the Periodical Press: Newspapers and Annuals

From the beginning of the English language press, English language newspapers published poetry, reviews of poetry, and poetic controversy. When they developed in India in the 1830s, literary annuals were intertwined with the newspapers, reprinting poems from them, advertising in them, and competing with British and American annuals that were also extensively advertised and reviewed.

According to Mohit Moitra, in 1830 there were sixteen Bangla newspapers and periodicals; nineteen more were started between 1831 and 1833. There were, in addition, thirty-three English language dailies and periodicals in Bengal alone.[6] From the beginning, English language newspapers frequently printed poetry, both poems "borrowed" from British publications and original verse composed in India. In India as in America, no copyright law discouraged wholesale appropriation.[7] As we saw in the cases of Anna Maria, Sir William Jones, and John Horsford in chapter 1 and Henry Derozio and Emma Roberts in chapter 2, newspapers provided not only access to British verse but also an important means for poets in India to publish their own work.

In addition, newspapers encouraged literary controversy. In the 1810s, for example, the *Calcutta Journal* printed numerous poems and tried to provoke literary dispute. It printed a lengthy exchange on Byron's *Childe Harold,* it discussed the contributions of the British in India to the Burns memorial in Edinburgh (1818, 777), and it celebrated Indian fundraising to support blind Irish musicians and the "revival of our national instrument, the Harp" (March, 18, 1832, 143).[8] The editors noted with pleasure the accomplishments of the literary societies of Madras and Bombay and lamented that Calcutta boasted only the Asiatic Society, whose proceedings were too abstruse to interest a broad public. Moreover, the *Calcutta Journal,* which called itself a "Political, Commercial, and Literary Gazette," published numerous poems and reviews. The *India Gazette,* likewise, had its poet's corner. A later incarnation of this paper was David Lester Richardson's *Calcutta Literary Gazette,* a weekly he began editing in 1833 as a literary supplement.

Richardson's *Calcutta Literary Gazette,* like the *Calcutta Journal* and many other newspapers, included poems, reviews, and excerpts from the British press, along with original articles written in India. Numerous of these poems were then reprinted by Richardson in *The Bengal Annual* and *The Orient Pearl.* These Calcutta annuals were a further development from Richardson's newspaper publication, and they imitated and competed with literary annuals published in London and the United States.

The advent of the London annuals on Indian shores was an occasion for significant advertising in the *Calcutta Gazette* and other newspapers. The British and American annuals were typically published in November (dated for the next year) to catch the Christmas book trade; they were advertised some weeks later upon arrival in Calcutta.[9] For example, the booksellers at the St. Andrew's Library offered on February 15, 1834, a long list of annuals "for 1834 and preceding years." Among them were *Ackermann's Forget-Me-Not,* the *Juvenile Forget-Me-Not,* the homegrown *Bengal Annual, The Amulet, The Bijou, The Botanic Annual, Biblical Annual, The Christmas Box,* and *Comic Offering,* just to cite the beginning of their long alphabetical list.[10] The merchants listed in detail the plates to be included in the Daniells' *Oriental Annual* for 1834 and in *Ackermann's Forget-Me-Not,* which included a number of Scottish subjects. The preceding week, the St. Andrew's Library had listed the plates appearing in the Daniells' *Annual, Ackermann's, Friendship's Offering,* and the *Landscape Annual.* Obviously Derozio and Emma Roberts were not the only residents of north India intent on pursuing the engravings available in these publications. To judge by the St. Andrew's Library's estimation of the market, readers in

India clamored for annuals on account of their engravings, their literary contents, and their status as a commodity—a lovely thing to repose upon the drawing room table.

In this climate, Richardson ventured his own two annuals: *The Bengal Annual* (begun in 1830) and *The Orient Pearl* (begun in 1834). The prefaces to these productions indicate Richardson's hopes that his collections of poems, essays, and fiction might find readers both in India and in Britain. He promoted his annuals in his *Literary Gazette* and in other newspapers. For example, to evade shameless self-promotion yet take advantage of the new year's trade, Richardson reprinted in his *Gazette* a review of *The Bengal Annual* that had originally seen print in the *Government Gazette*. This review itself allows us to understand the constraints on Indian publishing in English at this point and also to see how even British-born poets thought themselves at a disadvantage vis-à-vis the metropole. It points as well to the book as commodity and cultural marker. The reviewer in the *Government Gazette* notes with sorrow that Richardson's productions took various sizes in different years: "[T]hey all differ in their proportions. This, we think, is a pity—since, on a library shelf, instead of agreeing in form—they appear, like the three degrees of comparison, large, less, least." Nor, the reviewer noted, was there an agreeable flyleaf for inscription. In these complaints we see the reviewer's understanding of the annuals' place in the market—as gift books understood to become part of a permanent library.[11] The reviewer goes on to praise the literary productions in the volume, particularly those of Horace Hayman Wilson, Henry Meredith Parker, and Emma Roberts.

Indeed, the reviewer expresses a happy surprise that Richardson found to hand more than enough talent and good will for his annual: "[I]nstead of being pinched as to his means of eking out a volume, [he] has absolutely been rather perplexed by the abundance of materials pouring in upon him. In a word, the vein has been merely opened, and the volumes that have appeared, are only, it strikes us, specimens of inexhaustible literary ore, that lies in the Indian mine." The reviewer can only hope that as gifts to friends or family in Britain the annual can create an interest in all things Indian, an interest the reviewer finds sadly lacking, for the English public "do view India with a cold askance and step-mother-like regard" (*Literary Gazette*, January 1, 1833, 11). Though he does not expect to return "home," the reviewer nonetheless longs for recognition from the "step-mother" country.

However they were received in the "step-mother" country, the Calcutta annuals were widely distributed in India, and the productions of the press from the three presidencies—Calcutta, Bombay, and Madras—were exchanged on a regular basis. Newspapers blithely reprinted stories from other papers and reviewed each other's productions as well as locally published volumes. These exchanges were clearly aimed at boosting sales and distribution through the creation of a common English language literary culture. Like Richardson's *Gazette*, other newspapers in the presidencies regularly took note of each other and of the latest news from the London and Edinburgh and, to a lesser extent, Irish and American press. Newspapers and literary annuals were, then, intertwined in readership, advertising, and reviewing. Richardson was quick to reprint favorable notices from the Calcutta, the Indian, and the foreign press. *The Bengal Annual* for 1835, for example, contained favorable notices of Richardson's *Literary Gazette* from the London *Court Journal,* the *Delhi Gazette,* and the Madras *Literary Gazette.* All the poets I discuss in the first two sections of this book—Jones, Horsford, Anna Maria, Roberts, Derozio, Parker, Richardson, Kasiprasad Ghosh, Mary Carshore, and Madhusudan Dutt—published first in newspapers. All of those poets active in the 1830s—Roberts, Derozio, Parker, Richardson, and Ghosh—were also represented in *The Bengal Annual* and *The Orient Pearl.* And Roberts, Ghosh, Derozio, and Richardson all were additionally published in London annuals, which were then sold in India.

Literary annuals in India, then, were crucial outlets in the 1830s for English language poetry. In Britain, the proliferation of annuals did not contribute markedly to the lasting contours of a poetic canon—there were too many, with too many poets, and their verse became associated with feminine sentimentalism and was eventually marginalized by the literary establishment.[12] In India, though, the apparatus of canon formation was far less powerful; the number of poets publishing in English, considerably smaller; and the lasting impact of the annuals in the formation of a poetic canon, proportionately larger. Although all the important British annuals were marketed to India, Indian production, as far as I can deduce, was limited initially to the two annuals edited by Richardson. Interestingly, however, the general impact of the annuals is attested in Indian English language publishing even now. As late as 1885, Rudyard Kipling and his family published *Quartette* as the Christmas annual of Lahore's *Civil and Military Gazette.* Even in the twenty-first century, the English language newspapers of Calcutta, the *Telegraph* and the *Statesman,* still produce literary annuals to coincide, not with Christmas, but with the October Durga puja, the city's most important festival. Poetry has now given place to fiction and the essay, but the tradition of an annual literary compendium—of English language writing—continues.

Poetry for Purchase: Booksellers, Auctions, and the Canon of Probate

The publication of newspaper poetry and the advertising and content of literary annuals are not the only sources that allow us to understand the development of an English language poetic canon in nineteenth-century India. Booksellers' advertisements and catalogues and auction advertisements demonstrate that a wide variety of poetry, both homegrown and imported, was readily available for purchase or on loan to those with appropriate literacy and cash. And probated wills give us a useful cross-section of books actually bought and retained, at least by those British residents who died in India and were possessed of considerable resources.[13]

As in Britain, so in India by 1820 locally printed books were often published with advertisements for and even catalogs listing the publisher's other titles. While many of these catalogs were excised in binding, some do remain. Such catalogues reveal what titles publishers and booksellers commonly stocked. A particularly striking midcentury example is the 1848 catalogue of new books available from the publisher and bookseller P. S. D'Rozario. The catalogue appeared bound at the back of Richardson's *Literary Chit-Chat, with Miscellaneous Poems and an Appendix of Prose Papers*, published in the same year by D'Rozario. That D'Rozario took on the publication of Richardson's book is not surprising, for as a school principal the poet no doubt was responsible for his students' and colleagues' purchases of books and art materials from D'Rozario. The D'Rozario catalog seems aimed directly at middle-class British readers, at teachers and parents of young children and students, and at Indian readers and libraries seeking comprehensive and useful works at reasonable prices.[14] Here I think we see a marked expansion of the audience for English language works; as books became less expensive and as India recovered from the collapse of commerce in the 1830s, English language readers could afford more works of reference and instruction, and more belletristic texts as well. The D'Rozario catalog indicates the growing importance of English language education. It is by now also a truism that British women began to come to India in greater numbers after about 1820 and that this transformed the old acceptance of long-term sexual and domestic liaisons between British men and Indian women. But a little noticed effect of this shift was an increase in the number of English speaking children who stayed in India at least through the early stages of their education, an education supervised by parents or governesses or schoolteachers. If we add this group to the increase in private and government-sponsored English-medium education for nonnative speakers, the increase in mission schools, and a growing if proportionately small population literate in English, it is no wonder that D'Rozario found a profitable market niche in improving English books. Along with practical instruction, D'Rozario also evidently sold a great deal of poetry at midcentury.

The D'Rozario catalog for 1848 lists twenty-three pages of new books, the greater portion "offered for sale at and below the London publishing prices." The flavor is caught by the beginning (and most expensive) offering, the seventh edition of the *Encyclopedia Britannica*, and by the last, Whittock's *London New Juvenile Drawing Book.* In between are numerous informational titles, from Chambers's various encyclopedias to Mangnall's questions, alongside many other reference works. Poetry figures more importantly than fiction, especially through the anthology or collection of gems, recitation pieces, and other forms of multiauthor publishing. Complete sets or collections of Burns, Cowper, Dryden, Gay, Goldsmith, Milton, Moore, Ossian, Pope, Scott, and Sigourney are accompanied by Johnson's *Lives of the Poets* and, more surprisingly, Schlegel's course of *Lectures on Dramatic Art and Literature.* This list is clearly aimed at the "improving" books market, whether for self-improvement or for use in schools. The list also reflects the large number of Scottish readers and the literary conservatism of school curricula.

A different sort of evidence about books available for purchase is provided by newspaper advertisement, including both booksellers' advertisements and auction advertisements. In the 1830s, the *Calcutta Literary Gazette* published regular advertisements for the British Library (which both loaned and sold books) and for St. Andrew's Library, a similar establishment. The British Library, for example, advertised in 1834 a full column length of books, including Lyell's *Principles of Geology* (1830), various literary annuals, and such titles as *Men and Manners in America* (1833). Anchoring their advertisement was a double bill for Byron's works in "Murray's new and beautiful edition, just completed in 17 volumes" and *The Byron Gallery,* which included no fewer than thirty plates to "add fresh charms to Byron's deathless verse" (January 4, 1834, 15). The latter two items were far more expensive than the literary annuals, priced at 68 rupees for Byron's works and 24 for the *Gallery.* A schoolbook, Lennie's *Principles of English Grammar,* advertised in the next number was, by contrast, priced at 1 rupee, 4 annas, with a discount by the dozen. The British Library advertised books for loan as well as for sale, and the differences in the two lists reflects what Mr. Mudie also discovered, the rereading principle. Customers of the British Library clearly borrowed novels and bought reference books, annuals, books of prints, and editions of poetry. But if one could, in flush times, lay out a small fortune for seventeen volumes of Byron, could one hang onto them?

If one bought books, especially during the 1810s and 1820s when they were quite expensive, there was no guarantee one could keep them. In colonial India, as now, both bankruptcies and the need to pay creditors occasioned auctions. So did British residents' departure from India. A man might collect books, but reversals of fortune dispersed them, and no doubt at a loss. What happened, I wonder, to George Addison's books, carefully hoarded in Murshidabad, when his indigo plantation failed? Very few volumes would have fit in his trunk as he embarked for Java. And of the books left behind, even those stored in the metal boxes recommended for the purpose, how many fell prey to damp and bookworm? If the condition of books still preserved in the National Library in Calcutta from the period is any measure, his precious books would like as not quickly have become waste paper, unless, of course, they found another home, either by auction or by inheritance after his death.

In fact, we do have some records of auctions and bequests of books from the first half of the century. In the 1820s and 1830s, Messrs. Tulloh and Co. advertised extensively in the *Calcutta Gazette* and sold at auction everything from indigo factories to warm clothes to ale. Goods at auction also included new and used books. Tulloh advertised whole libraries, and on occasion the titles were listed. These lists, naturally, are fairly miscellaneous and cannot be taken wholly to represent even collections at auction, but poetry figures in about the same proportion in these advertisements as it does in wills. In the *Calcutta Gazette* in the late 1820s, we see a series of libraries sold at auction, owing no doubt in part to the wave of bankruptcies that followed on the Anglo-Burmese War (1824–26) and to the collapse of the indigo trade (Webster). Tulloh, for example, advertised on October 28, 1828, the sale at auction of a shipment of new books, including various of Walter Scott's works, Moore's *Melodies,* Mrs.

Hemans's *Poems,* Leigh Hunt's biography of Byron, and novels including *The Prairie, Red Wood,* and *Hope Leslie.* An auction two weeks later brought various collections of books "for peremptory sale"—the first selection was from the "valuable library belong to Doyl Chund Dhur" and another came from an unnamed owner of a "small collection of scarce and valuable books," which included C. F. Volney's *View of the United States,* Joanna Baillie's *Metrical Legends,* and books on Shakespeare (*Calcutta Gazette,* October 28 and November 4, 1828).

Often, libraries were advertised under a general description; by contrast, probated wills often provide information that is more detailed. We can now understand with reasonable exactitude at least one subset of the purchase or possession of English language books in the nineteenth century; Matthew Adams has done an extraordinary statistical analysis of book ownership in British India between 1780 and 1850, as established by probated wills. This analysis, as he points out, is limited to book ownership by Europeans, and it necessarily underestimates such ownership, for many books were not listed singly or perhaps at all. Moreover, not all wills of Europeans who died in India—Emma Roberts's, for example—were probated in India. Nonetheless, enough data is available from more than a thousand probate inventories to provide an important snapshot of the books thought important over the period. The variety of authors tallied by Adams makes clear the varied views of the books' possessors: Adam Smith, William Robertson, Edward Gibbon, Edmund Burke appear on the list, but so too do Thomas Paine, William Godwin, Mary Wollstonecraft, C. F. Volney, Richard Carlile, Robert Owen, and William Cobbett. Not surprisingly, dictionaries and Bibles were thought appropriate books to purchase, keep, and bequeath, though the works of Pope outnumber the Bible in wills probated from 1780 through 1782.

Adams has done a frequency study of the most popular titles. Only in the eighteenth century do novels figure among the top twenty most frequently occurring titles in probated wills (the two novels are Sterne's *Tristram Shandy* and *Sentimental Journey*). Voltaire, Montesquieu, Chesterfield, Hume, and Swift, along with Shakespeare and Milton, also figure in the top twenty lists in the eighteenth century, indicating the importance of an Enlightenment canon. Twenty years later, in 1802–4, Sir William Jones's *Works* and Thompson's *Seasons,* along with the *Spectator,* take an important role. The major change in the top twenty list for 1824–26 is the ascendancy of Walter Scott, whose works accompany those of Shakespeare, Pope, Sir William Jones, and Byron. This pattern persists in 1846–48, when Scott's *Works,* Byron's *Works* and *Don Juan,* Pope's *Works,* Virgil's works, and Burns's round out the additions. Notably, in the 1846–48 probated wills, the Enlightenment canon has been replaced, or at least surpassed in numbers owned, by English poetry, by Virgil, and by Paley's works. Adams argues that the data effectively counters contemporary profiles of readership by Emma Roberts and others that "underline the disproportionate significance on the subcontinent of works 'of a light and desultory description.'" It may also be true that patrons borrowed and shared novels but bought and retained collections of poetry.

Adams also documents the shift in the range of languages found in the samples and in the range of dictionaries over time. Between 1780 and 1820, he argues, "the reading profile was to become richer, more linguistically complex, as Latin, Hindustani, and to a lesser extent Greek rose in popularity to challenge . . . Persian . . . while minor European and Indian languages also began to make some headway." This expansion reflects the expansion of print, Adams argues, as well as the "perceived need for an increased supply of dictionaries in a diverse range of languages." Thus, it is not the Anglicist/Orientalist debate—famously encapsulated in Macaulay's minute on Indian education—that shaped European reading habits but rather an increased emphasis on Indian vernaculars and on classical and modern European languages in the context of an "expanding language community."

What we see in Adams's statistics, then, is a profile, however partial, of the libraries of men who were likely either to set or to implement educational policy in India. Their taste likewise affected the choices of libraries and, to a lesser extent, of booksellers. No wonder, then, that in the first half of the nineteenth century, poetry rather than fiction was the dominant belletristic genre when English language writers of whatever cultural background sought literary fame. The canon of probate, as I call it, was especially important for those whom Rosinka Chaudhuri has described as the "gentlemen poets" of India, those Indians (and I would add "East Indians") who sought upward mobility through education.

Borrowed Poems: Lending Libraries

Those who aspired to achievement, if not fame, as poets writing in English included, of course, British men and women of both the upper and middle classes, "East Indian" men, and relatively well-to-do Indian men. For all these groups, libraries also provided important access to books. This period saw the rapid growth of libraries serving all these groups, sometimes at once and sometimes separately. By 1850 there were lending libraries for fee, more or less scholarly libraries, and public libraries in the presidencies and even in the countryside, in addition to school libraries.

Following on Priya Joshi's outstanding work on fiction in Indian libraries after 1850, I have surveyed the role of poetry in the first half of the century in as many libraries as I could. Not all records are complete, of course, and, as Joshi has persuasively argued, the presence of books in a library is no guarantee that the books were read or read often. Notwithstanding these difficulties, I find that poetry clearly bulked large as a source of reading in the first half of the century and was gradually eclipsed by fiction in the second half.

Although the majority of Indian libraries (not counting private libraries owned by members of the elite) were established after 1857, a number, including both public and subscription libraries, were established earlier. Booksellers in Calcutta, including Thacker, Spink and Co., and the British Library, also loaned books by subscription.

Private clubs created libraries of their own (these include the Bengal Club, established in 1827, for British patrons only; the Calcutta Lyceum in the 1830s; the Mechanics Institute, established in 1839; and the Dalhousie Institute, established in 1859 for Indian men).[15] The most important library in Calcutta was no doubt the Calcutta Public Library, established in 1836 in the wake of the Metcalfe Press Law. Joshi describes this library as having been "insistent on the liberality of its provisions, as well as being expressly set up with the fiscal, political, and ideological collaboration between Indians and the British" (53). Joshi goes on to point out that the Bombay General Library (almost exclusively for Indian users) and the Madras Literary Society (almost exclusively for British users) had preceded it at the beginning of the decade (54). The success of the Calcutta Public Library led to substantial public libraries for Indian users in the next two decades, including ones at Midnapore, Jessore, Rangpur, Bogra, Barishal, Houghly, Krishnanagar, Konnagar, and Uttapara (Joshi, 54). We have full catalogues available for the Calcutta Public Library from 1855 and the Uttapara Library (founded in 1859) from 1902. The former is, of course, by far the better source for understanding the role of poetry in English at midcentury and before, but the Uttapara Catalogue is also of interest, as we can at least extrapolate from dates of publication what a poetic canon might have looked like in the early years of the library.

To start with the most complex data, the Uttapara Catalogue lists twenty-six pages of novels and tales as opposed to eight pages of poetry and drama. Printed Persian and Latin books are given four pages and magazines and periodicals three pages (but of course many more volumes); in separate but overlapping categories, the catalog lists two pages of gazettes and newspapers and five of "reviews and other periodicals." Clearly, periodicals and literary texts constituted a significant part of the holdings (the catalog of books other than Sanskrit and Bengali books runs to 192 pages; Sanskrit and Bengali books amount to 76 pages). Roughly speaking, at Uttapara, English books outnumbered Sanskrit and Bengali books two to one, and English language fiction outnumbered poetry three to one (though not necessarily in total number of volumes, as many entries for poetry included multivolume collected works). Many of the Sanskrit and Bengali texts, however, were poetic texts, and this means that a simple census of English titles substantially underestimates the overall presence of poetry in the collection.

On the whole, the catalog supports Joshi's contention that Indian readers of English were particularly interested in popular fiction, including—from the first half of the century at Uttapara—Marie Corelli, Dumas, Edgeworth, Scott, and Marryat. But it suggests that poetry was also important, and in a range of languages. What is striking about the selection of poetry in the Uttapara library is its relative comprehensiveness. The number of early or first editions of British poets, moreover, is astonishing and indicates either substantial bequests or library supervisors who were keenly attuned to the newest and most interesting British poetry, or both. The library purchased or was given numerous early nineteenth-century and first editions of

Keats, Shelley, Wordsworth, Coleridge, Landon, Wordsworth, Scott, and Joanna Baillie. Byron figured largely, not surprisingly. But Crabbe, Reginald Heber, Bowles, and Butler also figure, along with the earlier canonical poets. Although we cannot tell when these books were purchased or donated or how often they were read, nonetheless, we can conjecture that these editions were probably on the library's shelves shortly after its founding.

In short, at Uttapara, readers who were interested in poetry could find the entirety of the British romantic canon at their fingertips, along with numerous volumes of poetry in translation ranging from James Atkinson's translation of Firdausī's *Sháh Námeh* (1832) to versions of Dante, Petrarch, and Pindar. If Uttapara is a guide, the country towns around Calcutta were home to a small but serious group who were readers of English language verse.

The Calcutta Public Library catalogue is perhaps more helpful than the Uttapara catalog for gaining an understanding of available books in the first half of the nineteenth century, for it is better organized and dates from 1855. The catalogue indicates the extraordinary depth of the library's holdings by midcentury and runs to 632 pages of small print. English books outnumbered other languages by five to one, but the library had significant holdings in Greek and Latin, French, Italian, Spanish and Portuguese, Hebrew, and "Oriental" languages—mostly Sanskrit and Bengali. Poetry and drama run to 18 pages and "Prose Works of the Imagination" to 65 pages, though again the poetry entries are often for collected works, with multiple volumes listed as a single item. Fiction outnumbers poetry two to one, but only when we exclude poetry in classical and oriental languages and count multivolume editions as one item.

Readership is a different matter. Joshi has shown from records of the Calcutta Public Library's Committee on Selection that patrons were complaining by 1850 about the paucity of popular fiction; partly in consequence, she argues, the percentage of Indian subscribers fell over the following decades as the library's committee high-handedly ignored their request for a broader range of books (57). Joshi characterizes as futile the library's efforts to edify public taste through deemphasizing fiction over the next decades, and she notes that new institutions were established in the 1850s and 1860s to cater to Indian reading tastes. While it is clear that patrons read much fiction even in the first decade after the library's founding in 1836, it is true of the Calcutta Public Library as of the Uttapara library that there were, for those who wished them, significant holdings in poetry. At the Calcutta library before 1855, we can see holdings similar to those at Uttapara, with the addition of Barry Cornwall, Thomas Chatterton, a collection of British ballads, Percy's *Reliques*, and Mary Tighe, among others. Moreover, the dates on the volumes of poetry suggest an ongoing program of buying new work, for the 1855 catalogue includes Matthew Arnold's *Empedocles on Etna* (1852) and *The Strayed Reveller* (1849), along with Elizabeth Barrett Browning's *Casa Guidi Windows* (1851), Barry Cornwall's *English Songs* (1851), Tennyson's *In Memoriam* (1850, two copies), and Wordsworth's *Prelude* (1850). English poetry published in India or by residents of India is also represented, though in smaller numbers, including works by James Atkinson, James Hutchinson, Krishna Mohun Bannerjea, Shoshee Chunder Dutt, and several anonymous volumes. Clearly the Calcutta librarians, like the librarians at Uttapara, paid close attention to the British literary scene and bought poetry with discrimination and with remarkable speed after its publication.

That such purchases were important to aspiring poets is clear from the letters of Michael Madhusudan Dutt. I discuss Madhusudan's poetry at length in the next chapter, but here we might think of him as a reader—and as a failing literary entrepreneur. At the end of 1847, the youthful Madhusudan sailed from Calcutta to Madras, where evidently he hoped to find employment. His conversion to Christianity in 1843 had resulted in his quitting Hindu College and later enrolling in Bishop's College. By 1847 Madhusudan found that he had to leave Bishop's College, where he was on the verge of taking his last examinations, probably on account of his continuing quarrel with his father, who had himself experienced financial reverses. With little cash and high hopes, Madhusudan embarked for Madras, where he eventually found employment as a teacher. But the young poet apparently also made off with books. In a letter responding to a call to pay his fines, among other things, he described having published at Madras his first collection of poetry, *The Captive Ladie* (1849), which he hoped his friend Gour Bysack would be able to sell for him in Calcutta (Murshid, *Heart,* 76–77).

Although he obtained no subscribers in advance for this book, Madhusudan imagined that Gour could procure them post facto, despite the fact that Gour was hounding him for the money that Gour said he owed to the Calcutta Public Library. Madhusudan, ever in debt, denied owing anything, at the same time asking Gour to send him money and the books he left behind at the college:

> Pray let me have the money as early as you can. . . . So much for business. Printing, my friend, is as dear, here, as possible. What could I do? My printer is impatient. I am sure you can ask some friends to get you a few purchases. I make you my plenipotentiary to sell the books at any rate you like; only let me have money to pay my printer. As regards my liabilities to the public library, I am not aware of owing them anything, beyond some money, which I had promised to pay them as a *donation.*

Madhusudan went on to beg Gour to forward, along with the books, a parcel his mother made up for him, and he admitted, reluctantly, that his friend must have been "disappointed" by his poem. "Remember, my friend," he told Gour, "that I published it for the sake of attracting some notice, in order to better my prospects and not exactly for fame. However, what is done, is done." Almost as an apparent afterthought he added, "Do you know that I expect to be a father soon? Heigh ho! My stars are brightening. I trust I have answered every thing in your letter and that you will never cease to believe me. Ever your affectionate." A postscript adds, "I left a Persian book behind me in Bp's College. Ask Mr. Walker to send that book to you, and do you enclose it in my mother's parcel" (Murshid, *Heart*, 76–77).

The expectant father and worried poet, or expectant poet and worried father-to-be, thus entreated and cajoled his friend in Calcutta to make him right with the library, with other debts of honor, with his mother, and with his old tutor and to send books and sell books. "Dear Gour" clearly had his hands full. Madhusudan, I strongly suspect, had been availing himself of library privileges and absconded with the poems he could not afford to buy. Be that as it may, his debt of honor to the library, like most of the many debts he incurred throughout his life, could only be repaid in kind—through a voracious devouring and remaking of the British poetic tradition. Madhusudan's *Captive Ladie* received mixed reviews indeed, and its reception was one factor that caused him to turn to writing in Bangla. Madhusudan was certainly anxious about his pecuniary and literary future. The literary powers that be, back in Calcutta, were variously optimistic or skeptical of the whole English language literary enterprise.

The Anxiety of Reading English Poems in India

At almost any period since the development of print as commodity, opinions about the state of literary culture have been divided, but the 1840s in India were an especially anxious time in this regard. The growth of books and periodicals as commodities available to a widening audience was itself enough to generate social anxiety. One might draw a parallel between the anxiety attached to books and the unease directed at education. We could extend Foucault's argument that schools and school reform were coeval to a similar argument that commodity book culture was coeval with attempts to reform or control reading. In nineteenth-century India, the anxieties about reading (and about writing poetry) are marked. They parallel and on occasion entail the kinds of anxiety experienced in Britain, which focused on gender and class. Another focus of such anxiety was couched in a lament about quality. Often these anxieties—about gender, class, ethnicity, and aesthetic quality—were expressed in terms of each other.

In the 1820s and 1830s in India, much was available to read in English, but commentators were prone to lament its quality and its distribution. Emma Roberts provides a wonderfully comic picture of book hawkers in Calcutta, selling what can only be imagined as the nineteenth-century equivalent of today's remainders. In *Scenes and Characteristics of Hindostan* (1835), she declared that "certainly, in the streets of Calcutta, those who run may read; for books are thrust into the palanquin-doors, or the windows of a carriage . . . by natives, who make a point of presenting the title-pages and the engravings upside down. Some of these books seem to be worthy of the Minerva press in its worst days; and it is rather curious that novels, which are never heard of in England, half-bound in the common pale blue covers so long exploded, and which do not figure in any of the advertisements ostentatiously put forth on the wrappers of magazines, &c., are hawked about in the highways and byways of Calcutta" (3:11–12).

But such cheap goods—though ubiquitous—were by no means the only ones available. As Roberts found, "the most expensive standard works" along with numerous less expensive American editions were readily available in Calcutta. For readers outside of the major cities, books could be had by mail order from the presidencies or from London direct, or by "book club" special order at a discount from either. In the cities, as we have seen, books soon became available both in public libraries and, as in earlier decades, in private lending collections. Roberts was of a divided mind about the readily available reading matter, though she described the ways in which such matter was indispensable, in any of its forms, to readers of European literatures in the countryside. Here she echoed George Addison, who (as we see in chapter 1) lived for literary friendship more successfully than for indigo.

If junk and high culture were readily available and if, as the *Government Gazette* noted, there was no shortage of homegrown poets writing English, nonetheless beauty—or literary significance—was very much in the eye of the beholder. And commercial or pecuniary success in writing poetry became increasingly problematic as the number of imported books increased and publication by subscription declined.

The development of the book as commodity entailed anxieties for writers and for their critics as well. The anonymous Calcutta reviewer of *India, a Poem in Three Cantos, by a Young Civilian of Bengal* (London, 1834) lamented that "any volume of poems *printed* in Calcutta (it could not be *published* in the true sense of the word) is quite 'as good as manuscript.' The only way to circulate poetry here, is to print it in the periodicals" (*Calcutta Literary Gazette,* August 23, 1834, 127).

By the 1840s, increased literary production by Indians and by the British in India was being matched by the rapid increase in the importation of reading matter. Whereas Emma Roberts and George Addison were happy to borrow books from friends in the mofussil or "up country" and looked forward to their advent by post, by 1840 such reading was taken for granted. But in the same way that Roberts was of a divided mind about reading in India, so too in the 1840s did opinions differ as to the meaning of this rapidly developing literary scene: some were anxious; some were celebratory.

The contrast might be illustrated by the pronouncements of John Kaye and "Dr. Grant" in the late 1840s as they surveyed recent years in Indian literary culture. Kaye, best known today as a historian of India, published a novel and a volume of poems and contributed verse to Richardson's annuals; he was also the founder of the *Calcutta Review* (1844). His essay on "English Literature in India" appeared in the *Review* in 1846, Grant's in 1848. Kaye provides a general survey of the reading available in India in European languages; he points out that steam transport has made new books and newspapers plentiful. The "stream of intelligence pours in with the utmost regularity," he says. Every month, readers receive a fresh supply of the best products of the "English, Scottish and Irish press." They have the leisure to read and do read. Although Calcutta is "in advance" of other Indian cities and the countryside in its reading habits, "there is scarcely a remote station in India, which has not its well-supplied

Book-Club. Some of these are furnished direct from London; others receive their supplies from the Booksellers at the Presidencies." Scarcely a regiment lacks a good store of books, periodicals, and papers, Kaye says, and Murray's Home and Colonial Library and Chapman and Hall's Foreign Library have added to the variety.[16]

Grant, in contrast, reviewing in 1848 David Lester Richardson's *Literary Leaves, Literary Chit-Chat,* and *Notices of the British Poets,* was less sanguine. The latter book collected the biographical notices Richardson had prepared for inclusion in his anthology of British poetry, a task he had initially undertaken at Macaulay's behest. Perusing Richardson's volumes incites Grant's deep distrust of poetry in general and its role among young Indian men (including, most likely, Richardson's students). Grant finds poetry barely tolerable even for British men, whom he implies are less likely than Indians and East Indians to be corrupted by verse.

In an essay largely critical of Richardson and all his works, Grant describes what he sees as the deplorable state of the Indian reading public.[17] Grant feels a special anathema toward young men who strongly resemble the students and graduates of Hindu College. They, like British expatriates of literary leanings, are merely ostentatious, pretending to literary importance. "Notwithstanding young Bengal pretensions—there is really no demand [in India] for literature in its various branches—and this is one grand difficulty in the path of the literary man in India," Grant writes. "Nevertheless, the pursuit has been beneficial for man. It is a noble refuge, from ennui, and temptation, and idleness, and vice." Grant displays at once the evangelical distrust of literary texts and the Benthamite contempt for poetry. He admits that literary men—that is, British literary men—can take up literature more safely than, say, drink or gambling or women.

But when it comes to young men born in India, even literature's harmless pleasures seem dangerous (this is 1848, after all) and the young men themselves are dismissed in thoroughly racist terms. Grant can tolerate British expatriates with literary pretensions, but he finds the native born at once dangerous and silly: "'Fire in each eye, and paper in each hand,' our Calcutta juvenile aspirants do indeed 'rave, recite, and madden round the land.' . . . Of varied race and complexion they deem themselves perfect masters of English composition. Some of them never grope their way thro' jungly dingles of mediocrity. Embarking on a little catamaran or shell of knowledge, like boys disporting in a punt, they deem that they have made the voyage around the world of literature, when they have only made the circuit of a tank."[18] One imagines that in describing "our Calcutta juvenile aspirants," Grant might have had in mind Richardson's current students, perhaps including Madhusudan Dutt, who had published poems in various periodicals. He might even have been thinking of Derozio's student Kasiprasad Ghosh (whom I discuss in the next chapter), who at this point in his career was editing the *Hindu Intelligencer.*

In any case, Grant is made deeply uneasy by "young Bengal pretensions." As Rosinka Chaudhuri has shown, 1848 was the point at which the term "Young Bengal," in parallel to Mazzini's "Young Italy," was adopted by commentators on the literary scene in Calcutta to describe the radical westernized young men who had been a source of consternation in Bengal since the time of Derozio. "Young Bengal" in this sense was "certainly not exclusively a reference to Derozio's students" but went well beyond that group from the 1830s and had current referents in the 1840s. Chaudhuri summarizes several letters published in the *Bengal Hurkaru* in 1848, in which the writer (in terms very similar to Grant's) chides the English-educated youths of Calcutta as "young men of wit, intelligence, quick perception and great influence in the community to which [they] belong." But the writer declares that they "still seem indifferent to the public weal, totally heedless of what misery befalls [their] priest ridden country" (quoted in Chaudhuri, *Derozio*, lx). Chaudhuri goes on to reference Shoshee Chunder Dutt's 1854 essay "Young Bengal, or the Hopes of India," which distinguishes between the "liberal and magnanimous" Young Bengal and "insolent and profligate" youth, between the "hard-reading" and the "hard-drinking" (lxii).

Though clearly many young men associated with "Young Bengal" were indeed hard drinking, their hard reading and their writing, perhaps more than anything else, was what disturbed the anonymous writer in the *Hurkaru* and even more profoundly disturbed Dr. Grant. Their forays into what Grant contemptuously called the "jungly dingles of mediocrity" occasioned anxiety among both British commentators and orthodox Hindus.[19] But Grant's racism is curious here—who exactly did he mean when he mocked the literary aspirations of young men of "varied race and complexion"? It is possible that even seventeen years after his death, Derozio still excited Grant's ire. But it is equally possible that Grant was alluding to such little-known poets as T. W. Smyth, a friend of Derozio's, and Henry Page, both of whom published volumes of verse in the 1840s.

Smyth could have been one of those whom Grant derided as of "varied race and complexion,"[20] although it is difficult to say with certainty. Smyth clearly was, like Grant, of an evangelical persuasion, for in 1839 Smyth joined various British men and also Krishna Mohan Bannerjee (Derozio's former student and the most famous high-caste Christian convert in Bengal) on the Committee of the Calcutta Bible Association. Smyth's volume of verse, *Ella, or A Tale of the Waldensian Martyrs; and Other Poems* (1843), clearly indicated his piety, but in its antiestablishment tendencies, one can see Smyth's alliance to radical Christian politics. For reasons of race or class or religion, or all three, Smyth staked out a territory that the much more conservative Dr. Grant would have abhorred. Given his interest in the Waldensian martyrs, Smyth's evangelical views were probably of a dissenting sort, and he, like Derozio's family, is likely to have been connected to the Calcutta Baptists. Among the miscellaneous poems appearing in *Ella* is an amazing excoriation of the empire and of Queen Victoria herself.

Smyth's views on Victoria could certainly have given Dr. Grant apoplexy. When I came across this poem in the Carey Library at Serampore College, I realized how limited our understanding of the politics of English language poetry in India has been.

My colleague Hena Basu, who has worked in Bengal libraries for thirty years, assisting scholars in many fields, began to laugh aloud at Smyth's diatribe, which imagines the young Queen Victoria called to meet her maker. "On the Late Attempted Assassination of the Queen" is the most radical poem I have read written in English in India in the first half of the century. In it, Smyth recounts the attempt on Victoria's life (probably the first in 1840) and declares that she has been spared by God to redress the wrongs she has allowed to accrue in the empire:

X
See India groaning under countless ills,
        Cathay well drugg'd with opium and with blood,
The heathen martyr'd, while the Christian kills,
        With war and havoc roaring in a flood;
Oh! sin out-sinning persecution's sin!
The brand of double infamy burnt in!
XI
Look on Cabool!—and in Victoria's reign?—
        Shall this be told posterity, ev'n this?
Oh sov'reign sacred! lov'd and honor'd Queen!
        Be not thy name a mark for history's hiss!—
Think too, what He might think—thy Maker!—King!
Before whom summon'd, what art thou?
                —a thing
XII
Of dust,—a worm, a something, nothing now,
        Then, less than nothingness—a shadow flown—
A phantom pale with her undiadem'd brow
        Thy breath a bubble; and thy glory gone—
Thy scepter broken—shot to dust thy throne,
        Thy stewardship demanded now and done!

(153)

Victoria before the throne of God, sent to the last judgment with the sins of the empire on her head, can only be a "thing / Of dust,—a worm, a something." Clearly, Smyth takes an apocalyptic view of empire and holds the monarch personally responsible for the opium trade, the wars that supported it, and "countless ills" unspecified. If Grant was reading *Ella,* it is little wonder that he resorted to racist epithets, deriding poets lost in the "jungly dingles of mediocrity": better to dismiss views like Smyth's than to legitimate them by opposition.

The sole extant copy I have found of Smyth's volume was bound with that of a person who probably was his friend and certainly was associated with "Young Bengal."[21]

Henry Page, a friend of Derozio's, may have been the child of an Anglo-Indian mother and a British father, for in the title poem of *The Land of Poesy* (1842) he laments that India has been laid "grov'ling low / Upon a field of endless woe" by British conquest.[22] Indeed, both of these poets take a dim view of British imperialism.

Although little information about Page's education is available, he likely considered himself "East Indian," or simply Indian. Page's father, Henry Page Senior, was born in the west country of England, went to India, and ended his life as the fort adjutant at Monghyr in Bengal (now Munger in Bihar). The senior Page evidently was a dissipated youth who reformed himself through religion; although initially baptized as an Anglican, he became a Baptist and was baptized once more, evidently with much of his family, which probably included five children. The children appear to have been raised speaking Bangla or Hindustani, for the senior Page wrote to his wife, Jane, that he wished his daughter Charlotte to learn to say her prayers and read the Bible in English.[23] I conjecture that Jane, the poet's mother, was a native speaker of Bangla or Hindustani and was quite possibly of mixed Indian and British parentage. Her son, Henry Page, Jr., writes about Derozio and very much in his vein, clearly considering India his "native land." Whatever his family of origin, Henry Page, Jr., identified himself as Indian and imagined poetry creating the social and political awakening that would make such an identification a matter of great pride.

Page's "Land of Poesy" is a long poem in three books, and Book I, like Derozio's sonnets, imagines poetry reviving or re-creating the India that he claimed as his country:

> India, my country! once how bright,
> How spotless was thy fame!—
> Not brighter heav'n's ethereal light!—
> And oh! how matchless was thy might!
> Ere yet thy victors came,
> From Albion, o'er the tossing wave,
> In England's pow'r array'd,
> And to the summer breezes gave
> Their banners. . .
> . . . .
> Oh! I would drop a burning tear
> Upon thy listless breast
> To rouse the pride that slumbers there,
> And passions wake which should not share
> So long inglorious rest;—
> I'd tell thee what thou once hadst been—
> A nation great and free!—
> On earth, like some far-famed queen,

Amidst her loyal subjects seen
In new-born majesty!

(7)

With poetic sleight of hand, Page replaces Queen Victoria with India, personified as the queen of a new nation accepting the homage of her subjects. Later in the century, when nationalists invoked the metaphor of India as woman, the trope of mother India allied the domestic to the national; here the female personification of India is understood quite differently. India is herself an empress or will again become one; she only waits for her people to awaken and her poets to take up the harp again.

Page places himself directly in the line of Derozio as poet of the nation and evokes him by name at the end of Book III, lamenting Derozio's untimely death and wishing for his return in spirit. If indeed Derozio's spirit might return (implicitly inspiring Page), if such a spirit could be revived,

full well I know,
All India would awaking feel
A pride it could not then conceal,
All India's bosom glow
With fire to strike the harp again
He oft had woke to happy strain.

And may this be?—perhaps not so,
And yet methinks there are
Some few who *feel*—else why this slow
Returning hope comes even now
To cheer me from afar?

(89)

"The Land of Poesy," which ends shortly after these lines, is followed in Page's book with an elegy for Derozio. Here, once more, the poet imagines Derozio's spirit as the soul of patriotism. He describes his hero in the highest terms as the "Pride of the East":

One gifted mind, unfetter'd, rang'd
Beyond oblivion's grasp;
And Pride, that long had been estrang'd,
With one convulsive gasp,
Rose from the gloomy depths of time,
And breath'd another soul,
With thoughts that in a patriot's heart
Would brook no stern control!

. . . .

And thus, O Minstrel of the East!
Thy sun was clouded o'er;
But tho' thy strain hath hapless ceas'd
And thou art now no more,
An echo still in every heart
Shall breathe sweet melody,
And many a tear unbidden start
To thy sad memory!

(96–97)

Page dates his poem August 2, 1841. Though no particular course of political action is implied in Page's verse, the poet aligns himself with a project of bardic nationalism. Derozio is the brightest star in this patriotic firmament, and Page hopes against hope to join him.

If Henry Page and T. W. Smyth are among the young men of "varied race and complexion" who "rave, recite and madden round the land," one can see how Dr. Grant, who is obviously writing from an evangelical but thoroughly imperialist point of view, might have taken exception to them. Whatever the case, Grant sees the only hope for India's literature in a Christian awakening.

If young men who wrote poems in Bengal met with Grant's disapproval, David Lester Richardson, too, was unacceptable, at least in 1848. Grant very likely found him insufficiently Christian, but the *Calcutta Review*'s Dr. Grant is probably the same John Peter Grant who shortly became (or was already) embroiled in a dispute over Richardson's work as principal of Hindu College.[24] Such disputes were certainly important to the editor of the *Calcutta Review,* who succeeded John Kaye and published Grant's essay; he was none other than Alexander Duff, the head of the Free Church Institution, who reportedly had serious disagreements with Richardson. So it is possible that Dr. Grant's review of Richardson's poetry and his larger ruminations on the English language literary scene were shaped, in part, by the various internecine squabbles among the educators and divines of Calcutta. Clearly, neither Richardson's politically tame poetry nor the "ravings" of young men such as Smyth and Page comforted Grant. While Kaye looked on the literary scene with a comfortable composure and Roberts had mixed feelings about its contours but seemed to view Derozio as an equal, Grant was made anxious by new voices and attitudes.

Poetry in the Curriculum: Examinations, Anthologies, and Editors

David Lester Richardson's apparent falling afoul of the powers that be in Calcutta in the late 1840s—he was accused of neglecting his duties, and rumors circulated about his "mode of life"—led to his resignation from Calcutta's most important educational establishment for the education of young Hindu men, Hindu College, where Derozio and David Hare had preceded him a generation earlier (Sanial, 80). After a period as editor of the *Bengal Hurkaru*, Richardson came to head a new college, the Hindu Metropolitan College. But from 1833 on, when he was invalided from his post in the Bengal Native Infantry, he had been a central actor in what was always a drama in English language publishing and education. Richardson combined an aversion to political controversy with a passion for poetry, and one can only speculate what real or rumored personal failings led to his offending of John Drinkwater Bethune and Alexander Duff; Richardson's enthusiasm for students, though inevitably patronizing in its language, clearly evinced a serious respect for their intelligence and learning.[25] Richardson's primary goal (though he was asked to teach history, literature, and moral philosophy) was evidently to evoke his students' love of poetry. To that end, he significantly shaped an English language curriculum that broader indications suggest was already attuned to the study of poetry. Poetry was crucial in the mid-nineteenth-century English-medium curriculum, and Richardson became central to its cultural success.[26]

One could argue that the formative impact of poetry, especially of British poetry, lay in the schools. It is easy to forget, given the near disappearance of poetry from most schooling in the twenty-first-century United States, Shakespeare aside, that in the English speaking world of the nineteenth century, poetry was a significant part of the curriculum, particularly as it was integral to studies of classical languages, literature, and elocution.

In India, we can certainly see Gauri Viswanathan's point that the development of curricula in British literature was "invented" for colonial purposes; yet, of course, literary education was not limited to the formal curriculum. As we saw with Derozio's Academic Association, the understanding of literature and philosophy was significantly shaped by pupils and teachers outside of officially sanctioned curricula and examinations. Looking at the details of poetry in English-medium curricula at this period is useful nonetheless, for the growth in English language schools paralleled in its rapidity the growth of the world of print.[27]

The languages curriculum at Calcutta University provides a glimpse into how such curricula would have been prepared by other schooling. In the first year of the new university's degree examinations (1858), the subjects for the bachelor of arts were listed as follows for languages:

English:	Shakespeare, *Macbeth*
	Dryden, *Cymon and Iphigenia; The Flower and the Leaf*
	Addison, *Essays from the* Spectator
Greek:	Sophocles, *Antigone*
	Herodotus, Book 7, *Polymnia;* Book 8, *Urania*

Latin:	Virgil, *Aeneid,* Books 1 to 6
	Cicero, *Four Orations against Catiline*

Examinations were also offered in Hebrew, Arabic, Persian, Sanskrit, Bengali, Hindi (no texts listed), and Urdu (no texts listed). Papers were to include grammar, idiom, and translation. Almost two decades later, the curriculum had moved little—it was more comprehensive but scarcely more daring. The examinations in English for 1876 included poems by Cowper, Crabbe, Goldsmith, Southey, Johnson's lives of Addison and John Gay, and two stories by Washington Irving, a rare foray into America.

Obviously the informal curriculum of Hindu College in the time of Derozio was much more daring and varied than the examinations at the new university in 1858. Though perhaps less daring than the informal curriculum, even the formal curriculum of Hindu College in the time of David Lester Richardson (1836–43 and 1848–49) was still in some measure shaped by the vision of its founder, David Hare. Scholarship examination questions were posed on the following topics in 1846: Hamlet paraphrased and discussed; the poetry of Milton and Gray; Bacon's prose; and English history emphasizing Tudor/Stuart history (focusing on the Court of the Star Chamber and habeas corpus) and the English revolution. Clearly, Hindu College encouraged, implicitly if not explicitly, comparisons between British rights and liberties and the Indian scene. Shakespeare, Milton, and Bacon formed a literary and philosophical—if not explicitly political—triumvirate.

In contrast, in the same year, the Free Church Institution—the institution closest to Alexander Duff's heart and a much smaller school—inculcated religion through curriculum including the Bible, the catechism, *Pilgrim's Progress,* Butler's *Analogy of Religion,* Locke's *Reasonableness of Christianity,* Robert Boyle's *Veneration Due to God,* and so forth, along with moral philosophy. It required along with these texts Bengali translation, Greek (the New Testament book of Acts and Xenophon), poetry by Thomas Campbell, and James Thomson's *Castle of Indolence.* The competitive examinations at the Free Church Institution included questions in religion and moral philosophy, mathematics, astronomy and mechanics, Whately's *Rhetoric,* and topics from Milton, Young, Campbell, and Thomson.[28]

Obviously, the secular education at Hindu College and at the government colleges differed significantly from the inculcation of religion at the Free Church Institution or, for that matter, at Bishop's College, as is evident in the experience of Madhusudan Dutt, who moved from Hindu College to Bishop's College as a result of his conversion of Christianity. Perhaps because of the breadth of its curricula, even before the time of Derozio and certainly beyond it, Hindu College took the lead in the formation of poetic taste. Both the formal and the informal curriculum granted poetry significant, if somewhat different, roles.

The most striking example of the bridge between informal and formal curricula is the case of Richardson's anthology, *Selections from the British Poets,* first published in

1840. Richardson undertook the anthology at the request of the Committee of Public Instruction and of Macaulay, who was then president of the committee. Richardson avowed diplomatically that he took advantage of several of Macaulay's suggestions and goes on to say in his introduction to the anthology that after Macaulay's departure he added biographical and critical notices. Reviewing the British competition in anthologies and lives of poets from Dr. Johnson to Hazlitt, Richardson claims that his is the "first attempt to comprise in one volume an uninterrupted series of specimens *from Chaucer to the latest living poets*" (5). In a spirited defense of the study of poetry—contra the claims of utilitarians and evangelicals alike—Richardson evokes philosophers and poets from Aristotle to Isaac Watts, from Bacon to John Wesley, and even Bentham himself (in a footnote) to defend the pleasures, beauty, and moral usefulness of studying poetry.

Richardson takes on the school principal's task in the end, for he argues that Indian students will find his anthology especially useful and affordable. The latter claim is probably attributable to the fact that the book's cost was in part defrayed by the Committee of Public Instruction and the Calcutta School Book Society (*Selections*, 17). To the latter (particularly its secretary, the Rev. Mr. Pearce), Richardson is eager to argue for the morality of poetry. He has, he says, been mindful of the reverend's concerns, but though he has "taken the liberty of suppressing objectionable passages," he could not, he says, "be so ridiculously presumptuous as to supply their place" (18). These assurances are sandwiched between larger pedagogical reflections. His reflections are an amalgam of condescension toward "the natives," real delight in and belief in the aesthetic and moral usefulness of poetry, and sensible attitudes toward pedagogy. In the first place, Richardson defends teaching poetry in addition to science and practical subjects, implying at once that both British administrators and Indian parents are wont to advocate a curriculum that neglects poetry in favor of practical subjects. He echoes the common notion that Bengalis are "too apt to think that the loss of riches is the loss of every thing" (16). And in an argument Macaulay would have approved, he declares that "Indian students read our English poets, as English collegians read the poets of Greece or Rome, not only to familiarize their minds with beautiful images and pure and noble thoughts, but to acquire a thorough knowledge of the language in which the poetry is embodied" (16). But at heart Richardson has a more idealist goal in mind, hoping to inculcate a "sense of intellectual beauty," not by force or severity but by close reading and enthusiastic instruction. This practice "enforces attention and accustoms the youthful reader to think for himself" (19). And finally, Richardson argues that because his anthology is arranged chronologically, the student will begin at the end, such that the last selections will be the first read. Among the poets Richardson lists as appropriate for beginners are Gay, Green, Tickell, Addison, Parnell, Swift, Goldsmith, Cowper, Beattie, Scott, Crabbe, Hemans, Rogers, Montgomery, and Southey. He clearly sought language and subject matter that his young students would find accessible. Richardson was best known for his enthusiastic teaching of Milton and Shakespeare and Pope, who are given significant representation in his collection.

Pedagogy for beginners aside, the final poems in the volume comprise a wide and significant representation of British poetry after 1800 plus a selection of old English ballads, poems of Ossian, miscellaneous Scottish songs, translations from European, Greek, and Latin poetry, and a substantial selection of English language poetry written in India. Among eighteenth-century poets, Burns, Bowles, Sir William Jones, Goldsmith, and Chatterton get substantial space; among nineteenth-century British poets, Richardson made substantial selections, including long stretches of *Childe Harold* and *Don Juan*, the complete *Lay of the Last Minstrel*, significant work by Shelley, Keats, Crabbe, Coleridge, Wordsworth, Felicia Hemans, Campbell, Moore, L.E.L., and even poems from Charles and Alfred Tennyson, Ebenezer Elliott, Thomas Hood, and Barry Cornwall.

The most intriguing section of the volume, however, "British-Indian Poetry: Specimens of British Poets Once or Still Resident in the East Indies," is the first anthology of Indian English poetry; it includes along with the titular "British Poets" resident in India poems by Kasiprasad Ghosh and Derozio.[29] Richardson's ambitions, as he tacitly acknowledged, went well beyond a textbook, for the volume of more than 1,600 double-columned pages clearly was designed to provide a library between its covers. Despite his condescension toward the very material considerations that plagued his students and himself, Richardson's enthusiasm for verse had a significant impact on his students, including Madhusudan Dutt.

By the time Madhusudan was studying at Hindu College in the late 1830s and 1840s, readers of English had a wide and readily available selection of the British poetic canon available in accessible forms. Both the proliferation of English language print and the formal and informal curricula of English-medium schools, along with new technologies of publishing and distribution, made available to English speakers in India a wide variety of poetic texts. What poets made of this situation varied much by social location, material circumstance, and relative economic and political empowerment and disempowerment. What critics made of the scene of writing was also a complex matter.

Teacher as Poet: David Lester Richardson, Henry Meredith Parker, and the Conventions of Exile

For Sir William Jones in the late eighteenth century, an immersion in Indian classical and modern languages and culture led to a series of poems made from the fabric of orientalist learning. Despite Jones's place as the "first poet" of English India, the great majority of English language poets in midcentury India were more attuned to the concerns that are evident in Horsford's work, concerns of a more personal and less learned sort. As we have seen, topical political terrain was crucial for Derozio and Roberts, as for Smyth and Page, but for most poets of British origin exploring politics was less important than charting an affective landscape of the emotions. David Lester Richardson and Henry Meredith Parker created poems along these lines, though Parker was more willing than Richardson to engage, however lightly, political topics.

Richardson's "Stanzas on a Late Attempt to Shoot the Queen" (1842) and Parker's "Young India: A Bengal Eclogue" (1831) engage satirically with current events and, implicitly, with the English-educated youths of Calcutta. Richardson's poem is unusual among his texts in being satirical, and its difference from T. W. Smyth's verses on the same subject is striking. Not surprisingly, given "The Warrior's Farewell to the Family Bard," patriotism is triumphant for D.L.R. His satire (dated Calcutta, July 18, 1842) lacks Smyth's fire but is proleptical of Kipling's *Barrack-Room Ballads.* Richardson initially takes the common soldier's view:

> The Queen's luckless soldier for twelve-pence a day,
>   As a butt for a bullet must stand,—
> But he's not of the same flesh and blood you will say
>   As the lady that rules o'er the land.
>
> . . . .
>
> Yet where's the great difference 'twixt Soldier and Queen?
>   The difference is all the in the pay;
> His is less than two guineas a month it is seen,
>   And hers is a thousand a day!
>
> (*Literary Chit-Chat,* 416)

Despite the leveling premise of the poem, Richardson comes round to praise for the queen, who after all displays " a courage that charms the beholder." In contrast to Henry Page, Richardson concludes that Victoria is worth her pay.

Henry Meredith Parker's "Young India: A Bengal Eclogue" is a more pointed satiric poem than Richardson's odd foray in the genre. Parker's "Eclogue" was first published in 1831, within the period of Derozio's greatest influence. It was then reprinted along with his most amusing "Decline and Fall of Ghosts" in *Bole Ponjis.* In his "Eclogue," Parker ridicules the students of Hindu College for adopting Western manners and mores and for writing English poetry. Parker shared Dr. Grant's ability to mock Calcutta youth but was both more generous and less racist, subjecting the young not to slurs but to a parody. Parker satirizes the preferred curriculum of the Hindu College (or, as he calls it, the "Anglo Indian" College), mocking his originals Hari Mohan Bose and Shyam Chand, whom he calls Hurry and Sam—as they make their way through mutton chops to beef steak, against all religious law.[30] They also make their way through English and Roman literature, among other mangled knowledge:

> Was it for this we learned the world was round,
> That twenty shillings sterling make a pound;

That spinning jennies, Sam, were not young ladies,
And what a science is, and what a trade is?
Was it for this my essay, proved, (signed Justus)
That Dryden wrote his Virgil for Augustus?
Was it for this we thought Crabbe's Penseroso
And Samson Agonisthes, rather so so;
Scott's Comus dull, but Milton's song divine
Of Johnny Gilpin, very very fine?

(*Bole Ponjis,* 1:227)

There is a humor in this mockery that I take to be more affectionate than patronizing, more amusement than ridicule, for all its Byronic and hudibrastic rhyming. Certainly Parker works in the vein of satire that had remained important from the beginning of English verse in India, making fun of the excesses of the young—only here the youths are not "griffins" from Britain but local teenagers educated in British tradition. The griffin's debt, drink, and womanizing are replaced by tumblers of beer and books.

Parker wrote numerous more serious poems, some of which Richardson anthologized in his *Selections.* Parker's early volume, *The Draught of Immortality* (1827), included Byronic echoes, a long translation from the *Mahābhārata* (the title poem), and a variety of ballads and songs. The *Quarterly Oriental Magazine* singled out for praise his poems on the Greeks at Missolonghi and on Simon Bolivar, two lyrics that would have been especially pleasing to Parker's friends Derozio and Kasiprasad Ghosh. Derozio, as we have seen, was writing very similar poems at the time.[31] Parker writes that Bolivar was motivated not by an ignoble ambition but by a "holier cause": "'Twas freedom—country, laws, / Gave the word!" Bolivar's hand "rent the leaden chain" and saved his country from slavery (*Draught,* 99).[32] Parker's politics place him somewhere between Derozio (or T. W. Smyth and Henry Page) and Richardson. A political spectrum of English language poetry and its critics in the 1840s then might be represented by Grant on the conservative end, Richardson in the middle with Parker on the slightly more critical side, and Smyth (and perhaps Page) at the more radical end.

Despite his skepticism about British intentions in India, however, Parker shared with Richardson an energy for furthering the dominant tropes of British Indian poetry. His early volume tried all of them on.[33] His sequence of poems "The Indian Day" (1827), reprinted by Richardson in his anthology, rather ably describes the course of a day, only to end with the trope of exile, a trope the poem does not quite own. The conventional attitude is attributed to a generic "exile" who muses on his lonely state. The poem asks, "What to him are these, / The East's resplendent skies and fragrant trees, / This clime of flowers and stars?—Alas! 'tis not his own" (*Draught,* 124). Perhaps the exile of this poem is Richardson, or the avatar of Richardson, and not Parker himself. Or perhaps there is no "Parker" but only a collection of attitudes, tropes, and genres ranging from a translation of Hāfiz to a poem admiring Indian bravery ("The

Widow of the Mysore Hill: A Fact"), to a cheering imperialist ditty, to the impersonation of Persian poetry in "The Indian Lover's Song."

This last is one of the most effective in the volume, demonstrating that the poet might well have been a musician, for he seems more comfortable with song than with other genres. The Indian lover is surely as Irish as he is Indian, a close cousin to Tom Moore:

> Hasten, love, the sun hath set,
> And the moon, through twilight beaming,
> On the mosque's white minaret,
> Now in silver light is streaming.
>
> All is hush'd in deep repose;
> Silence rests on field and dwelling,
> Save where bulbul to the rose
> Is a love-tale sweetly telling.
>
> Save the ripple, faint and far,
> Of the river softly gilding;
> Soft as thine own murmurs are,
> When my kisses gently chiding.
>
> (*Draught,* 130)

Parker tries on various poetic guises with remarkable facility, which makes all the more amusing Theodore Douglas Dunn's conclusion in his 1917 retrospective of British poets in India that Parker was the first "distinctly original" among these poets (*Bengali,* 352).

Perhaps Parker's metrical and intellectual facility gives his work more purchase on a distinctive reality than Richardson's. In contrast, Richardson's poetic—rather than pedagogical—contributions to English verse in India were constrained by his more conventional poetic practice and his inveterate homesickness.[34] He also rang the changes on themes we have seen in the poetry of Roberts and Derozio—the Indian landscape, sati, ruins, and so forth. Richardson's tendency to moralize a scene, an event, an emotion, or a historical circumstance limited his poetry in a way that, paradoxically, did not unduly circumscribe his taste as an editor and teacher. His volumes' various titles—*Literary Recreations* (1852), *Literary Chit-Chat* (1848), and *Literary Leaves* (1836)—indicate his miscellaneous approach. He made no particular effort to shape an oeuvre through a politics or aesthetics; this made him an open-minded editor but lent his poetry an occasional quality. Nonetheless, some of Richardson's most moving poems are expressive of his separation from his children.

Typical are two poems that establish exile as the leitmotif of Indian English verse. The first also demonstrates that homesickness, even for an Englishman, could be filtered through bardic tropes. "Sonnet: On Hearing Captain James Glencairn Burns Sing (in India) His Father's Songs" captures the affective impact of "native song," though it elides differences between England (Richardson's "home") and Scotland:

> How dream-like is the sound of native song
> Heard on a foreign shore! The wanderer's ear
> Drinks wild enchantment,—swiftly fade the drear
> And cold realities that round him throng,
> While in the sweet delirium, deep and strong,
> The past is present and the distant near!
>
> (*Literary Recreations,* 35)

Indeed, Burns's "lays," the poet declares, are still more dear "when heard by exiles parted long / From all that love hath hallowed." Moreover, James Burns awakens a sense of holy awe and trembling in the poet's heart, for "filial echoes" move him. The Scottish son of the famous father evokes filial piety, bardic nationalism, and a longing for the parent country. The bard, here, obviously is quite different from the poet extolled by Derozio or Page—for the tropes of the Scottish bard are assimilated to an undifferentiated British homesickness.

Richardson's children were more of an inspiration than Burns. Two poems collected in *Literary Recreations* can represent the range of these concerns. The first, "England and Bengal," is a longish poem in two parts, contrasting a rural English landscape with the banks of the Ganges and conceding beauties to each scene. Richardson lovingly describes the flora of Bengal (he was later to write a book on Indian flowers and flower gardens, which is still sought after), but he comes in the end to a highly idealized celebration of an unspecified rural English landscape. "I can love all lovely lands," he writes, "But England most" (*Literary Recreations,* 26). The English landscape is wholly idealized, unlike the Bengali one:

> How proud a sight to English eyes
> Are England's village families!
> The patriarch, with his silver hair,
> The matron grave, the maiden fair

And so on, with well-scrubbed cherubs winding their way to church. He imagines, finally, his own "sweet children" running across a smooth lawn while old friends look on smiling from the cottage door.

Here we have the quintessence of versified homesickness filtered through a conventional haze of imagination. Richardson's landscape is ideology *pur.* These lines are not too far off from Emma Roberts's somewhat more nuanced (or contradictory) graveyard reflections or Felicia Hemans's poems of the same period. That such poems have a fill-in-the-blank quality is evident in the context of Indian English verse published at least from the 1820s on; one "R.," for example, published a strikingly similar poem, "Written on Leaving England for India," in the *Oriental Herald* of 1825. R. begins,

> Yon rural cot's a peasant's home,
> Who would not from his dear vale roam,
> Nor cross the wide Atlantic wave
> For all that wealth or fame e'er gave.

The poet evokes the "tender wife, and rosy boy," the loving "calm domestic sphere," and concludes:

> Though many yield to prouder star,
> Rove distant realms, or toil in war,
> Are there on earth could envy not
> Such happy loves, such tranquil lot.[35]

Ironically, the poem is datelined Camberwell, which even then was fast becoming a London suburb.

Richardson's essay "Arrival in England" takes the opposite point in the "exile's" life: not departure but return. This essay underscores the way that England must be imagined through the rural in order to remain a longed-for destination, for the urban is too close to the twin economic realities of empire and industry. In a piece collected in *Literary Recreations,* Richardson wrote with delight about the "clean cottages" and quiet meadows between Southampton and London—but upon arriving in the metropole, he says, "I got into the restless and mighty heart of the over-grown metropole of England—of the world rather—and witnessed the signs of eager toil and feverish rivalry, and observed the desperate struggles of many thousands of intelligent human beings to support a bare animal existence" (676–77).

Some of Richardson's sonnets on similar themes strike a different note from his "homesick" poems on England and Bengal. His sonnets "by a British-Indian exile to his distant children" actually create an identification with India, acknowledging the paradox that India is home yet not home when children are absent. In contrast to John Horsford (who, we have seen, clearly had no thought of returning to Britain and reared his children in India), Richardson did struggle to return. But he was, as his letters to Leigh Hunt reveal, unable to find sufficiently remunerative work to support his family.[36] The sonnets to his children were written just prior to this home leave, which he was granted on account of ill health. They begin,

> My sad heart sickens in this solitude—
> Home is no longer home,—yet eloquent
> Are these lone walls of by-gone merriment.
>
> (*Recreations,* 125)

Here home is double—home was an Indian home when his children were present, but India is home no longer. The sonnets seem to me to have been influenced by Wordsworth and perhaps too by Coleridge's "Dejection"; certainly dejection is the dominant mood here. Longing for his children, Richardson laments,

> Memories sad intrude
> Like silent ghosts, where late the air was rent
> With shouts of joy—where merriest hours I spent
> With merriest playmates in their merriest mood!
>
> (*Recreations*, 125)

The second of the three sonnets in the sequence calls up the vision of his children. "Fancy's art" transcends all other magic, Richardson writes, so that "Not mirrored shapes—realities ye seem! / Sweet ones!" (*Recreations*, 125). Finally, in the third and final sonnet of the sequence, the vision fades:

> I hear the waves upon the sad sea-shore—
> And ah! my visionary group hath fled!
> To me those dear existences are dead;
> For distance is a death that all deplore
> Who part as we have parted, never more
> To meet as we have met—alas! instead
> Each with a sadder heart, a graver head—
> So different, though the same!
>
> (*Recreations*, 125)

Imagining the passage of time, Richardson acknowledges that home, though remade in England, and family, though reunited at length, will never be the same. In his work, feeling comes in aid of feeling, or as he put it in the prologue to his first book, "Affection lights a brighter flame / Than ever blazed by art."[37] In his sonnets, he rewrites Wordsworth's "Ode, Intimations of Immorality," but the childhood that fades is not so often Richardson's own as the early years of his children, whom he will only meet again when they and he have sadder hearts and graver heads.

This vision of exile—in which the beautiful but emotionally empty country of exile (India) is contrasted to the still more beautiful and emotionally satisfying country of origin (England)—is sometimes complicated or even reversed in Richardson's work. An unusual but striking example of a more complex, or perhaps contradictory, approach comes in a pair of sonnets comparing London to Calcutta ("London, in the Morning" and "View of Calcutta"). The first is clearly a rewriting of Wordsworth's sonnet "Composed upon Westminster Bridge."[38] Richardson's London sonnet, written a generation after Wordsworth's, takes a dimmer—a more polluted view—of the same. "London, in the Morning" begins thus:

The morning wakes, and through the misty air
In sickly radiance struggles—like the dawn
Of sorrow-shrouded hope.

(*Literary Leaves,* 228)

The Thames is laden with a "wealth bourne" from every "port and clime" but suffused by a "pallid glare" of early light. Soon, the poet writes, the streets will "teem" with careworn people and "eager throngs shall meet where dusky marts / Resound like ocean caverns" (*Literary Leaves,* 228). The poet, not unlike John Leyden years earlier, moralizes the scene, asking how many hearts have been brought "by lust of gold" to seek the prizes they once scorned.

The country from which one is exiled, then, can be idealized only when it is represented as a rural scene. The center of imperial commerce is another matter altogether. Richardson views the second city of empire, on the other side of the globe, more positively than London but within a context that exemplifies the essential ambiguities of empire. Does the British poet expect—or the British reader imagined by this poet expect—exotic animals, deserted ruins, natural and sublime landscapes? The poet seems to reject the cliché, but then he in turn imagines empire as a dominion of peace and good cheer. "View of Calcutta," in consequence, is one of Richardson's oddest poems; it critiques metropolitan expectations only to replace them with the equally clichéd myth of the empire as a happy family. The poet writes of Calcutta,

Here Passion's restless eye and spirit rude
May greet no kindred images of power
To fear or wonder ministrant.—No tower,
Time-struck and tenantless, here seems to brood,
In the dread mystery of solitude,
O'er human pride departed—no rocks lower
O'er ravenous billows—no vast hollow wood
Rings with the lion's thunder—no dark bower
The crouching tiger haunts—no gloomy cave
Glitters with savage eyes!—But all the scene
Is calm and cheerful. At the mild command
Of Britain's sons, the skilful and the brave,
Fair Palace-structures decorate the land,
And proud ships float on Hooghly's breast serene.

(*Literary Leaves,* 228)

In an unexpected reversal, Richardson finds the sublime in London, the beautiful in India. He locates the heart of darkness, or at least what he calls "Babel," in the metropole; yet the ex-soldier elides the violence that conquered India. London bespeaks violence; Calcutta is material evidence of "mild command," the skilled architecture of the brave.

Richardson was devoted to bringing British poetry to his "exile," even as his exile was lifelong, amounting then not to exile but to home. One imagines that his respect for his students' intelligence, his dedication to a pedagogy that fostered their thinking, and his obvious love for his subject combined to make him both popular and effective among his students and respected as a literary editor. Both Richardson and Parker went "home," that is, to London, with Parker living to excoriate British imperialists as an "empire of the middle classes" and Richardson, briefly, to edit a newspaper aimed at the very exiles he no doubt had begun to miss.

FROM THE DAYS in the 1810s when George Addison begged and borrowed books in the countryside and cajoled the clerks of his indigo plantation to hand-copy his *Moofussil Magazine* to Richardson's multifarious publishing and pedagogical adventures in the middle decades of the century, English poetry became steadily more important in India. It formed a crucial part of the formal and informal curricula of English education; it inspired the "hard-drinking" and "hard-reading" of Young Bengal. Though numerically never dominant, English poetry had prestige, and volumes of poetry and periodical verses were made ever cheaper and more available in the English language print explosion.

Clearly, though, poetry could be seen as the most conventional of genres, creating a readily duplicated set of tropes and themes—the national bard, the trauma of exile, adventure, the longed-for rural cot, the historical ruin, absent or star-crossed lovers—each trope or theme taking on its characteristic coloring in the Indian context. At the same time, the very conventionality of poetry in this period made for plentiful contradictions. Calcutta, or the banks of the Ganges, somehow appeared more beautiful than not; the empire of the "middle classes" turned out to be a surprisingly violent affair; East Indian "madmen" could readily imagine the last judgment passed on Queen Victoria long before Disraeli made her an empress. Englishmen such as Parker and Richardson and young men of more radical leanings made "voyages around the world of literature," disporting not in a tank but in the silty roads of the Hooghly and the reaches of the Thames.

Kasiprasad Ghosh. From a painting by J. Drummond, engraved by J. Cochran, *Fisher's Drawing Room Scrap-Book* (London: Fisher, Son, and Jackson, 1835).

FOUR

Sighing, or Not, for Albion

Kasiprasad Ghosh, Michael Madhusudan Dutt, and Mary Carshore

Consider the advice Thomas Carlyle gave to David Lester Richardson in 1838. In characteristic prophetic form yet with Scottish good sense, Carlyle rejected Richardson's complaint that he had been "exiled" to India. "You feel yourself an exile in the East; but in the West too it is exile," Carlyle told his correspondent. "I know not where under the sun it is not exile." Then, stepping down from his pulpit—since exile was simply the human condition—the elder man offered the younger some sound advice: "As for you, my dear Sir, you have other work to do in the East than grieve. Are there not beautiful things there, glorious things, wanting only an eye to note them, a hand to record them. . . . I mean what I say. The East has its own phases; there are things there which the West yet knows not of; and one heaven covers both. He that has an eye, let him look."[1]

Richardson was never wholly able to take Carlyle's advice, though he did sometimes look attentively—at Indian gardens, at the banks of the Ganges, at smoggy London. The three poets whom I discuss in this chapter, in contrast, could never neatly assume the rhetorical position of the exile, nor for the most part did they wish to. Kasiprasad Ghosh, Michael Madhusudan Dutt, and Mary Carshore were born and died in India. Of the three, only Madhusudan left the subcontinent. He studied for the bar in England and lived in France, but only after writing virtually all of his poetry in English and in Bangla.

Though they came from differing social locations and had access to different kinds of education and to different social and economic institutions, these three poets negotiated, in their lived experience and in their experiments with poetic form and language, complexities of identity and agency that Richardson sought to finesse or, as an Englishman, was entitled to ignore. Their poems are more than performances of identity, even of hybrid identities, though this can be a significant dimension of their verses; for all were very young when they wrote the poems I discuss here. Despite their youth and the questions of identity that accompany it, these three poets created complex kinds of mimesis and complex relationships between imitation and identity in their different approaches to English verse.

In varying degrees, Kasiprasad, Madhusudan, and Carshore were also implicated in the literary and educational institutions represented by Richardson: Kasiprasad published in the *Calcutta Literary Gazette* and in Richardson's annuals; Mary Carshore was reviewed (not very favorably) by D.L.R.; and Madhusudan studied under Richardson at Hindu College. Yet none of the three, except Madhusudan in his early poetry, exhibited the kind of exilic lament common to the men who, like Richardson, served in the Bengal Army or in the East India Company's service. Instead, set apart by ethnicity or religion or language or gender or some combination of these, each poet needed to remake English language verse at an oblique angle to the centers of colonial power.

Kasiprasad Ghosh (1809–1873), an exact contemporary of Derozio but also his student at Hindu College, published *The Sháïr; and Other Poems* in 1830. In the preface to his volume, Kasiprasad described himself as the "first Hindu who has ventured to publish a volume of English Poems." From 1846 through 1857, Kasiprasad published a weekly newspaper, the *Hindu Intelligencer,* and he contributed poems to Richardson's *Bengal Annual* and to his anthology of British poetry. Kasiprasad's younger contemporary Michael Madhusudan Dutt (1824–1873) likewise studied at Hindu College, but under Richardson, who by the time of Michael's matriculation was principal of the college. Although Michael was one of the more interesting Indian poets in English in the nineteenth century, his lasting importance rests on his position as the outstanding writer of vernacular Bangla poetry in midcentury. I parallel Michael with his contemporary Mary Seyers Carshore (1829–1857), the daughter of an East India Company official. As far as I can determine, Carshore was the only woman of British parentage who lived her entire life in India in the nineteenth century and published a volume of poetry. Her *Songs of the East,* published in Calcutta in 1855, was reviewed by Richardson shortly before her death at Jhansi during the uprising of 1857.

Kasiprasad, Michael Madhusudan, and Carshore were differently situated with respect to British institutions and to new global technologies of publishing and distribution. Like Derozio and Roberts, each found the possibilities for poetry both generated and constrained by social location, access to education, and the colonial distribution of power. Whereas Kasiprasad Ghosh and Mary Carshore seem to have felt firmly tied to their natal shores—despite the obstacles to their success in English verse—Michael Madhusudan in his youth identified more strongly with Britain, though such an identification was both temporary and a mixed blessing.

Like Derozio and Roberts, Kasiprasad, Michael Madhusudan, and Mary Cashore engaged with a polyglot cultural moment. And for them it was also a moment of important developments in the technologies of printing and global communication. While each of these poets wrote some fine English verse, neither their achievements nor their failures can be understood apart from the complex literary culture they, differentially, shared. I agree with Rosinka Chaudhuri that attributing failure to Ghosh or Michael Dutt as English language poets elides their significant "engagement with colonial rule, an engagement that was problematic and marginal, but which, in its foreshadowing of an indigenous liberal, secular consciousness, would be ultimately subversive" (*Gentlemen,* 80).[2] For the modern reader, Kasiprasad Ghosh and Madhusudan Dutt have at least the advantage of being understood and discussed in the context of Indian or Bengali nationalism; Carshore remains virtually unknown. Taken together, these three poets represent the possibilities and the challenges of making English language verse in mid-nineteenth-century India.

Colonial Mimesis, Gendered Mimicry, and Poetic Exercise

If imitation is the sincerest form of flattery, we know in our hearts that virtually all flattery—even flattery we might take to be sincere—is best understood through a filter that assumes it to be less genuine than it appears. Let the poet who imitates and the critic who describes the imitation beware. In the wake of Franz Fanon, Homi Bhabha, and V. S. Naipaul, moreover, it is impossible to think of imitation, or mimesis, or mimicry in the colonial context apart from postmodern understandings of the subject. I evoke here, necessarily, Bhabha's definition(s) of mimicry: that complex function of discipline in the Foucauldian sense, of regulation, and of recalcitrance. Bhabha speaks of mimicry as a "secret act of revenge" and allies it with the transgressive mimicry of the "missing person," the creation of the minor or minority (*Location,* 55–63, 86). Here I make use of this notion of mimicry, but I argue that such ideas cannot be deployed only to describe the texts of the "colonized." It is not always easy, as we see in the cases of Henry Page or Derozio, to say who in fact is "colonized." Moreover, I read mimicry, following the work of Luce Irigaray (who in turn relies on Karen Horney and Simone de Beauvoir), as arising in situations of domination/subordination, of which gender subordination is a cardinal instance. So, for Irigaray, women become "women" in a process of mimesis. Mimicry, in Bhabha's sense of recalcitrant repetition, must be traced as a function of domination along more than one vector.

Finally, in addition to the "mimicry" of racial/cultural subordination and of gender, there was within literary culture at this period a further element of subordination, bringing with it a further impulsion toward recalcitrant mimesis. For as literary culture moved from a patronage to a commodity economy, the poet's work became allied to the affective realm and thus feminized. As a result, male poets in the metropole made "defensive" claims to power (for example, Shelley's unacknowledged legislators, Arnold's masculinist poetics, and the invention of the term *poetess*). These male claims to poetic power operated within a discourse that feminized all poets.[3]

Although poets in the metropole came to negotiate poetry within the discourses of feminization and compensatory masculinity, poets in India found themselves in complex relations to these discourses. Female poets writing in English, all of whom were of British extraction in the first two-thirds of the century, were doubly feminized or subordinated—by gender and by vocation. Men who *identified* themselves with India were already feminized by the tropes of colonial/racial subordination (for example, the Bengali babu and the East Indian), but they worked within local cultures that had no use or need for the British and American discourse feminizing poetry. In sum, the mimicry of race or of ethnicity or of cultural authority among the poets I discuss was not always obvious but operated differentially. Moreover, gendered mimicry was as important as the colonial mimicry of the colonized, and the colonial poet who imitated the feminized metropolitan poet was subject to a metropolitan masculinist critique.

At the same time, men educated in Indian English-medium schools were brought up within a larger cultural ethos that emphasized public performance of poetry (in Persian, Sanskrit, and vernacular literate traditions, as well as in purely oral popular traditions). Their English language schooling further equated intellectual accomplishment with poetic performance. In 1829, for example, the Bengali press *(Samachar Chandrika)* covered the public examination and prize presentations for Hindu College and recounted by name the students accomplished in the recitation of English poetry. By the newspaper's count, twenty-eight students participated in the recitation; a further public prize-giving involved recitation of Shakespeare.[4] Such proceedings were typical and were considered crucial to a boy's literary, rhetorical, and linguistic training.

In addition to colonial mimicry and actual performance, the colonial poetic text had a third element of imitation. Here I want to distinguish between imitation and mimicry, though recognizing that such a distinction is more heuristic than absolute. Each of the poets I discuss engaged in imitation as a form of poetic affiliation and engaged in mimicry as a form of recalcitrance, often in the same text.[5] We could think of this as a kind of layered mimesis.

For making poetry, imitation is crucial. Poets may be born, but their verses are, at least at the beginning, stolen. And so imitation among these three young poets was often a matter of setting themselves imitative exercises in verse. Like Derozio, they exhibited their debts in paratexts (epigraphs, dedications, and footnotes) and in their choice of verse forms. Their choices of form, along with the themes and topoi they addressed, tell us much about the scene of colonial writing. Kasiprasad, Madhusudan, and Carshore establish differing poetic identities through differing modes and objects of imitation. Kasiprasad Ghosh creates an implicit argument for the virtues of Hindu religious and ethnic identity through prosodic experiment; Madhusudan Dutt, worshipping at the shrine of Wordsworth and Milton, re-creates the possibility of Indian epic but under the sign of a romantic reading of Christian epic; Mary Carshore remakes the masculine discourse of exile by establishing a profoundly local poetics that functions at once as domestic and a questioning of the domestic.

Youthful Virtuosity: Kasiprasad Ghosh's *The Sháïr; and Other Poems*

Kasiprasad Ghosh matriculated at Hindu College in 1821 and nine years later published *The Sháïr and Other Poems.* As Rosinka Chaudhuri has noted, we do not know many details of Kasiprasad's life; my discussion here builds upon her work in *Gentlemen Poets* and scattered information about his later views. As Chaudhuri argues, Ghosh's poems imitated the orientalist practices of his time, from their subject matter to their learned footnotes. She cites Henry Meredith Parker's "Draught of Immortality," Horace Hayman Wilson's translations, and Sir William Jones's hymns as particularly important influences on Kasiprasad, and she notes, as well, that Kasiprasad (like Derozio) deployed the topoi of the bardic harp (*Gentlemen,* 71–77).

Kasiprasad was a student during Derozio's youthful teaching career, but one suspects, given their identical age, that he would have regarded Derozio more as peer than mentor. Clearly, the two poets shared common reading, yet Kasiprasad was less inclined than Derozio to direct his curiosity toward Europe. He was more interested in making English language verse answer to his situation as the son of a fairly traditional Brahmin family. His verse, like Derozio's, responds to the tropes of bardic nationalism and to the conventions of British eighteenth-century and romantic poetry. But while Derozio builds a protonationalist discourse from the elements of Enlightenment skepticism, Kasiprasad creates a defense of Indian culture through metrical experimentation.

Whatever his differences from Derozio, Kasiprasad shared with him an unapologetic approach to the apology. Both of them performed well the aspiring poet's apologia, a ritual repetition of humility that simultaneously stakes out poetic territory. The volume I discuss here, *The Sháïr; and Other Poems* (1830), was Kasiprasad's only book of English poetry. The volume consists of a preface; "The Sháïr" (a poem of nearly eighty pages at the beginning of the volume); nearly fifty pages of short verses appearing in the middle and at the end of the volume; and a series of eleven poems on Hindu festivals, plus accompanying notes. Both the paratexts and the poetic texts of Ghosh's volume engage the colonial scene through mimesis in its several senses.

The preface, the dedications, and the notes to *The Sháïr* create a paratextual apparatus through which the poet "places" himself, entering the world of English belles lettres by exploiting its tropes and conventions. First, in his brief preface, the author performs the role of Indian poet writing in English, which he and Derozio—differently—pioneered. He takes up the position of the colonial subject seeking and acknowledging the support of the British authorities. Then, with wonderful chutzpah, he takes on the discourses of orientalism and creates himself, despite his youth, as an authority in this realm. We might regard the preface and his other paratexts—dedications and notes—as a species of auto-orientalism, a particularly adept version of the performance of orientalist poetics. For Kasiprasad, the performance of orientalist poetics was, perforce, also a performance of identity.

The preface, dedications, and notes to *The Sháïr* all show us the poet "placing himself" for the reader, acknowledging his difference from the expected. I reproduce the first paragraph of the preface here in its entirety:

> In publishing this small volume of Poems, the Author, though apprehensive of making any general apologies, deems it still necessary to premise briefly

> and simply, that being the first Hindu who has ventured to publish a volume of English Poems; and having received his education at the Anglo-Indian College of Calcutta, in English only, among the other languages of Europe which are taught along with it as essential for the acquirement of the recondite learning of the West; the Author is perfectly conscious of the imperfections which must have occurred in this little work, but for which a sufficient plea will, he hopes, be proved in the circumstances just before mentioned.

This elaborate hypotactic sentence, the most Latinate of English syntax, does exceptionally well what prefatory apologies always do: it demonstrates that, while obligatory, no apology is in fact necessary. If "the Author" deems it necessary to "premise" his identity "briefly and simply," it is true that the apology is more brief than simple. The piling up of clauses and phrases on "this little work" has the effect of making a modest apology and a large claim. In fact, though the author does not claim to have studied "the other languages of Europe . . . essential for the acquirement of the recondite learning of the West," his English prose is syntactically recondite and promises learning enough to bolster any "small volume of Poems." Moreover, the author tells us that he is "the first Hindu who has ventured to publish a volume of English Poems," and thus he claims a space for a new subject position, a new poetry, a new poetics. Moreover, he claims to be not the first *Indian* poet in English, which would raise the awkward question of how to place his friend Derozio, but rather the "first Hindu" poet publishing a volume in English. This distinction is not merely semantic; it constitutes an implicit claim for the cultural and religious significance of Kasiprasad's series of poems on Hindu festivals. At the same time, it provides an unsettling context for the volume's title poem.

The basic story of "The Sháïr" is a simple one, but its emplotment involves formal overdetermination, even multiplication. First, the poem hovers generically between the Oriental verse tale (as practiced by Moore, and Byron, and Southey) and the narrative frame that constitutes an excuse for inset lyrics (as practiced by Landon). Second, in "The Sháïr" we are introduced to three poets. An unnamed poetic narrator, whom the dedications ask us to identify as Kasiprasad himself, introduces and dedicates each canto; his story is taken up by a Persian bard, or "sháïr," named Hassan, who takes his love, Zeeran, into a grove. There he tells her the story of "the Sháïr" (the poet) and his love, Amrita (divine ambrosia, nectar of the gods). In other words, the poem involves three poets (two characters and a voice). The narrative itself—unlike the orientalist narratives of Southey, Byron, and Moore—is not an adventure but an allegory. Though it is certainly not brilliant verse (I will refrain from quoting the more bathetic lines), "The Sháïr" attempts a complex iteration, a mimesis of mimesis.

The uneasy iterations of both the title poem and the volume as a whole are indicated in its multiple intertexts and dedications and even in the poet's preface to the volume. Having told us in the first paragraph of his preface that he is the "first Hindu" to publish a volume of English verse in India, the poet goes on in the second paragraph to explain the title of the volume and its longest poem. He had intended a different name for his text:

> The original title of the first poem in the book, was "The Minstrel;" but the Author having observed that persons wholly unacquainted with it, upon hearing its name only, mistook it for an imitation of some English poem of the same name, such as Dr. Beattie's "Minstrel;" he subsequently altered and called it by its present title "The Sháïr," the Persian term for a minstrel or a bard, and the reason of his adopting the Persian word is, that Hassan, who narrates the poem, is a Mussulman, and therefore calls the Hero of it a Sháïr or a bard.

Thus, the poet who disclaims in the first paragraph of his preface a knowledge of other European languages than English, all the while demonstrating his competence with Latinate syntax, in the second paragraph disclaims affiliation with bardic nationalism only to reclaim that as well. His poem is not "an imitation of some English poem of the same name." Indeed. It is, rather, an imitation of various English poems with various names that play on the bardic trope.

Even as Kasiprasad's preface provides an interesting imitation of bardic nationalism and commentary on this imitation, his other paratexts—dedications and footnotes—establish a complex web of intertexts and claim a unique space for poetic performance. In a profusion of dedications the poet commends the volume as a whole and then each of the three cantos of the title poem. These dedications acknowledge obligatory debts and create a web of affiliation. The volume as a whole is dedicated by permission to "The Right Honorable Lord W. C. Bentinck . . . Governor General of India" by "His Lordship's Most Obedient Servant The Author." This obligatory dedication is a good match for Emma Roberts's dedication of her Calcutta volume to Lady Bentinck; for each poet, the dedication appears as a sign, not so much of "obedience" as of access.[6] Kasiprasad's further dedications in the volume are more personal than this one and mark his literary debts and affiliations.

Canto 1 of "The Sháïr" is prefaced by a dedication to Horace Hayman Wilson, who had suggested to Kasiprasad that he write a reply to James Mill's history of India (as a member of the board of Hindu College, Wilson had encouraged both Kasiprasad and Derozio). Not only had Wilson defended Derozio from alarmed parents, but his enthusiasm for books and learning also served as encouragement to Kasiprasad. From 1811, Wilson had been secretary of the Asiatic Society of Bengal; he had translated Kālidāsa's *Meghaduta* (*The Cloud Messenger,* 1813); and published in 1827 *Select Specimens of the Theatre of the Hindus.* In 1830 when Kasiprasad published *The Sháïr,* Wilson was on the eve of issuing a revised edition of his *Sanskrit-English Dictionary* (1831). In evoking Wilson on the very first page of his volume, then, Kasiprasad is at once acknowledging a British mentor and evoking Sanskrit learning. Interestingly, he does not praise Wilson or even address him directly but instead takes a page from Derozio's book as he commences:

To Horace Hayman Wilson, Esq.

Harp of my country! Pride of yore!
Whose sweetest notes are heard no more!
O! give me once to touch thy strings,
Where tuneful sweetness ever clings.
Though hands that far superior were
Once waked the sleeping sweetness there;
Yet if my scanty skill can make
One note, however faint, awake,
My weak endeavour will not be
In vain;—'tis all I wish from thee.

(*The Sháïr*, 1)

Here the poet acknowledges Wilson by nodding toward Wilson's translations of great Sanskrit poetry; then he takes up the bardic harp.

Kasiprasad's address to the harp evokes Derozio and, beyond Derozio, British poetic tradition. A similar allusion occurs on the volume's title page, where Kasiprasad takes an epigraph from the beginning of Byron's *Childe Harold's Pilgrimage:* "Nor mote my shell awake the weary Nine, / To grace so plain a tale—this lowly lay of mine." Through his dedication and through the romantic trope of the harp, Kasiprasad engages the orientalist notion that India's poetic grandeur lay in the past. The poetry of *The Sháïr* at once affirms and refutes this problematic idea.

Bardic nationalism shapes the paratexts even beyond the first canto of "The Sháïr." The second and third cantos of the title poem, likewise, have their dedicatees: James Young for the second and Henry Meredith Parker for the third. The dedication to Parker evokes Parker's poems from *The Draught of Immortality* (1827), particularly his lyric sequence "The Indian Day." The allusion to Parker leads the poet to reiterate the trope of the dejected bard but to combine that trope with an allegory of poetry and nation. Beginning the third canto of "The Sháïr," Kasiprasad hails the setting sun, which lights the waves of the Ganges as a lotus folds its petals on the waters. He likens the lotus to a young widow dressed in a white sari who, at evening, lets down her hair. The image at once alludes to Parker's poetry and prefigures the death of the Sháïr in canto 3. It perhaps even creates a personification of India.[7] In canto 3, the Sháïr, like his lover in the previous cantos, dies; he flings himself from a cliff in the manner of Sappho (Landon's Sappho and Derozio's version of Landon's Sappho):

He sung how in his wild despair,
        Bidding adieu to life and woe,
The bard himself had plunged where
        The ocean's heaving billows flow.

(54)

The Sapphic bard owes much to Landon's abandoned women. But in the image of the lotus as widow, the bard also figures India through Hindu ritual. This is recalcitrant mimesis indeed. By the poem's end, precursor poets and poetry have drowned themselves. If the harp of India is the "pride of yore," the young Indian poet is the position of both lamenting and reviving the past.[8]

This double task of lamenting and reviving the past, of acknowledging and disavowing debts, is forwarded in the endnotes and footnotes as well as in the dedications and preface of Kasiprasad's volume. Many of the poems in the volume are accompanied by such notes, which serve to establish the poet's credentials as an orientalist and as a Hindu poet. It is not surprising, then, that the most substantial notes are attached to the sequence on Hindu festivals and to a short poem, "The Viná." The notes to the former, forty-four of them, run to more than twenty pages of small type. They are addressed, like the poem's dedications, to "the European reader" (189). More than half the notes seem to address a European reader who does not reside in India, for they explain matters that would be common knowledge to any resident of the subcontinent. For example, the poet notes that almost all Hindu festivals take place "on the days of the Hindu lunar year, which commences from the new moon of the month of Baisákh (April, May)" (189). Later, the poet provides geographical notes, such as this one: "The *Yamuná,* or as it is called by foreigners the Jumna, washes the borders of *Vrindavána,* or Brindabund, situated on the west side of the river.—Vide Hamilton's Gazetteer, page 151. The place is celebrated as the scene of the youthful sports of KRISHNA, with the GOPIS or milk-maids, which are generally too well known to the European community to require a description by the translation of the Songs of JAYADEVA by Sir William Jones" (192). This note is addressed first to the European reader and then to European orientalists. Similarly addressing the learned, Kasiprasad glosses an allusion to Kama by reference to Wilson's quotation of Jones's hymn in the footnotes to Wilson's translation of *The Cloud Messenger.* The *Asiatic Researches* are liberally referenced throughout.

Moreover, as we see in the note about the Yamuna, Kasiprasad regularly uses diacritics in his transliterations. This practice confirms for his readers Kasiprasad's orientalist learning and, I would imagine, reflects his training in Sanskrit, which had begun by the time he published this volume.[9] Kasiprasad's diacritics have the effect of claiming native scholarly knowledge.[10] In the notes, then, as in the prefaces and dedication to the volume, Kasiprasad at once acknowledges debts and seeks to establish his authority—most particularly his authority as a "Hindu poet."[11]

Internal evidence suggests that the title poem in the volume was written before the poems on Hindu festivals, for the management of tropes and versification is less skilled than in the later poems. "The Sháïr" raises questions about mimicry and imitation through the central figure of the bard—questions that, I argue below, are much more elegantly resolved in the poems on Hindu festivals. The beginning of canto 3 of "The Sháïr" figures poetry as a widow in white, a lotus in the Ganges, and the trope returns at the very end of the poem, which features a lament for the abandoned harp. Given that three poets figure in the narrative, precisely who takes up the harp here is not clear. The poet Hassan recounts the Sháïr's liebestod, which ends with praise of Ganga, or the Ganges (a metonymy of India), in these lines:

Where many sacred rivers lave
  Full many a wood or mountain green;
Where pines and citrons towering wave
  In rural grandeur—stately scene!
Land of the Gods and lofty name;
  Land of the fair and beauty's spell;
Land of the bards of mighty fame;
  My native land! for e'er farewell!

(69)

The poet Hassan then comments,

So tender is a poet's soul
It cannot brook the world's controul.
'Tis like the fragrant lotus white
Expanding full to fancy's light

(73)

The lotus, "tender, sweetest," cannot bear the ruthless power of the storm and is "pitilessly snapped away" (74). Finally, it is either Hassan or the poet's own voice that concludes in a final stanza commemorating the harp. Here the harp has become a "vin," or vina, hanging on an unnamed tree. But sadly, the instrument is entwined with (British?) ivy and eaten by a (Bengali?) worm:

Here ends my long and mournful tale
Of him who lived beside that vale.
There see his Vin is hanging by
    The mountain's lonely brow
And, Time and Air as o'er it fly,
    Is sadly mouldering now.

. . . .

The envious ivy's ringlets twine
Around the Vin of note divine.
The worm has formed his little cell
Where tuneful sweetness loved to dwell!

(77)

This mix of imagery owes a great deal to British poetry.[12] It also implies that the vina is a synecdoche for the book itself. If India is the woman and the river, the lotus and the stream, and if the harp or vina is metonymically the spirit of poetry, then the poet is left in a difficult place. He must reverse the destruction of the ivy and the worm. The young poet must play at once the vina and the harp.

The series of eleven poems on Hindu festivals is Ghosh's attempt to reverse the vina's decay, to rescue the harp from silence. The paratexts connected to the poems on Hindu festivals are the vehicles for this double voicing. They at once apologize and construct. In the general preface to the volume, in the table of contents, and in the endnotes to the poems, the young poet mimes the poetic neophyte and the accomplished Hindu scholar and prosodist.

The poems on Hindu festivals are discussed at the end of the author's preface after his apology and his defense of the volume's title. At the end of the preface, Ghosh describes the circumstances in which he wrote the Hindu festivals:

> The Author's motive of [for] writing the "Hindu Festivals," almost all the principal ones of which will be found in the subsequent pages of this volume, is nothing else but this: Being one day in conversation with a friend on the subject of publishing his poems, he was suggested [spoken to about] the importance and utility of writing something by way of national poetry; and having then no other Indian subject at hand which he could make a choice of, but the Hindu Festivals; an account of which he had promised to write for the Calcutta Literary Gazette; he versified them into small pieces of poetry, which were published in that journal. Some additions to, and alterations in them, have been afterwards made while these pages were in the course of printing.[13]

This paragraph appears on a verso sheet (ii) facing the table of contents on the recto. The contents page lists the poems in the festivals series by number and with only the transliterated Sanskrit names—"Dasabará," "Rás Yátrá," and so forth. The English subtitles appear only with the texts. The poet's account of the offhand and occasional nature of these poems is belied not only by the admission that they have been revised and supplemented for book publication but also by his bilingual strategy. He performs the work of apology only to redefine the bard—establishing himself in the process as a maker and a scholar.

Ghosh's poems on Hindu festivals incorporate the traditions of orientalist verse, but at an oblique angle. For all that he calls them "small pieces of poetry," in practice he seeks to transmute the tropes of a predominantly Christian British verse. Chaudhuri both cites and critiques Lotika Basu's argument that Ghosh's poetry is merely an employment of conventional epithets "out of sympathy" with Indian institutions; instead, Chaudhuri identifies "cultural and intellectual commerce that underlies Kasiprasad's verse, which was one of the earliest manifestation of such transactions in the history of colonial India" (*Gentlemen,* 79). The coin of this transaction was poetic form.

If we attend to these poems' forms, we can see a very young poet (Kasiprasad was a mere twenty-one years old at the time of the volume's publication) attempting a kind of poetic tour de force. The poems create a calendar of the Bengali religious year.[14] Each poem takes its own form, betraying the young author's study of Murray's handbook to prosody.[15] The first poem is in iambic tetrameter couplets; the second, in alternating stanzas of iambic and trochaic meter; the third, in stanzas of eight iambic lines rhyming *aaabcccb,* with a repeating reversed foot in lines one and five; the fourth poem, in Spenserian stanza; the fifth, in common meter; and so on. Such stanzaic variety constitutes a virtuoso performance, and while not all the sections work equally well, the fourth poem, "Janmáshtami, or Janma Yátrá festival in commemoration of the birth of Krishna, and number ten, "Káli Pujá," are worth special notice.

In "Janmáshtami," the Spenserian stanza looks in two directions—toward Spenser and early modern English poetics and also toward the revival of the form by Byron in *Childe Harold,* Keats in "The Eve of St. Agnes," and Shelley in *The Revolt of Islam* and "Adonais." In applying the Spenserian stanza to Krishna's birth, the poet may be referring as well to Milton's "Ode on the Morning of Christ's Nativity." Ghosh evokes the most elaborate of English stanzaic forms and the tropes of the Christian nativity pastoral to celebrate Krishna's advent. Stanza three, for example, reads:

> But hark! what noise invades the peaceful ear?
> What shouts and joyful acclamations rise?
> Why sounds of cymbals, drums, and pipes appear
> As if to rend the vault of yonder skies?
> Why should the people with astonished eyes
> Crowd to the place where Nanda doth reside?
> Why many a learned, holy sage there hies
> Whose wealth is prayer and virtue is whose guide?
> 'Tis Krishna born to crush the demons and their pride.
>
> (136)

As if to underline the parallel yet claim pride of place for Vaishnava piety, the next stanza describes the god as "power supreme revealed on earth, / In mortal dress" (136). Demons, not unlike the demons in Milton's hymn, shrink from the news. Then, to seal the likeness between nativity stories, we are told,

> Look, look how beautiful! The new-born boy
> Reclines upon its mother's cautious arm,
> 'Like young Hope resting in the breast of Joy.'

Finally, the poem ends on a prophetic note, for the wicked "king of demons foul" will "even like a meteor from its blazing state, . . . fall to nothing" by the hand "Of Vishnu great and Bhagavati's high command" (138). The poem is dated December 19, 1829, while the other poem about the baby Krishna, number seven (which commemorates "the swinging of Krishna in the cradle while a child"), is dated January 4, 1830, just before Epiphany, and is a songlike tribute to the young god, to those who tend him, and to attendant nature. Clearly, Ghosh varies the stanza structure in these poems to create decorum of theme and form.

A similar performative effect is obvious in poem ten, "Káli Pujá; or Syáma Pujá, a festival in honour of Kali or Syama, an emanation from the head of Durga and the goddess of war." The poem is in quatrains rhyming *abab;* their meter is a variation of anapestic trimeter alternating with anapestic dimeter. (I read the poem as anapestic though Ghosh adds an initial unaccented syllable at the head of each line.) I quote here the first and last stanzas:

> Most terrible Power! surrounding thee dance
> The direful disasters of war;
> Like lightning terrific thy ominous glance
> Doth pierce through the heart from afar.
>
> . . . .
>
> O! thou art all darkness, delusion and dread,
> Great Káli! most terrible Power!
> Thou hast sprung from the beautiful Párvati's head
> When wrath on her forehead did lower.[16]
>
> (155, 157)

Here Kali, an emanation of Durga (who is especially important in the religious practice of West Bengal), appears in what is clearly designed to be a martial meter.

"Káli Pujá" is the penultimate poem in the series and contrasts with the poems that precede and follow it. The preceding poem, "Jhulana Yátrá," celebrates Krishna's "gambols" with the gopīs, and the last poem in the series, "Ashayá Tritiyá," imagines the beginning of creation and the "commencement of the Satya Yuga or golden age." These two poems, flanking the martial celebration of Kali, contrast with the Kali poem in form, metrical realization, and tone.

The "Jhulana Yátrá," as befits its erotic theme, draws upon Persian tropes for love (bulbuls and roses), but it is dated, interestingly, December 25, 1829, further emphasizing for an English-speaking audience Krishna's religious significance. The poem lacks the emotional immediacy of Vaishnava devotional verse, but it attempts to bring together the lyric impulse of Krishna's love play with a stately religious resonance. This distinction from Vaishnava tradition may also reflect Ghosh's understanding of the disjunction between the devotion represented in the rasa līlā and the straightlaced

Christianity of colonial Calvinists. For an English-speaking audience, Ghosh diminishes the erotic core of this traditional subject in favor of a more generalized claim to religious power.

I quote here the last two stanzas to show how Ghosh's versification achieves these goals. In stanza four, the poet deliberately plays with reversed feet at the beginnings of lines to imitate the feel of Krishna swinging in the grove, while the final stanza returns to a more regular realization of the meter to establish a dignified closure.

IV

High on a throne of glittering gold,
    Beset with pearls and diamonds bright,
And borne by strings of wondrous mould,
    Hung from a vault of azure light;
Young Krishna proves his various love
    Unto the maids of lovely smiles,
And swinging gaily in that grove,
    The five bright nights in joy beguiles.

V

Soft music breathes her mellow note,
    As if it were a heavenly strain,
At midnight's solemn hour afloat,
    And kissing just this world of pain.
And sweeter songs are merrily sung,
    Than those by Kinnaur-chorus given,
As if in emulation flung
    To echo in great Indra's heaven.

(154–55)

The double quatrains in long meter are welded together not only by a rather elegant metrical realization but also by the assonance of the *b* and *d* rhymes in stanza four and the consonance of the *b* and *d* rhymes in stanza five. This acoustic complexity matches the rhetorical claims of the final stanza.

In one sense, Lotika Basu is right about Ghosh's poems; they are quite unlike Vaishnava poetry, for example, if we take that tradition to be an "Indian institution." But I would argue that however obliquely related these poetic forms are to "Indian institutions," Ghosh knew what he was about. His footnotes invoke the orientalist tradition; his prosodic experiments stretch well beyond even that. His effort was directed at presenting his audience with virtuoso performance of songs with markedly different meanings from traditional English verse. While Sir William Jones made multiple analogies between Indian, Greek, and European religious traditions, Ghosh is not content with analogy. Krishna is not the Indian Jesus; to the contrary, the poem suggests, by implication, that Jesus is the Christian Krishna.

The cumulative effect of Ghosh's poems is not finally to suggest an anthropological sort of interest in Hindu festivals and customs, a kind of auto-ethnography with a secular or at least a secularly self-critical basis. Nor is it, finally, I think, a kind of mimetic performance in which the Indian dancer puts on a costume for the Western observer. The poems may appear in this way—and even be introduced in this way in the author's preface—but the datelines and the versification here create a different kind of meaning as well, an excess of meanings made possible only through metrical performance. The whole tenor of the poems is one of high seriousness; the series re-creates through imitating English verse the author's religious values. That Ghosh is described a few years later by European writers as having "lapsed back into Hindu ways" (Roselli, 207) is not surprising.

Ghosh seems to have been, despite or in addition to his English education, firmly connected to Hindu religious tradition. Eventually he became persuaded that resistance to British efforts at "reform"—particularly related to women's education, child marriage, and widow remarriage—was central to maintaining one's identity and culture. A. F. Salahuddin Ahmed argues that Kasiprasad was one "whose conservatism was strengthened by English education" (197). And John Roselli, in his study of William Bentinck, shows that because of his religious scruples, Kasiprasad refused to accompany the governor on a tour of north India. Moreover, according to Ram Copal Sanyal, after publishing English language poetry in the *Bengal Hurkaru, John Bull,* the *Literary Gazette,* and other periodicals and founding the *Hindu Intelligencer,* the first English (but not bilingual) native paper, Kasiprasad nonetheless aligned himself with the Dharma Sabha. According to Sanyal, he "opposed female education, and the late Mr. Bethune found in him a stout opponent to his philanthropic efforts to ameliorate the condition of the Hindu woman. . . . [He] lent his ready pen against such social movements as the remarriage of widows and the suppression of polygamy." Sanyal goes on to characterize Kasiprasad as "an earnest advocate of his country's cause" who "never shrunk from exposing abuses and oppressions" (250–51). The poems on Hindu festivals, I would argue, are poetic evidence of the young poet's future political and cultural views.

Not that metropolitan reviewers or Calcutta commentators fully captured the subtlety of the young poet's work. Their job was complicated by the poet's inability to "edit" himself: some dreadful lines were allowed to see the light of day. Ghosh's volume was received in London through a filter of orientalist expectation, and it was praised in the Bengali press as an example of Indian success at the heart of the colonizer's language. Ghosh's layered mimesis, his imitations of English verse forms, and the often recalcitrant mimesis of his paratexts allowed critics to find what they would. And because his bad lines were so bad at the same time that his mimetic strategies were so subtle, his work was appreciated only for the most superficial reasons. Ghosh's poetry, with its layered and contradictory mimetic strategies, was illegible in its time.

Some metropolitan reviewers praised (and dismissed) Ghosh along the lines of Dr. Johnson's dancing dog—remarkable verse for a Hindu—while others were more objective and more generous. The *Athenaeum* faulted Ghosh for not being sufficiently "national"—a version of the criticism Richardson faced a few months later when British reviewers complained that the *Bengal Annual* was not sufficiently Indian.[17] In 1831, for example, the (London) *Literary Gazette* reviewed Ghosh's volume alongside Derozio's *Fakeer of Jungheera.* The reviewer derided both volumes for their imitativeness, which was merely a pastiche in the reviewer's mind of much better British orientalist poems: "Both these works are literary curiosities, as the productions of native East Indians. They are curious, however, only as regards their writers; for both oriental histories and oriental imagers, Sir W. Jones, Southey, and Moore, have already made familiar to English readers. Indeed it is from their works that our present aspirants have drawn their inspiration; and we are chiefly reminded with how much more grace and power the gorgeous fictions of the East have been before employed" (no. 746, May 7, 1831, 296). The reviewer went on to deride one of Kasiprasad's least happy metaphors and to proclaim that both his work and Derozio's should have been "inscribed to Moore," if gratitude were possible among poets. The reviewer seems to have overlooked the actual inscriptions, notes, and epigraphs plenteously employed by both poets, so eager was he to draw an unfavorable comparison between these new Indian writers and British orientalist poets.

A more sympathetic reviewer praised Ghosh in Parbury's *Asiatic Journal,* a London-based publication that nevertheless defined its audience globally, calling itself the *Asiatic Journal and Monthly Register for British and Foreign India, China and Australasia.* Despite his praise, the reviewer treated Ghosh with Johnsonian condescension:

> But a few years back, such a prodigy in literature, as a volume of English poems, written by a Hindu, printed at an Indian press, clothed not merely in the English language but in its genuine idiom, and displaying as large a share of accuracy and even elegance of composition, as many of our writers of verses can boast, whose productions find admission into albums and annuals, would have excited at least as much astonishment and interest as a camelopard, a pair of united twins, or even a Malay mermaid. If, in this age of changes and of wonders, such an event is not likely to provoke surprise and admiration, none who take an interest in the welfare of our Hindu fellow-subjects can fail to experience pleasure in finding that the Hindu mind is apt to receive the seeds of European learning, and that, by the strenuous efforts of our Indian government, English literature is likely to take permanent root amongst the natives of Hindustan.[18]

It is curious that although Ghosh declares himself in his preface to be writing a national poetry and although he takes up the vina in an assertion of national or protonational cultural power, the reviewer misses the point.

Parbury's reviewer praises Ghosh's technical accomplishments but overlooks the subject matter of Hindu festivals: "The diction is easy and fluent; the rhyme is seldom defective; the pauses are often musical; the construction is almost always regular, and even in the higher attributes of poetry, the thoughts and sentiments, there is often a justness and boldness, which show that the author's understanding is of no mean rank" (105). Ghosh's metrical skill, however, is marred in this reviewer's mind by the fact that he has modeled his work on "the namby-pamby compositions, which the complaisance of public taste suffers to be dignified with the name of poetry. We have no doubt, that after a diligent course of application to the true models of English poetry,—the authors who deserve to be called our classics,—Kasiprasad Ghosh will be competent to take a station much above those writers whom he seems to imitate" (106).

Here, then, is the panoply of critical premises encountered by a young Indian poet in metropolitan reviews. First, there is condescension—that an Indian can indeed write English poetry at all is prodigious, or might once have been thought prodigious. Second is misreading or reading around implications of such English poetry—the Hindu festivals are ignored, "The Sháïr" is (rightly) found imitative. Third, the poet is dragged into the gendered discourses of English literary culture—he has mistakenly enrolled in the "namby-pamby" school of English poetry. As Steven Jones has shown, by 1830 this "school" was being satirized as the school of Wordsworth; Francis Jeffrey and others had come to diminish the "Lakers," as Byron called them, by linking them to eighteenth-century satires against the original Namby Pamby (Ambrose Phillips). Thus Ghosh is implicated in what Stevens calls the culture wars of the first half of the nineteenth century. He is said (with little basis, as far as I can see) to have aligned himself with sentiment, with feminized and infantilized verse. One imagines that his identity as a Bengali babu was enough, in itself, to feminize him in the eyes of metropolitan reviewers.

Reviews of Ghosh's work in Calcutta were more positive. The *Calcutta Literary Gazette* observed in a long biographical piece accompanied by a portrait that his volume was characterized by "richness of fancy and harmony of meter." The *Gazette* did note, however, in summarizing the London critics that they were "naturally astonished at the general purity and accuracy of our poet's English" (November 1, 1834, 278–79). Even before his volume was published, the Bangla newspaper *Samachar Chandrika* commented that Ghosh's poetry—forthcoming as a volume—should acquire "unprecedented fame"; like the London papers but with a celebratory rather than a condescending tone, the paper observed that Ghosh's work takes on the toughest challenge in English—writing excellent poetry. For them, perhaps, the virtuosic quality of *The Sháïr* was clear.[19]

Although the London reviews might characterize it as dangerously imitative of namby-pamby poetry, Ghosh's volume took on imitation in a much more complex way than this. In the context of Ghosh's declared intention of writing "something by way of a national poetry," the poems show us deliberate acts of appropriation and imitation, mimicry of the English Oriental tale, imitation of prosodic models, and something else—the recalcitrant mimesis of a young man's metrical tour de force. Ghosh's volume is not merely imitative, in a negative sense, though it is full of infelicities and poems that we should understand as juvenilia. Rather, the poet makes subtle rhetorical moves. His study of prosody paid off, not just in the skill of many of his lines but in the way his understanding of English language prosody allowed him to revise poetic tradition more broadly. The paratextual mimicry of the position of the colonized but educated poet—acknowledging his debts in various inscriptions and epigraphs—was matched by the imitation of English verse forms. This layered mimesis, combining subtle recalcitrance and overt imitation, made Kasiprasad's poetry a curiosity for the metropolitan reader and an exemplum in the Bangla press. For the "postcolonial reader," I would argue, the double voicings of Kasiprasad's verse can be read against the grain of his volume's paratexts and against the grain of the volume's reception. The "Hindu Festivals" are a tour de force in more ways than one.

The Futility of Anglophilia: Michael Madhusudan Dutt

In the year that Kasiprasad Ghosh published *The Sháïr*, Madhusudan Dutt was six years old and Mary Seyers was an infant. Madhusudan was born in 1824 in a village near Jessore, Bengal (now in Bangladesh). Mary Seyers, later Mary Carshore, was born to Irish Catholic parents in Calcutta in 1829. About the time she reached her teens, Seyers's family left the city for the North West Provinces and then went to live in Fatehpur in what is now Uttar Pradesh, where her father was an official of the East India Company administering revenues of the opium trade. At roughly the same time, Madhusudan's father, and then his whole family, moved to Calcutta, where Raj Narain practiced law. Each of these two poets could be understood, like Kasiprasad, as a "first": Michael was the first modern Bangla poet—eventually—and Mary Carshore the first woman born of British parents in India to publish a volume of verse. But such descriptions do not capture the complexity of their circumstances. Michael, like Kasiprasad Ghosh, was situated obliquely with respect to the dominant linguistic and economic institutions of his time; as a woman and a Catholic, Mary Seyers was, at least with respect to education, still further outside of the linguistic arena that provided the context for Indian English verse.

The cultural, political, and religious climate of India shifted significantly between the publication of Derozio's (1827, 1828) and Ghosh's volumes of verse (1830) and the publication of Michael Madhusudan's (1849) and Mary Carshore's (1855), and it was to shift again with the uprising of 1857. The rise of the evangelical party within the British establishment caused a concomitant growth in Christian evangelical piety in India. From founders of the Baptist mission in Serampore to a second generation, from the large number of freethinkers to increased piety among the officers and the civilians in the British establishment, from the cooperation of Moravians and Baptists to the increasing influence of the Free Church of Scotland, the evangelical influence became more pervasive, more conservative, more outspoken, and more middle class. The rhetorical gestures of the radicals Whigs and freethinkers—the emphasis on "liberty" and the spread of English values and ideas, especially freedom of thought and speech—became for the most part only ritual gestures. The evangelical party in

Michael Madhusudan Dutt, with a portrait of Milton. Painting, n.d.

England, as exemplified in William Wilberforce and Thomas Babington Macaulay's father, Zachary, had agitated for the abolition of slavery—and of sati—in similar terms. But with the outlawing of the British slave trade and then of slavery in British colonies and with Bentinck's prohibition of sati in 1829, the rhetoric of freedom was for British evangelicals attached to no particular goal. Although U.S. slavery was still abhorred (Lincoln would issue the Emancipation Proclamation in 1863), the issue had less salience in India than it might have had. Moreover, the political rhetoric of Byron or Shelley, which had focused on repression in England after the Peterloo Massacre (1819), diminished in importance. Other causes, in India and England, took shape, but they tended not to be argued in the Enlightenment language of liberty. For both Michael Madhusudan and Mary Carshore, the economic shakeout of the late 1820s and 1830s, the rise of evangelical religion among company servants and army officers, and the proliferation of print media created both obvious and subtle shifts in the literary landscape, as did the fluid condition of British poetry in this period.

Young poets such as Madhusudan and Carshore, who began writing in India in the 1840s, were two generations away from the orientalist poems of Sir William Jones and a generation away from Byron and his contemporaries—Keats died in 1821, Shelley in 1822, Felicia Hemans in 1835, and Landon in 1838. Yet all these influences were still felt in Indian English belletristic writing. Both Michael Madhusudan and Mary Carshore, from widely different educational and family backgrounds, sought with varying success to mold these influences to their own purposes as English language poets in India. Like Kasiprasad, they engaged in multiple mimetic strategies.

Paradoxically, it was not Carshore but Madhusudan whose early career was shaped by Anglophilia. Virtually every scholar of Indian English literature has read his youthful poem "I Sigh for Albion's Distant Shore":

> Father, mother, sister, all
> Do love me and I love them too
> Yet oft the tear-drops rush and fall
> From my sad eyes like winter's dew.
> And, oh! I sigh for Albion's strand
> As if she were my native land!
>
> (*Madhusūdana racanābalī*, 438)

Though Madhusudan had no sister, the meter of his plaint demanded one, and he supplied her—creating for himself a mimetic family. Despite this fabrication, Madhusudan's longing for England, as his translator Clinton Seely puts it, is "heartfelt." As Seely argues, it is as if Madhusudan "had two native lands, England and Bengal, emotionally as well as intellectually, though to date he had never left Bengal" (16). In 1841, when he wrote these lines, the poet was a seventeen-year-old student at Hindu College, imbibing the tradition of British poetry from David Lester Richardson, whom he much admired. Madhusudan is not simply expressing his heartfelt Anglophilia here; he is also echoing Richardson's own poetry of exile.

Indeed, Richardson's influence was so pervasive that Madhusudan took his teacher's departure from Hindu College very hard. In late 1842, Richardson took a leave of absence and subsequently sailed for London, and Madhusudan used his departure as yet another excuse for skipping classes. Like many another boy of his age, he vowed to skip school, writing to his best friend, Gour Bysack, on November 25, "I believe you recollect my once hinting to you of a resolution or rather desire of keeping away from college, during D. L. R.'s absence. Now I have made up my mind to do it, that is, I will not go to college until D. L. R.'s return, be it of whatever duration—I don't care. I have no great liking for any of my fellow collegians, except a few souls who love me, and whom I love;—and I hate the damned fellow Kerr [the vice principal who soon replaced Richardson]" (*Heart,* 28). Madhusudan reiterated these sentiments two days later, while asking Gour to return his copy of "Tom's" *Life of Byron* (that is, Thomas Moore's biography of Byron), which the two were then reading. At the same time, Madhusudan conceded that he missed his friends, and his resolution to skip school almost gave way to the desire for Gour's company. But then, later that evening, in another letter, he recounted a more serious cause for consternation—he was to be married.

Although child marriage, arranged by the children's parents, was the norm at this point among a certain class of Bengali Hindus, Madhusudan rebelled. Whether he resisted out of a desire for romance or a desire to travel abroad was is unclear. In a letter dated November 27, 1842, he informed Bysack that the prospect of marriage

> harrows up my blood and makes my hair stand like quills on the fretful porcupine! My betrothed is the daughter of a rich zemindar;—poor girl! What a deal of misery is in store for her in the ever-inexplorable womb of Futurity! You know my desire for leaving this country is too firmly rooted to be removed. The sun may forget to rise, but I cannot remove it from my heart. Depend upon it—in the course of a year or two more—I must either be in England or cease "to be" at all;—one of these must be done! (*Heart,* 33)

Madhusudan cast himself as an imprisoned Hamlet, his betrothed bidding fair to become Ophelia. This crisis seems, according to his biographers, to have precipitated Madhusudan's conversion to Christianity. Clinton Seely, in his introduction to Michael's epic, and Ghulam Murshid argue that Madhusudan came to believe seriously in the new religion he professed, but they speculate that he may also have believed that his conversion might produce from church officials some financial support for his study in England, a prospect that even in the 1840s was still highly unusual for Indians.[20] At any rate, shortly after this exchange with Gour, Madhusudan was baptized, resulting in a break with his family and most of his old friends and the necessity of withdrawing from Hindu College (which at the time admitted only Hindu students). Some months later, the poet enrolled at Bishop's College, with support from his father, with whom he had partially reconciled.

In the course of his education at these two institutions, and perhaps even earlier at another Calcutta academy or with a munshi near Jessore, Madhusudan learned Persian, followed by English, Latin, and Greek; he studied English at Hindu College along with Bangla (which, according to Murshid's biography, he did not take very seriously), then returned to the study of the Greek and Latin classics at Bishop's College. On leaving Bishop's College without completing his final examinations, possibly because of a quarrel with his father, Madhusudan moved to Madras, where in a letter to Gour he laid out an even more ambitious course of study, indicating, if not achievement in multiple classical and vernacular language, a strong sense that to be equipped for poetry (or schoolteaching, for that matter), one must master them.

He sketched out for Gour the ambitious program he intended to undertake to remake Bangla for great poetry: "I devote several hours daily to Tamil. My life is more busy than that of a school boy. Here is my routine: 6–8 Hebrew, 8–12 School [he was teaching at the Madras Orphan Asylum], 12–2 Greek, 2–5 Telugu and Sanskrit, 5–7 Latin, 7–10 English. Am I not preparing for the great object of embellishing the tongue of my fathers?" (August 18, 1849, *Heart*, 78). As Paula Richman has argued, Madhusudan gives evidence through these letters that even in Madras, where he published his book of English verse, he was considering shifting his poetic endeavors from English to Bangla.

Here, I would argue, Madhusudan was responding to the tepid Calcutta reception of his first book, which had just been published. In particular, he was responding to the famous advice forwarded to him by his friend Gour from John Drinkwater Bethune, president of the Council of Education (and sometime opponent of D.L.R.). On reading *The Captive Ladie*, Bethune declared that the poet should "employ his time to better advantage than in writing English poetry" (quoted in Seely, 26). Bethune went on to tell Madhusudan's friend Gour that Madhusudan's book of English poems was a neat exercise but fundamentally wrongheaded. Gour relayed the comments to his friend this way: "As an occasional exercise and proof of his proficiency in the language, such specimens may be allowed. But he could render far greater service to his country and have a better chance of achieving a lasting reputation for himself, if he will employ the taste and talents, which he has cultivated by the study of English, in improving the standard and adding to the stock of the poems of his own language, if poetry, at all events, he must write" (quoted in Seely, 26). Gour underlined Bethune's advice in terms that would have come home to his friend: "We do not want another Byron or another Shelley in English; what we lack is a Byron or a Shelley in Bengali literature" (quoted in Seely, 26–27).

This advice is often singled out as a famous turning point in the history of Bangla literature. Michael followed it to good account, writing the first sonnets in Bangla, followed by Bangla plays and then by long poems, most notably his famous epic, the *Meghanadavadha kavya (The Slaying of Meghanada).* Here I want to read Madhusudan's response to this advice backward, into his English poetry, as well as forward toward his Bangla epic.

It is important to remember that Gour challenged Madhusudan to become the "Byron or Shelley of Bengal"—a sobriquet even now liberally applied to Michael by literary Bengalis. And the advice was administered, like all their correspondence, in English. In this sense, Madhusudan's turn toward Bangla was framed, not cleanly, as a nationalist turn rejecting the colonizer's language, but as a strategic intervention in the literary scene. And the Bangla poetry itself, from the point of view of form, involved complex layers of mimesis. So did the English poetry.

Even in preparing himself to embellish the tongue of his fathers, Michael followed the example of the poets most admired by Richardson, whom he always referred to by his poetic signature, D.L.R. Clearly, Madhusudan was imbued with Richardson's taste: a great admiration for Milton and Wordsworth. Madhusudan's program of language study suggests that he wished to rival the learning of Milton. His enthusiasm for Milton, and for Wordsworth (another admirer of Milton), shaped both his self-imposed curriculum and his poetic practice in English and in Bangla. Milton's great learning and way of bringing that learning to bear on his verse clearly shaped Michael's desire to study—at once—Hebrew, Sanskrit, and Latin.[21]

Like Kasiprasad, Madhusudan developed his poetic sense, first in English and later in Bangla, through metrical imitation and experimentation. For him, Milton was a metrical model. As he later argued with respect to his Bangla poem *Tilottama sambhava kavya* (1860), he hoped to teach his Bengali readers a new tune. He wrote to a correspondent, "If your friends know English, let them read the *Paradise Lost,* and they will find how the verse, in which the Bengali poetaster writes, is constructed. The fact is, my dear fellow, that the prevalence of Blank Verse in this country is simply a question of time. Let your friends guide their voices by the pause (as in English blank verse) and they will soon swear this is the noblest measure in the language. My advice is Read, Read, Read. Teach your ears the new tune and then you will find out what it is" (*Madhusūdana racanābalī,* "Introduction," n.p.). Such exhortation is of a piece with his declaration that "the best writer of Blank Verse in English is the toughest of poets—mean old John Milton!" (*Madhusūdana racanābalī,* "Introduction," n.p.). This new determination to bring European and Indian classical languages to bear on Bangla poetry can best be understood as a transformation of Madhusudan's practice in his early verse, which was itself heavily indebted to Milton as well as to the English romantic poets.

Madhusudan's early poems in English clearly owed much to Richardson's poetic practice and to Richardson's version of the canon of British literature. The debt to Richardson is clear from the first lines of the first poem in Madhusudan's collected works:

> Though in a distant clime I roam,
> By Fate exiled from thee;
> And tho' the sweets of native home
> Are thus estranged from me

So the youthful poet rings the changes on exile and imagined love, comforted in his "exile" by the recollection of his "fond sweet blue-eyed maid" (*Madhusūdana racanābalī*, 435). At this point, Madhusudan had no experience of exile or of a "blue-eyed maid" (as far as I know). Although requiring a poet to write only from experience would be silly, I think this verse is evidence of a very young poet imitating the practice of a favorite teacher.

The "exile's" sentiment is reiterated in yet another early poem, this one an English sonnet: "Oft like a sad imprisoned bird I sigh / To leave this land, though my own land it be." The sonnet, dated Kidderpore 1842, is reminiscent both of Shelley's "England in 1819" (for it is a Shakespearean sonnet) and of Wordsworth's diction:

> For I have dreamed of climes more bright and free
> Where virtue dwells and heaven-born liberty
> Makes even the lowest happy;—where the eye
> Doth sicken not to see man bend the knee
> To sordid interest:—climes where science thrives,
> And genius doth receive her guerdon meet
>
> (*Madhusūdana racanābalī*, 449)

In his early English poems, Madhusudan attempted both Shakespearean and Petrarchan sonnets; he followed Richardson's practice of composing sonnets in both forms and also imitating the poems of Milton, Keats, Shelley, and Wordsworth. Later on, Madhusudan was to write a series of Petrarchan sonnets in Bangla, in addition to employing the blank verse of Wordsworth and, especially, Milton in his Bangla epic.

Two other early poems are especially interesting as layered imitations. Like Kasiprasad, and possibly imitating him along with Richardson and Richardson's British predecessors, Michael attempted the Spenserian stanza. In an unfinished early poem, "The Upsori," he imitates a double handful of English language poems (see *Madhusūdana racanābalī*, 457–63). A pastiche of Keats, Spenser, and Shakespeare but with an unlikely hero, "The Upsori" depicts a renunciant who visits a Kali temple. It reverses the specular gaze of Keats's "Eve of St. Agnes," and gives to the "upsori" *(apsara)* the role of Keats's Porphyro or Shakespeare's Romeo and to the young sadhu the role of erotic object. A similar reversal comes in another early poem, one more closely allied to the Oriental tale, "King Porus, A Legend of Old."

"King Porus" is both a prelude to Madhusudan's "Captive Ladie" and an earnest of his later device of reversing the culturally expected alignment of poetic sympathies. "King Porus," a relatively long narrative beginning in tetrameter couplets, evokes Shakespeare, Byron, and "liberty." In epigraphs to the poem, Madhusudan alludes to Shakespeare's Hamlet and to Byron's "Giaour." He quotes Byron's line "When shall such [a] hero live again?" The allusion is to Byron's allusion to the death of Themistocles, the hero who helped to free Greece from the threat of Persian invasion. In "The

Giaour," Byron implies that modern Greece once again needs heroes on the scale of Themistocles.[22] Adopting Byron's epigraph to describe his own hero, Madhusudan engages in a curious layering of historical referents. He equates Byron's Themistocles with India's Porus, who famously fought and lost to Alexander at the battle of the Hydaspes (Jhelum River) in BCE 326. Madhusudan's King Porus, then, is the equal of Themistocles in heroism. But it is notable that Porus resisted an invader from the West (the Macedonian invasion of what is now the Punjab), while Themistocles resisted the Persian advance from the East. As in Derozio's evocation of the Greeks and the Persians, the Byronic epigraph seems to equate the "Indian" hero Porus and the Greek Themistocles; yet Porus is acclaimed for resisting the army of Greece. Perhaps, then, in his choice of hero Madhusudan is both imitating and remaking Byron. "King Porus" is surely a poem of recalcitrant mimesis; its metaphors resist interpretive closure.

To make the layers of historical reference in "King Porus" still more confusing, Porus is characterized in a metaphor suggesting that he and his warriors usurped the place of both Greek *and* English heroes:

> Then lion-like, each warrior brave
> Rush'd on the coming foe,
> To strike for Freedom—or the grave!
> Oh Death! upon thy gory altar
> What blood-libations freely flow'd!
> Oh Earth! on that bright morn, what thousands
> Rendered to thee the dust they ow'd!—
> But 'fore the Macedonians,
> —Like autumn-leaves by Simom's driven
> Fell Brama's hardy sons,—
> Proud mountain oaks by thunders riven—
> And for their country's freedom bled—
> And made on gore their glorious bed.
>
> (*Madhusūdana racanābalī*, "King Porus," II, 464)

Thus, Porus and his men are Brahma's "hardy sons," but they are characterized as lions and oaks as well. If they have lost to Alexander, they have fought under the signs of British nationalism: the lion and the oak. So the hero is marked metaphorically as a British one, though his victory is a beacon of Indian "freedom."

Later in the poem, the metaphors again occur. The Miltonic Alexander, whom Madhusudan calls "th' Emathian conqueror," confronts and saves the life of his wounded opponent Porus, whom he must perforce admire.

> V
> Like to a lion chain'd,
> That, tho' faint—bleeding stands in pride—

With eyes where unsubdued
Yet flash'd the fire-looks that defied—
Kind Porus boldly went.
Where 'midst the gay and glittering crowd
Sat god-like Alexander,
While 'round Earth's mightiest monarchs bow'd:
He couched not as a slave—
He stooped not—bent not there his knee,—
But stood—as stands an oak,
Unbent—in native majesty!
"How should I treat thee?" ask'd
The mighty king of Macedon,—
"Aye—as a king!"—respons'd
In royal pride Ind's haughty son.
The king was pleased,
And him released.
Thus India's crown was lost and won.

(*Madhusūdana racanābalī,* "King Porus," V, 466)

Never mind that, despite his undoubted heroism, Porus became a vassal of Alexander. Here Madhusudan attempts to redouble Porus's stature by likening him to the lion and the oak.

The metaphors prove recalcitrant, however, for in the poem's final stanza all this metaphorical glory is taken away. The tone is that of the poem's other epigraph, from *Hamlet,* "We ne'er shall look upon his like again." The poem concludes on a bleak note. Porus is gone. "Fair Freedom" is gone. India's past glory is bathed in twilight gloom. India now "standest like a lofty tree / Shorn of fruits—blossoms—leaves and all . . . / Despised and scorned e'en in thy fall" (*Madhusūdana racanābalī,* "King Porus," VI, 466). Thus the paratexts—the epigraphs from Shakespeare and Byron—and the allusions in "King Porus" create a multilayered mimetic palimpsest. Byron is commandeered to Indian protonationalist goals, as are the topoi of British nationalism. Yet the poem ends with a kind of romantic apotheosis confirming, if anything, only the poet's ability to marshal his metaphors and Miltonic epithets.

The strategy in "King Porus" is repeated in the title poem of Madhusudan's volume, *The Captive Ladie* (1849). Whereas Kasiprasad Ghosh's first volume had been somewhat uneven (bathetic lines side by side with metrical virtuosity), Madhusudan's is more than uneven. "The Captive Ladie," though historically interesting, in many places scarcely rises above doggerel; the poet had talent in English verse, indubitably, but the volume on my reading reveals that it was written in haste and, most likely, scarcely revised.

Murshid's biographical work and Madhusudan's letters indicate that *The Captive Ladie* was written under a kind of duress in Madras, at a time when the author was a poorly paid teacher. He had married after only a few weeks in the city one Rebecca

McTavish, a young student at the Madras Male and Female Orphan Asylum School, where he taught.[23] Though his financial circumstances were extremely precarious before his marriage, he was shortly to become a father. His first volume was a none-too-successful attempt to raise his prestige and, with luck, a bit of cash. In a letter to Gour Bysack about his efforts, Madhusudan wrote,

> You will, I am sure, be surprised to hear that, though beset by all manner of troubles, I have managed to prepare a volume for the press. This will be my first regular effort as an author. The volume will consist of a tale in two cantos, yclept the "Captive Ladie" and a short poem or two. I must give a description of my "Captive." It contains about twelve hundred lines of good, bad and indifferent octo-syllabic verse and (truth, 'pon my honour!) was written in less than three weeks. . . . I wrote it for the pages of a local paper, the editor of which, one of the most eminent in India, has been blowing my trumpet like a jolly fellow. It has excited great attention here, and many persons of superior judgement and acquirements have induced me to republish it in a *bookish* form. (*Heart,* 62)

I love the play of *bookish* here, for Madhusudan's poem is indeed bookish, made possible by intertexts provided by Byron, Southey, and the played-out tropes of bardic nationalism.

Madhusudan's title poem commences where "King Porus" left off. *The Captive Ladie,* a small volume (really a chapbook of eighty pages), begins with an introductory verse in which the poet, though he appears to be a barren (oak?) tree, nevertheless puts out new leaves. Such renewal allows him to take up the bardic lyre:

> IX
> Though bitter be the echo of the tale
>   Of my youth's wither'd spring—I sigh not now;
> For I am as a tree when some sweet gale
>   Doth sweep away the sēre leaves from each bough,
> And wake far greener charms to re-adorn its brow!
> X
> Then come and list thee to the minstrel-lyre
>   And Lay of Eld of this my father-land,
> When first, as unchain'd demons, breathing fire,
>   Wild, stranger foe-men trod her sunny strand,
> And pluckt her brightest gems with rude, unspairing [*sic*] hand
>
> (*Captive Ladie,* "To —," 480)

In this pastiche of Shelley, Southey, Landon, and who knows what else, the poet himself becomes a revivified Porus, an oak putting out new leaves.

The tale of "The Captive Ladie" follows in octosyllabic couplets, as good and indifferent as Madhusudan described them. Each canto is prefaced with an epigraph, the first from "The Giaour" and the second from Tom Moore's *Lallah Rookh.* Madhusudan unfolds a narrative within a narrative. Canto 1 has the poet of the introduction virtually transformed into a "minstrel," who is, of course, a warrior in disguise come to rescue his beloved, imprisoned by her evil father in a "donjon." The minstrel mysteriously rescues his lady from the tower, only to meet a cruel fate in the second canto, for now the warrior minstrel, Baiza, is surrounded by Muslim foes. His lady love has a dream vision that the Hindu gods Kali, Shiva, and so forth desert her one by one; at last the warrior (and his bride) cast themselves upon the blazing pyre built for him by his Muslim enemies. This is a reprise of the double self-immolation scene popular with male poets in India (and done in a different mode by Emma Roberts); the source is Alexander Dow, whose *History of Hindostan* (1803) inspired poets from Byron to Southey to Landon. Madhusudan quotes Dow in the numerous footnotes to these cantos, which consist largely of explications of allusions to Hindu deities. In the notes, he recapitulates Dow's story: "It was in those days a custom of the Hindus, that whatever Raja was twice worsted by the Mussulmen, should be, by that disgrace, rendered unfit for further command. Jeipal in compliance to this custom, having raised his son to the government, ordered a funeral pile to be prepared upon which he sacrificed himself to his Gods. Dow's Ferishta, Vol. I. 45. (Third Edition)."[24]

As ever in Indian imitations of British Oriental tales, layer piles upon layer and the plot cannot lie comfortably down with intertexts. In addition to the intertexts suggested in the poem's epigraphs, the second canto begins with a kind of pastiche of Oriental tales, along with a heady dose of Robert Burns. As the Muslim foe surrounds Delhi, the poet laments:

> And there be blood on land and wave,
> And many a dead without a grave—
> And there be blood in grove and bow'r,
> And fane and altar, leaf and flow'r
> . . . .
> And well hath Valour battled there,
> With fiery hope,—in calm despair,
> To conquer, save, or proudly die,
> For death-less fame—or liberty!
>
> (*Madhusūdana racanābalī*, 495)

The canto continues in the vein, cutting back and forth between the Muslim conquerors and the lamented conquered, until the poet exclaims,

Oh!—Who can look upon the plain,
Where sleep the glorious—mighty slain,—
Brave hearts that for their country bled

(*Madhusūdana racanābalī*, 497)

One senses in these lines and others like them the poet casting about for a subject suitable to the combination of languages he brings to it.

The footnotes to "The Captive Ladie" indicate the cultural and linguistic layers that eventually led to Madhusudan's epic, *The Slaying of Meghanada*. In the first canto, the disguised minstrel sings under his lady's tower a lay comprising numerous traditional stories, including the story of Rama and Sita. Madhusudan glosses the minstrel's production this way:

> This is the subject of the Ramayana of Valmiki. The abduction of Seeta—the Indian Helen, and wife of Rama—by Ravena King of Ceylon. Seeta was taken away from the forest where Rama resided during his banishment from his kingdom. The consequence is well known.[25]
>
> Ilion, Ilion
> Fatalis, incestusque judex,
> Et mulier peregrina, vertit
> In pulverum!
>
> (*Madhusūdana racanābalī*, "The Captive Ladie," 509)

Madhusudan ends his note with this famous passage from Horace's third ode, in which Juno alludes to the judgment of Paris, fatal to Ilion, which now is dust; as in "The Captive Ladie," love is itself fatal. In a later note (canto 1, note r), Madhusudan quotes Horace Hayman Wilson's essay on the *Mahābhārata* from the *Asiatic Researches*, then comments that though these stories "have not escaped the Dramatist, yet they are oftener *recited* by Pundits than subjected to scenic representation." "The Captive Ladie" comes down to a pastiche drawn from Greek, Latin, Scots, and English intertexts and from English language versions and probably Bangla oral versions of Indian epics. The footnotes nod toward a more unified poetry to come, in Madhusudan's Bangla dramas and in his Bangla literary epic.

There is one more intertext in *The Captive Ladie:* the author's name. Clinton Seely points out that, despite what many have said, Madhusudan did not choose this name upon his baptism, nor was such a choice required. Rather, his English name appears for the first time in the marriage register in Madras and, in abbreviated form (M. M. S. Dutt), on the cover of *The Captive Ladie* (Seely, 20–21). Critics, including Seely, have wondered about this choice, while acknowledging the audacity of christening oneself after the prince of archangels. But I would argue that Michael's chosen name nods not so much to a biblical as to a literary intertext, that is, not just to the biblical archangel but to Milton's Michael. Specifically, we should think of "Michael" in the context of a passage in *Paradise Lost* that was congruent with David Lester Richardson's poetry of exile and Madhusudan's epic ambitions; for it is Michael whom God sends to usher Adam and Eve into exile. Before they are exiled from Paradise, the archangel Michael famously shows Adam the future history of the world, "all Earth's kingdoms, and their glory." Michael leads Adam to a summit from which his eye "might there command wherever stood / City of old or modern fame, the seat / Of mightiest empire" (11:384–87). In a prefiguration of empire and of orientalist scholarship, Adam's view extends from Samarcand to Agra and Lahore, to Moscow, onward toward Turkistan, and thence to Africa. Milton's Michael is thus the agent at once of exile and of empire.

That "Madhusudan" should become "Michael," then, indicates the poet's epic ambitions—ambitions that were reiterated some years later on another domestic occasion, when Michael Madhusudan named a son (by his second partner) Frederick Milton Dutt (Murshid, *Heart,* 172n). Frederick Milton was born in the same month, July 1861, that the final cantos of the *Meghanadavadha kavya* appeared in print. We might say that Madhusudan's Milton was born in the flesh and reborn in a book at the same time.

But "Milton's" identity, like Madhusudan's son's identity, is multilayered. The *Meghanadavadha* begins this way (in Seely's translation):

> When in face-to-face combat Vīrabāhu, crown-gem of
> warriors, fell and went before his time to Yama's city—
> speak, O goddess of ambrosial speech—which best of warriors
> did the foe of Rāghava, treasure-trove among that clan
> of Rākṣasas, designate commander, then send fresh to
> the battle? . . . .
> . . . . I, who am
> ignorant, praise your lotus feet and call upon you once
> more, white-limbed Bhāratī! Come, chaste woman, favor me, your
> servant as you once sat on Vālmīki's tongue
>
> (*Slaying,* 71)

Or in William Radice's translation:

> I adore your lotus-feet, base-minded as I am, I call you again,
> White-armed Bharati! In the same way, mother,
> That you came and sat on the tongue of Valmiki (as on a lotus-seat) when,
> With the sharpest of arrows, in the deep forest, the huntsman pierced the heron when the heron was with its mate,
> Come, chaste one, and do kindness to your servant.[26]

In his prefatory study, Seely makes clear that Madhusudan combines epic traditions from classical, British, Italian, and Indian sources to create his verse form (a Bangla version of blank verse) and his narrative strategy. Seely shows that the poem begins by echoing the beginning of *Paradise Lost* and ends by "evoking the cremation scene from the final book of the Iliad"; in the middle, it remakes Dante's path to the underworld. As Seely argues, "The evident presences of Milton-Tasso-Homer-Virgil-Dante notwithstanding, Datta's [Dutt's] epic remains throughout, and through and through, a partial embodiment of the *Ramayana.* In narrating this episode from the Ramayana—the slaying of Meghanada (resonant with, intentionally, the slaying of Priam's son Hector)—Datta shows sympathy for the traditionally opposing side, that of Lanka's King Ravana and his Rakshasa clan, in much the way Milton makes sympathetic his Satan" (33).

But Satan is most sympathetic, not in Milton but in the unmentioned additional intertexts for Madhusudan's poem—the romantic rereadings or misprisions of Milton. It is not so much Milton's Satan as Blake's and Shelley's that Madhusudan acknowledges. If British romantic poets viewed Milton as "of the devil's party without knowing it," Madhusudan remakes his partial *Rāmāyaṇa* in their light. As in the mini-narratives "King Porus" and "The Captive Ladie," but more effectively, partly because he follows—and revises—a traditional narrative and partly because he is writing Bangla, Madhusudan linked multiple epic traditions as he had come to know them. Like his archangelic namesake, he set out, in the *Meghanadavadha kavya,* to tell a story of exile and of empire.

The appeal of Christianity for Madhusudan would appear to have been as literary as religious; it enabled his procedure of importing Milton into the *Rāmāyaṇa,* recasting the *Rāmāyaṇa* metrically and in terms of its narrative allegiances along the lines of a British romantic reading of Milton. Such an approach to mimesis is glimpsed in the footnotes to *The Captive Ladie,* written during Madhusudan's sojourn in Madras, and in the colonial mimicry of his famous (or infamous) "The Anglo-Saxon and the Hindu." In this essay, a lecture presented in Madras, Madhusudan extols the vigor and virtues of the "Anglo-Saxon," presenting his own history of world conquerors as if he were Milton's Michael, whom he explicitly evokes. Indeed, the "Anglo-Saxon" is able to stand for all the British because Madhusudan is imitating, almost channeling, Thomas Carlyle's *Past and Present* (1843). Carlyle's prose, though less ironic in *Past and Present* than in *Sartor Resartus,* is never far from the corrosions of irony; and in this essay, Madhusudan's language is so over the top, the mimicry of Carlyle so complete (right down to Carlyle's race thinking and his syntactic tics), that one can only wonder what ironies attend the double voicing of his mimicry. It is the mission of the Anglo-Saxon, the poet concludes in his lecture, "to renovate, to regenerate, to Christianize the Hindu—to churn this vast ocean that it may restore the things of beauty now buried in its liquid wilderness; and nobly is he seconded—will be seconded, by the Sciences and the Literature of his sea-girt father-land—the Literature of his country" (*Madhusūdana racanābalī,* 529). For, as Madhusudan argues at the commencement of the essay, the Hindu is "an untuned harp, an unstrung lute," an old oak with fallen leaves and withered arms. Even in Madras, Michael Madhusudan is haunted by the leafless oak, the bardic hero, the defeated Porus. He is haunted equally by the prophetic language of his predecessor Carlyle.

Madhusudan's poems, written in English in Madras and in Bangla after his return to Calcutta, were his curious answer to the challenge of restringing the "Hindu harp." He himself was, at this point, neither an Anglo-Saxon nor a Hindu, yet he sought the kind of "renovation" that he called for in the lecture. Though Anglo-Saxon only in affiliation—or through mimicry, to put it less kindly—Michael Madhusudan certainly imagined himself, like the gods of the *Mahābhārata,* churning the "vast ocean" of Indian story. Madhusudan's turn to Bangla poetry, then, became a mimesis of a Christianized, rather than a Christian, Hindu epic. If Michael wished to become the Carlyle of Madras, this masquerade (or, as Carlyle would have called it, rhodomontade) resulted in a romantic reading of Milton and, eventually, in a modern remaking of a *Rāmāyaṇa.* Michael Madhusudan's mimetic strategies made possible an implicit argument that the *Meghanadavadha kavya* was the *Paradise Lost* of Bengal *and* that *Paradise Lost* was the *Rāmāyaṇa* of Britain.

Neither Epic nor Exile: Mary Carshore and the Poetics of Domesticity

In the invocation to the muse at the beginning of *The Slaying of Meghanada,* Michael Madhusudan prayed to "white-limbed Bhāratī," that is, to the goddess Sarasvatī:

> Let me, Mother, sing this epic song
> filled with virile *rasa.* . . . .
> You come also, goddess, you who are the honeybee
> Imagination! Glean honey from the flower garden
> of the poet's mind and form your honeycomb from which the
> folks of Gauḍa might in bliss sip nectar ever after.
>
> (71, lines 25–30)

Epic power is envisioned as "virile rasa," or *vīra rasa,* the determining quintessence of heroic verse. Even Michael's Carlylean mimesis in prose was a matter of taking on *vīra rasa,* the heroic aesthetic. In his lecture, as in his epic, Michael fused the masculinized poetics of British criticism—which we have already seen operating in the metropolitan criticism of Kasiprasad's namby-pamby models—with an Indian aesthetic.

But for Mary Carshore, Madhusudan's contemporary, such a stance was, by virtue of her gender and education, entirely impossible. If we think of colonial mimesis in both its cultural and its aesthetic senses—as mimicry and poetic imitation—for Kasiprasad and Madhusudan, various possibilities, however limited, were available.

Though they could never be, in the eyes of their British counterparts, equal in cultural or political terms, they could become educated in the conquerors' languages and in Indian classical languages. Men such as Wilson, Parker, and Richardson, too, had access to multiple European and Indian languages. Kasiprasad and Madhusudan, too, learned Indian and European classical and modern languages, but Mary Carshore, as far as I can determine, was literate only in English. For Carshore, colonial mimicry was complicated by gender and by her consequent lack of access either to classical learning or to literacy in any Indian vernacular other than English. According to her sister's biographical introduction in the 1871 second edition of her book, *Songs of the East,* Carshore had a bit less than two years of formal education. She attended briefly with a handful of other girls the Loretto Convent, which had just started a school in Calcutta when she was in her teens.

Consequently, Carshore's intervention in British orientalist poetics takes a different tack from that of her contemporaries. Rather than citing, acknowledging, or augmenting orientalist learning, she argues from experience. Although in the notes to her first volume of poetry Carshore sometimes takes the stance of the Western Christian poet describing an alien country, this voice does not predominate in the poetic texts or even in the notes. India was the only country Carshore knew or was likely to know, and although it was hers by birth and experience, it was neither hers to command nor entirely hers linguistically. Far from having a classical education in any language, far from being able to create a *vīra rasa* or comfortably to take up the subject position of the male British poet, Carshore was caught betwixt and between. Though a fair number of the poems in the first edition of her work (published in 1855) did not rise above average album verse, the better among them re-created domestic scenes in a songlike or straightforward idiom, claiming for themselves a space deliberately gendered. The layered mimicry that engages colonial power relations and the elaborate imitation of English versification that we see in Kasiprasad's or Michael Madhusudan's poems do not often enter Carshore's work; instead, I would describe her texts as *gendered* mimicry, the mimesis of domesticity.

The beginning of the only volume that Carshore herself saw through the press is certainly a gendered performance. It is also an attack on the conventions of British orientalism. The volume begins with exactly the kind of apology that was conventional in books of its time and place. The poet limits her claims. In this paratextual mimicry of femininity, the poet situates herself as an "authoress":

> In submitting this little work to the public, tho' greatly encouraged by the partial and favorable opinions and suggestions of friends, who in defiance of all past warnings, will now and ever after persist in seeing with none but their own partial eyes,—the Authoress, it will readily be supposed, must naturally feel a diffidence and hesitation in thus venturing to appear before the world, and cannot be without many doubts and fears as to her success;

> yet, notwithstanding, these have not sufficed to scare her from the task to which more powerful motives urged her on, nor can she with any truth affirm, that her feelings are now entirely of distrust and diffidence; no, "but with a hope" she gives forth her unpretending little volume, trusting that a kind and indulgent public will give it a favorable reception. Born and reared on Indian soil, she cannot boast an extensive or intimate acquaintance with the literature of the West, and her only object in publishing the following tales and songs has been, to give a more correct idea of native customs and manners, than she has yet observed Europeans to possess, seconded of course by that instinctive thirst for fame implanted in the human breast. This acknowledgement she trusts will disarm the severity of those who might otherwise be disposed to be too critical. Rajapore, 25th Sept. 1854[27]

In this prefatory apology, the author, or "authoress," claims the authority of experience rather than education. Experience, she implies, constitutes the major part of her education and suffices to correct the excesses of orientalist verse.

A second layer of paratextual mimesis is presented in Carshore's dedication. Carshore does not choose as a dedicatee a woman who, like Emma Roberts's Lady Bentinck, can reasonably be thought to command immediate social power. Rather, Carshore's dedicatee is both more powerful than any British woman in India and less important to the poet's actual situation. Significantly for Mary Carshore, her dedicatee combined conservative Catholicism with the glamour of a star. Carshore inscribes her volume and her first poem to the Empress Eugenie, the half Scottish, part Spanish, part Belgian bride of Napoleon III. Following this inscription, the first poem in the volume, addressed to the empress, begins by evoking a male poet in "the East," who died trying to praise the empress. Carshore characterizes herself as a "less adventurous minstrel" who tunes her lyre and offers a "wreath" of songs, or, perhaps, just a wreath of weeds.

Following this humble dedicatory poem, however, is one that speaks to the second goal of the poet's efforts, to her admission that she has an "instinctive thirst for fame." In "A Tale of Cashmere," Carshore takes on the demigod of orientalist poetics himself, Tom Moore, and chastises *Lalla Rookh* for its ignorance:

> There's a valley so bright in the beautiful east,
> Where the roses bloom wild 'neath the wanderer's feet.
> O! a breath of that vale is to pilgrims a feast,
> The flowers are so fragrant, the air is so sweet;
> And the maids are so fair, that the spirits of bliss
> Have deserted Elysium to win but their kiss;
> And the sons of the west pause in glory's career,
> To look back with sighs on the vale of Cashmere.
> Thus sang the sweet minstrel of Erin one day,

And how sweet and how precious, tho' false is his lay;
Yes, false tho' still sweet, for the valley so blest
Is trampled with scorn by the sons of the west.
And the maidens, tho' beauteous, are dusky, not fair,
And the roses, tho' bright, not uncultured, grow there;
Yet all is not false that the minstrel has sung,
Save the veil of poetic enchantment he flung.

(30)

Moore should have known, the poet says, that maidens in the Vale of Kashmir do not need fair skin to be lovely; he should have known that maidens and youths there do not disport together. The poet proposes to correct Moore's errors: "Let my muse then confine her to genuine truths / And sing the sad tale of a daughter of earth" (30). Carshore's tale, as it turns out, is one of a young woman betrayed; she is virtually sold by her father and her husband to a raja, and then, unable to produce sons, she is neglected and ridiculed by her marital family, whereupon she loses her mind. The Vale of Kashmir, moreover, has been "trampled with scorn by the sons of the west" (possibly an allusion to the First Anglo-Sikh War, 1845–46, as well as to earlier conflicts). Moore's Oriental tale is wrong on several counts, the poet says—it ignores the violence of Western conquest, and it ignores the subjection and seclusion of women.

Like the orientalist poets, Carshore loads her poems with notes, but rather than the usual set of orientalist citations, hers are a correction. Her notes admit that Moore rightly evoked the beauties of Kashmir, but they declare that he was wrong on other counts:

> The natural beauties of the valley are of course here alluded to: the climate is one of the finest in the world, and the rare birds, the rich fruits, and the delicious flowers, cannot sufficiently be extolled; but as to "young people" meeting in "cool, shining walks" by moonlight, after having slept out the day "and waked to moonlight and to play," and "maids and matrons" leaving their "veils at home" and wandering about at night to amuse themselves, it is all as little like truth as the tales of the Arabian Nights, though it sounds very sweet in a poetical romance. It is marvellous how travellers delight in misleading people with their incredible "facts" of other countries, and above all, it is wonderful with what facility these monstrous facts are received when they relate to the east. This class (that is the travelling) are to be blamed of course, not Moore, for any mistakes of the above kind. (145)

Carshore ridicules the traveling class, ostensibly exempting Moore from her strictures but at the same time suggesting that he has relied on useless sources and created poetry with little regard to the truth.

This satiric take on the Irish poet got Carshore in trouble with the impresario of Calcutta letters, David Lester Richardson. Although Carshore's volume was reviewed, generally positively, in the periodical press when it was published in Calcutta, Richardson took exception. In the "learned" notes that provoked Richardson's criticism, Carshore went against the grain of the common British understanding of India: she refused, in some measure, to romanticize sexual relations, and she refused the British typology of Indian religions, which demanded identification of individuals as either Hindu or Muslim. Possibly because of her familiarity with the North West Provinces, Carshore argued in her notes that Moore was wrong—Hindu and Muslim folk practices or rituals are sometimes shared and, in the particular festival he describes, often were. According to Carshore's sister, Richardson "took umbrage at the idea of a debutante daring to find fault with Moore and himself" (*Songs,* 2nd ed., ix).

In dismissing Carshore, Richardson valued books over experience and his own authority over voices from beyond his world of belles lettres. Carshore's sister quotes Richardson's defense of Moore: "Moore prepared himself for the writing of 'Lalla Rookh' by long and laborious reading. He himself narrates that Sir James Mackintosh was asked by Colonel Wilks, the Historian of British India, whether it was true that the poet had never been in the East. Sir James replied, 'Never.' 'Well, that shows me,' said Colonel Wilks, 'that reading over D'Herbelot is as good as riding on the back of a camel'" (*Songs,* 2nd ed., x). The collective authority of Colonel Wilks, James Mackintosh, D'Herbelot, and Richardson combine to suggest that education trumps actual experience: it was better to read about camels than actually to ride them. Moreover, Richardson seems to have been exercised that a young woman poet would question him.

Carshore took on Richardson and Moore not only in her preface and her long Oriental tale but also in her lyrics and notes. Carshore's sister quotes almost the entirety of Richardson's review and argues that Mary challenged both Richardson and Moore in her poem "The Beara Festival." In this poem's notes, Carshore again argues from experience rather than from books: "Much has been said about the Beara or floating lamp, but I have never yet seen a correct description. Moore mentions that Lalla Rookh saw a solitary hindoo girl bring her lamp to the river. D. L. R. says the same, whereas the Beara festival is a Moslem feast that takes place once a year in the monsoons, when hundreds and thousands of females offer their vows to the patron of rivers" (*Songs,* 1st ed., 147). To this argument Richardson responded by reprinting his own poems and long passages from Moore as well. He went on at length, drawing testimony from Horace Hayman Wilson, "a high authority on all Oriental customs" (*Songs,* 2nd ed., xii). Then, quoting a "Hindu friend" (Kasiprasad perhaps?), Richardson reversed himself, conceding that the Beara festival is Muslim in origin. Richardson states, finally, that the custom of women lighting lamps to make wishes for the future is likely to be widely shared across religious lines. Carshore's sister dismissed Richardson's quibbles in a very short paragraph that reads entire: "So much for D.L.R." (*Songs,* 2nd ed., xiv).

The paratexts to Carshore's *Songs of the East*—in both editions—suggest the ways in which she and her sister placed the poet in a world of experience outside of the world of orientalist learning. This world of experience, though deeply literary (as their paratextual arguments show), is nonetheless presented as faithfully mimetic of domesticity. As in the complex relationship of texts and paratexts—particularly in the ironic footnotes of Letitia Landon—such "mimesis" has an elsewhere.

Aside from Carshore's many songs, which I do not discuss here, "The Beara Festival" and other domestic and elegiac poems can represent Carshore's means of entering the literary scene. Her poems assume less than her male counterparts' texts do—less knowledge, less power, less authority—even as she argues for a kind of experiential authority. The actual plot of "The Beara Festival," for example, foregrounds the status of European knowledge and the gendered constraints of married life that apply to both Indian and European women. The festival itself is one when "proud and lowly, loftiest and least, / Matron and Moslem maiden pay their vows" by floating lamps on the water and making wishes for the future (*Songs,* 1st ed., 114–15). The poet speaker of "The Beara Festival" positions herself as one of a band of Europeans, not all of whom understand the language of the songs they overhear as they watch the festival. The songs, then, require translation: "One who stood there, / Then rendered him in his own native tongue. / Thus artlessly the simple words she sung" (116). For the male listener, the poems require translation. The Muslim singer, a young and "artless" matron, longs not for a lover, as is usual in orientalist versions of this scene, but for a happy marriage. Like Carshore herself at this point in her life, the singer is newly wed, and she propitiates the heavenly powers for a happy future, while lamenting her departure from a beloved home. The poem ends with the poet's reflection on the young matron's song. The speaker of the poem, like the young singer, has watched the lighted lamps float out of sight. But the speaker refuses any easy assumption about her own or the singer's future:

> How eager eyes all watched the lonely light,
> As jocundly it glided out of sight;
> But was the omen's promise all fulfilled?
> O! who may say, perchance it was, perchance
> In vain, the maiden all her hopes did build
> Upon it, and with disappointed glance,
> Saw them all fade away. Such is, alas!
> Many a heart's sad history: let it pass.
>
> (117–18)

"Let it pass," the speaker concludes. The poem, thus, remakes the orientalist footnote and refuses the romance plot. But it also creates instability between the mimesis of gendered domesticity and the potential implication for the male listener that cultural meanings are lost in translation. Even in "The Beara Festival," mimesis shades into translation. Domesticity may not be quite what it seems. Carshore operates at an oblique angle to orientalist conventions.

The doubleness of domestic mimicry is more sophisticated in one of Carshore's later poems, where the affective core of the poem is conveyed in a kind of urbane new voice, more like Shelley's "To Jane—An Invitation" than like the self-dramatizing poetry of L.E.L. This voice is glimpsed in the first edition of *Songs* in such poems as "To Annie," but the most sophisticated version of it comes in "Poetical Letter to Mrs. V. . . ." in the second edition of Carshore's work. This poem recounts a visit from the poet's friend, Mrs. V., the addressee of her poetic letter. It concludes,

> Thou art no fancied shape of dreams
> To vanish with the morning gleams;
> No bright, illusive beau ideal,
> But loving, true, unchanged and real;
> And I shall see thee yet again
> To know and love thee better then;
> O my dear Lady,—writing dear,
> My heart cries dearest low and clear,
> But then 'tis always best to show
> Less than is felt,—than once to know,
> You feel not half of what you say.
> O my dear Lady, therefore, pray,
> Think of me sometimes as you may,
> And when your nightly prayer is given,
> Repeat my lowly name to heaven,
> Thus wilt thou, when at closing day
> Thy better thoughts resume their sway,
> Think of me, tho' I merit not
> From thee—from any one—a thought,
> For I with traits of good and ill,
> And all my faults, I love thee still;
> And will, tho' fate and distance sever,
> Affectionately yours, be ever
> Mary Carshore.
>
> (*Songs*, 2nd ed., 157–58)

Here the poet melds the domestic and the urbane, self-reflexiveness and the re-creation of emotion. Mrs. V. evidently accompanied her husband, who was presumably traveling on the East India Company's business; the poem is written after the poet assures herself by looking at the imprint of Mrs. V.'s "vanished tent" on the grounds of her house that this delightful visit has actually occurred.[28] As in "The Beara Festival," Carshore stakes a position outside the romance plot. She imaginatively inhabits the tent, not of an orientalist hero but of a company official, creating a longed-for and intense relationship with another woman.

In contrast to this affirmative poem are several that are more elegiac, significant among them "Lines to a Withered Shamrock," "To Clarence in His Grave," and "The Ivied Harp." The first takes on the elegiac trope of exile (to rewrite it), the second harkens back to Roberts's "deathscapes," and the third laments the death of Letitia Landon—implicitly figuring the poet's own situation.

In "Lines to a Withered Shamrock," Carshore takes up the perennial colonial trope of exile, giving it a specifically Irish valence. The occasion is the poet finding a dried shamrock leaf folded into an old letter. The poem is a colloquy between the speaker and the shamrock. The speaker, however, is not an exile. Rather, the speaker imagines another person who can be comforted by an absent sister's gift. The shamrock has the effect of teaching an exile to "forget the while" his "weary part" (*Songs*, 2nd ed., 165). While an imagined Ireland remains unaltered—nothing is changed on "Erin's sainted shore"—the speaker of the poem has no direct connection to the home country. The withered shamrock then becomes a metonymy for the speaker's "parent stem." As in every other poem of exile from Ireland, the verses evoke not famine, emigration, or industrialization but lost rural peace. Landscape, after all, can more easily be imagined to remain "unaltered" than family can. In "Lines to a Withered Shamrock," the elegiac is easily contained by the letter, in both its literal and its figurative sense. The withered leaf scarcely stains the page.

Containment is more difficult in the poems lamenting the death of Carshore's first child, Clarence, who was born while his father was deeply in debt and on trial for some kind of criminal offense. After Clarence's early death, the family moved away from their first home, and the poet laments not only his death but also separation from his grave. The trope of exile, as we saw in Roberts's poems and as it functioned for many other European poets, often depended on the survivor's separation from the remains of the dead. Such separation was usually understood as exile from the mother country or from those left behind upon one's return to the mother country. For Carshore, though, this trope is reprised as mother love; exile becomes separation between mother earth and an earthly mother. "To Clarence in His Grave" casts the poet as a ghost, haunting the lost sepulcher of her son. Did I dream, the speaker asks, that we would "quit that home thou mad'st bright, to find / Another far from thee"? And so the speaker can only haunt the plot. She is a "ghost of fond maternal love":

> tho' removed so far,
> My spirit haunts that sacred spot,
> There memory's treasures are
> Too dearly valued to be e'er forgot.
>
> And tho' I may not steep
> Thy urn with tears of grief o'er past delight,

Around it still I creep
In dreams and waking fancies of the night.

(*Songs,* 2nd ed., 158)

The lost child becomes a hermit, a kind of sannyāsin, living alone beneath his monument, while the earth holds the child "on its parent breast" (*Songs,* 2nd ed., 159).

Exile, always a trope depending on the domestic and the sentimental, is transformed both in the lines to a shamrock and again in "To Clarence in His Grave." Perhaps Carlyle and Carshore were in agreement, one proceeding from philosophical reflection and the other from domestic experience, that all is exile.

The odd thing about "To Clarence in His Grave" is not its sentiment but rather its verse form. Rarely do English quatrains consist of short lines, in the first and third positions, alternating with long lines in the second and fourth positions. Here the lines are alternating trimeter and pentameter, a reversed and lengthened version of long meter (alternate lines of tetrameter and trimeter). The effect is odd, off-kilter, disturbing. The versification provides a metrical counterpart to the "haunting" described in the poem. Like the still more disturbing description of the death of Carshore's husband and other children in her sister's prefatory memoir, this poem indicates an excess just beyond the reach of domesticity. The masque of domesticity, ultimately, cannot fully domesticate the affective life.

Of course, the past grand master of this conundrum of domesticity was Letitia Landon, and I would argue that Mary Carshore's most interesting poem about colonial poetics is her elegy for Landon. Even the title is overdetermined: "The Ivied Harp." Bardic nationalism is turned to gendered mimicry; national identification is given over to transperipheral affective links. The poem is written in anapestic tetrameter couplets, like Byron's "Destruction of Sennacharib" and Kasiprasad Ghosh's "Káli Pujá." Although any poem in this meter threatens descent to bathos or doggerel, the end of "The Ivied Harp" redeems its earlier metrical infelicities. Landon, famously, had died at Cape Coast Castle, West Africa (now Ghana), in suspicious circumstances; suicide, murder, and accidental death by an overdose of prussic acid were contending explanations. She was buried after a hurried inquest within the walls of the fort, which was commanded by her husband, George Maclean. Rather than erecting a monument, Maclean covered the grave with courtyard pavers. Of this famous resting place, Mary Carshore read a firsthand account. Lamenting Landon's death, Carshore evokes Landon's "harp" now "untuned and unstrung," covered with clinging ivy. Landon's early death is bad enough, Carshore implies, but her exposed grave—baked by "fierce Africa's ray"—adds insult to injury. Paths intersect in this courtyard, with the result that "feet undiverted tread o'er it each day." "Rude strangers" trample the grave, and none can wake the poet again. Carshore, at least, can protest—as one colonial poet to another, one speaking in place of another, one speaking in the voice of another. Could Landon, the "minstrel," awake to behold such unkindness,

her heartstrings would break.
But the spirit is departed of heavenly flame,
Whose halo illumined the temple of fame,
To regions from whence it can never return,
Neglect as ye will the cold dust of the urn.
Then rest secure, England! thy accuser is far,
E'en her ashes repose 'neath a strange foreign star,
Then rest thee unquestioned, there's none to upbraid thee,
Since they dare not to tell thee the things that degrade thee,
The living thou feedest with vain empty breath,
And 'tis thus thou rewardest thy children in death.

(*Songs,* 1st ed., 123)

The conclusion to "The Ivied Harp," which comes near the end of the first edition of Carshore's poetry, reinforces Carshore's critique of Moore and orientalist poetics. People of the traveling kind, the itinerant English or their homebound cousins in general, have no idea what empire can mean. Their protestations and response to such poetry as Landon's or, we might add, Carshore's consist of "vain empty breath." The mother country cares nothing for its poetic offspring.

It was left to Carshore—and to her sister—to take care of her poetic progeny. Carshore was in fact to describe her second manuscript of verse as her "child." According to her sister, during the uprising of 1857 she buried it under a bench in her garden. Like Landon, Carshore became a poet from beyond the colonial grave, for her sister retrieved and published her last work.

Nevertheless, when her sister recast Mary's life into the plot of sentimental domesticity, the critical thrust of poems on the order of "The Ivied Harp" was blunted. Much like Charlotte Brontë memorializing and domesticating Emily, Carshore's sister asked the reader to reconstruct the poet as a youthful martyr and faithful mother. In contrast, Mary Carshore herself identified with Landon and like Landon engaged in a mimesis of sentiment and femininity. Marginalized by gender, education, and location, Mary Carshore both furthered and critiqued the intellectual structures that created the possibility for her work.

Layered Mimicry, Layered Memory

All three of these poets—Kasiprasad Ghosh, Michael Madhusudan Dutt, and Mary Seyers Carshore—engaged in poetic imitation and recalcitrant mimesis. Writing English verse, for each of them, entailed engagement with a variety of texts, sometimes in multiple languages. It required young poets to make space for themselves within a variety of discourses—orientalist, religious, critical, and domestic—discourses that also claimed to define them. For each writer, education, access to languages, gender, and economic circumstances opened or precluded poetic possibilities. Writing English poetry itself entailed multiple and sometimes contradictory identifications—these poets cannot be defined simply as Hindu or Anglican or Catholic; Irish or "native"; even, given the relentless gendering of poetry and the Bengali babu, masculine or feminine. Although many of the poems I discuss here might be dismissed as juvenilia, these poets' youthful works reveal the multiple layers of mimesis and poetic imitation that constitute the colonial poet's art.

PART THREE

Nationalisms, Religion, and Aestheticism in the Late Nineteenth Century

Cover of *The Dutt Family Album* (London: Longmans, Green, 1870).

FIVE

From Christian Piety to Cosmopolitan Nationalisms

The Dutt Family Album *and the Poems of Mary E. Leslie and Toru Dutt*

In 1824, Reginald Heber, then bishop of Calcutta, strolling on the banks of the Ganges, found himself in much the same place that Sir William Jones had occupied a generation earlier.[1] In his perambulatory verse "Plassey-Plain," Jones had turned the eighteenth-century prospect poem into gentle satire. His poem became at once a compliment to Lady Jones on her escape from danger, a botanical catalogue, and a send-up of literary and scientific scholarship. Heber also engaged the prospect poem but to different ends, for Heber's frame of reference was neither scientific nor linguistic but religious.

In his most famous poem about his time in India, "An Evening Walk in Bengal," Heber, like Jones, responded to perceived dangers, but he promised his companion that all was safe, for tigers and snakes no longer threatened. "Taught by recent harm to shun / The thunders of the English gun," the tiger kept its distance. Heber coaxed his timid companion, "Come boldly on!" (64). Like many a British poet before him, he noted the beauties of Indian flora and fauna, peacocks and peepuls. And like many of his contemporaries, he found that singing the beauties of Bengal evoked the note of exile:

> So rich a shade, so green a sod
> Our English fairies never trod!
> Yet who in Indian bowers has stood,
> But thought on England's "good greenwood!"
> And bless'd, beneath the palmy shade,
> Her hazel and her hawthorn glade,
> And breath'd a prayer, (how oft in vain!)
> To gaze upon her oaks again?
>
> (64)

The poet's reverie of home is broken by the "jackal's cry," which leads him back to an alienated present. Yet in a second turn, the poet hears the nightingale—"it is—it must be—Philomel!" All this emotional reflection leads him to moralize the prospect:

> And we must early sleep to find
> Betimes the morning's healthy wind.
> But oh! with thankful hearts confess
> E'en here there may be happiness;
> And He, the bounteous Sire, has given
> His peace on earth,—his hope of Heaven!
>
> (66)

The prospect poem is shaped, in the end, by Heber's Christian piety.

In his short time in India (1823–26), Heber earned a reputation as a humane and open-minded Christian, as evidenced by famous dinners to which he invited persons who would not otherwise have been willing to meet each other and by his indefatigable travels to Anglican congregations throughout India. His ecumenical cast of mind tempered his evangelical zeal. But Heber's broad-mindedness was, by midcentury, not the dominant tone of Indian Christianity. Later English language poets found religious discourse more dogmatic and, often, more polemical than in Heber's time.[2]

Religious questions came to shape English language poetry in significant ways in mid- to late nineteenth-century India. The previous chapter traces some of these threads in describing the increasing importance of evangelicalism, the conversion of Madhusudan Dutt, and the reframing of Hindu practices by Kasiprasad Ghosh in a deliberate response to orientalist and Christian poetics. In particular, Christianity over the course of the century (as is evident in the case of Michael Madhusudan) became increasingly identified with Englishness. When Portuguese Catholic, Moravian, and Danish Protestant missionaries became outnumbered by increasing numbers of evangelical clergy in the Church of England and by mostly British missionaries sponsored by the London Missionary Society (LMS) and the Church Missionary Society (CMS), the English nationalist identification of Christianity increased. Madhusudan Dutt, in sighing for "Albion"—and in acting out his youthful rebellion—found conversion to be an appropriate response; for him, English language poetry and religion were inextricably mixed. Indeed, for Madhusudan (and others who followed), Christianity could not be taken largely for granted, as it was by his teacher David Lester Richardson, who seems to have transmitted a passion for Milton to his students much more directly than a passion for any particular religious dogma.

For a number of poets after 1857, Christianity shaped a sense of poetic tradition and of social identity. The impact of Christianity is particularly evident in the concerto grosso of Dutts—brothers and nephews—whose understandings of poetry were formed at Hindu College under Richardson. Though there are differences among them, in emphasis, in expression of piety, and in poetic skill, Govin Chunder, Hur Chunder, Greece Chunder, and Shoshee Chunder Dutt were profoundly affected by what amounted to their joint family's group conversion to Christianity.[3] In contrast, but sharing mutatis mutandis much of the Dutts' evangelical sensibility, is Mary E. Leslie, after Heber the most able Christian devotional poet in nineteenth-century India. At the end of the century we find Toru Dutt, the best known and by far the most talented of these poets, whose world view was equally shaped by the Christianity of her father, Govin Chunder, and by the cosmopolitan education that fed a voracious intellectual curiosity.

The elder Dutts' poetry is, from a postcolonial perspective, very nearly embarrassing. Though some of it is skilled, its sentiments—to me, as to many critics—sometimes invite condescension. Here I have tried to take their poetry seriously and, where possible, initially on its own terms, though this has not always been easy. As Rosinka Chaudhuri has argued, aesthetic (or, I would add, formalist) readings of their poems often result in judgments that they were "imitative" or conventional, but such readings, she argues, occlude the ways in which the Dutts' poems were "sites of colonial conflict and interchange" (*Gentlemen*, 140). Chaudhuri has shown how the Dutts' historical poems recalled Walter Scott and older English language Indian poetry and drew heavily on Tod's *Annals and Antiquities of Rajasthan,* along with more recently published English works, particularly Mountstuart Elphinstone's *History of India* and Grant Duff's history of the Marathas. As she points out, these narrative tropes and this version of Anglophilia had come to seem outmoded by the 1870s. In describing their poetry as sites of colonial conflict, she brilliantly argues that the Dutts' fascination with Mughal/Rajput conflicts in their imitations of Scott drew a triple parallel among the ostensible orientalist subject, the internal colonization of Scotland, and the colonization of India. But I argue, in addition, that their volumes, on the whole, are so permeated with Christian and perforce Anglophile piety that the oppositional subtexts of their historical poetry are overwritten by Christian apologetics.

A different kind of postcolonial discomfort accompanies, for me, the reading of Mary Eliza Leslie's poems, for Leslie re-creates recent events—the rising of 1857—in interchangeable codes of Christian martyrdom and British heroism. Leslie's bloody-minded treatment of the events of 1857 is in some ways complementary to and in some ways antithetical to her devotional poetry. Although, like Heber's, Leslie's poems have entered Protestant hymnals, her devotional verse is more formally various than either the Dutts' or Heber's and thus less suited than Heber's to hymnology. Her rhymed incidents from Tod's *Annals,* like the Dutts' versions, are highly conventional though told from a female perspective. Ironically, however, while several of the Dutts traveled to Europe and studied in England, Mary Leslie's experience seems, except for a childhood trip to Britain, to have been wholly confined to Bihar and Bengal. The daughter and granddaughter of missionaries, Leslie was both religiously and geographically parochial.

In contrast to the somewhat older Mary Leslie and though she too was raised in a highly pious household, Toru Dutt packed into a short life considerable travel and learning. She had to contend ideologically, as well, with a family as much divided as united by religion. Although much of her father's family converted to Christianity, her mother's did not, and her grandmother's persistence in Hindu religious practices was a source of pain and contradiction. This combination of influences seems to have kept Toru from recapitulating her uncles' dogmatism. Her education in Calcutta, in France, and in the higher lectures for women at Cambridge opened intellectual vistas unavailable to most British or Indian women writing in the last decades of the century.

In the poems of the elder Dutts and of Mary Leslie, the strands of nationalism and religious piety are inextricably twisted; each feels both at home and alienated in India—whether the alienation be that of Indian Anglophilia or, for Leslie, a Calvinist conviction of spiritual unworthiness. In the next generation, Toru Dutt managed these elements by taking her religion more for granted, if seriously, and, like Derozio, by triangulating an understanding of poetry and politics through an international context. Her uncles, by contrast, focused necessarily on making their way as poets, intellectuals, and professionals in a society controlled by the British and on defending their family decision to convert to Christianity. While Toru was able to play with language and form to achieve a kind of intellectual and linguistic flexibility, her uncles worked within conventions in a way that feels like poetry wearing an uncomfortable set of clothes.

The kinds of religious piety represented by the elder Dutts and by Mary Leslie, are, as I imply in earlier chapters, by no means the only ways that Christianity figured in the Indian literary scene. Certainly, Sir William Jones's piety was of quite a different kind, intellectually speaking, from the poets I am concerned with here. His mixture of deism and Anglican Christianity, his admiration for other religions, and his broad interests in the moral philosophy and religious art of Indian and Persian traditions made his pious endeavors to improve the dating of the biblical flood an enterprise very different from activities inspired by missionary zeal. Similarly, the radical Protestantism of the early Calcutta Baptists—and its origins in working-class British life and in the East Indian community—made for an evangelicalism sometimes more politically radical than Mary Leslie's. This more radical background, along with his education in the philosophy of the Scottish Enlightenment and in late eighteenth-century political radicalism, shaped the poetry of H. L. V. Derozio. As I argue in chapter 2, Derozio's friends who remained Christian—the poets T. W. Smyth and William Page—were openly critical of British imperial power in part because of their religious convictions. Although clearly Christianity in India maintained and deepened this sort of radical critique—witness the career of C. F. Andrews as the most notable example in the twentieth century—in the mid-nineteenth century, Christianity most frequently wore the face of evangelical piety. The resulting poetry was heavily influenced by the dogmatic codes and dominant tropes of missionary zeal, tropes that in the Dutts' poetry proved remarkably durable.

By 1870, the elder Dutts had been writing poems for many years, some published in newspapers, some shared among family and friends. They had, earlier, brought out two volumes of youthful verse. Shoshee Chunder—who does not appear in the family collection—had published *Miscellaneous Verses* (Calcutta, 1848), and Hur Chunder had put together a collection titled *Fugitive Pieces* (Calcutta, 1841). *The Dutt Family Album,* published in London in 1870, was an altogether more elaborate affair. At 210 pages, it is bound in a green cloth cover, with the title and cover art embossed in gold. Red and blue ornamental capitals adorn the words *Dutt* and *Album.* In the tendrils entwining the title perch four golden birds, a group of three—representing the brothers Govin, Hur, and Greece—and a single bird on a higher branch of the family tree representing their nephew Omesh. The title, cover, and paratexts of the volume attest to the diffidence with which it was assembled and the mix of ambition and modesty that characterizes some of its verse. These paratexts speak to the simultaneous intellectual complexity and dogmatic simplification in the poetic texts.

As in many similar volumes, the Dutts' paratexts are as revealing as the poems they preface. Even the title is a kind of curiosity, connoting at once the public and the private, bespeaking the personal album or commonplace book and the old-fashioned genre of the annual gift book. Despite its iconographical cover, the volume contains no indication of the authors' full names, no indication of which poet wrote which poems. Rather, the poetic texts are framed by two epigraphs and an anonymous author's preface. The first epigraph appears on the verso of the half title page. It is taken from Leigh Hunt and may allude, when appropriated in this context, equally to English and Persian poetic traditions: "Not oaks alone are trees, nor roses flowers, / Much humble wealth makes rich this world of ours." British poets only by affiliation, who unlike British orientalists were not deeply immersed in Persian poetry, the Dutts make indirect links to traditions they cannot entirely claim.[4] Their productions are neither oaks nor roses, British nor Persian, epic nor ghazal.

The second epigraph to the *Dutt Family Album* appears on the title page and is equally problematic. It reproduces a quatrain from Richard Chenevix Trench, dean of Westminster and, after 1864, archbishop of Dublin:

> I liken thy outgoing, O my book,
> To the impatience of a little brook,
> Which might with flowers have lingered pleasantly,
> Yet toils to perish in the mighty sea.

This second epigraph the Dutts took from Trench's untitled sonnet, first published in 1838 in *Sabbation, Honor Neale and Other Poems,* and then reprinted in numerous editions of Trench's poetry. The passage in its original context no doubt appealed to the

Dutts' piety, as many of Trench's poems are explicitly religious or devotional. In both epigraphs, the Dutts minimize their own work before the reader can experience it.

This modesty is reiterated in the brief preface to *The Dutt Family Album*, a preface that reads all the more uncomfortably on account of its self-conscious presentation of the work as a novelty. The author(s) of the preface write, as is traditional, in the third person:

> The writers of the following pages are aware that bad poetry is intolerable, and that mediocre poetry deserves perhaps even a harsher epithet. There is a glut of both in the market. But they venture on publication, not because they think their verses good, but in the hope that their book will be regarded, in some respects, as a curiosity. They are foreigners, natives of India, of different ages, and in different walks of life, yet of one family, in whom the ties of blood relationship have been drawn closer by the holy bond of Christian brotherhood. As foreigners educated out of England, they solicit the indulgence of British critics to poems which on these grounds alone may, it is hoped, have some title to their attention.

The preface, quoted here in its entirety, like the epigraphs, draws equal attention to the poems' modest claims and to their religious significance.

In one of the few reviews of the volume, the *Athenaeum*'s reader followed the Dutts' lead, paraphrasing the preface and calling the volume "creditable to foreigners educated out of England." The reviewer went on, however, to claim that the volume was insufficiently foreign. Here the Dutts faced the same metropolitan demand that confronted their teacher David Lester Richardson in the 1830s, when reviewers complained that his *Bengal Annual* was insufficiently Indian. The reviewer argued that in the *Family Album*, "we might expect to meet with distinct characteristics, some gleam of foreign light, some robustness of native thought or expression. Instead we have imitative and artificial verse; but the poems are readable,—a merit that cannot be ascribed to most books of poetry." The reviewer, finally, was made uncomfortable by the fact that the Dutts' conversion had made them "ashamed of their former faith" (*Athenaeum*, no. 2254 [December 30, 1870]: 885–86). Given the tenor of many of the *Album*'s poems, the discomfort shared by authors and reviewer is unsurprising. The preface does not fairly reflect the variety of topics and influences touched on in the poems; yet, like the *Athenaeum* review, it identifies the dominant problematic that shapes the volume—the Dutts' conversion to Christianity.

The Dutts' conversion was, in the small world of Calcutta Christianity, quite dramatic, and it caused both the unusual sense of family cohesion displayed in the *Album*'s preface and an unusual sense of familial alienation from the dominant culture. We cannot know exactly what led to the family's decision, but some evidence does remain. The story, as it has survived, is narrated within the contexts of missionary ideology and thus deemphasizes the social and intellectual consequences of this action. To understand it, we have to go back three generations. In brief, the grandfather of Govin, Hur, and Greece Chunder Dutt (hence the great-grandfather of Toru Dutt) was a pious Hindu. Nilmoni Dutt, nonetheless, was great friends with Rammohun Roy and quite interested in the ideas motivating what became the Brahmo Samaj. Not surprisingly, Nilmoni's son Rasamoy was a collector of English books and an important advocate of education. According to Harihar Das, Rasamoy "was catholic in his views and opposed the extravagance in connexion with Hindu Pujas and ceremonials which had involved his father in pecuniary difficulties" (5). As commissioner to the Court of Requests, Rasamoy held a responsible position; he managed through his intellectual and business acumen to restore the family fortunes. At his death in 1854, his sons performed the usual funeral rites, but the eldest, Kishen, was taken ill with a fever in the process. On his deathbed a few days later, Kishen asked his brother Girish (or Greece)—who was not yet a Christian—to read the baptismal service and to baptize him. As recounted in a letter of Dr. W. S. Mackay's, dated June 29, 1854, Kishen then "called all his family around him, and . . . bore dying testimony to Christ, and besought his family to embrace the Gospel" (H. Das, 8). Mackay continued, "It appeared old Rasamoy himself had been a careful reader of the Bible, and that he had made all the ladies of the family write out the whole of the Psalms in Bengalee" (H. Das, 8). Mackay attributed Kishen's conversion to a deathbed "dream or vision of another world."

Thus, Rasamoy and Kishen were responsible for bringing the remaining brothers and their wives (at least nominally) into the Scottish church. When Mackay visited the family shortly after Kishen's death, he "found that all the brothers and most of their sons were so far believers in Christianity that they were making preparations in their families, getting their affairs in order, and conversing with their wives, with a view of coming over to the Lord in a body—their cousin, Shoshee Chunder Dutt, with them." Mackay went on, "The wives were willing to remain with their husbands, but are still firm idolaters. . . . If the whole family are baptized together, you may suppose what an excitement it will produce; for, take them all in all, they are the most distinguished Hindoo family under British rule" (H. Das, 9). Thus, the Reverend Mackay, superintendent of the Church of Scotland's mission school in Calcutta, alluded to the significant social as well as the religious consequences of conversion. Although Mackay read these consequences positively, as a victory for the church, the detail of his narrative indicates the seriousness of this family decision.

Mackay's language makes the baptism of the Dutts sound like a death or preparation for going on a long journey. The brothers and their sons needed, Mackay observed, to get their "affairs in order" and to make preparations in their families. Indeed, though Mackay did not say so, their conversion entailed something akin to social death. As Toru Dutt's letters, written years later, make clear, the brothers—while retaining their employment in various government offices—would have lost caste and social status through their conversion. At a stroke, they made their children unmarriageable within the Hindu community, drove a division between their joint family and the families of their wives, and possibly created a rift within their joint family itself. As Mackay wrote, all the brothers and "most of the sons" were persuaded of the truth of Christianity. As for the wives, they did as they were bid, however reluctantly.

For the women of the Dutt family, the consequences of the Dutt brothers' Anglophilia and their conversion were both positive and negative: positive in that the women had greater access to literacy—some became literate in multiple languages—and negative in that they were excluded from the networks of sociality that would have allowed them to arrange successful marriages for their children. More than twenty years after this conversion, Toru Dutt wrote to her favorite correspondent, Mary Martin, saying that she wished Martin to come out to India for an extended visit, as "we do not visit any people about the neighborhood except Uncle Girish." "Do you know," Toru wrote, "I am getting to love our lonely life too much, and . . . I want a little shaking up, before I become quite an anchorite!" (October 31, 1876; *Letters,* 233). The same theme is struck in an earlier letter, where it is coupled with the issue of marriage. Having visited a Parsi family of their acquaintance, Toru described how the daughter of the family exclaimed (in English) that Toru remained unmarried. Recounting the incident to Mary Martin, Toru commented, "Marriage, you must know is a great thing among the Hindus. An unmarried girl of fifteen is never heard of in our country. If any friend of my grandmother's happens to see me, the first question is if I am married; and considerable astonishment, and perhaps a little scandal, follows the reply" (May 3, 1876; *Letters,* 152). She also makes clear that the family was not visiting among their Hindu acquaintances. In other letters, Toru mentions being excluded from weddings and other ritual gatherings, but her grandmother (her mother's mother) seems to have provided a continuing link to social life. Although Toru mentioned, on more than one occasion, her desire that her grandmother, too, become a Christian, she seems to have benefited from her grandmother's continuing love for her daughter's family as well as from the social network of her grandmother's extended family. Nonetheless, the conversion in itself made it relatively unlikely that either Toru or her sister, Aru, could marry well or easily; it significantly limited their social world in India, though it did create an entrée to clerical social circles when they were abroad.[5]

Toru's father, Govin, gives touching evidence of these concerns in *The Dutt Family Album.* His poem "The Hindu Convert to His Wife" makes clear the consequences of conversion. The poet, or "Hindu convert," addresses his spouse:

> Nay, part not so—one moment stay,
> Repel me not with scorn.
> Like others, wilt thou turn away,
> And leave me quite forlorn?
> Wilt thou too join the scoffing crowd,
> The cold, the heartless, and the proud,
> Who curse the hallowed morn,

When, daring idols to disown,
I knelt before the Saviour's throne?

(28)

Govin goes on to recall their marital love and their mutual grief over the death of their son, and he describes this new division between them over religion, which drives him to "despair." The poet recalls Jesus's saying that even the sparrow "cannot fall / Unmarked by Him that cares for all" (31). He concludes, though grieved, that he will continue to pray, hoping that Jesus will "constrain thee, love, to bless His Name" (31). Govin characterizes himself as a sinner who meets "no kindness here"; he sheds no tears at being ostracized in the wider world, being grieved chiefly by division between himself and his wife. But the sense of alienation conveyed in the poem is palpable.

A similar sense of alienation sounds a dominant note in the *Album* from its very beginning. The first poem, "Home," also by Govin, takes its shape from the romantic topoi of recollecting an absent place.

No picture from the master hand
    Of Gainsborough or Cuyp may vie
With that which at my soul's command
    Appears before mine inward eye
In foreign climes when doomed to roam—
Its scene my own dear native home.

What though no cloud-like hills uprear
    Their serried heights sublime afar!
What though the ocean be not near,
    With wave and wind in constant war!
Nor rock nor sea could add a grace,
So perfect seems the hallowed place.

Casuarinas in solemn range
    At distance look like verdant hills,
And winds draw from them music strange,
    Such as the tide makes when it fills
Some shingle-strown and land-girt bay
From men and cities far away.

(1)

Here Govin reverses the trope he learned so well from David Lester Richardson, the trope of exile. The poem commences by redefining exile, and his English verse is flavored by D.L.R.'s influence even as the poles of home and foreign are reversed. Home is clearly Bengal and exile "a foreign clime," presumably a European clime, given the examples of Gainsborough and Cuyp.

But the mental calisthenics involved in recapitulating the trope of exile in "Home" go beyond a simple reversal. The dyad of home and exile—let's say Bengal and southern England—is always already a representation. Rather than England or the low countries serving for comparison to "home," the poet understands home through visual, and also verbal, representations of European landscape. As memory supplies the Bengali landscape to the mind's eye, it is laid over the European landscape almost as a transparency, its contours matching European contours, but with a difference. The casuarinas serve as hills, as oceans, as shingle-strewn shores. In the next stanza, native tropical and imported temperate vegetation of Bengal—mangoes, bamboos, palms, plums, and peach trees—become the nest of home, surrounded by the fields of Bengal, which stretch before the mind's eye like an "emerald sea." The cattle munching the greensward are, presumably, nothing like Cuyp's but nonetheless substitute for them.

> And at high noon when every tree
> Stands brooding on its round of shade
> And cattle to the shelter flee
> And there, in groups recumbent laid,
> Gaze ruminant—what deep repose
> Lies on the landscape as it glows!
>
> (2)

The "emerald sea" of vegetation and the brooding cattle surround the family house.

Finally, at the poem's end, all landscape is shrunk to—and expanded to—family:

> As round me cluster those I love,
> And eye meets eye in glances bright,
> I feel that earth itself may be
> Lit up with heaven's own radiancy.
>
> (2)

Thus the European landscape is layered over, first by a Bengali landscape and then by the interior of the nest (evoking the volume's cover), sheltering the family—the poetic Dutts, the family circle, "heaven's own radiancy." The alienation from Bengal is marked by the peculiarities of recollection and by the shrinking of landscape to the domestic nest. The poet cannot possess even the Bengali landscape the way Wordsworth or Coleridge might have possessed the English landscape. The next lines in *The Dutt Family Album* prove that the nest is as fragile as the recollection of landscape.[6]

"Home" functions as part of a diptych; it is paired with the poem that follows and comments upon it. The second poem has no real title of its own and is simply called "Lines, written some time after." "Lines," rather than reversing the tropes of colonial verse, directly echoes the poetry of metropolitan culture, particularly that of Milton and Matthew Arnold. It takes as its starting point—though it does not say so directly—the death of Govin's only son, Abju. In contrast to "Home," in "Lines . . . sometime after" both nature and family are dark to the poet; peace is nowhere to be found; paradise is lost. In his grief the poet moralizes, paraphrasing Milton:

> 'A kingdom is to me my mind,'
> The shadow of one sorrow flung
> Athwart it, makes this change unkind.
>
> (3)

The next stanza—looking for consolation—quotes directly from Arnold's "Stanzas from the Grand Chartreuse":

> Well, be it so. We have on earth
> No city for continuous stay;
> As children of the second birth
> We seek another far away
>
> (3)

Arnold's emblematic landscape is crossed with the allegorical landscape of *Pilgrim's Progress,* as Govin dares to hope for reunification in heaven, where the scattered "pearls" of his family will once more be united.

Govin's allusion to Bunyan's allegorical landscape is by no means the only way *Pilgrim's Progress* features in *The Dutt Family Album.* Bunyan's place is part of a larger Calvinist and evangelical landscape in the collection. Although critics have scarcely noticed it, the social and theological contexts of the Dutts' conversion were crucial to their poetry. The family was baptized in the Scottish Church, within a tradition that emphasized Calvinist dogma (H. Das, 10).[7] Later, Govin Chunder Dutt and his family attended various Anglican churches both in England and in India. Toru Dutt's letters speak of attending St. Paul's Church when the family lived in Cambridge and of attending both the Old Mission Church and St. John's in Calcutta. *The Dutt Family Album* and even Shoshee Chunder Dutt's second volume, *A Vision of Sumeru,* reveal the impact of a Calvinist missionary spirit on the elder generation.

In *The Dutt Family Album,* the model of *Pilgrim's Progress* underlies several poems, while missionary language and attitudes inflect others. Govin's "Sonnet, Written on the Fly-leaf of Alford's New Testament" takes its epigraph from Bunyan, quoting the passage where "the shepherds" give Pilgrim a mirror in which he glimpses heaven. Govin addresses Alford as his "dear Guide," and both Alford's commentary and the Testament become a mirror in which the poet sees

> Beulah's trim orchard walks—the path serene
> Of crystal waters, and the city door,
> With dome and minaret crowned and foliage green.
>
> (21)

Like the oaks and roses of the volume's epigraph, heaven, too, seems an interesting mix of trim orchard walks and minarets. But though they could assimilate minarets to Beulah, the Dutt brothers could not rest easy in the vision. The missionary's specters—Hindu "idols"—remained.

If we had to distill the poems of *The Dutt Family Album* to their most religious, or perhaps iconic, core, we could do no better than "Lines, Written While on a Visit to Kalighat." Kalighat, the most important temple in Kolkata to this day, makes an odd but logical destination for a "Hindu convert," as Govin called himself. Through the nineteenth century, there was much controversy about government contribution to pujas, and the offerings to Kali at her temple were particularly appalling to missionary sensibilities, as they involved animal sacrifice (primarily of goats).[8] Only the temple of Jagannātha (whom Victorian missionaries called Juggernaut) in Puri inspired a more horrified response. The Dutt poet who wrote "On a Visit to Kalighat" echoed a century of British missionary reaction to the shrine:

> Still grim Idolatry with pomp,
> O'er India's realm doth reign;
> Still in its fell and baneful power
> Is owned in palace, hut, and bower,
> In city, town, and plain.
>
> Where'er we turn we see them rise,
> Those temples huge and grand,
> To hideous idols consecrate:
> For man's degraded state!
> Oh, woe to this fair land!
>
> But most they fear that goddess dread,
> Reeking with blood and wine,
> And prince and peasant trembling bring
> Their rich or humble offering
> To her ensanguined shrine.
>
> (24)

Though lamenting the willful errancy of the inhabitants of India, the poet, finally, prays that God's love and grace will allow his countrymen to open their "blinded eyes." His poem concludes with a plea that God should "send freedom to the slave" (25). Here is the ultimate transformation of eighteenth-century radicalism: Jones's republicanism and Derozio's plea for freedom have become a plea for religious conversion. The Dutts' religion is reduced to a politics of contending sovereignty—local custom versus God. And the transgressive potential of Kali worship is emphasized in a way that calls attention to its Christian counterpart: rather than milk, Kali is offered here a mix of blood and wine.[9]

A more moderate (and perhaps later) poem, "The Caves of Elephanta," strikes a related but different note, perhaps because the old religious shrines of Elephanta are described as having been deserted. Their glorious carving has been marred by the "guns of Portugal" and the graffiti of travelers; the poem moralizes the ruins as a testimony to the futility of human fame:

> And now the remnant—Pride—behold!
> A lonely wilderness again.
> Where are the gems and cloth of gold?
> Where is the king and all his train?
>
> The guns of Portugal have done
> Their shattering work amid these gods;
> The banyan lo! a niche hath won,
> And to the south wind's whisper nods
>
> (66)

Though "The Caves of Elephanta" alludes to blood sacrifice, the Christian zeal inspired in the visit to Kalighat is tempered to a reflection on the mortality of all human projects. Do we glimpse, too, a moment when the poet, though Christian, is allowed to lament the "guns" of empire?

Not every scene in *The Dutt Family Album* is moralized in quite the same way as Kalighat or the ruins of Elephanta, but the missionary seriousness and Calvinist ethos of the Dutts' conversion never entirely disappeared. This ethos, and the long reach of David Lester Richardson's admiration for Milton, continues in Shoshee Chunder Dutt's collection, *A Vision of Sumeru and Other Poems.*

A Vision of Sumeru and Other Poems: Bringing Milton to the Mountain

Shoshee Chunder Dutt was not included in *The Dutt Family Album,* but his work betrays a sensibility similar to that of his first cousins. Shoshee Chunder was the child of Nilmoni Dutt's youngest son, Pitamber, and became a justice of the peace in Calcutta. Like his cousins, he published verse, beginning with *Miscellaneous Verses* (1848); his longest collection of poetry, *A Vision of Sumeru and Other Poems* (1878), reprinted earlier work and included a newer long poem that represented the enthusiasm of the Dutts' conversion. This poem, which lent its title to the whole volume, was also perhaps Shoshee's dialogue with his cousin Govin's late study of Sanskrit and his niece Toru's and nephew Romesh's interest in translating Sanskrit verse.[10]

Shoshee's *Vision of Sumeru* draws on and responds to these family interests and to his own religious and academic background. The volume is divided into four major sections: the long title poem, a section of Indian ballads, a collection titled "Lays of Ancient Greece" (frankly imitative of Macaulay's famous *Lays of Ancient Rome*), and a section of miscellaneous poems. The contradictions among these endeavors are too numerous to describe briefly. On the one hand, the construction of the Indian ballads suggests participation in the important nineteenth-century discourse that—spinning out of Tod's *Annals and Antiquities of Rajasthan* and similar works—established a story of "India" oppressed first by "Moguls" and then by Pashtuns. "India," thus, is defined as Hindu. At the same time, as a Christian, Shoshee must reject his own narrative, for a renovated or free India would need to make room for or, better, be made over by Christian belief and practice. And finally, cohering with neither of these narratives, there is a remnant of an older, Enlightenment discourse, which suggests the power of science to create a new India.[11]

The "Indian Ballads" incorporate these contradictions whole, rather like a snake swallowing a teapot. The first and last poems of this section reframe the heroic central poem in a highly peculiar way. The first, "Address to the Ganges," is an early poem. It begins by evoking ancient Indian heroism:

> Canst thou forget the glorious past?
>   When, mighty as a god,
> With hands and heart unfetter'd yet,
> And eyes with slavish tears unwet,
>   Each sable warrior trod
> Thy sacred shore; before the blast
> Of Moslem conquest hurried by;
> Ere yet the Mogul spear was nigh.
>
> (81)

No lines are spared to lament—equally—the British conquest of India. Though the "savage Tártár" conqueror comes in for a disapproving stanza, he is followed immediately by those dominant Christian missionary icons of Indian degradation—sati and infanticide, each given its own stanza. The poet then turns against his own recital of India's woes:

> But why recount our woes and shame?
>   Upon thy sacred shore
> Be mine to dream of glories past,
> To grieve those glories could not last,
>   And muse on days of yore!
> For ever harp on former fame,

Remembering still those spirits brave
Who sleep beneath thy boist'rous wave.

(84)

Shoshee's harp does in fact harp on this nostalgia, though it sounds discordant in the company of burning widows and murdered infants.

Very similar tropes shape the last poem in "Indian Ballads." In "My Native Land," Shoshee, like Henry Meredith Parker before him, characterizes India as a widow. Nonetheless, the poet exclaims, "I feel the dagger's edge, the dart / That rankles in thy widow'd heart" (142). And he concludes,

I cannot choose but love thee yet;
And, while I rove thy fragrant meads along,
I only wish I could forget
That thy sun hath for ever set,
Sweet land of love and song!

(142)

Here, as in other poems in the volume, Shoshee Chunder seems to consign India to a long and ignominious future, a future of slavery.

Other poems in *A Vision of Sumeru* including "Sonnets:—India" envision a free India whose future is guided by "Science." "My Native Land" is significantly bleaker than the sonnets, but for its footnote. As is the case with so many of these English language poems, in "My Native Land" the paratext is as important as the text. To counter his assertion that India's sun has "forever set," Shoshee appends this note to his poem's last stanza:

> The following beautiful stanza was added, to a presentation copy of the poem, by the late Rev. J. H. Parker:—

"Nay, not *for ever* set the sun;
Truth's brighter, holier sun shall rise to shine:—
See, even now, the dawn begun,
A glorious course thou yet may'st run,
Beneath the beamings of that 'Sun
Of Righteousness' Divine."

(142)

Like the intrusion of sati and infanticide in "Address to the Ganges," so Reverend Parker's optimistic stanza strikes a contradictory note. Similar contradictions plague the volume's title poem, caught as it is between the claims of Christian dogmatism and Hindu protonationalism.

"A Vision of Sumeru," the volume's title poem, is peculiar in many ways, drawing on traditions of orientalist poetry and translation, on traditional descriptions of Hindu deities, and on the dominant tropes of missionary and evangelical Christian literature. Like Michael Madhusudan Dutt, Shoshee Chunder reveals his debt to David Lester Richardson's and the Dutt family's fascination with Milton, for "A Vision of Sumeru" parallels *Paradise Lost* in its story of gods (or angels) exiled from heaven.[12] In place of Milton's Satan, we have Brahma, who here plays the role of a central commanding deity. In place of Milton's muse Urania, we have Sarasvatī, the Indian goddess of music and learning. Shoshee's muse, however, lures him into a paradoxical situation. Unlike Milton's Urania, whom no one would have taken for the object of European devotion in the seventeenth century, Sarasvatī was and still is venerated in Bengal. Though the poet consigns her to hell at the poem's end, he continues to call upon her aid.

Shoshee's poem is full of such paradoxes, ones that Michael Madhusudan overcame by simply ignoring his professed Christianity in most of his poetry. When he did reprise Milton, Michael Madhusudan read him through a romantic lens, a Blakean kind of lens that revised the meanings of Satan. In the *Meghanadavadha kavya,* as discussed in chapter 4, Michael re-created the *Rāmāyaṇa* on this romantic model (and in part on a Bengali model as well), making a sympathetic hero not of Rama but of Rāvaṇa. One could say that Michael was deliberately of the devil's party. Of Shoshee Chunder Dutt, by contrast, we might say, as Blake said of Milton, that he was of the devil's party and did *not* know it. "A Vision of Sumeru" is of Brahma's party in spite of itself. The purport of Shoshee Chunder's poem is to describe Jehovah/Jesus as a divine power superseding Indian deities. But the narration of Jesus's victory makes problematic the poem's dogmatic claims.

"A Vision of Sumeru" is caught between two religious traditions and two formal allegiances. At about two thousand lines in three cantos of irregular stanzas, the poem lies formally between a long irregular ode and an epic episode. Its formal instability mirrors fundamental thematic and even theological instabilities. The poem begins by describing Brahma's ire at not being properly worshipped by humans in India. Then follows the convocation of the gods on Mount Sumeru; the sending of Brahma's emissary Māruti (known as Pāvana or, more familiarly, Hanumān, though Shoshee does not use his most common name) to earth to investigate the cause of this neglect; and the response of the gods when Māruti reports that Brahma has been superseded by Jesus. In the last canto, Brahma and the gods descend in warlike array from Sumeru to battle Jesus, only to be conquered without a shot by the victorious—and very Victorian—messiah.[13] Rather than Jesus being assimilated into the Hindu pantheon, as he in fact was from time to time in India, he instead informs Brahma that Jehovah *created* the Hindu pantheon. Jesus declares that Jehovah long ago called the Hindu deities forth "to rule o'er men." He tells the gods that they have forgotten "the day, / Forgotten too [their] Maker's name" and laid an "impious claim" to Jehovah's power. Like

Satan rising against Milton's god, so too have Brahma and the other gods risen against the Almighty, the poet implies. Jesus has been commissioned by Jehovah to consign the gods to hell.

The poet narrates a colloquy of the Hindu gods on Mount Sumeru and describes their subsequent descent to earth. He has Jesus, who appears only in sections 30 and 31, assert but not narrate the Hindu deities' coming demise. Jesus sends the Hindu pantheon packing:

> Immortal life to ye belong,
> Go taste immortal pains,
> With sighs, and wails, and blasphemies,
> Amid the funeral screams of hell.
>
> (77)

These lines end section 31. Section 32 begins abruptly: "My dream is o'er; Sumeru's gods— / Sumeru's self hath past [*sic*] away" (77). The Hindu gods are no more, the poet claims.

But the poem performs exactly what it claims cannot and should not be performed—the restoration of the Hindu pantheon (could we think of it as mythological Bollywood?). For even after the gods of Sumeru are consigned to Hell, the poet lovingly describes them. He dwells, for the second time, on the beauties of Lakshmi and Uma, the "Cinnaras mild / And Apsarás born of the main." He concludes,

> And never more ye may behold
>   The gods and sprites so deft
> Wanton upon the craggy mound,
>   Or in the woody glades,
> Or happy walks, and sylvan shades,
>   Move loftily and slow;
> Or where resistless torrents sweep,
> Or milder streamlets gently flow,
> Or where the ocean surges bound,
>   Fit haunts for such as they!
>   Sing songs, or play, or sleep,
> In morning hour, or at bright noon,
> Or when the mists of evening close,
>   Or 'neath the autumn moon.
> That day, when Bruhmá was uncrown'd,
> With him to hell they did depart,
> By fiery tempest whirl'd away;
> Eternal justice doom'd them all

Who had their lot together wound,
And none may them again recall
To envied bliss, and boundless power,
And dignity sublime.

(78)

Here and in the lines preceding these, Shoshee Chunder *shows* the beauties of Sumeru, reprises them, recalls them one final time in the poem; he only *tells* of the gods' consignment to hell. The moral climax of the poet's story is, in fact, not narrated but described. Jesus speaks God's doom, and we are to presume that his will is done, but Brahma and his train (like Michael Madhusudan's Rāvaṇa or Shelley's version of Milton's Satan) are the poem's real heroes. Here the narrative organization of the poem exceeds its dogmatic claims. The reprise of the gods' multiple powers and beauties has more rhetorical power than Jesus's judgment.

Near the poem's conclusion, the poet attempts to compensate for this evident contradiction with exclamatory verse, recurring again to the ending of his "dream." "My dream is o'er," he writes at the conclusion of "A Vision of Sumeru," and every "art of man" that attempts to restore service to the ancient gods is "fruitless now and vain":

Glory on earth! Jehovah's sway
Alone endureth now!
Alone it passeth not away!

(79)

In the final stanza of his longest poem, the poet appeals—to the reader, one presumes—"ah! do not deem / The poet's dream an idle song, / And nothingness, and phantasy" (79). And yet it is precisely as fantasy that the poem makes its strongest gestures.

Only within a framework of domesticity, within the tropes of evangelical missionizing, not within any frame of heroic action, can the poem narrate Christian activity. Here Shoshee seems to share Govin's conflation of Christianity and domesticity. In canto 2, Māruti, investigating the sources of Brahma's complaints, comes upon a Brahmin boy in prayer. Truth comes out of the mouth of babes; the young boy tells Māruti that Jehovah is everywhere and, in a pathos that descends to almost incoherent doggerel, describes Jesus's birth:

'Twas many, many years ago,
The time was winter wild,
Jehovah's son a babe when lay;
While stars look'd down in mute amaze,
Or wand'ring show'd towards Him the way

(49)

This description of the incarnation and the claim at the conclusion of three cantos that "a light o'er India sheds its gleam" constitute the triumph of the poet's beliefs, beliefs that, manifestly, had little impact in the country as a whole. Shoshee Chunder writes with the zeal of a convert, yet one can sense—despite the poem's religious claims—the impact on the poet of the very "phantasy" to which at such length he bids adieu.

Mary E. Leslie: Home and Jesus, Devotion and Violence

At the end of his volume of verse, Shoshee Chunder Dutt appended a "prize poem" written by his grandson Shuteesh to celebrate the arrival of the Prince of Wales in India. Whether or not the proud grandfather entirely shared his grandson's enthusiasm for Queen Victoria, as expressed metrically in Shuteesh's poem, the entire Dutt clan was so willing over the years to praise British power that Rosinka Chaudhuri has aptly characterized their time as "loyal hours" (*Gentlemen*, 127–58). We see a similar loyal sentiment in Greece Chunder Dutt's late poem on the Taj Mahal (published in his collection *Cherry Stones*, 1881), where he—in an unintentionally amusing moment—compares Shāh Jāhan's great mausoleum to Victoria's monument to Alfred at Frogmore. A more believable, and somewhat more nuanced, note of loyalty is struck in *The Dutt Family Album*, when the writer extols the virtues of George Canning during the uprising of 1857. As Chaudhuri points out, Bengalis generally did not support the rebellion of 1857 (*Gentlemen*, 127–58). In *The Dutt Family Album*, the Dutts endorse the sense of justice that earned Canning, among British hawks, the sobriquet "Clemency Canning." The poem "To Lord Canning, during the Mutiny" at once promotes justice (including legal but not summary punishment of those responsible for the mutiny) and professes loyalty. Anglophilia, horror at British vengeance during the mutiny, and Christianity coexist in uneasy mixture. Thus, the elder Dutts engaged the political context of their times. Mary Leslie, too, wrote topical political poems that blended nationalism and religion, but for her the codes of Christian virtue allowed little room for ambivalence in either political or devotional texts.

Leslie's war poems—for such we have to call them—developed an unambiguous view of the uprising of 1857. In her verse, British soldiers are heroes; British women are pitiable victims and noble nurses; and God at the end is entrusted with bringing a Christian future to India. Leslie's meditation on the mutiny was published in the immediate aftermath of the fighting. Her volume *Sorrows, Aspirations, and Legends from India*, begins with an untitled sequence of thirty-six sonnets narrating the events of the year 1857, from spring through New Year's Day 1858. Leslie's response to the uprising, like the rest of her poetry, was profoundly shaped by her family background and education and by her place in a personal religious network extending into the British Army and administration. Though biographical details about Leslie are sketchy, they are crucial to understanding her response to the events of 1857: her father's position clearly shaped her understanding of politics, poetry, and religion.

Born on January 13, 1834, at Monghyr in what is now Bihar, Mary Eliza Leslie was the daughter of Andrew Leslie, a Scotsman who had gone to India in 1824 as a Baptist missionary (Burrage, 201). Andrew Leslie began life as a printer, but after becoming connected to a Baptist congregation, he conceived a plan to go to India as a missionary. Following some delay, his application was approved, and he was sent to study at Bristol Academy, to prepare himself to go to India—not as a printer but, with a considerable rise in status, as an ordained minister. Apparently Andrew Leslie was an enthusiastic student, for the memorials published at his death in 1870 mention his extensive knowledge, his elegant scholarship, and his "masterly English style." The extent of his language training is unclear, but it probably included the classics—at least at a beginning level—and certainly included a knowledge of Hindustani as well as Bangla. He is recorded as having revised a Hindi New Testament. Leslie is likely to have been a product of good Scottish primary schooling and of serious self-education, for his memorialist says that before his conversion he had "drunk deep of the poisonous streams of skepticism and universalism"—in other words, those same texts that shaped David Hare and Derozio (*Baptist Magazine* 62 [1870]: 808). On his ordination, Andrew and his first wife, also characterized as a missionary, departed for India, where he was posted to Monghyr. There he led a congregation, oversaw schools, and proselytized the hill tribes. After his wife's death in 1826, he remarried; his second wife was another missionary, the daughter of "his eminent predecessor," the Baptist missionary John Chamberlain, according to church records. With her he had two children who survived at his death in 1870: a son and Mary Eliza. When Mary was seven years old, the family took a year of home leave in England, returning to Calcutta in 1842, when Andrew was called to the pulpit of the Lower Circular Road Baptist Church (*Baptist Magazine* 62 [1870]: 808). According to his successor, Thomas Evans, Andrew Leslie led a "mixed" congregation, which invited the participation of members of the Brahmo Samaj.[14]

Exactly what education Andrew Leslie provided his daughter is unclear, but it appears to have been reasonably extensive. Her first published volume of verse featured a long title poem, "Ina," which contained notes and epigraphs in Greek, Italian, and German—including quotations from Goethe, Tasso, and the *Iliad.* Her other volumes, too, indicate wide reading, though they restrict themselves to familiar orientalist or Christian devotional topoi. At the same time, Mary Leslie's missionary writings, which I believe to be largely autobiographical, make clear that she both read and wrote Bangla and possibly other Indian vernacular languages.[15]

The foundation of her knowledge, however, was clearly pious. Her family was devout and had its social life in Indian evangelical Christian circles. As was the case with Mary Carshore, Mary Leslie probably had no expectation of living in Britain, a country of which she had little direct experience. The parameters of her thought and adult world lay wholly in Bengal, so far as I can tell. Her sense of home was formed in a childhood love of India and a simultaneous sense of alienation shaped by being part of a minority religious community. There is a kind of paradox here. The Baptists in Bengal were certainly not a state religion but instead tended to see themselves in a more international frame than did the evangelicals of the Church of England. They had extensive ties with Baptists in the United States, for example, and there was coming and going among British cities, Philadelphia, and Calcutta. Yet as Christians and by racial and cultural identification, British Baptists identified themselves with British national interests. This identification is particularly clear in Leslie's poems on the uprising of 1857, which she, nonetheless, calls "the Sorrow." These poems are framed in part by Leslie's family connections to leading figures in the conflict. Though she was not directly involved in it, Leslie seems to have experienced the violence of 1857 as trauma—and perhaps this trauma owes its force to the identification of British governance in north India at this time with evangelical earnestness.

One of the most famous and prolonged battles of the uprising was the siege of Lucknow, from July through November 1857, and this event is a primary focus in *Sorrows, Aspirations, and Legends.* The history of the siege came to form a centerpiece of "Mutiny" lore and patriotic gore in the 1860s and 1870s and inspired in Britain poems too numerous to name (among them Tennyson's "Havelock"). Leslie's sonnets, published in 1858 in London, were both timely and topical. But her choice of subject, I believe, was more personal than strategic.

Lucknow was the capital of the state of Oudh (now Awadh), the center of resistance to the British. Oudh had been high-handedly annexed by the East India Company in 1856, upon which, much wealth was confiscated, the nawab exiled to Calcutta, and a good portion of his army rendered unemployed or awkwardly absorbed into the company's army. Resentments ran high. Particularly important to Mary Leslie were two British figures in this story: Sir Henry Lawrence had been appointed as the chief administrator of Oudh in an attempt to quell dissatisfaction and avert incipient rebellion; and Henry Havelock, adjutant general to the British Army, famously led the relief of Lucknow. Havelock died at the end of that campaign while overseeing the evacuation of civilians. He had become close to Andrew Leslie when Mary was a child at Monghyr. Memorials to Andrew Leslie emphasize his crucial role in Havelock's religious life, as the agent of Havelock's decision to join the Baptist Church. In his later years, Havelock became well known for his attentions to the spiritual welfare of the men under his command and for his many acts of piety. He served with Henry Lawrence in the Burmese war, in which he temporarily converted the chief pagoda at Rangoon to a Christian chapel. Shortly after his death, the *Baptist Magazine* described Havelock as "every inch a soldier, and every inch a Christian." The writer declared, "His sterling piety, combined as it was with chivalrous daring and military genius, has naturally led to the association of his name with the great men of the Commonwealth, whose worth is the more appreciated in proportion to the liberality of the age. Havelock exhibited all the strength of their religious feelings without any of the vagaries of their enthusiasm. He was a Puritan of the true Cromwellian stamp" (50 [1858]: 209). Even more than Havelock, Henry Lawrence was known throughout North India for his piety and for the earnestness of the young officers and administrators with whom he surrounded himself in the Punjab. Though committed to the evangelical wing of the Anglican Church, he and his wife, Honoria, made common cause with other evangelicals in many missionary and social projects.

Mary Leslie, then, takes these two men as the heroes of her sequence of sonnets. Lawrence figures at the beginning (for he died shortly after the siege of Lucknow commenced) and Havelock toward the end. Lawrence is described as the pole star, the unchanging guide (now in heaven) to those below, who are surrounded by "woe and massacre." While other heavenly lights may wander, "thou alone / Remainest never changing," the poet says (*Sorrows,* 9). Almost simultaneously with Lawrence's death at Lucknow, the siege of Cawnpore (now Kanpur) came to an end with an infamous massacre of women and children, who were butchered and thrown into a well, and with the equally infamous retaliation against both soldiers and noncombatants by British forces. Before advancing on Lucknow, Henry Havelock led the raid that recaptured Cawnpore. Leslie treats Cawnpore and Lucknow similarly, praising feminine purity and heroism and masculine rescue of the innocent. Immediately preceding her sonnet on Lawrence's death, Leslie pauses to lament the massacre at Cawnpore. She has no word to say about the brutal British retaliation for the massacre, only characterizing Nana Sahib's forces as "fiends."

The whole of the massacre is understood in Christian terms. In the eighth sonnet, the poet describes the wails of victims blown on a "crimson" wind, while angels step "down Heaven's ladder stair" to comfort "their heart's wild, bird-like throbbings" (10). The next sonnet describes a British clergyman reading the Bible to his fellows at Cawnpore; his words call up a "better land" where no "hellish treachery" is with "malignant hatred coldly planned" (11). And finally, Leslie commemorates the dead British women and children:

> And nought remains but the wet, bloody floor,
> And little rings of soft, white baby-hair
> Mingled with long, dark tresses, dimmed with gore,
> In hopeless tangles scattered here and there,
> And God's own blessed Book of holy lore,
> Sole comforter amid that deep despair.
>
> (13)

Omitting Havelock's relief of Cawnpore, in the next sonnet Leslie turns toward Lucknow, commemorating Lawrence's death; then in the two sonnets that follow—XIII and XIV—she prays for divine (and therefore earthly) vengeance. The poet admits some surprise at her own bloodthirstiness but subsumes any misgivings in the first-person plural pronoun: "And we, who little thought such cry would spring / From our hearts even in their wildest hours, / Catch up the burning spirit" (16). This desire for vengeance turns into a celebration of the "heroes" and "heroines" of Lucknow in the sonnets that follow.

The heroines of Lucknow are portrayed as succoring angels. Meanwhile, the heroes have for "months of woe and dread / Like lions stood most gloriously at bay" (30). The greatest hero, however, is Henry Havelock, whose death is commemorated in a poem that—like so many others in this sequence—rhymes *head, shed, dread, red,* and by implication, *dead.* The second of the two poems on Havelock frames the war entirely in biblical terms, for in this sonnet God calls his servant home. Although Havelock died before he could hear of the ways his nation honored him, the poet argues, there was "no more fitting hour" for the hero's death. Havelock has successfully snatched his compatriots "from the tiger's power," and he is granted the best reward:

> For God said softly to him:—"Come and rest,
> Thou Good and Faithful! Close beside my throne
> A seat stands vacant for an honoured guest.
> A victor's crown, woven for one alone,
> Lie waiting on it." So, his work-toil done,
> He entered the great glory and was blest!
>
> (32)

While Havelock is taken to heaven, the poet herself is left grieved and bereft at the bitter end of a bitter year. Renewal, with a new year, cannot at first even be imagined—for the uprising has called into question the whole imperial enterprise.

The penultimate sonnet in "Sorrows" dwells on the gap between present distress and previous aspirations, while the concluding sonnet can only turn to highly conventionalized Christian tropes in order to create a final consolation. Key rhymes in the penultimate sonnet (XXXV)—*one* and *moan, tears* and *years*—capture the basic emotion. The two quatrains of the octave and the octave and sestet are strongly enjambed, unusually for Leslie:

> We lift our voices, praying:—Let the gone
> Be gone, O God. O fling Thou down and break
> Our cup of sorrow, so that none may take
> Hereafter ought like it to look upon,
> And, tasting, drink with deep and bitter moan.
> Pity us, O our God. These moments rake
> The smouldering embers up, and darkly make
> Past agonies remembered one by one
> Too vividly for utterance, and hot tears
> Come rushing into lately dried-up eyes,
> To think our first glorious Hundred Years
> Of rule, aye widening under Eastern skies,
> Not ending with loud, jubilant heart-cheers,
> But with deep griefs, and wailings, and low sighs.
>
> (37)

This bleak penultimate poem, more clear-eyed than the celebrations of heroism, admits of a future beyond vengeance, but its tempered grief is reversed in the last poem of the sequence by Christian platitudes and toothless prophecy.

The final sonnet, or "sorrow," begins, improbably, "Yet turn we hopefully to Thee." The reader is assured, "Before / The dawning hour the thickest darkness reigns," for God will surely "bring rare glory" to replace such suffering. As if this assurance were not enough, or were not problematic enough, the poet goes on to declare,

India's idol fanes
Shall crumble into dust; her bloody stains
Fade away silently; her Bramin lore
Be aye forgotten; Peace shall spread her wings
Silver-soft over her; dread Caste shall be
Among the long-departed, perished things;
And 'mid the joy and blessedness shall He,
Lord of earth's lords, and King of all earth's kings,
Commence His reign of glorious majesty!

(38)

Earthly justice from the British, it is tempting to say, is impossible for Leslie to imagine. So, like Shoshee Chunder Dutt, she imagines the Christianization of India. All political matters, the province of earthly kings and lords, are swept away in an attempt at eschatological vision.

Gautam Chakravarty, one of the very few recent critics who has read Leslie's volume, argues that her poetry suggests the passing away of the old Mughal order in the face of British triumphalism. Leslie's description of the desolation of Delhi in this sonnet sequence, Chakravarty argues, invokes the "topology of the Anglo-Indian picturesque, that with its fetish for ruined palaces, fortresses, temples and mosques, is a visual equivalent of orientalist nostalgia, and an Asiatic recension of the metropolitan picturesque" (106). In fact, I would argue, what undergirds most of these poems is not the recension of the metropolitan picturesque—as we see in Emma Roberts's work—but rather an eschatological sublime. One face of that sublime is British jingoism; yet because India was the only place that Leslie ever called home, the poem is driven, finally, into an end time, outside of and transcending political history.

The poet, of course, could not and did not live in such an unearthly space, and it should be no surprise that her last published volume of verse, *Heart Echoes from the East; or, Sacred Lyrics and Sonnets,* moves into an entirely personal mode—the mode of devotional verse. The two most interesting reviews of this volume read its devotional qualities in quite different ways. The *Calcutta Review* argued,

> The great characteristic of this volume is its extreme individual, meditative pietism. The authoress never goes out of herself. The utterance of her own

> thoughts, feelings, and desires about herself fills almost every page. We mention this as a peculiarity; we do not speak of it as necessarily a defect. It may be that her own nature is intensely subjective and individualized; or, perhaps, she has never come beneath influences which draw the thoughts and feelings toward the outward world; or it may be, that she designed to give unity to her volume, by excluding from it whatever was foreign to her own personal relations to the religious life. We suspect the second conjecture to be nearest the truth. (72 [June 1861]: 39)

Nonetheless, the reviewer went on to suggest that Leslie's range was "greatly limited and restricted" and to imagine that she had not experienced any "strong or over-mastering passions" (39). The London reviewer for the *Eclectic Review*, by contrast, read Leslie's last book of verse as dealing with the "profound and touching spiritualities of devotional experience." And whereas the Calcutta reviewer read her verse as "mechanical" (largely, I think, because of her metrical experimentation), the London reviewer twice compared her verse to the "quaintness" of George Herbert (*Eclectic Review*, n.s., 5 [1861]: 603).

Leslie's devotional verse not only moves from the explicitly political to the personal but also is directed at a different audience or subset of that audience which she might have anticipated for her earlier volume. When *Heart Echoes from the East* was issued in London in 1861 by the evangelical publisher James Nisbet, it was directed to a sabbatarian audience. By the 1860s, devout evangelicals had made Sabbath keeping an important political issue and a crucial part of their devotional practice. Not only did they discourage public amusements or secular entertainments on Sunday, but they extended these exclusions to secular reading. Thus, sabbatarians typically read only religious literature on Sundays, and poets such as Christina Rossetti divided their verse into devotional and secular, publishing them in separate volumes. Leslie too followed this practice, as is clear from explicit references to "Sabbath hours" in many of these poems (*Heart*, 27, 43). Moreover, she frames the first section of the volume, "Lyrics," with two quatrains from John Keble's *Christian Year*, the century's best-loved book of devotional verse. It is a fascinating paradox that *Heart Echoes from the East*, though more explicitly religious—or devotional—than Leslie's earlier volumes, is much less dogmatic. Perhaps in examining her own religious experience Leslie became less demanding of others, less interested in their conforming to Christian ideology or approved behaviors. Nor does the coupling of nation and religion persist in this volume.

Virtually all of Leslie's poems that have achieved any longevity appear in "Lyrics." The most often reprinted among these is "The Gathering Home," a poem whose missionary background is subsumed into Christian allegory. It begins,

> They are gathering homeward from every land
> One by one,
> As their weary feet touch the shining strand
> One by one,

Their brows are enclosed in a golden crown,
Their travel-stained garments are all laid down,
And clothed in white raiment they rest on the mead,
Where the Lamb loveth His chosen to lead,
One by one.
Before they rest they pass through the strife
One by one,
Through the waters of death they enter life
One by one.
To some are the floods of the river still
As they ford on their way to the heavenly hill,
To others the waves run fiercely and wild,
Yet all reach the home of the Undefiled
One by one.

We too shall come to that river side
One by one,
We are nearer its waters each eventide
One by one,
We can hear the noise and dash of the stream
Now and again through our life's deep dream,
Sometimes the floods all the banks o'erflow,
Sometimes in ripples the small waves go
One by one.

(45)

A missionary context for this verse is readily imaginable but not crucial, for the sense of exile is extended to the human spiritual condition and then rendered in terms that Bunyan would have found familiar.

Similarly, the opening lines of the sixth poem in the series—"I am alone, O Saviour; all my doors— / My heart's doors—are closed and barred at this still time"—have a missionary context, but they render religious questions personal. In this poem the poet alludes to the apostle Thomas, who in the traditional story was thought to have preached on the Malabar coast of India and there to have been martyred. Leslie likens her doubt to Thomas's and takes comfort in the idea that Thomas found comfort and "lived calmly on a life of holy faith" before his death beneath "tropic suns" (17). But the question of doubt—rather than dogmatism—dominates these poems, and in the very next lyric, Leslie prays that the "unbelief which rises high" can be remedied, and both the reapers (herself) and the sheaves (those she loves) be blessed. If we read this as an allegory of the "mission field," it nonetheless remains a tempered prayer for success, the missionary being in as much need of succor as the obvious unbeliever:

"Lord, I believe; help thou my unbelief!"
  With faltering tones I say this faltering prayer;—
  Let all I bring to Thee Thy mercy share,
Bind thou my loved in Thy salvation's sheaf!

(19)

Whereas *Sorrows, Aspirations, and Legends* prophesies Christ's kingdom in India, these later lyrics refrain from any such claims. Exile is the human condition and doubt the constant companion even of one who hopes to reap a harvest of souls.

Such a tone of humility is struck at the beginning of the volume, where the poet claims not to bring golden sheaves or ripe fruit to her master but only "some simple field-flowers," a "slight and fragile token" (*Heart,* 6). And she likens herself to the child whose fond mother praises the gift. Here the poem moves both toward and away from the conventions of sentimental verse as it allows its feeling to be constrained by a devotional decorum. Perhaps this decorum is what the *Calcutta Review* disliked, but in my view, many of these poems are saved from bathos either by a devotional restraint or by metrical experimentation. The introductory poem, despite an awkward reference to "wheaten ears with gleaming golden," becomes stronger as it progresses, until finally the poet makes an offering of her verses to Christ:

O more than mother dear, than mother tender,
    Receive my offering,
And smile upon it, till amid Thy splendour,
    Within the angel-ring,
I take the crown Thou givest; and straight bending
    In adoration deep,
Cast it before Thee, while the songs ascending,
    The crystal arches sweep.

(7)

Here the poet echoes the most famous hymn by a poet whose work she undoubtedly admired: Heber's hymn for Trinity Sunday, "Holy, Holy, Holy." Indeed, Leslie's volume is indebted to Heber and Keble and also to Luther's Bible, which is quoted in the German. Each poem or sonnet is prefaced by a brief quotation, either from the Bible in English or German or, more occasionally, from liturgy or other sources. In its frequent biblical quotation, the volume's design is true to its Baptist roots, emphasizing the text of the Bible itself. At the same time, the collection has a Christian ecumenical feel—beginning as it does with an epigraph from Keble and with allusions to Heber.

Though God is more than mother in the opening poem of *Heart Echoes,* God becomes a father when the poet is most conscious of sin. In the course of the volume, the poet becomes metaphorically not the daughter but the wayward son of this stern and watchful parent. Here the allegory of Christian devotion meets the Indian poetry of exile in a most curious way. In poem number 46, which begins "All, all is dark, for I have sinned," the poet presents herself as a willful boy child who longs to caress and be caressed by the father. The father, though still watchful to snatch the child from danger, turns away from the child's affection. The poet likens herself explicitly to the boy and in the next stanzas asserts,

E'en so I feel Thy guarding arms enfold
        Now as before,
I still can trust Thee, though Thou dost withhold
        Aught token more
Of the deep love,—the tenderness untold
        Of Thy heart's core.
Yet Father, I am desolate; O turn
        On Him Thine eyes
Who for me in the garden by the burn
        Did agonize,
And, interceding, even now doth yearn
        In Thy far skies.
And then look on me; O my God, the smile
        Will surely come
Back to Thy face, and I, the same glad while
        As to my home,
Will nestle on Thy breast, in sad exile
        No more to roam.

(115)

The homeless child is exiled, banished from affection, sternly watched over, in a relationship that he/she must nevertheless try to construe positively.

Jesus, in contrast, agonizes in the garden—"by the burn"—on behalf of the child. Suddenly Christ lives in Scotland, his Gethsemane, opening through that landscape a door to heaven and to reunification with a now affectionate father. The poet experiences exile from a home that was never home—Scotland. Simultaneously she experiences alienation within a place that is home and not home—Calcutta. She experiences spiritual divorce from the divine, understood as disruption within the family. And further, she is divorced from her very self as a woman within a patriarchal religious tradition—for she must become a boy to be beloved finally of the father. On all these counts, the poet inhabits an alien world. She has no need of the Calvinist contempt for the earthly—though she has that too—in order to feel profoundly exiled from any available social or political world.

Even the sanguinary rhetoric of *Sorrows, Aspirations, and Legends* can, in this perspective, be read as Leslie's colonial mimicry, her attempt by overreading and overwriting to become at "home." But such rhetoric, from a Christian woman, was by its excess over the top. It was too bald to admit of recuperation by the very British reviewers and divines whom she must have hoped to please.

Toru Dutt: A Daughter's Incisive Imaginings, a Father's Gleaning

Mary Leslie's "wheaten ears with gleaming golden" become something else again in Toru Dutt's *Sheaf Gleaned in French Fields,* published in Calcutta some fifteen years after Leslie's devotional verse. Like *The Dutt Family Album,* and in contrast to the deliberate solitariness of *Heart Echoes, A Sheaf Gleaned in French Fields* (1876) can be considered a family effort. Many critics, following the lead of Edmund Gosse, have considered the volume as preparatory to the collection of Toru's original English poems; but, in agreement with Tricia Lootens, I believe that *A Sheaf,* which comprises more than 150 translations of mostly contemporary French poetry, can more usefully be read as part of a single effort alongside Toru's later volume, *Ancient Ballads and Legends of Hindustan. A Sheaf* reveals the family dedication to writing poetry in English, as made clear in Aru's contributions, in Toru's notes, and in the dedicatory poems to the sisters' parents. Aru and Toru conceived the volume as a joint enterprise, and when it was published after Aru's death it contained both a number of her translations and her sister's heartfelt acknowledgment of her own personal and poetic loss. *A Sheaf* also evidences Toru's ability, even as a very young woman, to radically remake the religious, political, and cultural parameters of her father's and uncles' verse. Christian tropes, like the tropes of Anglo-Indian verse more generally, are remade in an incipient cosmopolitan poetics.

At the time of her early death, Toru was preparing additional translations against a possible second edition of *A Sheaf,* studying Sanskrit with a pandit along with her father, Govin, and writing the poems that became *Ancient Ballads and Legends.*[16] The first edition of *A Sheaf* was the only volume whose publication Toru was able to oversee; her father assembled from manuscripts and periodicals the later volume of original English language poetry, and he facilitated the publication from manuscript of her two works of fiction (*Bianca; or, The Spanish Maiden,* written in English, and *Le journal de Mlle. d'Arvers,* written in French). The publication of Toru's posthumous work was very much an effort of international collaboration, with the significant cooperation of Edmund Gosse, who had famously reviewed *A Sheaf,* after plucking it from the pile of books for review at the *Examiner* office, and of Clarisse Bader, a French writer whose history of illustrious women of India Toru had hoped to translate.[17]

Although I emphasize Toru's role in shaping *A Sheaf Gleaned in French Fields,* the volume clearly was, like *The Dutt Family Album,* a family affair in its inception, its production, and its publication. Toru contributed the largest number of poems to the volume, but Aru and Govin contributed translations as well, and no doubt the three poets shared draft translations among themselves. Govin's influence is also felt in the very conception of the volume, a result of the sisters' unusual education. Govin was most encouraging of both his daughters' efforts. After an unsuccessful year in Bombay—where Govin sought the promotions he deserved in the East India Company's service and probably also a more welcoming environment for a Christian family—and after the death of his only son, Abju, Govin took his wife and daughters to Europe. On the advice of some Christian missionary friends, they initially settled in the south of France, where Toru and her older sister, Aru, studied in a *pensionnat* while Govin took a French tutor. Learning French, thus, was a family project. Some months later, the family moved on to London, their original goal—and after several months moved yet again in 1871 to the more congenial atmosphere of Cambridge.

There is no doubt that Govin recognized the extraordinary talents of his daughters and that he devoted much love, energy, and money to their education, permitting them a degree of freedom not always accorded their British counterparts. For nearly two years, Toru and Aru attended the Higher Lectures for women at Cambridge, where they met, among others, Anne Clough, who had just become head of the newly founded Newnham College. The sisters studied French as well as other subjects, and they had, in addition, private tuition in piano and voice.

On the one hand, it is clear that their parents intended the sisters to become accomplished young ladies on the Victorian model; on the other hand, it is clear that Toru at least had ambitions to become a learned woman, on the model of Elizabeth Barrett Browning and Louise-Victorine Ackermann, whom she may possibly have met while the family lived in Nice. Mme. Ackermann, who lived in Nice in the 1860s and early 1870s, was a poet of considerable distinction, imitating Victor Hugo in her earlier work and later writing a philosophical poetry that was widely praised (and also deplored for its anticlerical skepticism). Barrett Browning and Ackermann provided models for Toru, as she makes clear in the notes to *A Sheaf*. There she describes Ackermann as "a scholar of the first order, with Latin, Greek, Hebrew and Sanskrit, and even (so it is reported) Chinese. No English authoress, not even Mrs. Browning, is her equal in point of erudition" (210).[18] If this kind of learning was Toru's goal, Govin did all in his power to further it.[19] When Aru became increasingly ill from tuberculosis, the family moved from Cambridge to Hastings, and thence home to Calcutta. *A Sheaf Gleaned in French Fields* was commenced during this period but was completed by Toru—with assistance, it seems clear, from Govin—after Aru's death. *A Sheaf* arose from family enterprise and family pieties; it also constitutes what Byram Talookdar characterizes as a "bold and fearless" entrance into the world of letters (10).

As Tricia Lootens notes, the first edition of *A Sheaf* contained little by way of apologetic or poetess-like paratexts. It did not, in Lootens's words, offer the "panoply of modest feminine self-display" common to volumes of verse by women ("Bengal," 581). As Lootens points out, the subsequent London edition (Kegan Paul, 1880) included a photograph of Toru and Aru and a prefatory memoir by Govin. *Ancient Ballads and Legends* was similarly prefaced, but with a now famous memoir by Edmund Gosse. Unlike *Ancient Ballads*, *A Sheaf Gleaned in French Fields* is naked with respect to the author's biographical paratexts. The paratextual elements are integrated with the text itself, by way of introductory and concluding poems and in a note. The minimalist paratexts of the first edition also diverge from the practice I have traced in virtually all other volumes of English language verse written in nineteenth-century India. Though it is always dangerous to argue from absence, I think Toru's omission of the apologies that were typical both of Indian English verse and of British women's verse in this period signals a bid for intellectual, critical, and political seriousness. It signals that this is poetry to be reckoned with. Toru balances family piety—in both its senses—with more ambitious goals.

Toru's letters to Mary Martin, a friend from her Cambridge days, indicate Govin's crucial role in seeing *A Sheaf* into print. On November 23, 1875, a few months before its publication, Toru wrote to Mary Martin, "Papa showed my book of French translations to a publisher here; but Calcutta publishers are a very timid class of people, not at all enterprising, and they are besides more given to the sale of books than publishing new ones. The publisher referred Papa to another one, who, he said, knew more about these things, and was a better judge in such matters. Of course he praised the translations very much, and was half willing to take them and publish the book" (Dutt, *Letters,* 119). Evidently Govin's efforts with a second publisher met with no greater success, for he appears to have subsidized its publication at the Saptahik Sambad Press, which also published numerous texts for the Calcutta Christian Book and Tract Society.[20] The typography, design, and textual editing are much cleaner than is often the case in books of the period, indicating how much time the author (and perhaps her father, too) took over the volume. Toru, at any rate, described the most amusing typographical errors to Mary Martin, laughing with her over one passage in which children at their devotions declare, "[We] never lift our heads while prying / Just before we go to bed" (January 13, 1876; *Letters,* 124).

The importance of family to the volume is indicated as well in the first and last poems included. In the first, Toru translates a poem whose author, X. Labenski, had dedicated to her mother. Here the mother's temperament is likened to a tranquil lake, which becomes invisible to the poet's mind when it is troubled by "discords of the earth" but afterward "gleams in my heart, as sunlight after rain" (*Sheaf,* viii). The companion poem is the last in the volume, an original sonnet by Toru, with its title in French and text in English:

> À mon Père
>
> The flowers look loveliest in their native soil
> Amid their kindred branches; plucked, they fade,
> And lose the colours Nature on them laid,
> Though bound in garlands with assiduous toil.
> Pleasant it was, afar from all turmoil,

To wander through the valley, now in shade
And now in sunshine, where these blossoms made
A Paradise, and gather in my spoil.
But better than myself no man can know
How tarnished have become their tender hues
E'en in the gathering, and how dimmed their glow!
Wouldst thou again new life in them infuse,
Thou who has seen them where they brightly blow?
Ask Memory. She shall help my stammering Muse.

(*Sheaf*, 187)

This is as close as Toru Dutt comes to crafting an apology for poetry, yet instead of minimizing her strength or ambition, as either a Bengali writing in English or a woman, Toru claims more than she gives up. On a personal level, France and the study of French seem a pleasant valley but also a lost paradise, perhaps a place and time before Aru's illness. In the context of her and her father's study of Sanskrit, Toru's observation that "flowers look loveliest in their native soil" is particularly telling: French poems are best written in France, Sanskrit poems in India, and English poems in England, the poem seems to suggest.

But for a migratory poet, one who at the age of twenty had lived half her teenaged years outside of Bengal and whose family was intent on migrating once more, this equation seems too simple. All metaphor is a species of translation, the garland of translated flowers included. The poet registers her seriousness as a translator with a combination of assurance and the masculine pronoun. She has gathered in her "spoil," despite knowing—"no man" better—how gathering, or translating, dims the glow and tarnishes tender hues. One might argue, as various critics have, that modern Bangla verse should have been Toru's "native soil"; there the flowers would, presumably, have remained unfaded in their native paradise. But the fact that "À mon Père" comes at the end of a long volume of *translations* suggests that "Memory," or Mnemosyne, the mother of the Muses, may "infuse" translation with new life. It is not a mother tongue but mother/memory/Mnemosyne and a father's love that are evoked in this final poem.

The metaphor of translation as flower gathering touches, too, on the volume's title, a title derived, as in Leslie's poems, from missionary tropes. Toru's title alludes to the biblical story of Ruth, itself a story of multiple migrations: Ruth married the son of Naomi, who had come with his family to Moab to escape famine in Judah; when she and Naomi both were widowed, Ruth left her home country following Naomi to glean in the fields of Judah, protected finally by Naomi's kinsman Boaz. For missionary Christians, Ruth signified the faithful believer gathering the scattered harvest of souls to be won in alien places. But missionary language is not the only intertext here. Ruth, the stranger, signified for Keats in "Ode to a Nightingale" the meeting of art and mortality. She gathers the end of harvest, hard-won sustenance "amid the alien corn." At once like Ruth and like Keats himself, Toru recuperated loss through memory and through poetry.[21] By publishing Aru's translations and one of her father's among her own, she gathered a sheaf, and in raising them toward her father she made good—not the missionary's task but the remembrance of an earthly Paradise.

The crucial paratexts in *A Sheaf Gleaned in French Fields* are the volume's title and its learned footnotes.[22] The biographical paratext enters only in the note to "À mon Père," which then constitutes the final words of the volume. Here Toru explains why several of the volume's poems are signed "A.":

> The writer of these pages has only to add here, that the pieces signed A are by her dear and only sister Arû who fell asleep in Jesus on the 23rd July 1874, at the early age of twenty years. The last piece she translated was Colinette. Had she lived this book with her help might have been better, and the writer might perhaps have had less reason to be ashamed of it, and less occasion to ask for the reader's indulgence. Alas!
>
> "Of all sad words of tongue and pen
> The saddest are these,—it might have been."
>
> (233)

Toru ends this note and her book with a quotation not from a British but from an American poet, John Greenleaf Whittier, whose "Maud Muller" was quite popular at midcentury. The footnotes, thus, provide a familial paratext, a necessary explanation of painful reality, deferred to the very last possible textual moment.

Though they create a biographical paratext, the footnotes to *A Sheaf* also function importantly outside the context of family devotion, for they are extensive, and as Lootens suggests, serious, daring, witty—an exhibition of "panache" ("Bengal," 581). In their extended interchange with the translated texts, the notes allow the poet to triangulate metropolitan/colonial relations.

Although it is beyond my scope here to offer a systematic reading of the many political and literary complexities of Toru's two volumes of verse, I want to focus on the way both *A Sheaf* and *Ancient Ballads* triangulate metropolitan/colonial relations and, through translation and political commentary, claim the English language—and to a lesser extent Christianity—outside of, or at least in opposition to, a dyadic power dynamic.[23] Toru's notes, the texts themselves, and even the selection of texts translated create a complex cultural and political terrain.

As Lootens points out, Toru Dutt identified passionately with the French, if complexly with French republicanism. Dutt told her cousin Omesh that while he was a "quite a republican," she was not.[24] Perhaps here Toru followed, in part, the lead of her hero Elizabeth Barrett Browning, who upon Napoleon III's coup d'état professed (to her husband's dismay) her admiration for Napoleon III and whose generally democratic principles were thus rendered problematic, at least from Robert Browning's point of view. Exactly placing Toru's feelings toward post-Napoleonic France is problematic. On the one hand, despite her declaration that she was not such a republican as her cousin, Toru was famously to translate Victor Hugo, including his satire on Napoleon III, whom she, in the best spirit of republican repudiation, called Tom Thumb. On the other hand, in her letters Toru compares Hugo both favorably and unfavorably with Alphonse de Lamartine. Here both her class politics and her religious politics seem to get the better of her admiration for Hugo. Lamartine, she says, will be less harmful to young people than is Hugo—perhaps ignoring or acknowledging the fact of her own youth (*Letters,* 298). Lamartine is less "bad" than Hugo, as Toru puts it, meaning either that he is less racy or that he is more Christian than the poet she so much admires. Hugo, nonetheless, holds a prominent place in Toru's translations, and her admiration for Hugo harkens back to an earlier moment in English language poetry in India—to Derozio's turn to Byron's support of Greek independence. In much the same way that Derozio imagined the Greek struggle via Byron, so too did Toru engage with Hugo's opposition to Louis Napoleon. Whether or not she was a republican, she found Hugo a compelling figure. She declared in her letters to Mary Martin that Hugo's *Les châtiments* was very beautiful (Dutt, *Letters,* 85). Translations from *Les châtiments* and from Hugo's *L'année terrible* prove the centerpieces of *A Sheaf,* underlining the political valence of Toru's France, for the former is concerned with Louis Napoleon's coup d'état while the latter treats the Franco-Prussian War. However weak-kneed a republican she might have been, Toru clearly lamented the disasters of the war.

The choice of poems in *A Sheaf,* however complex or conflicted their politics, is anything but haphazard. Toru reported to Mary Martin that her father liked best of the entire volume two of Hugo's longer poems that she translated: "A Souvenir of the Night of the 4th" from *Les châtiments* and "On the Barricade" from *L'année terrible* (Dutt, *Letters,* 143). Both turn on the deaths of children. The first is a scathing attack on what is now called "collateral damage"—the death of a seven-year-old child during Louis Napoleon's coup. The second celebrates the pathetic heroism of a child of twelve who is executed with his friends during the war with Prussia.

A passage from "A Souvenir of the Night of the 4th" plays ironically on *souvenir* in its English and French senses, memento and memory. Toru's translation is no apolitical tourism, as her choice of texts and mode of translation make clear. In "A Souvenir," a small child has been killed and his adoptive mother laments, only to be sarcastically comforted with these words:

> Mother, you understand no politics,—
> Monsieur Napoleon, that's his true name, sticks
> To his rights. Look, he is poor, and a prince,
> He loves palaces he enjoyed long since,
> It suits him to have horses, servants, gold

For his table, his hunt, his play high and bold,
His alcove rich-decked, his furniture brave,
And by the same occasion he may save
The Family, Society, and the Church,
Should not the eagle on the high rock perch?
Should he not take advantage of the time
When all ends can be served?

(*Sheaf*, 122–23)

Toru's note to this poem says much, and that to the advantage of neither Louis Napoleon nor English poetry:

> Like Tennyson's *In Memoriam, Les Châtiments* of Victor Hugo harps upon one subject. A great sorrow inspired the muse of the one, a great public wrong that of the other. But in Tennyson's poem, exquisite as it is, the monotony palls at last, while in Hugo's the variety is infinite; hence the superiority of the latter. Disdainful, sarcastic, pathetic, sublime, by turns, the book is a master-piece of its kind. The piece translated here is about the child killed in the Carrefour Tiquetonne on the 4th December 1851, during the street-fights consequent on the *coup d'état* of Napoleon III. Victor Hugo alludes to it in another piece in the *Châtiments.* (224)

Toru Dutt, a poet who resolutely refused to lament her own great sorrows, thus turned for comfort and challenge not to the author of *In Memoriam* and "Havelock" and "Ode on the Death of the Duke of Wellington" but to Hugo.

Disdainful, sarcastic, pathetic, sublime by turns: none of these attitudes was wholly appropriate to the British poetess, none led to simple colonial mimicry or loyal celebrations of Canning, and none led to devotional verse.[25] That these selections from Hugo were Govin's favorite poems from Toru's collection suggests that her father's political views had more complexity than meets the eye. Hugo was clearly Toru's favorite among the poets she translated, and the inclusion of thirty of his poems creates a highly politicized ground to her volume.

The personal and the political—and a transformation of religious language—are blended, I think, for Toru Dutt in this love of Hugo. *Les châtiments,* Toru's favorite volume of his verse, is, after all, a poetry of exile. From this volume, she chose to translate "Après le coup d'état" and "Lines," both describing the poet's exile to the Isle of Jersey. Here England represents freedom, but the poem can be read more broadly as expressing a poet's longing for the freedom of his country. Hugo describes this freedom in precisely the biblical terms that would have been resonant for the Dutts. In "Lines," Hugo compares the Isle of Jersey to St. John's Patmos, as he watches the seagulls rise like souls that "from trials upward soar" (*Sheaf,* 7). Most of all, the poet says, he loves the rocks, the "thunder-shock / Of waves eternally that moan"; exile is conceived in terms of mother love, as the poet says remorse has "such a cry, and such a force— / Wail mothers thus for children gone!" (*Sheaf,* 7). The trope of exile, with a specifically Christian reference, is refracted here in translation through a triple nationalism: Hugo's thanksgiving for English freedom, his hope for French recovery of freedom, and—by implication—Toru's hopes for India.

A similar triangulation, both political and poetic, is at work in the lyric poems of *Ancient Ballads and Legends of Hindustan.* In "France, 1870," the poet alludes to the defeats in the Franco-Prussian War; France is fallen, but "Levite England passes her by" (129). No Good Samaritan arrives to succor those in need. A second poem, "On the Fly-Leaf of Erckmann-Chatrain's Novel Entitled 'Madame Thérèse,'" recalls at the moment of the Franco-Prussian War the early hope of the French Revolution. The recollection of past hope, of the revolution, is not quite bitter but nearly so:

> When rose high your Marseillaise
> Man knew his right to earth's remotest bound,
> And tyrants trembled. Yours alone the praise!
> Ah, had a Washington but then be found!
>
> (134)

Had France found a Washington, rather than a Napoleon, tyranny would have been averted. But at least at the time of the revolution, "man knew his right to earth's remotest bound"; even in Bengal, revolutionary republicanism had its proponents in the century before Toru was born, as she no doubt knew from her reading of Derozio.[26] Not that these sentiments meant that Toru would claim to be a "rank democrat" like Hugo or a fervent republican, as she called her cousin Omesh. But they do align her with her poetic predecessors, however unstable or inarticulate her politics might have been.

Ancient Ballads and Legends of Hindustan continues the political triangulation effected by *A Sheaf Gleaned in French Fields* even as it enacts a second one (for it triangulates folk tales and stories from the *Purāṇas* through Milton and the orientalist narrative poem) and even a third (as it translates the flora of Bengal through the tropes of British romantic poetics).

Chandani Lokugé has detailed the layers of literary borrowings—both oral and written, Indian and European—that went into the making of the lyrics and the narratives that Govin collected and published after his daughter's death. She concludes, limning the dominant narrative, that in *Ancient Ballads,* Toru had come home to India both intellectually and physically: "By whatever convoluted route Toru actively reawakened to her country's literature; when she did, it sparked off her creativity in ways that were spontaneous, innovative, and daring. *Ancient Ballads* embraces all her creative inspirations and skills. In a final glorious burst of creative energy [she had not long to live], she shares with us experiences held most precious from childhood memory deeply centred in the family and family home, to timeless Indian epics that, in her dexterous hands, take on contemporary socio-political and religious significance" (xl–xli). Here Lokugé repeats—in a different tone—a version of the praise for Toru that appeared in Edmund Gosse's memoir prefacing the posthumous London edition of these poems. But as Lootens, following the work of Meenakshi Mukherjee and of Malashri Lal, puts it, home (India) and language (English, Sanskrit, Bangla, French) was a complex and multiple place for Toru Dutt. Perhaps, Lootens argues, Toru did come "home" in her final book: "home, that is, to a multiply translated realm within which popular Bengali, Sanskrit, and English traditions claimed intimate place" ("Bengal," 575). For Lokugé, Toru is at once a multilingual and migrant poet and a poet through whom we can touch "memory deeply centred in the family" and "timeless Indian epics." The halo of nationalist ideology here makes family and timeless India amount to the same thing. Hence, Lokugé can only depict Toru as "an innocent forerunner to 'the idea of the modern,' at the centre of which is a 'mélange, adulteration, impurity, pick 'n' mix' that Salman Rushdie provocatively recommends" (xliii). One wonders, could an attentive reader of Baudelaire really be an "innocent" forerunner of modernism? Toru Dutt was no "innocent" modern but instead a remarkably self-assured one, who could only call home a polyglot and contradictory space.

Alpana Sharma makes much the same point in her essay "In-Between Modernity: Toru Dutt (1856–1877) from a Postcolonial Perspective." Sharma argues that Toru's narrative poems in *Ancient Ballads and Legends* occupy a "risky in-between position."[27] Though they derived from a long history of oral and written tradition and also in part from the Oriental tale, they do not attempt the same kind of heroic narrative that we see in the work of Toru's "uncle" Shoshee.[28] One wonders whether, in this light, the poet would have approved of Govin's title for her volume. As many have noted, the title emphasizes ballads and legends but omits mention of the lyric poems.[29] Moreover, unlike Shoshee's volume, Toru's volume is not actually concerned with "Hindustan," with victory and defeat among Mughals, Rajputs, Marathas, and the like. Walter Scott and Southey, the long orientalist tradition of translation from Persian tales, and the versification of Indian martial history or legend are absent here. The narrative is simplified, in a sense, and the poems emphasize not martial conquest but interior moral drama. Were there space here, it would be useful to trace the ways in which Toru modifies her sources and casts them in terms of a spiritual, internal drama that has its own Christian resonance. The poems, although they may have a nationalist agenda, have no place for the notion that India equals Hindustan. To the contrary, the narratives are almost entirely about personal moral struggles and the nature of duty and familial love. If there is a political agenda here—and Tricia Lootens and Alpana Sharma, among others, have argued that there is—it is filtered through or created in domestic metaphors and in the issue of translation as a politics.[30]

Indian and East Indian Christian poets had for years proposed the "renovation of India," often politically, as in the case of T. W. Smyth, but always in explicitly Christian terms, as in Shoshee's "Vision of Sumeru." Toru's approach in the poems that constitute *Ancient Ballads and Legends* is much more subtle and much less dogmatic. A semi-republican in politics, a Christian in her way, and surrounded by examples of family duty and devotion, she constructed legends that work on the moral imagination and the domestic emotions. Yet Toru, like T. W. Smith and Henry Page, also took up the notion of the bard, as she certainly had encountered it not only in Scott's work but especially in that of Derozio, on whom she wrote an important essay in the *Bengal Magazine* (H. Das, 43).

Though a systematic reading of Toru's narrative poems is beyond my scope here, I want briefly to follow the lead of Tricia Lootens and Meenakshi Mukherjee in arguing for the complexity of these narratives—and to add that they were also shaped in complex ways by Toru's version of rethinking both Christian ethics and gender politics. First, however, I want to deal briefly with critical approaches that have had considerable longevity. Toru's narrative poems are generally framed by two variants on a biographical story, each of which has important truths and can also create curiously partial readings. In the first, Toru is seen as returning to her mother tongue and almost literally to her mother's tongue. The poem "Sîta" underwrites this narrative, as it depicts the genesis of the stories Toru tells; in that poem, Sita, the much traduced heroine of Rāmāyaṇa, is less important than the domestic scene of tale telling. "It is an old, old story, and the lay / Which has evoked sad Sîta from the past / Is by a mother sung. . . ." (*Ancient Ballads*, 122). This line, broken by an ellipsis, replicates the broken family circle, for the poem celebrates her mother's telling of stories to her three young children, two of whom are no longer alive. In the critical narrative built on this scene, Toru's poems are a return home, to her mother tongue and her mother's telling, and this return is read as a reaffirmation of nation. In a second critical approach, the genesis of these narrative poems is ascribed to Toru's study of Sanskrit with her father, and the tales are sometimes described as all translations from the Sanskrit. The turn from French to Sanskrit is also read as an affirmation of nation. There is truth in this narrative as well, but I would argue that Toru's retelling of familiar Indian stories is doing cultural work that is more complex: remaking ideas of community, language, gender, domesticity, ethics, and religion. No simple notion of "the nation" contains them.

Lootens and Mukherjee provide us a way out of this rather too easy understanding of Toru's narrative poems as a form of nationalist celebration. Lootens, in fact, argues that Toru's narratives need to be understood as taking up the problematic of bardic nationalism but also as raising questions. "Whose ancient ballads were these?" Lootens asks. "Like her career itself, Dutt's reception seems calculated to dramatize the instability of national affiliations and appropriations" ("Alien," 297). What would a "female Indian bard who writes in English" and in French mean: "What might it mean to be a bard whose 'nation' was already being moved to seek unity, in part, through processes of translation?" (297). Mukherjee responds to the dominant narratives of Toru Dutt's reception from a different and equally useful point of view.

She argues that Toru's ten months or so of Sanskrit study would not have "given her enough proficiency in the language to translate or adapt from the original" in most cases (97) and that instead Toru was for the most part adapting from oral retellings of traditional Bangla stories, her mother's famous storytelling. In Mukherjee's view, Toru's choice of tales and her re-creation of them reveal both the complex placement (which Lootens also acknowledges) and her specifically Bengali context. Mukherjee argues that Toru was not about creating a "pan-Indian" idiom for "purposes of national projection" and was not about evoking a notion of "Indianness" in this sense; rather, "despite her western orientation" she "remained curiously local in her conflation of India with Bengal" (106). And Mukherjee goes on (as Sharma, Lootens, and Natalie Phillips do) to read "Savitri" as foregrounding issues of female agency. In addition, she reads Toru's poems "Buttoo" and "The Royal Ascetic and the Hind" as critiques of caste in the first instance and of religious asceticism in the second. Mukherjee argues that "to praise Toru Dutt for upholding the so-called 'Indian tradition' which is predicated upon caste and gender hierarchy seems somewhat anomalous when in an understated way she carries out a running critique of conventional scriptural wisdom—an enterprise made quite remarkable by the fact that most of these poems were written before she was twenty" (107–8).

I think we can see both "Buttoo" and "The Royal Ascetic and the Hind" as part of Toru's work toward critiquing and celebrating "domestic" social and religious practices, taking the term *domestic* in both its household and its national senses. Just as Derozio and Henry Page reimagined India through their freethinking or Christian lenses, without imagining such transformation as somehow un-Indian, so too may Toru be harking back not to the orientalist traditions that Mary Carshore also critiqued but to the Bengali-born freethinking of Rammohun Roy and the Brahmo Samaj reformers. Opening a space for female agency in the context of celebrating a broken and now lost domestic felicity, Toru defends a notion of love against both ascetic practices and male codes of honor and of caste.

As Mukherjee points out, "Buttoo" can be read as a rejection of caste and patriarchal (master/disciple) relationships. In Toru's story, a young low-caste man is rejected as a disciple of a master archer but perfects his art in the forest under the statue of the master that he creates. Buttoo, the rejected hunter's son, muses, with mingled shame, pride, and anger:

> "My place I gather is not here;
> No matter,—what is rank or caste?
> In us is honour, or disgrace,
> Not out of us," 'twas thus he mused,
> "The question is,—not wealth or place,
> But gifts well used, or gifts abused."
>
> (*Ancient Ballads*, 78)

Years later, when Buttoo's perfection is revealed to the master, who has taken Arjuna for a disciple, the master extracts a vow of obedience from the willing young man—who then is forced to cut off his own thumb. No one is to rival the beloved Arjuna. Toru's understatement only makes more powerful the arbitrary cruelty of the master. Similarly, in "The Royal Ascetic and the Hind," Toru critiques what she regards as social and religious practices that deny the power of love; in "The Royal Ascetic," she brings to the narrative a more explicitly Christian subtext than in "Buttoo," for the whole poem, a translation from the *Vishnu Purāṇa* (book 2, chapter 13), is framed by the poet in a way that reiterates a common Christian critique of Hindu ascetic practices. The "royal ascetic," faulted by orthodox Hindus for worldly attachment to a deer, is praised by the poet for beginning to discover that god is a god of love. Toru Dutt does not deride the "Brahman sage" of old, who wrote the "pious chronicle" of her source, but she claims to be one of those "who happier, / Live under the holiest dispensation" (69). Toru's understanding of a Christian dispensation grounds a critique of Hindu asceticism.

Another of Toru's narratives, "Jogadhya Uma," focuses not on patriarchal law (caste, discipleship, even asceticism) but on domesticity of a curious kind. This poem is linked more directly than many of the other narratives to the lyrics of *Ancient Ballads and Legends.* Mukherjee observes of "Jogadhya Uma" that it "narrates a specifically Bengali tale, centring upon a pair of white shell-bangles, which are auspicious markers of a woman's married status only in Bengal—with no such ritual significance attached to them in any other part of India. Also, conceiving the goddess Uma or Durga in purely domestic and familiar terms (as a married daughter in this case) is an exclusively Bengali practice which Toru Dutt does not subsume in a larger Hindu ethos of Devi-worship" (105). Mukherjee's reading suggests a properly Bengali, rather than a pan-Indian, reading of the poem. I believe, too, that the poem is tricky to interpret because it is at once Bengali, "Indian" in the sense that being taken into English makes it so, and domestic and familial. In Toru's narrative, a peddler encounters Uma, the kindly form of Durga, who buys the shell bracelets from him, sending him to the local priest for payment and claiming to be the priest's daughter. Priest and peddler go in quest of the woman once the priest recognizes her for the goddess she is, but Uma eludes them. Finally her arm rises from the water at the ghat, and the very vision of it provides a magical power enabling future prosperity and happiness. The daughter goddess vanishes but has left behind her emblems of purity and a future of good fortune. The peddler's shells are, at least metaphorically, transformed into lotus blossoms—and a recognition of the divine Bengali daughter's power confers blessings on the two men who receive the flowers as a memento of their vision:

> A wide ripple tost and swung the blossoms
> The blossoms on that liquid plain,
> And lo! the arm so fair and young
> Sank in the waters down again.
>
> (63)

There is a kind of pathos here, certainly. Though the shell bangles are typical, as Mukherjee argues, of a Bengali married woman's ornaments, the poet compares Uma to the famously chaste Diana—asserting her virginal power. I would argue that in Toru's retelling of this story, the daughter's value does not hinge upon marriage (or, as in the traditional reading of Savitri, upon her fidelity to a husband). Rather, here the daughter's divine purity is at one with a prosperous landscape, for her bangles are transformed into lotus blossoms. The young and lovely spirit descends again into the waters.[31] As I suggest below, the lotus for Toru Dutt, as in Indian iconography generally, invites readings beyond the literal. The ending of "Jogadhya Uma" evokes the metaphors that appear in the most famous poems in *Ancient Ballads and Legends*—the lyrics.

We actually have very few original lyric poems from Toru's pen, and these—aside from "À mon Père"—come at the end of *Ancient Ballads and Legends.* Among them, the most often anthologized and discussed is "Our Casuarina Tree." Like Toru's translations, this poem too engages in a kind of triangulation, not through translation but through multiple layers of allusion. If we take the poem's title as a kind of paratext—whether or not Toru herself wrote the title—the key element is the plural first-person pronoun, *our.* The poem itself would better justify *my* or simply the definite article *the* or even nothing at all modifying the noun.[32] Despite the plural pronoun, all the persons with whom the casuarina tree was intimately shared—the poet's "sweet companions"—are gone; the plural gives them life and reconnects them to the family circle. (*Ancient Ballads,* 137). The tree itself has its own literary significance mediated through the British and Indian English poetic canon; both Govin and David Lester Richardson had written poems about casuarina trees, though neither is explicitly referenced here.

The poem's most important intertexts are Milton, Keats, and Wordsworth, a heavy load of allusion for a poem of five stanzas and fifty-five lines. "Our Casuarina Tree" begins with a Miltonic intertext:

> Like a huge Python, winding round and round
> The rugged trunk, indented deep with scars
> Up to its very summit near the stars,
> A creeper climbs, in whose embraces bound
> No other tree could live.
>
> (137)

Moreover, thanks to the tree, the garden overflows with Keatsian music, as if Heber's and Keats's nightingale has migrated to Toru's garden in Baugmaree: "With one sweet song that seems to have no close / Sung darkling from our tree, while men repose." The next stanza begins with dawn, "When first my casement is wide open thrown." But then something happens—Milton's Eden, Keats's fairyland, Heber's Philomel herself have given rise to an unexpected figure: "A grey baboon sits statue-like alone." Within the giant tree's shadow, water lilies bloom in the tank, "like snow enmassed."[33] The casuarina tree thus mixes allusive domains, tropical fauna, snow, Miltonic Eden, songbirds, and baboons. Perhaps it is appropriate that the casuarina is native not to Bengal but to Southeast Asia and Australasia; its Bangla name, *belati jhāu,* literally means "foreign tamarisk."

In the third stanza, the tree becomes marked by memory.

> But not because of its magnificence
> Dear is the Casuarina to my soul:
> Beneath it we have played; though years may roll,
> O sweet companions, loved with love intense,
> For your sakes, shall the tree be ever dear![34]
>
> (138)

The tree murmurs like the ocean heard on a "shingle-beach," and its lament, the poet believes, may "haply" reach to "the unknown land." We have Milton's Eden initially, here, obliquely, a hope of paradise, for the unknown land is "yet well-known to the eye of faith!" Toru presents the casuarina tree through Miltonic and Keatsian allusions, but the poem's most important intertext is Wordworth's. In "Our Casuarina Tree," the poet presents us with a Wordsworthian layering of landscape and memory. It is not just that the tree itself reminds the poet of her "sweet companions," but that its music reminds her of recalling the tree years earlier when she heard waves kiss "the classic shore / Of France or Italy." At that time, "before / Mine inner vision rose a form sublime, / Thy form, O Tree" (138).

From Eden, through death, to heaven, to the classic shores of France and Italy, to "my own loved native clime" came the music of the tree, its "eerie speech" evoking layered memory, layered allusions. Though this tree is surely identified with "my own loved native clime," and though the poet is surely praising it in terms that have since become part of a nationalist project, the poem ends with its own ambitions, the poet's desire to live on in her verse.[35] Like Keats, who had suffered the same lingering death as Aru, the poet seeks immortality—not in "blessed sleep" but in poetry. She quotes from Wordsworth's "Yew Trees," but in doing so, she expresses an aching desire for poetic fame like Keats's:

> Therefore I fain would consecrate a lay
> Unto thy honour, Tree, beloved of those
> Who now in blessed sleep, for aye, repose,
> Dearer than life to me, alas! were they!
> Mayst thou be numbered when my days are done
> With deathless trees—like those in Borrowdale,
> Under whose awful branches lingered pale
> "Fear, trembling Hope, and Death, the skeleton,
> And Time the shadow"; and though weak the verse
> That would thy beauty fain, oh fain rehearse,
> May Love defend thee from Oblivion's curse.
>
> (139)

This is not, perhaps, "modern" in the sense of modernist, but it is powerful on its own terms. It revises Milton and Wordsworth (and before him John Logan and Walter Scott, whose poems are antecedent to Wordsworth's). "Our Casuarina Tree" also captures but does not merely imitate the self-referential power of Keats's odes.

Toru's imagination, nonetheless, thinks much more through Christian tropes than did Keats's; and these tropes empower her final stanza. Love defending the living from a curse, blessed sleep—these Christian notions are here subsumed in the poet's longing for poetic immortality. The last stanza is made powerful, like the last two of Keats's "Ode to a Nightingale," by repetitions. The assonance (*Tree, sleep, trees, weak*), the skillful enjambment in five of the eleven lines and with it the strength of the syntax, and the deliberate repetition (*fain, fain, fain*) all enrich the stanza.[36] These sounds carry echoes with them, given the poem's subject, *fain* calling up the word *pain* and *sleep* the word *weep,* neither of which the poem speaks. But most of all, the stanza is unified in its quality of self-reflexivity. It quotes Wordsworth, modifying and appropriating "Yew Trees" while omitting two of the ghosts that haunt Wordsworth's landscape—Silence and Foresight. Neither of these does the poem claim, but rather only three of Wordsworth's figures—Fear, Hope, and Death—along with their shadow, Time. "Our Casuarina Tree" inhabits speech and memory, the world of poetry—not silence and foresight (the worlds perhaps of nature and morality). Not only is there an intertextual reflection in Toru's appropriation of Wordsworth, there is also a powerful reflexivity in the metaphor of the lay consecrated at the casuarina's temple. The final triple rhyme—*verse, rehearse, curse*—captures the poet's longing to make a poem against or in spite of "Time the shadow." The lay in the fane, the lay that would fain defeat oblivion, the poem of love and memory, acknowledges its own art in the insistence of the penultimate line. The poet's verse would "fain, oh fain rehearse" the beauties of Baugmaree, the memory of her lost loves, her family.

But behind the fane lingers another shadow—futility. Will this verse escape oblivion's curse, or is all effort vain? *Pain, vain, fane, fain.* "May Love defend thee from Oblivion's curse" is the last line of Toru Dutt's second, and final, book of poetry. Her editor—her father—placed "Our Casuarina Tree" at the very end of his daughter's career, and it might be understood as Toru's epitaph for herself. Little wonder, then, that both volumes of verse are filled with stories of parental affection.

The Flowers of Empire

The penultimate poem in *Ancient Ballads and Legends of Hindustan* might stand as an emblem of this chapter, for "The Lotus" examines the realms of psyche, religion, and nation with remarkable compression. Ostensibly, Toru's sonnet recapitulates an old poetic conceit: the contest of flowers, the lily and the rose. The contest is ancient, but the proximate sources for Toru's poem "The Lotus" are William Cowper's "The Lily and the Rose" and Tennyson's "Maud," especially the latter's famous lyric "Come into the Garden, Maud." Both of Toru's intertexts are exercises in imperial gardening. For

Tennyson, Maud's appearance in the garden is fully implicated in imperial politics, because the rose and lily (who are met in Maud's person) are in the end transformed into the "blood red blossom of war." Love and empire, love and war, Maud and the Crimea, indeed Maud and England itself become inextricable. In the psyche of Tennyson's speaker, the transfer of emotional energy from Maud to the Crimea provides the only hope of action in a corrupt and corrupting world. Tennyson's lily and rose fuse in a geopolitics of nation.

Cowper's poem also entails the politics of empire. "The Lily and the Rose" bespeaks a nation defined through its "flowers," its women, "the fairest British fair." In Cowper's contest of the flowers, lily and rose compete for power (or "empire," in the broad eighteenth-century sense of the word). The goddess Flora must resolve the dispute, creating a nation beyond faction:

> The Lily's height bespoke command,
> A fair, imperial flow'r;
> She seem'd design'd for Flora's hand,
> The sceptre of her pow'r.
>
> This civil bick'ring and debate
> The goddess chanc'd to hear,
> And flew to save, ere yet too late,
> The pride of the parterre.
>
> "Yours is," she said, "the nobler hue,
> And yours the statelier mien;
> And, till a third surpasses you,
> Let each be deem'd a queen."
>
> Thus, sooth'd and reconcil'd, each seeks
> The fairest British fair:
> The seat of empire is her cheeks,
> They reign united there.
>
> (*Poems*, 370)

If we read backward from Tennyson to Cowper to the traditional iconography of Christian piety, Toru's revision of Cowper's satire on "faction" has a vivid personal, political, and religious point.

The conflict in Toru Dutt's "Lotus" occurs not in Flora's garden—as in Cowper's poem—but in "Psyche's bower." If we take the lily and rose together as "the fairest British fair" and take the lily further as a traditional emblem of Christian purity and sacrifice, then Toru's poem makes a striking turn, for neither the lily nor the rose nor their combination in the "fairest British fair" wins the day. Rather, the lotus carries away the victory. Beginning in psychic conflict—the contentions of empire, the weight of Christian symbolism—the poem enacts a novel solution. Flora, judging the flowers of her garden, gives a lotus to Love, who has asked for the most beautiful blossom in her garden. The sestet begins with Love's request to Flora:

> "Give me a flower delicious as the rose
> And stately as the lily in her pride"—
> "But of what colour?"—"Rose-red," Love first chose,
> Then prayed,—"No, lily-white,—or, both provide";
> And Flora gave the lotus, "rose-red" dyed,
> And "lily-white,"—the queenliest flower that blows.
>
> (*Ancient Ballads*, 136)

If we read Toru's lotus as growing in her Indian context, then "fairest" fair is consistent with the iconography of the goddess Lakshmi, the goddess of wealth, beauty, and wisdom, for the lotus is crucial to Lakshmi's iconography. Lakshmi almost always appears, when alone, on a full bloomed lotus. Both in Hindu and in Buddhist texts, the lotus connotes purity and spiritual realization arising from the muck of creation. And so here, for Toru, Lakshmi—absent in name but likely present iconographically—takes dominion. The "fairest British fair," the lily and the rose, of Cowper's verse are eclipsed, though the poet admits that "bards of power" have "sung their claims" (136).

The psychic territory of religious conflict (the claims of the lily) and of empire (the claims of the rose, or the "British fair") are resolved within the bower of the Toru's sonnet. But they are resolved through an urbane and cosmopolitan textual play. It is not Flora's parterre, Cowper's and Tennyson's British ground, where the poet must reconcile or reject contradictory claims. Rather, it is "Psyche's bower," the place where multiple languages, locations, and religious and ideological claims compete. Toru Dutt, by triangulating these claims—through France, through worlds of translation—negotiated this bower with amazing success for one so young. Her uncles, like their contemporary Mary Leslie, found Psyche's bower something of a poetic wilderness. Dogmatic religious claims and the cultural and poetic displacements of writing poetry in a Christian tradition in India proved for Leslie and the elder Dutts a nearly insurmountable challenge. The flowers in the "sheaf" of the mission field, not the flowers of translation, are those whose glow has "dimmed" and whose "tender hues" have tarnished in the light of a later day.

Rabindranath Tagore. Frontispiece to Tagore's *Gitanjali,* by William Rothstein (London: Macmillan, 1913).

SIX

Cosmopolitanism, Nationalism, and Aestheticism in Fin-de-Siècle London

Manmohan Ghose, Sarojini Naidu, and Rabindranath Tagore

And rhyme shall rule o'er reason,
        And Swinburne over Time,
And panting poets seize on
        Each continent and clime;
Aching alliteration,
        Impotent indignation,
Eternal iteration,
        Wrapt in eternal rhyme.

—Laurence Binyon, "The Garden of Criticism," *Echoes*

The practices of literary culture, by contrast, are practices of attachment.

—Sheldon Pollock, "Cosmopolitan and Vernacular in History"

In the 1870s, writing in her garden at Baugmaree on the outskirts of Calcutta, Toru Dutt daringly claimed the lotus as the most beautiful flower—or poem—in Psyche's garden, surpassing the lily or the rose, surpassing the flowers of English poetic tradition, the roses of Cowper and Tennyson, and surpassing even the roses of the Persian tradition. Yet the victory of the lotus, the image of purity, belied the poetic practices of attachment and detachment, identification and disidentification that subtended the creation of this English sonnet from the outset. There was no Archimedean point from which Toru Dutt could claim a natural or single-minded attachment to her "native clime," as she called it in "Our Casuarina Tree." The garden at Baugmaree was already full of foreign transplants, the casuarina among them. By the time she wrote "The Lotus," Toru Dutt had seized on various "continents and climes," as Laurence Binyon would put it a decade later; her verse was to mark a cosmopolitan reality made from English language lyrics and in translations from French and from Sanskrit (Binyon, "Garden," 90).

In the years following the publication in London of Toru's posthumous book, *Ancient Ballads and Legends of Hindustan* (1882), the discourses of "native clime," nation, and purity took a further turn. Nation, gender, race, and religion were conflated in ways that framed the reception of poets writing in English through at least the 1910s. Issues of authenticity and cosmopolitan friendship were articulated in shifting nationalist contexts. The Ilbert Bill, proposed by Lord Ripon in 1883 to allow Indian judges to try British citizens, fanned racist discourse within the Anglo-Indian community and in Britain, which, in turn, provoked angry reaction on the subcontinent. Indian reaction to the Ilbert Bill and to the terrible famine in south India (1876–78), along with other issues, led to the formation of the Congress Party and to a new phase of Indian nationalism. The partition of Bengal in 1905 further galvanized nationalist opposition. As a result, the discourses of nation—both in Britain and, differently, in India—adumbrated the cultural power of "authenticity," which in turn shaped the canons of reception for Indian belletristic writing in English. At the same time, and paradoxically, the continuing movement of writers and artists from the subcontinent to Britain and vice versa expanded the reach of the kind of cosmopolitan sensibility we see in Toru Dutt and others.

The poets I discuss in this chapter, Manmohan Ghose (1869–1924), Sarojini Naidu (1879–1949), and Rabindranath Tagore (1861–1941), published their English language poetry in London or, in Tagore's case, almost simultaneously in London and the United States. Each of these poets encountered—furthered, resisted, managed, or was managed by—discourses of authenticity and the urgencies of nationalism. At the same time, their English language poetry emerged within a crucial nexus of friendship that at once exceeded and was shaped in these discourses.

Although the period of the fin de siècle was more intensely nationalist and racist than earlier decades, it still saw Indian poets writing in English remain invested in the tropes and structures of feeling that preceded them. Principal among these tropes was the trope of authenticity, which gained increasing power in India as it moved from the discourses of religious or regional identity to an identification of race, nation, and Hinduism.

Authenticity provided a conceptual structure through which a poet could claim to be (or, more often, could be claimed by others to be) "Indian." Srinivas Aravamudan reads the process as a late version of orientalism. He sees the discourses of orientalism with respect to India as moving through three phases: the "patronizing" orientalism of the early scholars; the "Romantic" sort "commenced by German Indologists and carried through" by Bankimchandra Chattopadhyay; and the "nationalist" style of Swami Vivekananda and Sri Aurobindo (Manmohan Ghose's brother). In this late nineteenth-century adaptation of orientalism, "pure roots are sometimes professed in relation to a background that is ironically hybridized" (Aravamudan, *Guru English*, 91). The past is read as a Hindu past, an estranged past that has been forgotten, and thus a present nationalism is conceived in terms of "essentialized civilizational characteristics" (74).

Aravamudan describes this notion of Indianness as a "fictive ethnicity."[1] In the reception of Indian English poets, I would argue, fictive ethnicity figures as the "authentic." Aravamudan shows how fictive ethnicity is crucial to the development of what he calls guru English. By the late nineteenth century, it had also become a dominant factor in the reception of Indian English language poetry. The more closely the poet approximated the role of guru or the more closely he or she represented the authentic Indian self, the more successful she or he could become. In short, to be legible, the poet had to *become* authentic. I have argued that this conceptual nexus, in its earlier forms, shaped the metropolitan reception of English language poetry written in India over the course of the long nineteenth century, from the reviews of Kasiprasad Ghosh to the reception of David Lester Richardson's poetry to the reception of Toru Dutt. But by the fin de siècle, the development of nationalist discourses in India and in Britain had further strengthened cultural demands that the poet from the subcontinent be "authentic."

The trope of authenticity, moreover, when understood through the metaphorical language of maternity, raised the question of where one's mother, real or imagined, might reside. The root metaphor of authenticity grounded in mother/family/identity was extended in metaphors of mother tongue and mother country and played out in actual relationships of actual individual families. To be authentic was to be "pure." To be taken as authentic, a poet must be read as if cultural purity were anywhere to be found.[2] Take, for example, Oscar Wilde's review of Manmohan Ghose's poetry. Though Manmohan had been brought to England at age ten and had lived over half his life in England when Wilde met him, though in his brown velvet suit he dressed as the perfect British aesthete, Wilde nonetheless felt compelled to describe his poems as arising from Ghose's "purely" Indian parentage. That these very different realms—language, nation, and family—were expressed in terms of each other implied that authenticity was ultimately biological, but the notion was and still is used to link together intractable realities. The incommensurability of language, nation, and family necessarily meant that authenticity, with its claim to be natural, was actually the reverse of "natural": it was ineluctably ideological and contradictory. Though Wilde used a claim for authenticity to read Ghose's poems, the same claim renders illegible other meanings in the poetry of fin-de-siècle Indian English, for this poetry is often more about estrangement than about comfort. The trope of authenticity was, equally, the trap of authenticity.

In short, Indian authenticity was coeval with structures of attitude and reference that subtended fictive ethnicity—with discourses that constructed and equated race, religion, and nation. And yet, to write English if you were an Indian poet at the fin de siècle was by definition to be "impure," mixed, complex, cosmopolitan. It was to participate in an already intertwined world of poetic forms, tropes, and discourses and an already impure scene of literary production and reception.

For Ghose, Naidu, and Tagore, the trope of authenticity functioned in both the production and the reception of poetry. But to read the fin de siècle solely in terms of authenticity not only renders illegible the textual marks of cultural interaction but also effaces the historical record of human generosity. In contrast to the discourse of authenticity, which is ultimately based in familial relationships, I want to pose a different realm, crucial to the three poets whom I discuss here: the realm of friendship.

Another way to describe the contrast between discourses of authenticity and the lived world of friendship is, in Saidian terms, to distinguish between filiation and affiliation. Here I think particularly powerful the process of affiliation that Homi Bhabha calls "shadowed mutuality." As Bhabha describes it, "a shadowed mutuality does not demean the dominated. . . . [I]t is a process of affiliation that conceives of sovereignty in ways that are different from the governing assumptions of ethnonationalist exclusivity. 'Shadowing' doggedly affirms the enduring hope for a politics of proximity in a current situation in which only polarization and alienation seem possible" ("Untimely Ends," 20). The dynamics of affiliation, of friendship, and of hospitality make for an understanding of literary culture that goes beyond or perhaps stands behind or beside the "governing assumptions of ethno-nationalist exclusivity."

Though discussion of friendship and affiliation can be characterized as optimistic if not utopian, I do not intend to be facile about friendship. Any experience of friendship is an experience of misunderstanding as well as understanding; like friendship—and as the precursors of friendship—the interactions we call hospitality have their own ambivalent core. As Émile Benveniste, Jacques Derrida, and Seyla Benhabib have argued, *hospis* (host) and *hostes* (enemy) have common roots (Derrida, *Hospitality,* 43–45). In Benhabib's words, hostility and hospitality are entangled with each other: "When the stranger (the guest) comes upon the shores of the other, the home of the other, there is also a moment of anxiety, generated by the undecidability of the other's (the host's) response. Will I be greeted with hospitality or rejected with hostility? Will you admit me beyond the threshold or will you keep me waiting at the door?" (156).

Once beyond the threshold, moreover, hospitality or shadowed mutuality also takes the form of mutual obligation. Such obligations were evident in the middle of the nineteenth century among poets in India who managed, more or less successfully, to cross cultural thresholds—Emma Roberts's obligations to Derozio, for example, or Kasiprasad Ghosh's friendship with Horace Hayman Wilson. By the beginning of the twentieth century, more Indian writers than ever before had begun to cross the actual thresholds of London's literary drawing rooms. Among them were those who established relations of reciprocal hospitality, mutuality, and even friendship. These networks of affiliation were created at the same time that British imperialism was entering its most ideologically violent stage and at the moment when resistance to the empire was, if anything, more immersed than before in discourses of authenticity. At the very time when the nationalist movements in Ireland and India were gaining important ground, at the moment when the language of "Mother India" was in the ascendant as a form of political resistance, poets developed networks of affiliation that both furthered the tropes of authenticity and exceeded them.

Manmohan Ghose, Sarojini Naidu, and Rabindranath Tagore each established a "shadowed mutuality" with British poets and artists, and each published poems that arose from this encounter. The relationships that enabled and at the same time disabled their English language poetry can best be understood not as a microcosm/macrocosm relationship of the home and the world but its refraction. As the connections between hostes and hospis, enemy and guest, remind us, friendships across empire might be characterized as a form of unhomeliness.

Unhomeliness is not the same thing as separation of home from the world, or of the individual from the home. Instead, it points to the permeability of the home and the world. As I have argued with respect to Toru Dutt and Michael Madhusudan Dutt and even with respect to a more obdurate figure such as David Lester Richardson or an isolated one such as Mary Carshore, unhomeliness, like the turtles the earth rests on, goes all the way down. While it has been fashionable to locate aporia everywhere—and certainly the morning paper is a good place to start on any given day—at the fin de siècle, we find the forces of nationalism, ethnography, and cultural institutions such as the exhibition and the museum, the technologies of communication and publishing, and travel itself creating cultural spaces where "unhomeliness" is not merely analyzable but bubbles up whenever the poet's pen touches paper. As Manmohan Ghose lamented, he was at home neither in India nor in England.[3] A different form of unhomeliness, one based in gender as much as in national location, is revealed in Sarojini Naidu's remark in a letter to Arthur Symons: "I have taught myself to be commonplace. . . . Everyone thinks I am so nice and cheerful, so 'brave,' all the banal things that are so comfortable to be. My mother knows me only as 'such a tranquil child, but so strong-willed.'"[4] And Tagore at great length, in a state of depression following the responses in Bengal and Britain to the Nobel Prize, turned unhomeliness into the central metaphor of his post-Nobel novel, *Bhaire Gaire (The Home and the World).* Indeed, Homi Bhabha's lengthy invocation of unhomeliness at the outset of *The Location of Culture* invokes, equally, Henry James's Isabel Archer and the heroine of Tagore's novel.

The English language poems of Manmohan Ghose, Naidu, and Tagore—lyrics arising from the ostensibly personal, lyrics deliberately bridging cultural gaps and psychic aporia—can be read as extended meditations upon, even theorizations of, unhomeliness. Unhomeliness in this sense is the opposite of authenticity; one is removed from one's imagined "author," whether cultural or familial. In negotiating authorship and cultural authority in England, these poets found personal networks to be of the first importance. The circumstances of their publication, though these entail discourses of authenticity, attest to the complexity of hospitality.

Unhomeliness at the fin de siècle was mediated through bardic tropes that had been transformed in each generation since the beginnings of English language poetry in India and through paratexts that were supposed to make familiar the unhomely. Bardic tropes, which had persisted since Derozio took up the harp of India, reappear in Ghose's and Naidu's poetry as fin-de-siècle Celticism; they emerge in Tagore's assimilation of the bard and the guru. Paratexts too have their mediating role—in the forewords and introductions by Laurence Binyon, Arthur Symons, and W. B. Yeats and in frontispieces showing a young Sarojini in aesthetic dress or in a sari and depicting Tagore in cross-legged meditative abstraction. The transformed bardic trope and the biographical paratext "place" the poet in an unhomely world. Gone is the intellectual mediation provided by the learned footnote, for these poets have assimilated their diction to a Georgian standard that assumes a transparency impossible to achieve. All three poets faced the continuing, if differently articulated, demand that they be authentic.

There are, of course, crucial differences between the Indian reception of all three writers and the ways they were perceived in Britain, and these differences provide the subtext of my argument. But it was in Britain that the first two poets made their reputations and in Britain that Tagore and his friends laid the groundwork for what became an international phenomenon.

It is important, then, to recall the situation of elite poetry in Britain at the turn of the century. All three of these writers published work in the context of a market for collectors' limited editions that was coupled with relatively difficult market conditions for poetry in the fin de siècle. All three were implicated in the ideological and material practices of turn-of-the-century aestheticism and the avant garde. Initially at any rate, they found a British audience whose expectations were attuned to practices created by such publishers as Elkin Mathews and John Lane, the Chiswick Press and other fine printing establishments, and institutions spawned by the Arts and Crafts movement (the Century Guild, its house in Fitzroy Square, and the related journal the *Hobby Horse*) and by the rise of other avant-garde journals, including the *Yellow Book* and the *Savoy*.

All three of these poets participated a world of literary sociality in which they functioned, to varying degrees, as the oriental other but in which they also found and created their own spaces for making art. Their London associates—British and American poets, artists, missionaries, critics, and journalists—were themselves, as often as not, critical of British culture and British imperialism. Nonetheless, literary relationships were frequently expressed in terms of colonial patronage for the colonized—which was virtually unavoidable in this period, whatever goodwill obtained on both sides. Such relationships therefore were characterized by some degree of mutual ambivalence, including ambivalence on the part of the self-critical British or American subject and ambivalence on the part of Indian poets, whose own positions vis-à-vis language, poetry, and art—as well as their social positions at "home"—were at best vexed and complicated. Other elements—particularly differences in gender, age, and class position—shaped the possibilities of social relationship.

Despite the potential for cultural misunderstanding and despite real differences of attitude and position, these ties of literary sociality can be seen as ties of personal affection and as professional relationships often conducted with integrity on both sides. It would be altogether too ironic to ignore the ways in which personal needs and delights, dependent on but never entirely reducible to larger cultural constraints, were figured in the creation of poems in this period.

Ghose, Naidu, and Tagore entered the milieu of fin-de-siècle London from different social positions. Common to the three, however, was Bengali ancestry and association with the progressive wing of high-caste Bengali culture, as exemplified in the Brahmo Samaj. Ghose and Tagore came from Bengali families who belonged to the Brahmo Samaj; indeed, Tagore's father and grandfather had founded Brahmo institutions.[5] Brahmo respect for selected traditions of European learning had far-reaching consequences for poets, including Manmohan and Sarojini, in that it formed their parents' educations and made both acceptable and inevitable their intimate encounter with British literary traditions.

Manmohan, Sarojini, and Rabindranath grew up in the second or third generation of families that had been, to different degrees, formed by their affiliation with Brahmo ideas. Manmohan Ghose's parents both belonged to the Brahmo Samaj. His father, Krishna Dhan, a civil medical doctor, had studied in Aberdeen, like many in the Bengal Medical Service, and in 1877 took his three very young sons to study in England, in part because of his belief in European education and in part because of their mother's mental illness. The three boys took different paths in later life, and their father left the Brahmo Samaj while they were in their teens to become a Buddhist. While Manmohan dedicated himself to belles lettres, to the extent that he could, his brothers Aravinda (later Sri Aurobindo) and Barindra Kumar had by about 1900 become revolutionaries. Both Manmohan and, later, his brother Aurobindo were drawn to serious religious reflection. In his early letters, Manmohan espouses a kind of rationalist yet pantheist understanding that sustained his verse.

Sarojini Naidu's upbringing was less embedded in Bengali Brahmo culture than Manmohan's or Rabindranath's, for she was raised in a religiously diverse community in Hyderabad. Her father, like Manmohan Ghose's, was a physician with significant Scottish connections; he had studied both in Edinburgh and in Bonn. While he lived in Europe, he placed his young bride in a Brahmo school for girls. Sarojini Chattopadhyay thus grew up in a freethinking family, but her experience was equally shaped by the culture of Hyderabad. Her father's eclectic group of friends included scholars, poets, scientists, and medical practitioners from various backgrounds, and, as he was employed by the nizam of Hyderabad, he had many Muslim friends.

While there are important commonalities among these poets, their differences are equally salient, especially with respect to poetic language. Indeed, Sarojini, unlike virtually any of the poets I discuss elsewhere in this volume, grew up multilingual in Urdu, Telugu, Hindi, and English; and as both her parents were Bengali, along with all her extended family, it seems logical to assume that she also spoke Bangla. She alone of the poets I discuss in this chapter read Persian and deeply appreciated Persian poetry. In contrast to Sarojini (who was sent to England at age sixteen) and Ghose (who was sent at age ten), both of whom began their writing careers by making English verse in

London, Rabindranath Tagore first traveled to Europe at eighteen and during his two years of study in Britain continued to write verse in Bangla. Moreover, Tagore's class position as a member of one of the most prominent families of Bengal shaped his understanding of his role as a poet quite differently from either of the other two. While Tagore principally wrote in and, many would say, invented modern Bangla, Ghose and Naidu, to my knowledge, published poetry only in English. Laurence Binyon reported that Ghose attempted poetry in Bangla but did not find it congenial.[6] Both Naidu and Ghose undertook English language poetry at a time when the urgencies of nationalism were coupled with traditional prejudices to make the effort, if not suspect, at least problematic. Within the scene of British reception and reputation, these decisions had complex ramifications. For an Indian writer of English verse in this period to escape the discourses of authenticity was impossible; within the parameters of affiliation, friendship, and hospitality persisted the shadows of unhomeliness. Of the three poets I discuss at length here, Manmohan Ghose experienced the most profound sense of estrangement.

Double Exile and the Lyric Impulse: Manmohan Ghose

In 1890, a slim volume came before the public, under the imprint of Basil Blackwell in Oxford and with a cover and title page designed by Selwyn Image. With its simple brown paper cover and unassuming size and its lovely typography, the volume was recognizably in the tradition of Ruskin's Oxford. Selwyn Image's work declared its connections to the new Century Guild, which he had helped to found to further the reach of the Arts and Crafts movement. On Image's cover, a quartet of graceful tulips alluded to the four young authors whose verses intertwined inside. Of the four, the moving spirit was Laurence Binyon, who was later to introduce the public to the complexities of Chinese and Japanese art as the keeper of Oriental prints and drawing in the British Museum.[7] The sole Indian poet in this group was Manmohan Ghose, who had been Binyon's closest friend during their teenaged years at St. Paul's School, Hammersmith. Ghose wrote from a position of estrangement from his homeland, his adopted land, and his family.

As adolescents, Manmohan and Binyon shared a passion for poetry, and they moved from the worship of Keats to a veneration for Arnold and, at least on Binyon's part, for Browning. Though Ghose's and Binyon's youthful and nearly exclusive friendship had changed by 1890 (Binyon had more money and more friends at Oxford, while Ghose scraped to make ends meet), the two friends still exerted a powerful influence on each other. Ghose left Oxford in the spring of 1890 about the time he was collaborating with Binyon on *Primavera.* Ghose wrote to his friend back in Oxford, "[Y]ou cannot imagine my isolation."[8] But Binyon soon introduced Ghose to the Fitzroy, the house taken by the Century Guild in Fitzroy Square, which had become a magnet for artists and poets. Probably through Binyon's introduction, Ghose also soon became a friend and admirer of Oscar Wilde. These and other connections led to a remarkable number of reviews for so slim a volume as *Primavera.*

Here I read *Primavera* in the context of Ghose's and Binyon's later works, for Binyon edited and saw through the press in London both of Ghose's subsequent collections. It is fair to say that without Binyon there would have been no public presence for Ghose's English language verse. The poems that Binyon edited are riven by a conflicted understanding of place, nation, and exile. They are influenced, too, by the final form of bardic nationalism and by a late form of transperipheral poetics, which conflated "race" and nation and suggested "racial" links between Indian and Celtic poets. For Manmohan, friendship created within an experience of double exile—exile from Bengal and then exile from Britain—shaped the development of verse; at the same time, discourses of nation and authenticity shaped its reception.

Binyon and Ghose, though they communicated less frequently in later years, each in his own way tried to foster an affiliative world he identified as the world of art. Both poets refused to submit art to the boundaries of nation. Binyon's late poems pose the terms of the shadowed mutuality that he and Manmohan Ghose found in their youth and that Binyon later found in Japanese and Chinese art. As Binyon wrote in a late poem, "Koya San," a meditation in the mountain temple complex central to Japanese Shingon Buddhism:

> Fragments we are, and none has seen the whole.
> Only some moment wins us to restore
> The touch of infinite companionship.
>
> (*Koya San,* VI, 12)

Binyon's and Ghose's companionship was broken and nearly destroyed by Ghose's return to India in 1893, but the threads of their exchange extended through the complex networks of literary sociality that made up fin-de-siècle London.

Three of the four *Primavera* poets as they matured came to understand their place in the world as profoundly and complexly global. In *Primavera,* all four gave evidence of their training in Greek and Latin, something that aligned Ghose with his peers but would seem to exceed the parameters of the "authentically" Indian. Ghose and Binyon, both excellent scholars, read Greats at Oxford—five terms of classical literature and seven of ancient history and philosophy (Hatcher, 19). Such training left indelible marks on their early efforts. So did Binyon's and Ghose's mutual enthusiasm for Matthew Arnold—not unrelated to their veneration for the classics. The volume began with Binyon's cousin Stephen Phillips's invocation to the muse who is said to have "fled" Europe. According to Phillips, the classical world, and all its freshness, is gone. Next Binyon struck his own Arnoldian note. For Binyon, unlike his cousin, it is not the beauty of the classical world that has fled. Rather, Binyon misses something more "Eastern" and sensual, the world of Bacchus, whom the poet describes as an "Eastern" deity:

When from the storied, sacred East afar,
Down Indian gorges clothed in green,
With flower-rein'd tigers and with ivory car
He came, the youthful god;
Beautiful Bacchus, ivy-crown'd, his hair
Blown on the wind, and flush'd limbs bare,
And lips apart, and radiant eyes,
And ears that caught the coming melodies

(*Primavera,* "Youth," 6–7)

Sadly, though, Binyon writes, "victorious youth" has given way to an aging world weighed down by "disenchanting years." Bacchus and his Titianesque pards, his Keatsian chariot, have gone. I would speculate that Binyon's Indian Bacchus combines versions of Manmohan Ghose and his own alter ego. Yet Ghose likewise proclaimed Arnoldian disenchantment.

Ghose's first poem in *Primavera,* immediately following Binyon's "Youth," reveals a highly conflicted young poet—conflicted about poetry, love, and fame—and afflicted with "unhomeliness." Although Binyon struck the note of Arnold's "Resignation," Ghose's untitled debut poem is much closer to Arnold's suicidal Empedocles. If not his best work, Ghose's poem is so symptomatic of later conflicts that it is worth quoting in full. The poet's emotional difficulties and his classical training emerge as tortured syntax:

'Tis my twentieth year: dim, now, youth stretches behind me;
Breaking fresh at my feet, lies, like an ocean, the world.
And despised seem, now, those quiet fields I have travell'd:
Eager to thee I turn, Life, and thy visions of joy.
Fame I see, with her wreath, far off approaching to crown me;
Love, whose starry eyes fever my heart with desire:
And impassion'd I yearn for the future, all unconscious,
Ah, poor dreamer! what ills life in its circle enfolds.
Not more restless the boy, whose eager, confident bosom
The wide, unknown sea fills with a hunger to roam.
Often beside the surge of the desolate ocean he paces;
Ingrate, dreams of a sky brighter, serener than his.
Passionate soul! light holds he a mother's tearful entreaties,
Lightly leaves he behind all the sad faces of home;
Never again, perchance, to behold them; lost in the tempest,
Or on some tropic shore dying in fever and pain.

(*Primavera,* "Youth," 10–11)

The youth or man in this poem exists not only in two times but also in two places and two states of mind. The relentless syntactic inversion creates an almost schizophrenic division. The eager boy on the implicitly British shore imagines leaving home for the world. But where exactly is he to locate home, and how is he to understand either home or world? Is his home England—which biographically speaking is the only home the poet has known for half his short life? And who then would be the lamenting mother—a person, a country, an imagined speaker's imagined parent?[9]

Ghose had the enormously complex emotional burden of coming to terms with a turbulent childhood, healing the pain of his early "exile" from Bengal to England, and accepting the prospect of being exiled yet again should he have to return to India. Like the imagined boy in this poem, Ghose, too, had left home, never to see his mother again, for she died, after a life of mental illness, long before his return to India. The syntax of the last two lines could be said to embody the poet's contradictions. The boy is to leave the sad faces of home "never again . . . to behold them; lost in the tempest / Or on some tropic shore dying." If we read beyond the semicolon, the syntax is thoroughly ambiguous. Will the boy die on a tropic shore, or will his family? Will the boy or his family be lost in the tempest? Even if we take punctuation to be more important than lineation and enjambment, we must reckon with a kind of odd mimicry effect as the young man envisions exactly that fate most often feared by the British boy going abroad. Ironically, it must be said, Ghose's speaker can only imagine the death most feared by the British colonizer—death by fever and pain.

In some ways this poem was indicative of Ghose's future—not death but double exile. In a letter to Laurence Binyon written during World War I, Ghose described the difficulty of his position, as a professor at Presidency College, Calcutta. "With English people in India," Ghose wrote, "there can be only a nodding acquaintance or official connection, and with Indians my purely English upbringing and breeding puts me out of harmony; denationalized, that is their word for me."[10]

To be denationalized for an Indian at the turn of the century was metaphorically to be motherless. The image of the mother subtends other poems in *Primavera* and later poems as well, perhaps because Ghose had neither a biological mother nor an ideological one in India. In Ghose's untitled poem about the seasons from *Primavera,* an implicitly maternal nature counsels her despairing son to follow the footsteps of a personified and rather Keatsian autumn. Mother nature nourishes and advises the aspiring poet yet teaches lessons in loss:

> Green still it is, where that fair goddess strays;
> 	Then follow, till around thee all be sere.
> Lose not a vision of her passing face;
> 	Nor miss the sound of her soft robes, that here
> Sweep over the wet leaves of the fast-falling year.
>
> (31)

And finally, in the volume's last poem, "Mentem Mortalia Tangunt," Ghose evokes, again, the Arnoldian estranging sea. Again maternal nature is both comforting and empty:

> What though we gaze with fear,
> So blank death seems to be;
> What though no land appear
> Beyond that lonely sea;
> Still in our hearts her cry doth stay
>
> (41)

Though maternal nature provides philosophical comfort, it does not provide emotional solace: "Her glorious works she works alone, / Unfathom'd and unknown!" (41).

Although the reviews of *Primavera* were positive, and the volume shortly went into a second edition, the reviewers could not ignore the question of the Indian poet's authenticity.[11] For Ghose, as for Sarojini Naidu some years later, reviewers felt the need to comment on the writer's "Indianness"—in marked contrast to the treatment of the other three authors, whose authenticity was assumed. The reviewer in the *Athenaeum* did call Ghose a true poet, but typically, what was given with one hand was taken away with the other: "What is published as English poetry must be judged as English poetry. But that is no hard law for Mr. Manmohan Ghose. He can lay no claim to ignorance of English. As a writer he simply is English."[12] As a writer yes, but as a man? Clearly, the slippage here between "English language" and Englishness is crucial.

A surprisingly similar stance was taken by Oscar Wilde. Wilde made much of Binyon's recent Newdigate Prize for poetry, but he singled out Ghose for praise, even as he too raised the inevitable question of the poet's "English":

> Particular interest attaches to Mr. Ghose's work. Born in India, of purely Indian parentage, he has been brought up entirely in England, and was educated at St. Paul's School, and his verses show us how quick and subtle are the intellectual sympathies of the Oriental mind, and suggest how close is the bond of union that may some day bind India to us by other methods than those of commerce and military strength. There is something charming in finding a young Indian using our language with such care for music and words as Mr. Ghose does.[13]

Even the sympathetic Wilde transformed Ghose's poems, which so much resemble those of his Oxford peers, into the subtle sympathies of the "Oriental mind." Here the subtlety, for better or worse, is Wilde's—an accusation of mimicry perhaps, as Wilde argued that though "purely Indian," Ghose can charm the British in "our language."[14] Contra Wilde, Ghose might have said, as Jacques Derrida was to put it many years later, my language is not my language.[15]

Ghose responded to this critical demand for empire by other methods by attempting to write a novel. As early as January 1888, two years before the publication of

Primavera, he was already writing Binyon about a projected novel and credited Binyon with having "showed great sagacity" by advising him to write prose, even a romance. The letter reveals the extent to which Ghose understood the literary enterprise simultaneously in classical and orientalist terms. Because fiction was "so much the rage," he argued hopefully that a prose romance might be the equal of poetry: "One thing distresses me, and that is, that I must perforce introduce those trifles, which seem inevitable in a novel. But there has been a Catullus, and perhaps it may be my happy fate to put poetry into the most trivial things. That objection too would not tell so much, choosing as I do an Indian subject, in which novelty would tend to magnify little things" (*Collected,* 1:156). Thus Ghose himself imagined that his "Indian subject" could lend significance to the detail. He faced, nonetheless, the problem of language. He told Binyon that he had already sketched a plot and "scrawled" a few scenes. But, he continued, "I only wait to know one thing,—what is the genuine Indian way of talking. This I can get alone by knowing Bengali, which I have sedulously set myself to learn. In the meantime I have read a story with Bengali conversational phrases literally translated. You cannot imagine how simple and Homeric some of them are. I think I could create a striking and novel effect by introducing these sometimes. As for the customs wherewith to colour the incidents, memory and imagination will easily supply those" (*Collected,* 1:157). Given the inevitably conflicted nature of this orientalizing project and Ghose's estrangement from vernacular Bangla, his projected romance got no further than a few fragmentary pages.

Consigning his prose romance to deserved oblivion, Ghose focused on poetry after leaving Oxford. On moving to London, he became associated with the Rhymers' Club.[16] Though Ghose's penury meant that his poems were not included in the first or the second *Book of the Rhymers' Club,* he shared with his fellow Rhymers an equal fascination for the classics and for the peripheries of the British Isles.[17] Like Lionel Johnson, John Todhunter, and Victor Plarr, Ghose was fascinated with the classics, though for him—as for many of the Rhymers—Keats was equally important. These qualities are best balanced in Ghose's early "Sapphics":

> Cease, O my spirit, cease this endless yearning!
> Idly thou seekest; gone is it; past hoping.
> That golden treasure: thine own sweet contentment
>   See shalt thou never.
>
> Glass'd in her waters, her own green haunts with music
> Shall the flown mavis fill again, and warbling
> Taste her old freedom: but oh, not the prisoned
>   Breast that is burning.
>
> Burning, Myvanwy, from that smile whose sweetness
> Makes mad the spirit and tells the trembling gazer
> Peace is gone from him, peace and every thankful
>   Moment forever.[18]

Ghose's classicism and his Keatsian diction are filtered through a romanticized Celticism that functioned much like its equivalent romanticized orientalism.

For Ghose, Keatsian delight, Celticism, and orientalism amounted to the same thing. We might call it bardic Celticism, tinged as always with an unacknowledged gendered subtext. Bardic Celtic Sapphics? Friendship with Wilde? Such gendered possibilities are contained in the medium of rhyme and in newly racialized theories of culture. Matthew Arnold's theories of poetry, together with the Celticism of the Rhymers' Club, accounted for Manmohan's fascination with the Celtic—a kind of thinking that also animated Sarojini Naidu's friendship with Arthur Symons. Arnold's essays in *On the Study of Celtic Literature* argue for the true virtue of English poetry being attributable to the Celtic or, in Arnold's equation, the Indo-European rather than the Germanic element of British letters. According to Arnold, Celtic poetry has style, penetrating passion, and melancholy. The Celtic element is "Titanism," Arnold says: "Woody Morven, and echoing Sora, and Selma with its silent halls! we all owe them a debt of gratitude, and when we are unjust enough to forget it, may the Muse forget us" (116).[19] This emotional identification of the Celtic and the "Indo-European" certainly would have provided Ghose with ample ground for understanding himself as entitled to poetic inspiration; in this kind of race thinking, Ghose was as close as, or perhaps even closer than, his British companions to supposed Indo-European roots of English language poetic energy.

But easy as it might have been for Arnold to posit Indo-European-Celtic verse, its practice was another thing. The Irish, Welsh, and Scottish flavor of the Rhymers' Club probably also would have heightened Ghose's attraction to the "Celtic." The moving spirits inaugurating the group's loose network were the three Irishmen: W. B. Yeats, T. W. Rolleston, and John Todhunter. Moreover, Ghose's poems, with a striking number of poems inspired by holidays in Wales, were in harmony as well with the defiantly Welsh Ernest Rhys. Had he the cash on hand, Ghose's Keatsian Celtic "Sapphics" might have kept good company in the first *Book of the Rhymers' Club* with Lionel Johnson's "Plato in London," Rhys's "Wedding of Pale Bronwen," G. A. Greene's "Keats's Grave," and Yeats's "Fairy Song" and "The Lake Isle of Innisfree." But lacking funds and called home by the illness of his father, Ghose reached the unhappy determination to return to India.

Binyon, when he came to edit a small volume (really a pamphlet) of Ghose's verse for Elkin Mathews' Shilling Garland in 1898, chose to end his selection with Manmohan's long lyric, "Exile." This poem, evidently written before Ghose left England, places the speaker on the seashore, where he remembers his home country while the breakers fling him back "with derisive laughter, / Shouting, 'Exile, back unto thy home!'" (*Love-Songs*, 38). The speaker then imagines a ship sailing away from him, a mere speck on the horizon, which he wishes good speed:

> Go, like lightning: be the imaginary
> Wings to bliss that exiles weary for.

Here, O hard compulsion, must I tarry.
Hie thee, hie thee, sweet ambassador!

Hasten, though the immeasurable distance
Break my heart, imploring, forced to stay;
Not a surge, and not a blast's resistance!
Quiet be the waters of thy way.

Mine alone be all this deaf commotion.
Let the breakers lash me with their scorn
O'er the unfooted, vast, relentless ocean
I would still remember, though I mourn.

(38–39)

Home, obviously, has no simple meaning here, as the breakers order the poet back to his "home" (that is, England, the land behind him) while the ship of imagination wings its way back to a home that he can no longer entirely claim.

Thus Ghose could be said to have neither a biological mother nor an ideological one in India; both the nationalist and the personal metaphors fail to account for his experience. The difficulty of his position was redoubled when after 1905 he found himself under suspicion because of the nationalist activities of his brothers. His brothers, Aravinda and Barindra Kumar, were both engaged in terrorist activity against the British; both were arrested in connection with the Alipore bombing, and, though Aravinda was finally acquitted of sedition for lack of evidence, fearing re-arrest he fled British India. Barindra was tried by the British, condemned to death, and, his sentence being commuted, transported for life. Manmohan, a great admirer of Milton, came under suspicion for an epic he was composing on the subject of Perseus and Medusa, and he agreed to abandon it (L. Ghose, *Collected,* 2:viii).

At best, Ghose's blank verse epic, *Perseus, the Gorgon-Slayer,* could have been a pyrrhic attempt at a very late Arnoldian classical revival, though of course Perseus can be read as "Asian" just as much as Greek. Though written in blank verse, Ghose's poem lacks the Miltonic vigor of Michael Madhusudan's Bangla epic. Given the highly abstract philosophical conception of the poem, it could have had little cultural resonance for British or Indian readers. Well might they look for an allegory of rebellion, but to little avail. Perhaps a more political and less philosophical allegory would have had more purchase on the (divided) minds of his audience, but Manmohan was unlikely to go the path of his brothers, particularly given his familial and financial responsibilities.[20]

It is not surprising, consequently, that Ghose's best poems are a series of late lyrics inspired by the tragic death of his wife after years of an illness, probably a mental illness, that had left her paralyzed. Written just a few years after Thomas Hardy's

Poems of 1912–13, they are, if less tormented, comparable in an intensity created over the remains of a relationship that, however important in retrospect, was at best vexed in the living.[21] Like Hardy's lyrics, if less assured, Ghose's achieve power through the accumulation of metrical invention coupled with a relative simplicity of diction. One stanza only will have to serve to give the flavor of these poems, more felt than the early Rhymers' Club poems and, at last, more skilled at running a complex syntax across a complex metrical pattern:

Face, to memory clear,
    That comes to thieve me
Into the fancy dear
    'Tis your lost eyes I see
Shining once more on me,—
    Your very lips I sight
Smiling the old delight!
    Dead face, in memory fair,
With the old brow, the old hair
    Triumphant; can you be,
Sweet shadowy witchery!
    Only an image vain,
Wrought as a balm for pain,
    Mirrored upon the brain,
Only to mock my sense
    With shadowy, intense
Thirst, rapture, then to fade
    How like an empty shade!
Then in the present cold,
    Heartbroken, lonely and old,
        Leave me?

(*Songs*, "Face, to Memory Clear," 113)

Lacking an intellectual community in India, Ghose never had the critical response—or perhaps the raw talent—that would have allowed him to grow as a poet. His English friendships, especially with Binyon, formed his verse but could not sustain him after his return to India. His last collection was edited posthumously by Binyon, and Binyon's final comments in his foreword best sum up their "shadowed mutuality": "I hope that fate, so malignant to him in his life-time, may not pursue him after death with the hasty and cheap criticism that his verse is neither Indian nor English, and so dismiss it. On the contrary, it is both Indian and English; that is its interest" (in *Songs*, 21).

Two years after Manmohan Ghose embarked for India, the sixteen-year-old Sarojini Chattopadhyay who would later publish her work as Sarojini Naidu appeared on the London literary scene. She was swept into the same constellation that had surrounded Manmohan Ghose. Immediately she became friends with two men, one of whom became a mentor and father figure, the other an intellectual and emotional companion. The first, Edmund Gosse, had daughters of a similar age and took the young poet seriously. His expectations had perhaps been shaped by his "discovery" of Toru Dutt, whose work he had championed despite the fact that they never met.[22] Gosse introduced Sarojini not only to his daughters but also to the most exciting poets in London. Among them was Arthur Symons, who became Sarojini's closest literary companion and who years later was to refer to her as "a little Indian princess, an old flame of mine" (letter to Julia Marlowe, April 2, 1914, *Selected Letters*).

Although Sarojini had a father figure in Gosse and although she lived in London with friends of her family and then at college in Cambridge, she had a remarkable amount of freedom, owing in part to her freethinking family. Sarojini was something of a child prodigy, both as a poet and as a scholar, and equally precocious socially. Her journey to England began when her father persuaded the nizam to grant her a scholarship to study at Cambridge, largely to separate her from Govindarajulu Naidu, his colleague, to whom the family strongly objected because of the differences in caste and in age between them. No doubt the fact that Naidu was not Bengali was also problematic.

So the young Sarojini found herself at the University of London and later in Cambridge. Although she wrote passionate letters to Naidu and suffered from their separation, her excitement at arriving in London was palpable. Clearly, she saw her arrival in highly literary terms. One of her early letters to Govindarajulu catalogs her enthusiasms:

> Shelley and Byron, Moore and Scott, Keats and Campbell and Wordsworth were a brilliant starry coterie, but even as brilliant as their coterie, though rather differently, are the new poets. Fancy the young, passionate, beautiful poets gathered together in a radiant galaxy. William Watson with his sublime, starry genius, Davidson with his wild, riotous, dazzling superabundant brilliance, Thompson with his rich, gorgeous, spiritual ecstasy of poetry, Yeats with his exquisite dreams and music, Norman Gale, redolent of springtime in the meadows and autumn in the orchard, Arthur Symons, the marvelous boy, with his passionate nature and fiery eyes, all gathered together in the friendly house of that dearest and lovingest of friends and rarest and most gifted of [geniuses] Edmund Gosse. Take too the older men, with their beautiful gifts—Swinburne, with his marvelous spirit, his

voluptuous ecstasy of word music, take that grand old Socialist William Morris hammering with golden thunders. . . . [W]ho says we have no rare geniuses and true poets in these days? (January 13, 1896, *Letters,* 2–3)[23]

Sarojini's list reads like a who's who of her early reading, and all her favorite poets living and dead become part of one brilliant "coterie." However loosely this might accord with literary history, it shows Sarojini's intuitive sense of the way literary sociality worked in her own time.[24] She understood the uses of poetic networks and the cultural importance of an avant garde.

The Rhymers' Club, still more than the loosely connected group in Gosse's drawing room, surely could be called a coterie, and Sarojini soon became part of their circle. Like Ghose, she was marginal to the club itself, but not on account of money—no women were admitted. Nonetheless, Sarojini became a great friend of Arthur Symons, who was famous for his poems about and reviews of fin-de-siècle dance halls. His most famous achievement is probably his early critical study *The Symbolist Movement in Literature* (1899). He was at once a "gifted man of letters" at the center of the art world and a figure of decadence, as Karl Beckson puts it.[25] Beckson concurs with Symons's self-characterization, for Symons wrote that he led a "double life," torn between the aesthetic and the transcendent. A similar doubleness formed Sarojini's aesthetic.

The "shadowed mutuality" of the young Indian poet and the English Decadent poet allowed each of them to explore their differently contradictory positions. The fin-de-siècle experience of unhomeliness—which might mean cultural alienation, linguistic alienation, or the limitations and exclusion of gender—forged an unlikely bond between them. Like Symons and like Manmohan Ghose before her, Sarojini too felt she led a double life. Like Manmohan, Sarojini described herself as between two cultures, but probably owing to her much stronger family and the stability of her early childhood, she was far less conflicted than he about her position, even as a teenager. In a fictional autobiography written, it seems certain, while she was in Europe during 1897, Sarojini describes her fictional alter ego Sunalini this way: "Unlike the girls of her own nation, she had been brought up in an atmosphere of large unconvention and culture and absolute freedom of thought and action; her education had been based, chiefly on European models, and yet she was totally unlike any European girl: she was not a type. She was a personality" ("Sunalini," 9). Sarojini goes on to describe how her fictional heroine falls ill, is tended by the doctor (her "brave lover"), and is then sent to Europe: "[T]hey brought her to the land she loved best next to her India" (11).[26] While Ghose experienced what he called double exile—at home neither in Britain nor in Bengal—Sarojini seemed determined to be at home, a circle whose center is everywhere and whose circumference is nowhere. In her later life, when she became a leader of the Congress Party and the independence movement, her numerous prison letters testify to this theme.

As a child she took hold of English, according to her own account, with a kind of vengeance that betrays not exile from a possible mother tongue but what, following

Sheldon Pollock, we might call a cosmopolitanism of the vernaculars.[27] Because she was, very probably, the most thoroughly multilingual poet writing English language poetry in India since William Jones and John Leyden, it is not surprising that choices among languages were crucial to her. In his introduction to her first volume of verse, *The Golden Threshold,* Symons quotes Sarojini saying that as a child she was "stubborn" and refused to speak English. "So one day," she wrote to Symons, "when I was nine years old my father punished me the only time I was ever punished by shutting me in a room alone for a whole day. I came out a full-blown linguist. I have never spoken any other language to him, or to my mother, who always speaks to me in Hindustani" (xx). She attributed scientific training to her father and poetic instinct to her mother, who "wrote some lovely Bengali lyrics in her youth" (xx). While one might well doubt this self-report—how many stubborn nine-year-olds would actually adhere to such a resolution?—her strong will was evident later, not only in her eventual marriage to Naidu but also, and more especially, in the complex cultural negotiations of her poetry.

The first volume Sarojini published in England, *The Golden Threshold* (1905), included one translation from Urdu and one from Persian. The poet divided her volume into three sections: the first two are "Folk Songs" and "Songs for Music," and the third is "Poems." The verses invoke or imitate traditional songs and move thence to occasional, nationalist, and domestic poetry in the last section. The last three poems in the collection—"To India" (a nationalist lyric), "The Royal Tombs of Golconda" (describing the most famous historical ruin of her city, Hyderabad), and "To a Buddha Seated on a Lotus"—evidence her attempt at both particularity and representativeness. Moving among the languages and cultures of India, yet within the medium of English language verse, the young poet is, from one perspective, trying on various kinds of cultural clothes; from another, she could be said to stitch a variegated wardrobe that she hopes will become positive emblems of cultural multiplicity.

The terms of this multiplicity can disconcert the twenty-first-century reader and can appear naïve; yet I want to suggest that Sarojini was both more critically self-reflective and more self-assured than Manmohan Ghose. This extraordinary assurance, along with a cultural and sexual negotiation, is evident equally in Sarojini's friendship with Arthur Symons and in her poems. Like Binyon and Ghose, Sarojini and Symons seem to have found a place of "shadowed mutuality."

The extraordinariness of this friendship might not be at first apparent: but imagine a very young woman in a silk sari flitting about London alone with the Decadent poet who was just about twice her age. Despite her on-again off-again romance by correspondence with Dr. Naidu while she was in England, Sarojini and Symons developed what I would call a passionate friendship. Their letters make clear that the two met at Gosse's and also that Sarojini visited Symons at his rooms in Fountain Court. In a letter to Symons from this period, Sarojini recalled Yeats reading aloud in Symons's room from Symons's *London Nights.* Symons, responding to her enthusiasm, sent her proofs of his volume *Amoris Victima* in July 1896, to which she replied with genuine enthusiasm yet in the tone not of his junior but of his equal: "[T]here will be divine heretics to whom your poems will come with a strange power and loveliness; there will be hearts deepened by sorrow and strengthened by tears that will vibrate in 'every little nerve' to your heart's expression. . . . [G]o on, dear poet, you have given us what is very beautiful and strong: but it is not yet your best" (Munro, 139). Symons might believe that she ran "on too fast, and enthusiastically," but, she reminded him, "you are a 'fiery Celt' . . . and can understand the incense youth offers to genius" (139). Like Ghose among the Irish and Welsh Rhymers, Sarojini claimed kinship with Symons as a fiery Celt.[28] Though she knew him less personally than Symons, Sarojini had a similar reaction to Yeats. In her unpublished poem "Alul," she describes Yeats as a child of the Druids whose eyes are "dark and prophet-like with fire."[29]

Symons and Sarojini each functioned as the other's shadow; their exchange of poems and of emotional intimacies allowed each to measure the cultural alterity of aestheticism against a wider interplay of difference and commonality. Each figured the other as the East to his West, the West to her East. As we will see, although Sarojini locates "Europe" in Symons, it is a particular kind of Europe, and as he locates "the East" in her, it too is a particular kind of "East." Among the extant papers, this version of alterity is clearest in Sarojini's last letter to Symons before her departure from London for India in 1898, and in Symons's introduction to her first volume of verse. Sarojini wrote to Symons on August 17, 1898,

> Dear, I will not see you before I go: I could not wish you good-by, perhaps a final good-by, in the formal presence of others: and let you go with all the things my heart longs to say unsaid, you will understand. . . . You will not drift away from me? I shall be so far away and it will be so easy for you, not to forget me, but to lose touch. . . . All your interests are in Europe: all your aspirations, your whole being is full of Europe, with nothing of the East in it? . . . I cannot write tonight. . . . I feel stupid with the suddenness of things: and, there is a curious pain at my heart. . . . My dear one, I wish I could have seen you once more, and laid my head on your head a moment in a century of blessing. . . . [I]t seems impossible to realize that I might never see you again, I who have loved you so . . . and trust you, and had no fear or shame, to tell you the most hidden things of my spirit. . . . [H]ow can I thank you that you have made it possible? that you have never misunderstood me?" (Munro, 145)

Some ten years later, Symons responded, introducing the book he had urged his friend to publish. While Naidu's second volume, *The Broken Wing,* would be published with a portrait frontispiece of the poet in a lovely sari, as if to guarantee the Easternness of its author, in this volume, *The Golden Threshold,* Symons provided a frontispiece drawing by John Butler Yeats of the poet in Western "aesthetic" dress and a verbal portrait of her in "Eastern" garments. Symons recalled Sarojini in London as almost a spirit of the East:

> She was dressed always in clinging dresses of Eastern silk, and as she was so small, and her long black hair hung straight down her back, you might have taken her for a child. She spoke little, and in a low voice. . . . Through that soul I seemed to touch and take hold upon the East. And first there was the wisdom of the East. . . . But there was something else, something hardly personal, . . . which I realized and wondered at, and admired, in her passionate tranquility of mind, before which everything mean and trivial and temporary caught fire and burnt away in smoke. (16)

Obviously this exchange, in which the two represented the "East" and "Europe" to each other, was key to their "shadowed mutuality." As a female poet, Sarojini was framed and reframed through the paratextual representation of her body—as an aesthete by J. B. Yeats, as the "East" by Symons. Transmuting the private into the public in his introduction, Symons emphasized the very qualities of passionate physical and intellectual intensity that clearly attracted them to each other, yet Symons attempted to transmute these qualities into the unlikely claim that the teenaged Sarojini allowed nothing to "disturb that fixed contemplation as of Buddha on his lotus throne" (17).

The claim that the teenaged Sarojini exhibited a Buddha-like tranquility is scarcely credible, but *The Golden Threshold*, published some seven years after her return to India, indeed is organized almost programmatically along the lines of a nationalist program, as the poet attempts to embody "the East" (or, rather, an imagined India) in her verse. *The Golden Threshold* moves from the idealized representation of village culture to a celebration of Sarojini's small children as future nationalists to the final evocation of an older wisdom in "To a Buddha Seated on a Lotus." Whether the arrangement of the poems was Symons's doing or Sarojini's is unclear, but in either case Symons and the poet transmute the personal into the spiritual, the aesthetic into the transcendent, and the Decadent into the nationalist.

Symons's introduction came seven years after Sarojini's departure for India. She left suddenly, I would argue, on a strategic double decision to marry Naidu, despite objections, and to pursue poetry within a deliberately nationalist context. The one poem that was published in Britain during Sarojini's stay, however, owes clear debts to Symons, to the poetry of decadence, and to the Paris Exposition of 1889 and provides matter to which she returns in later verse. At the same time, this poem rewrites the famous British obsession with the Indian "nautch." At the Exposition of 1889, Europe was transfixed by the advent of dancers from Java. The music of the gamelan famously inspired Claude Debussy, and the dancers were painted by many European artists, including John Singer Sargent and Henri de Toulouse-Lautrec. Symons's poem "Javanese Dancers" appeared in his collection *Silhouettes*, the second edition of which was published in 1896, about the time he met Sarojini. "Javanese Dancers," in turn, inspired Sarojini's "Indian Dancers," which was published first under the title "Eastern Dancers" in Symons's short-lived but influential magazine *The Savoy*. Curiously, it is the British decadent whose poem is the more restrained of the two, perhaps because Symons's speaker finds the dancers "disquieting," "stealthy," "unintelligible," and mysterious. Sarojini's poem, by contrast, creates dancers more clearly erotic than Symons's. Indeed, when publishing the poem in *The Savoy,* Symons toned down her first line. In "Eastern Dancers," the figures are "passionate spirits aflaming with fire"; in the book version, they have "passionate bosoms."

In both versions of "Indian Dancers," the positions of dancer and spectator are unstable. In the first stanza, subject and object, poet and dancer seem to merge:

> Eyes ravished with rapture, celestially panting,
> what passionate bosoms aflaming with
> fire
> Drink deep of the hush of the hyacinth
> heavens that glimmer around them in
> fountains of light;
> O wild and entrancing the strain of keen music
> that cleaveth the stars like a wail of
> desire,
> And beautiful dancers with houri-like faces
> bewitch the voluptuous watches of
> night.
>
> (*Golden Threshold,* 71)

In Symons's "Javanese Dancers," the roles of spectator and dancer are unmistakeable, for at the end of the poem the dancers are reduced to "little painted figures on a screen, / Or phantom-dancers haply seen / Among the shadows of a magic grove" (*Silhouettes,* 33). Sarojini's poem, by contrast, elides the distinction between the dancer and the speaker. Both the poet and the dancer could be said to "drink deep," and the poet/spectator, like the dancers themselves, is assimilated to the "voluptuous watches of night."

Moreover, Sarojini's rewriting of Symons is also a version of Symons's own self-rewriting, for he had made his reputation as a poet, for better or worse, writing about dance halls. *London Nights,* for example, included a series of five poems, "Décor de Theatre," one each for the Empire, the Tivoli, the Moulin Rouge, and so forth. The dancers of the European stage Symons knew well. When they turned to "Eastern" dancers, both Symons and Sarojini owed less to actual dancers than to their imaginations of what these dancers might represent. In these poems, the relations of culture and person, "orientalism" and the cultivation of metropolitan success, and love and physical distance are ineluctably confused. These poems are a variation—perhaps one might say an erotic variation—on what Srinivas Aravamudan calls "romantic orientalism."

In an analogous way, Naidu's second volume, *The Bird of Time* (1912), evokes an "Eastern" motif that owes its salience to a previous European appropriation of Asian poetry. Sarojini's paratexts confuse as much as they clarify. Sarojini took her title and her epigraph from Edward Fitzgerald's translation of *The Rubaiyat of Omar Khayyam:* "The bird of Time has but a little way / To Fly—and lo! the bird is on the wing." Ironically, Fitzgerald's English transcreation of Persian verse thus frames the poetry of one of the few English language poets at this point who was perfectly able to translate Persian poetry herself. But Sarojini's title was multiply mediated; it owed as much to the music of the composer Liza Lehmann as to Fitzgerald's volume. Naidu dedicated her poem "The Dance of Love" to the composer, whose immensely popular song cycle "In a Persian Garden" was based on Fitzgerald's *Rubaiyat.* "The Dance of Love" thus functions in Naidu's second volume in much the same way that "Indian Dancers" functions in the first: "The Dance of Love" equates poetry, music, and dance, and, as with "Indian Dancers," these forms are not particularized. Rather, the music of words is the counterpart of emotion, and dance is simply the trope that is used to evoke the music:

> Light bright and wind-blown lilies,
> The dancers sway and shine,
> Swift in a rhythmic circle,
> Soft in a rhythmic line
>
> (*Bird,* "Dance," 21)

Indeed, the most generous reading of Sarojini's poetry would view her volumes in light of a song cycle.

Critics have often remarked, usually negatively, on what Paranjape calls the "hedonistic self-abandon and escape from reality" evoked in poems on the order of "The Dance of Love" (*Selected Poetry,* 15). Paranjape analyzes this problematic as Naidu's attempt to offer "Indians a picture of themselves which they might be proud of," an "attractive image of India . . . traditional, vivid, vibrant, colorful, and joyous." I will return to the discourses of nationalism and oppression and to the justifiable argument that Sarojini's poems derive from an escapist aesthetic. But first I want to show that Sarojini created a paradoxical version of a Decadent fin-de-siècle aesthetic, an aesthetic conflating Urdu/Persian traditions with the kind of sensuality Symons represented.

The figure of the dancer, which appears with multiple transmutations in Sarojini's first two volumes, is key to the kind of impressionism that so influenced the young poet during her years in London. Her poems fit companionably beside Symons's in their attempts to evoke emotions through selective impressions of the city, and at their best they might well constitute a version of what Symons came to denominate Symbolism, "leading through beautiful things to the eternal beauty."[30] As R. K. R. Thornton and Ian Small have argued, the image of the dancer was to become "a central image of modernism"; the dancer is transformed into "a ritual figure who would be able to show both Yeats and Eliot how to hold the physical and the spiritual, the timeless and the temporal, in one moving image."[31]

What happened with Sarojini's poetry is analogous what happened to Symons's. Symons made his way as a critic—more so, really, than as a poet—by shaping the aesthetic that was the precursor of modernism. Sarojini returned to Hyderabad, to the world of the colony and to the newly adumbrating discourses of nationalism, and she too made her way as much from her prose—speeches and letters—as from her poetry. There was no cultural position from which Sarojini as a poet could make the kind of aesthetic move that Yeats made, creating a private symbolism that functioned in a larger cultural discourse and a diction that moved beyond the formulas of the aestheticism. Sarojini in India had no audience for this sort of English language verse; she had no Pound with whom to argue poems at Stone Cottage and no circle of artists and writers with whom to grow. Sarojini refused Manmohan Ghose's sense of isolation and Aurobindo's religious retreat, finding her métier not in the modernist lyric but in oratory. Her poems became a kind of political theater, I would argue, both on the page and on the platform.

If we take, for example, the rhetorical design of *The Bird of Time,* it is on the one hand a reprise of many of the tropes of Indian English poetry—star-crossed lovers divided by fate and religion, flowers and bird songs of spring, traditional folk songs (one might almost call them lyrical ballads), Rajput heroism, and the like. But at the same time, the volume works a thesis through its music, as the poet uses various forms and themes to create a theatre of national unity. The subtext of many of these poems is religious toleration; the volume wants to enact a pluralist national imaginary. Ironically, however, the factitious feeling of this verse indicates the power of communal discourse to suck in and deform secular nationalist discourse. In the end, *The Bird of Time* is less the rhetorical creation of an imagined community than an imaginative hope for a unified community.

Many of the poems in this and Sarojini's other volumes do voices, either by proposing particular actors or choral entities or, less often, by indicating dramatic speakers. The voices function, along with the lyric voice connecting them, as a panoply of Indian possibilities, the varied chorus imagined as national unity. *The Bird of Time* is divided into four parts, each contributing to a nationalist text or subtext but mediated by an aestheticized lyric voice.

Section 1, "Songs of Love and Death," begins with death and ends with love, mirroring the thematic insistence on hope for the nation as well as the person. Take, for instance, "An Indian Love Song," which carries the epigraph (in lieu of a note) "Written to an Indian tune." Here we have the tale of star-crossed lovers, Hindu and Muslim. But rather than use the octosyllabic couplets common to English orientalist verse, the poet uses a sixteen-syllable line and eschews story in favor of song. The song, moreover, is made to carry political weight in the last stanza, where the man speaks:

He:

What are the songs of my race, Beloved, what are my people to thee?
And what are thy shrine, and kine and kindred, what are thy gods to me?

Love recks not of feuds and bitter follies, of stranger, comrade or kin,
Alike in his ear sound the temple bells and the cry of the muezzin.
For Love shall cancel the ancient wrong and conquer the ancient rage,
Redeem with his tears the memoried sorrow that sullied a bygone age.

(17)

This poem could be read simply as love conquers all, especially if taken out of context. But it is followed a few pages later by "At Twilight," which carries the epigraph "On the way to Golconda" and reprises the concerns first mooted in the love poem.

"At Twilight" begins as the poet seeks "kind Death" in the shadow of the hills. English readers would know Golconda as a legendary source of wealth, especially diamonds, but on the outskirts of Hyderabad its ruins would have been at once an excursion destination and a reminder of the multiple layers of Muslim history in India. The poet asks,

Shall hope prevail where clamorous hate is rife,
Shall sweet love prosper or high dreams find place
Amid the tumult of reverberant strife
'Twixt ancient creeds, 'twixt race and ancient race,
That mars the grave, glad purposes of life

(25)

The poet's personal and unspecified grief mingles with this larger one as she passes a funeral procession. After four stanzas comes a row of ellipses marking a sudden turn, and the speaker's soul returns to a world of children's laughter, "love's delight," and "Winged dreams that blow their golden clarion, / And hope that conquers immemorial hate" (26). This section of the volume concludes with "A Rajput Love Song," "A Persian Love Song," and a short lyric titled "To Love," which is apparently meant as a summation of the preceding ones.

I will not read the rest of the volume in detail here. Section 2, "Songs of the Springtime," reprises the springtime tropes of Persian and Urdu poetry—bulbuls and roses—and celebrates, equally, nasturtiums, which represent for the poet, as she explains in a note beneath the verse, "the immortal women of Sanscrit legend and song" (47). Section 3, "Indian Folk-Songs: To Indian Tunes," carries on in a similar fashion, and although these songs primarily are sung or spoken in the voices of Hindu girls or even goddesses, they also include "Songs of My City." The final section of the volume, "Songs of Life," takes a more personal turn on the whole, yet even here the personal meditation on death or loneliness jostles with a deliberate political framing of its tropes. Indeed, the whole volume is not unlike Kasiprasad Ghosh's sequence on Hindu festivals though lacking the extended orientalist footnotes—which were no longer fashionable—and without a particularized religious meaning, save perhaps a very broadly understood Brahmo imagining of an impersonal and inclusive god.

The volume imagines that song can be, more or less, a universal solvent, like its own god dissolving personal pain and internecine conflict. In the last section of the volume, "The Call to Evening Prayer" would enact this desire. Each of the four stanzas of this poem re-creates a "call to evening prayer" for each of four religions: Muslim, Christian, Parsi, and Hindu/Brahmo. The first stanza sets a repeating pattern:

> Allah ho Akbar! Allah ho Akbar!
> From mosque and minar the muezzins are calling;
> Pour forth your praises, O Chosen of Islam;
> Swiftly the shadows of sunset are falling:
> Allah ho Akbar! Allah ho Akbar!
>
> (95)

The remaining stanzas make similar moves. The poem that follows "The Call to Evening Prayer," titled "In Salutation to the Eternal Peace," addresses a prayer to an unspecified deity, or a deified concept, in language derived partly from Sufi poetry: "For my glad heart is drunk and drenched with Thee / O inmost wine of living ecstasy!" (98). The final three poems of the volume, which become increasingly devoid of content, celebrate song itself.

The penultimate poem in *The Bird of Time*, "Farewell," in essence sends these leaves of poetry, these butterflies or birds of time, flying toward Europe. In her envoi, her "go little book," the poet attenuates her previous efforts to bind the political and the lyric in a theater of national unity; she has turned from her own context to the context of the fin-de-siècle aestheticism she has left behind in Europe. Like winter migrants turning home in spring, her birds wing back to the literary context from which they came—and in which their political subtexts were illegible. The poems are diminished to a "fragile storm of sighing leaves / Adrift upon the breeze." And finally the poet bids them farewell:

> Wild birds with eager wings outspread
> To seek an Alien sky,
> Sweet comrades of a lyric spring.
> My little songs, good-bye!
>
> (101)

This short effusion and another extolling the "rapture of Song" conclude the volume.

Naidu's alien sky, the home for the migrant that is not a home, was the publishing house of the metropole. *The Bird of Time* was published by William Heinemann in London and by John Lane in New York. The publishers framed the volume in much the same way the author did in "Farewell." "Farewell," like any envoi, hovers between text and paratext; it balances the blurbs from reviews of *The Golden Threshold,* which the publishers bound at the beginning of the second volume. Preceding the portrait of Sarojini in her sari, preceding Gosse's introduction, are snippets from ten periodicals (nine of them British) praising the poems' "delicacy," their charm, their mystic temper, their "something of the spirit." The nationalist program of the poems, never free from orientalist late romanticism itself, is thoroughly orientalized in these critical paratexts.

Even the snippets of criticism indicate the temper in which the poems were received. Despite the publisher's relentless pruning of their prose, the critics lose themselves in discourses of authenticity. The *Glasgow Herald* declared in Heinemann's blurb, "The pictures are of the East, it is true: but there is something fundamentally human in them that seems to prove that the best song knows nothing of East or West." The *Manchester Guardian* opined that the poetry is "always musical, its eastern colour is always fresh, and its firm touch is quick and delicate." The *Madras Times* still used the phrase "gifted poetess" (though L.E.L. and even Mrs. Browning had been dead for years), but its reviewer, too, needed to declare the poet's authenticity: "Though so perfect a mistress of the English language, she remains a true Indian in her thoughts and imagery. She gives us Indian pictures in English verse which have the ring of originality." And Milton Bromley, in *Poet Lore,* looked for exactly that which reviewers were to find in 1912 in Tagore's *Gitanjali:* Sarojini's poems, he said, "have the authentic lyric cry. But they have something more significant, something rarer. In the forms familiar to the West, she expresses something of the soul of the East. . . . Her particular quality is something subtle, something of the spirit woven in the very text of the verses."

Authenticity in the English language—for whom is it possible? Yeats (the Anglo-Irishman), Ernest Rhys (the Welshman in London), Arthur Symons (the Cornish man who rebelled against his parents' Wesleyan piety), Sarojini (the Indian woman born into a multilingual household), Tagore (who translated himself for British readers)? There is no good answer to a wrong question.

Perhaps we could argue that Sarojini experienced a kind of hybridity, but I think the notion of "shadowed mutuality" better conveys the kind of doubleness she experienced in London with Symons and even, perhaps, in India. Although Sarojini celebrated "mother India" in her oratorical platform poetry and in the introductory note to *The Broken Wing,* the metaphor could encompass neither her early experience of London nor her later experiences of married life, extramarital love, and feminist and nationalist activism.

In 1916, Sarojini visited the ailing Symons on a political trip to Europe. By then, she had written the best poetry of her life, probably about an affair with a younger Congress Party activist. Like Manmohan Ghose, Sarojini wrote some of her most powerful poems in midlife, and, like Ghose, she found her métier in English language love lyrics, particularly the sequence she called "The Temple."[32] Manmohan and Sarojini both, paradoxically, found themselves in the same place as Mary Leslie after

1857—unable to make satisfactory poetry of public concerns, driven back at last on the personal lyric. Sarojini's late sequence of love lyrics is hard to quote out of context, for it derives its power from a kind of accumulation of implied narrative and the vicissitudes of passion. Published in 1917, in *The Broken Wing*, Sarojini's last collection of any considerable merit, "The Temple: A Pilgrimage of Love," includes several moving poems. They exhibit a significant command of meter, diction, and especially syntax and lineation. In "The Menace of Love," for example, the speaker denounces her lover's ambivalence:

How long, O Love, shall ruthless pride avail you
Or wisdom shield you with her gracious wing,
When the sharp winds of memory shall assail you
In all the poignant malice of the spring?

All the sealed anguish of my blood shall taunt you
In the rich menace of red-flowering trees;
The yearning sorrow of my voice shall haunt you
In the low wailing of the midnight seas.

The tumult of your own wild heart shall smite you
With strong and sleepless pinions of desire,
The subtle hunger in your veins shall bite you
With swift and unrelenting fangs of fire.

When youth and spring and passion shall betray you
And mock your proud rebellion with defeat,
God knows, O Love, if I shall save or slay you
As you lie spent and broken at my feet!

(100)

One hopes that Symons, though he had experienced a devastating mental breakdown in the interim, could praise these poems of his old friend. Surely the poet of *Amoris Victima* might have appreciated Sarojini's late fire.

Sarojini Naidu would be characterized by reviewers on the subcontinent as "the Indian nightingale"—a figure problematic enough, though still current in schoolbooks and on Web sites. The contradictions in her poetics are thus elided—whoever could imagine a nightingale giving voice to an intractable political scene? And so, too, is rendered illegible the anger of "The Temple," which simmers with its rejection of her place as the "good mother," the faithful Savitri, the avatar of mother India. Who could imagine a nightingale being herself passionate pursuer as well as victim? In the ideological and actual prisons of "mother India," it was scandalous to think that a mother of her country might be unwilling to act Savitri's part in her personal life.[33]

Poetic Enterprise and Spiritual Teaching: Rabindranath Tagore Meets Yeats and Pound

It may be true that a great artist makes the taste by which she is appreciated; it is certainly true that many a good artist finds the social networks that enable his recognition and that with any luck these same networks may foster his artistic development. Such networks of affiliation, as I have argued with respect to Manmohan Ghose, can be tenuous and limited by financial stress, cultural misunderstanding, and historical shifts. They may prove a mixed blessing, as they were for Sarojini Naidu; her affiliation with Symons and the Decadents provided an aesthetic vocabulary that, coupled with Edmund Gosse's famous admonition that she should write about India, resulted in a poetry only partly legible in India or England and an aesthetic perhaps too limited by the codes and tropes of late nineteenth-century English language verse. Rabindranath Tagore, indubitably the towering figure in this chapter, also found London networks of affiliation a blessing and a curse.

In 1912, Tagore was a mature artist in command of his medium and well aware of the complexities of publication and reception. Because he continued principally to write in Bangla, his aesthetic practice was not as much shaped by metropolitan affiliations as were Ghose's and Naidu's. Though Tagore's poetry combined the influences of English romantic poetics, Bengali folk traditions, and Vaishnava poetry, his self-translations of these poems were clearly written with an expectation of the London market. If London was a blessing—launching the poet into international fame and enabling a life of international travel and literary friendship—it was also in its own way a curse, celebrity bringing with it strong adulation sometimes followed by equally strong disillusionment. Mary Lago has argued that "Tagore's introduction in England was a lesson in how not to present a poet to a new audience" *(India's Prisoner,* 73). My reading of Tagore's first English language volume, *Gitanjali,* through its Euro-American reception bears out her judgment.[34]

When he embarked for England in 1912, Rabindranath had already begun the translations that were to become an international phenomenon. I want here to trace the course of his London reception in 1912–13, rather than to offer an extended critical analysis of the volume, for the cultural imaginary in which Tagore was understood was a culmination of romantic orientalism. It provided a language for eliding and negotiating the increasingly vexed poetry of empire and, initially, for sidestepping political questions by transforming them into spiritual ones. Nonetheless, political events had their own insistence.

Tagore's volume was published just five years after Rudyard Kipling had received his own Nobel Prize and after Kipling had come to represent, for better and worse, the voice of empire. Tagore's advent on the British scene occurred precisely at the moment when the British government, in response to years of protest, rescinded the partition of Bengal and simultaneously decreed that the capital of British India would move from Calcutta to New Delhi. In Ireland, strikes, lockouts, and petitions evidenced similar unrest. The period 1912–13 was marked by extended debate in the British parliament of the third Irish Home Rule bill. At this point, the Irish Parliamentary Party held the balance of power in the Commons, and hence the contest over partition of Ulster grew intense.

As if to bracket these political developments, metropolitan readers found that *Gitanjali* could be understood as a collection reflecting the folk spirit of Bengal, as a Bengali analog to the Celtic twilight, or, in terms made familiar from theosophy, as a rendering of Asian mysticism. Their access to Tagore through his English self-translations rendered invisible (at least initially) his political and social context. Rabindranath's translation of metered Bangla verse into English prose poetry was in this milieu an effective if limited form of self-presentation. It certainly provided an entrée into already forming networks of affiliation, networks that also included a "shadowed mutuality."

Like Sarojini, Tagore was understood in London through a late romantic orientalism that guaranteed his authenticity; unlike Sarojini (who, as a woman, was diminished to a nightingale), Rabindranath stepped into the role of the bard. Especially for W. B. Yeats and Ezra Pound, the semicolonials in this scene, Tagore represented at first a living avatar of bardic nationalism—perhaps even the last gasp of bardic nationalism. So successful was Tagore's appearance in London, and subsequently in the United States, and so easily was he assimilated to the newer constructions of "guru" English that on the basis of a slim volume of self-translation, and that only, Tagore was awarded the Nobel Prize in Literature.

In London, Tagore immediately connected with the painter William Rothenstein, the founder of the India Society, and then with W. B. Yeats and Ezra Pound. Along with Arthur Henry Fox Strangeways, a retired English member of the Indian Civil Service, these three men basically engineered Tagore's reception. They made an unusual trio: a young American ambitious to create literary taste and his own fame; an Irish poet with a long and complex relationship to Irish nationalism and to Indian-influenced theosophy; and a middle-aged artist who had returned from several months in India to find his enthusiasm for Indian art incomprehensible to his peers.

Of the three, Rothenstein and Tagore achieved the strongest affiliation, for Rothenstein was by far the best equipped to understand Tagore. Rothenstein had visited India in 1910–11, traveling to various archaeological and religious sites from Ajanta to Benares, and he had met Tagore's nephew, the painter Abindranath, in Calcutta, where he also became acquainted with the poet.[35] On his return from India, Rothenstein experienced something of a crisis; he had missed Roger Fry's post-impressionist exhibition and found himself on the fringe of that circle. Except for Fry's generous review of his subsequent one-person show, Rothenstein found little sympathy for the paintings he had done in India. Indeed, Fry's review may point to the ways in which Rothenstein's understanding of his Indian subjects did not mesh with the expectations of his audience. As Fry pointed out, Rothenstein's failure to orientalize his subject or to seek the picturesque was the very quality that distanced him from the London audience. Of Rothenstein, Fry wrote, "One feels that the artist has had no idea of bringing back Oriental curiosities or *carnet de voyage*, but that he has succeeded, even in so short a visit, in submitting himself to the reality of what was before him, and rendering the life of his figures, and not only their appearance."[36]

Ironically, it was Tagore, not Rothenstein, who produced work suited to London tastes. Unlike Rothenstein, Tagore could represent "authenticity"—and be assimilated, whether or not by his own desire, into a late romantic orientalism. Moreover, because he could make use of his ambiguous and unhomely relationship to modern India, Tagore paradoxically appeared more "authentic" to European audiences than did the Anglophile Ghose or the resolutely at-home Sarojini. And he was, of course, much the greater artist.

Rothenstein, himself experiencing something of a crisis of artistic alienation, was just the person to prepare Tagore's success. Partly because his Indian paintings did not sell and partly in opposition to contempt for modern Indian art in official circles, Rothenstein threw his energies into the India Society, which was designed to defend Indian arts. In addition to his enthusiasm for ancient and contemporary Indian art, particularly that of Abindranath and the new Bengal school, Rothenstein was an ideal mediator between Tagore and London literary circles because he and his wife, Alice, had multiple literary connections, among them Laurence Binyon, Ford Maddox Hueffer, Arthur Symons, George Moore, John Lane (who became Rothenstein's publisher for a time), Max Beerbohm, and W. M. Rossetti. Indeed, Alice's father had been D. G. Rossetti's pupil. An actor of some talent, Alice had made her own way in the London art world.

As generous as Pound—but less judgmental—and relying on Alice's hospitality, Rothenstein found in Yeats and Pound perfect partners for what willy-nilly became a consuming enterprise. The Anglo-Irishman, the part-Jewish Englishman, the American, and the Bengali Brahmin each operated in a conflicted way within the parameters of British colonialism, both "internal" and "external." None of them could be construed as a nationalist *tout court;* yet each partly conceived himself in these terms, though imagining a meeting place for the arts beyond nationalisms. The famous episode of the farewell dinner to Tagore in London on September 5, 1913, sums it up: at the end of the festivities, Yeats, Rothenstein, and Tagore each attempted to sing a patriotic song, and each forgot the words (Speaight, 259).

It is ironic, then, that Tagore was lauded by both Yeats and Pound within the constructs of a bardic nationalism that had long subtended literary relations within the empire. Tagore appeared to his audience as something between a guru and a troubadour. His conquest of London, a conquest that owed itself equally to his "presence" and to those who made it felt, commenced in private readings and in a semipublic gathering. Rothenstein organized the private readings, and he and his friends, notably Yeats, orchestrated a dinner for more than seventy members of London's literary and artistic elite. The *London Times* on July 13, 1912, reported a large gathering attended by

"Messrs. J. W. Mackail, Herbert Trench, R. B. Cunninghame Graham, H. W. Nevinson, H. G. Wells, Cecil Sharp, J. D. Anderson, E. B. Havell, T. W. Arnold, R. Vaughan Williams and T. W. Rolleston." Yeats presided and delivered the toast, characterizing Tagore as a troubadour and saint. Yeats thus assimilated Tagore to his own project in the Celtic revival and, through an extended comparison to Thomas à Kempis, framed him as a religious teacher. The point of this enthusiasm for the Bengali poet—of whose real work Yeats could know little—was an implicit critique of contemporary British culture.[37]

Yeats's toast, moreover, was repeated at length and still more grandiloquently in his subsequent introduction to the India Society and Macmillan editions of *Gitanjali.* The first of these editions, printed at the Chiswick Press for members of the society and for resale, was (like *Primavera*) part of the culture of limited edition publishing. Yeats deployed the tropes of bardic nationalism, Pound's interest in the troubadours, and the implicit critique of commerce in aesthetic publishing to praise his new Indian colleague.

In the introduction to *Gitanjali,* Yeats imagined a literary culture where real men sing poems while traveling "on the highway" and "rowing upon rivers." These are not the poems, Yeats says, that will "lie in little well-printed books upon ladies' tables . . . or be carried about by students at the university" (S. Das, *English Writings,* 40). Yeats's adoption of Tagore reveals the contradictions implicit in the modern image of the bard and in the limited edition collector's book of poetry—one longs for the audience of the common man "on the highway" while making books that will only end up on the tables of "ladies" and "students at the university." Yeats went on to compare Tagore to Thomas à Kempis, St. Francis, and Blake, preparing the world to perceive Tagore as a source of Eastern wisdom.

No doubt the reception of Vivekananda at the Parliament of World Religions in Chicago in 1893 and Vivekananda's subsequent visits to Europe, along with the rise of theosophy and other forms of religious orientalism, played a part in this reception as well. The skeptical author of an article on Tagore in the *New York Times* of 1916, while denying the simple identification of poet and guru, succinctly described the milieu in which the celebration of the poet and the eventual backlash against him occurred: "One hesitates in classifying Tagore among the mystics. We have had our Blavatskys, our Swamis, and the writers of various theosophical diatribes, and about all these there is something that ever savors of the fad either in literature or religion. Faddism, however, *does not* apply to the appreciation of Tagore."[38]

However skeptical the *New York Times* may have been by 1916, clearly for Yeats and many others present at Tagore's early appearances in London, the troubadour cum Asian mystic was alive and well. Indeed, as Krishna Dutta and Andrew Robinson point out in their introduction to *Selected Letters of Rabindranath Tagore,* the Asian "mystic" became for many a kind of purified Christ figure. May Sinclair, for example, described in the *North American Review* (1913) hearing Yeats and Tagore read poetry, an occasion that "turned Mr. Rothenstein's drawing room into a holy temple" (659). She went on to discuss Tagore in terms of English devotional poetry but concluded that he exceeded the achievement of the English poets by combining religious expression of a high order with a simplicity that can be heard and understood as "the most natural thing in the world." In the "Western mind," she said, "there is a gulf fixed between the common human heart and Transcendent Being." In Tagore's work, she believed, one glimpses a world in which such a gulf need not exist. Sinclair is alone among all the reviewers of Tagore's *Gitanjali* in having actually read a good deal of Indian poetry in translation; she compared Tagore's verses to the Upanishads (and found them very different), and she discussed them in the context of Kabir, Chandidas, and Vaishnava poetry. Though Sinclair was more aware of Indian poetic traditions than the average European reviewer, her veneration of Tagore is of a piece with the admiration of critics and readers who soon tended to refer to Tagore's volume not by its title, *Gitanjali,* but as "the Gitanjali," rendering it at a stroke a sacred text.[39]

None of Tagore's other reviewers in 1912–13 seems to have followed Sinclair's lead in bridging the gulf between poetic traditions; nor did any reviewer pause long enough to discover Tagore as novelist or educational reformer. Hence the Indian poet was left to carry the burden of his problematic self-translations, and, in a media backlash after he received the Nobel Prize, he was subject to the contradictions within the poetry and guru businesses. How could he be a troubadour and mystic, as Yeats and May Sinclair would have proposed, and still sell the books that perforce must "lie upon ladies' tables"? How could a guru, whose cultural function was to be unlike the poet of Euro-American culture, be applauded after he garnered the highest European prize for his work? One might argue that in his very "unhomeliness" in a European drawing room, Tagore was too close to home.

When May Sinclair placed Tagore among the mystics and looked to the distant past of Indian poetry for analogs, she elided Tagore's modernism. When Pound and Yeats characterized Tagore as a troubadour in 1913, they placed him—as in many ways Tagore placed himself—in the equivocal position of a cultural survival who gestured toward the national spirit of a nation yet to come. In the cases of Ireland and India, such a gesture traced an imagined community over a ground of communal and revolutionary violence.

The mishaps of this bardic project were perhaps prognosticated at the very beginning of Tagore's metropolitan visit. When Tagore arrived in London on June 16, 1912, the day after a few of his poems (translated by Ajit Chakravarti) were published in *The Nation,* he brought with him a complete manuscript of *Gitanjali.* But the manuscript was left on the train by his son, only to be retrieved some hours later among the bowler hats and umbrellas of the lost property office (see S. Das, *English Writings,* 12–15). Unlike his first two trips to London, where he appeared as the image of the English gentleman, this time Tagore arrived in modified traditional garb. The social whirl that surrounded Tagore traded on the image of the bard plucked out of time and space, and it underwrote responses like Sinclair's. This image was given concrete form in Rothenstein's portraits of the poet, one of which appeared as a frontispiece both to the India Society's privately printed edition of *Gitanjali* and to the Macmillan trade edition.

Though he was not persuaded by Tagore as guru, Pound echoed Yeats's description of Tagore as troubadour. Pound's response to Tagore was itself a species of orientalist translation. His *Fortnightly* review reveals how the chronotope of the 1910s was a kind of Möbius strip circling the empire, its imagined past, and the European past. In his lengthy discussion of *Gitanjali,* Pound extended the comparison of Tagore to the troubadours of twelfth-century Provence and invoked Dante and Theocritus as well. The analogy on which he depended runs like this: Sanskrit is to Bangla as Latin is to Italian. Hence Tagore could be considered the Dante of Bengal. In a way, the comparison is apt—most critics concur that Tagore, along with the novelist Bankim Chandra Chattopadhyay, essentially created a modern Bangla literary vernacular. But of course, the very comparison with Dante elided both Tagore's real debts to medieval Vaishnava poetry (which Pound could not have understood) and the differences of several hundred years.

Though he argued that Tagore was making language new, Pound claimed still higher stakes than this in his *Fortnightly* piece. Pound shifted the ground of his comparison from Latin to Greek to account for Tagore's linguistic precision, a precision that Pound believed was founded on the flexibility and fluidity of an inflected language.[40] For Pound, Tagore combined the virtues of the troubadours, of Dante, and of the Greek poets whose musical modes are, in Pound's view, comparable to Indian ones. "We have now found our new Greece, suddenly," Pound wrote. Implicitly, Pound likened himself to Boccaccio hearing "for the first time the curious music of Theocritus." European humanism since Boccaccio, Pound suggested, has "run its course," and so we have the "corrective presented to us in this writing from Bengal" (574). And then, twisting the already twisted chronotope yet again, Pound suggested that "when I leave Mr. Tagore I feel exactly as if I were a barbarian clothed in skins, and carrying a stone war-club, the kind that is, where the stone is bound into a crotched stick with thongs" (575).

In encountering Tagore, then, Pound himself is—what? A native American encountering an ancient and sophisticated culture arriving on his shore? Or a European sophisticate jarred from his ennui by the presence of a simple spirit? Or a poet who is like enough to Dante to find in Tagore a kindred spirit to make language new? If Tagore is a lens through which Pound views poetic tradition, then surely it is a lens creating multiple distorted images.[41]

No poet, least of all one as complex and as complexly modern as Tagore, could support such images for long; but, for all the imprecision of these historical analogies, in one respect—the techniques of Bangla versification—Pound seems really to have attempted to understand Tagore's work. Pound's is the only English language review of Tagore's poetry from the decade that makes anything of the original verse. Pound's remarks are as detailed and accurate as can be expected of someone who did not speak Bangla. Here Pound's comparisons of Tagore, the Greeks, and the troubadours are pointed, and he describes Tagore's rhythms, meter, and rhymes in detail. Pound concludes that Bangla "has already found that sort of metric which we awhile back predicted or hoped for in English, where all the sorts of recurrence shall be weighted and balanced and coordinated" (578). Pound analyzed Tagore's metrics, comparing his lines of eleven and five syllables to Sapphics. Ironically, it is the contemporaneity of Tagore (Tagore's debts to European romanticism in his self-translation and the analogies between his prose poems and the French avant garde of the fin de siècle) to which Pound really responds. Pound's recognition of Tagore's contemporaneity, Tagore's modernity, is deflected by both his own and Tagore's own orientalism.

Pound's encounter with Tagore, ultimately, bore two kinds of fruit: first, a series of Pound's translations of the medieval Indian poet-saint Kabir, and second, Pound's rejection of the very sensation he had helped create, a rejection that, ultimately, provided a justification for Pound's turn to East Asia in *Cathay*. While reviewing Tagore in the *Fortnightly*, Pound was working on what he later called "Certain Poems of Kabir." Tagore likewise published Kabir translations, a volume of them, in the next year (1914)—issued like *Gitanjali* first in a limited edition by the India Society and later by Macmillan (London and New York, 1917). Both Tagore (with his co-translator Evelyn Underhill) and Pound (with his co-translator Kali Mohan Ghosh) relied on Kshiti Mohan Sen's four-part Bengali translation of Kabir, which had been published at Bolpur in 1910–11. Though according to Sisir Kumar Das many of these poems are not traditionally part of the Kabir canon, Kshiti Mohan Sen's work provided the path of transmission for Pound and Tagore. Both poets may have relied as well on the manuscript of English translations from Sen's text by Ajit Kumar Chakravarti; Tagore certainly did.[42] So we have a group of poems from early manuscripts attributed to Kabir, rendered into Bangla, thence into English, and into English again—a palimpsest of languages not unlike the one Pound later made from Fenellosa's notebooks. His encounter with Tagore, inspiring Pound's brief fling with Kabir, created a model for Pound's multilayered approach to Chinese translation.[43]

In fact, Pound was encountering Tagore's own version of a modernist aesthetic. The history of prose poetry and *vers libre* in Britain, France, and the United States demonstrates a like concatenation of influences; the act of translation, be it from Chinese to English, from Chinese to French, or, as here, from Bangla to English created linguistic and rhythmical triangulation that inspired English language innovation. Though Rabindranath was largely presented in the press as a guru and mystic, his English language poetry functioned both within and outside the orbit of this Euro-American aesthetic. To write free verse or prose poems (to "break the back" of the pentameter, as Pound put it), English language poets wrote as if they were translating from Asian languages. In *Gitanjali,* they found a fascinating example of what they were attempting; yet for the primitive, the exotic, or the oriental to remain a powerful catalyst for Euro-American art, it could not be acknowledged as equally engaged in a modernist project. Put another way, neither critical nor poetic avant-garde definitions of modernism could acknowledge contemporary "Asian" poetic innovation. At the foundations of American and British modernist poetics is an unacknowledged transformation of the multilayered translation and transmission histories that had characterized English language poetics in India for more than a century.[44] At its foundation lay not the primitive or the ancient but another modernism.

If we reverse the vector of attention from a Eurocentric to an Indian point—or poet—of origin, we might argue that Rabindranath Tagore created his own modernist poetic in the process of translation. Shortly after he published his volumes of English prose poem self-translations (*Gitanjali, The Gardener, The Crescent Moon, Fruit Gathering,* and *Lover's Gift and Crossing,* all published between 1912 and 1918), Rabindranath began to experiment with prose poetry in Bangla. He published these experiments in *Lipikā* in 1919. Though these poems went largely unremarked, ten years later, in the thick of the controversy over modernist Bengali poetics, Tagore began once more to write in this form, publishing a poetry "distinctly different from his earlier writings," as S. K. Das puts it (*History, Struggle for Freedom,* 214–16). Rabindranath's *gadya-kavitā* (prose poems) published in *Punaśca* responded to the young avant-garde poets in Bengal (including Buddadev Basu and Premendra Mitra) who adored T. S. Eliot and sought a new movement to counter the "Rabīndra Yug," as they called it.

Tagore also wrote a novel in response to the Bengali avant-garde movement. *Śeṣer Kabitā* (1929) was a brilliant send-up of these poets' practices and of his own, according to Das (*History, Struggle for Freedom,* 216). The novel revealed, moreover, Rabindranath's acute understanding of the way he had been understood as the "primitive" by Euro-American modernists, even as he was now the "Wordsworth" to young Bengali modernists. I quote here Das's translation of a passage in which the novel's hero, an Oxford-educated barrister, chairs a debate about poetry. Through this "hero," Rabindranath creates a hilarious and ironic critique of his own (non)place as a modernist poet. Tagore's barrister "hero" intones,

> The strongest objection against Rabindranath Tagore is that this gentleman, imitating old Wordsworth, insists most perversely on continuing. Many a time the messenger of Death has called to switch off the light, but even as the old man rises from his throne, he still clings to its arms. If he does not quit of his own accord, it becomes our duty to quit his court in a body. . . .
>
> My second contention against Rabindranath Tagore is that his literary creations are rounded or wave-like, like his handwritings, reminding one of roses and moons and female faces. Primitive, so to copy Nature's hand. From the new dictator we expect creations straight and sharp like thorns, like arrows, like spearheads. Not like flowers, but like a flash of lightning, like the pain of neuralgia—angular and piercing like a Gothic Church, not rounded like a temple porch. Even if they looked like a jute-mill or a government secretariat, I wouldn't mind. . . . Down with the witchery of rhythmic fetters. (S. Das, *History, Struggle for Freedom,* 216)

Tagore's brilliant send-up of the discourses of poetic modernism cuts multiple ways at once, from the troubles in the jute industry to the masculinist rhetoric of modernism to its primitivism to its unacknowledged roots in Ruskinian dogma.[45]

Tagore dissects here the ideological complexities of international modernism, creating in a novel the same kind of analysis we find decades later in Geeta Kapur's *When Was Modernism.* Kapur describes in theoretical terms the kind of situation in which Tagore found himself between 1913 and 1941: "[T]here is in India the double discourse of the national and the modern. It is a generative discourse and can yield multiple equations. Nationalism calls up the category of tradition, modernism catapults into internationalism. This then becomes a four-part equation enabling one to confront the question of 'invented traditions' that erupts during nationalism with current globalism and its improvisatory techniques of cultural appropriation" (288). Kapur urges a "continual double-take" in the locating "modernisms" (291).

If we look, again, at the practices of translation from Asian languages as they occur in English language modernist verse, we can see that Pound's and Tagore's translations from Kabir are not dissimilar. But if anything the prize for the more straightforward—shall we call it modernist?—language goes to Tagore. Consider poem VII from Pound and Ghose's "Certain Poems of Kabir":

> How shall it be severed,
> This love between thee and me?
> Thou art lord, and I servant,
> As the Chakora is servant of moonlight
> And watches it all the night long.
> The love between thee and me is from beginning to ending,
> How can it end in time?
> Saith Kabir: As the river is immersed in the ocean,
> My mind is immersed in thee.
>
> (612)

Compare Tagore's poem 33, *Man mast tab kyon bole:*

> Where is the need of words, when love has made drunken the heart?
>
> I have wrapped the diamond in my cloak; why open it again and again?
>
> When its load was light, the pan of the balance went up: now it is full, where is the need for weighing?
>
> The swan has taken its flight to the lake beyond the mountains; why should it search for the pools and ditches any more?
>
> Your Lord dwells within you: why need your outward eyes be opened?
>
> Kabir says: "Listen, my brother! my Lord, who ravishes my eyes, has united Himself with me."
>
> (*English Writings*, 514)

In his various approaches to Tagore and his interest in Kabir, Pound looked for ways to triangulate European tradition, but soon he moved away from what might have become a politically fraught fascination with India.

Indeed, the aftermath of Tagore's Nobel Prize and the backlash against the less effective self-translations that succeeded *Gitanjali* became a kind of monitory tale for Pound. As he wrote Margaret Anderson in February 1917, "I do not want to go Tagoring all over the place with bad copies of *Cathay* as he does with (dilutions of) diluted *Gitanjali,* or to eke out Cathay-light as the Celtic Twilight has been eked out" (*Pound: Little Review,* 16). This comment on *Cathay* is contemporaneous with a story Pound published in the May 1917 issues of *The Little Review.* This scurrilous "story" puns on Tagore in its title: "Jodindranath Mawhor's Occupation." Of this story, the less said the better, except to note that it was in extraordinarily bad taste. Here the title character is, at best, a lascivious and not very intelligent aesthete. Pound, one might argue, attacked the chimera that he himself had created in the public imagination. Pound's attack on Tagore continued in August 1917, again perhaps deliberately to distance Pound's new oriental fascination from his previous enthusiasm. In discussing *Certain Noble Plays of Japan* (note the similarity to "Certain Poems of Kabir") and *Noh, or Accomplishment,* Pound avers that this work is "infinitely better than Tagore and the back-wash from India" (*Pound: Little Review,* 8).

It is a shame, given Pound's willingness to investigate the originals of Tagore's Bengali songs, that he approached Tagore more as a project in puffery than as a project in translating verse. Tagore admitted later in life that he had done himself no favors with some of his self-translations. As Tagore's editor Sisir Kumar Das argues, in the volumes published after *Gitanjali,* Tagore's self-translation entailed a deliberate choice of simpler poems that represented Tagore's "stereotype" of what a British audience might appreciate.[46] Hence Tagore's later regret that "I have done great injustice to the translations" (letter to Chakravarti, October 23, 1834, quoted in S. Das, *English Writings,* 22).[47] William Radice and S. K. Das argue, however, that Tagore's injustice to himself is primarily in the later self-translations. Radice has recently argued, moreover, that the English poems of *Gitanjali* should be understood as inflected by Indian rhythms: the rhythms of Bangla verse and the rhythms of Indian English.[48]

It is unfortunate not only that Pound became unjust toward Tagore but also that readers assume that Tagore's self-translations should be heard in the mind's ear with the inflections of either standard British or American English. In the previous century, bardic nationalists in Britain could adopt orthographic conventions to shape the reading of their verse. At the turn of the twentieth century as an Indian bard-cum-guru, Tagore found such measures unavailable, particularly given the near universal British ridicule of what was then pejoratively called "babu English."

Instead of being understood through the simultaneous uncontemporaneities of international modernism, Tagore has most often been framed by the persistent trope of the romantic bard. At the end of *Gitanjali,* Tagore himself took on the bardic pose, or at least a position that translated as bardic for his British and American audiences:

> I dive down into the depth of the ocean of forms, hoping to gain the perfect pearl of the formless.
>
> ....
>
> Into the audience hall by the fathomless abyss where swells up the music of toneless strings I shall take this harp of my life.
>
> I shall tune it to the notes of for ever, and, when it has sobbed out its last utterance, lay down my silent harp at the feet of the silent.
>
> (poem 100 in *Gitanjali*, 92)

Here Tagore functions as Pound's and Yeats's troubadour, come back from an East that is uneasily pretending to be in the past. He carries a modern make of "harp" that in 1827 his predecessor in Indian English poetry, H. L. V. Derozio, called—with more explicit political resonance—the "harp of India."

Indeed, this poem, like many of the other translations in *Gitanjali,* exists necessarily between cultures, evoking one reading from those who had already encountered the Bangla originals or at least had a thorough understanding of the poem's original contexts and yet gesturing through the double language of their tropes toward the Euro-American context of their reception. Tagore's metaphors, inspired by Vaishnava poetry in the wider context of Brahmo religious practices but translated into English, are truly in motion between cultures. The flora of Bengal, so central to Tagore's art, is recapitulated in a language that, largely bereft of Bangla words and learned footnotes, naturally cannot convey its cultural specificity. Moreover, the religious tropes of the traveler and of the stranger seeking a home create metaphors of unhomeliness that resonate at once in religious and cultural registers.

The poems—which by rights should have been called *Gitanjali: Selected Poems*—appear as a single numbered sequence though they are drawn from several collections. While this typographical arrangement (and the lack of any cues to the poems' original provenance) might imply a metaphorical coherence, the poet moves freely, selecting poems from several volumes of his recent verse and depicting the lyric speaker/spiritual seeker as a cottager and as a traveler in alien lands. Of course, the metaphorical understanding of the poet's quest—for divine vision, religious understanding, human and divine love, and the feeling of being at home—means that these metaphors are not basically contradictory; following the poet's thought, we move constantly across thresholds. The speaker sometimes longs for the divine to cross his doorstep and sometimes describes himself as a traveler in alien lands. In poem 12, for instance, Tagore writes,

> The time that my journey takes is long and the way of it long.
>
> I came out on the chariot of the first gleam of light, and pursued my voyage through the wildernesses of worlds leaving my track on many a star and planet.

> It is the most distant course that comes nearest to thyself, and that training is the most intricate which leads to the utter simplicity of a tune.
>
> The traveller has to knock at every alien door to come to his own, and one has to wander through all the outer worlds to reach the innermost shrine at the end.
>
> My eyes strayed far and wide before I shut them and said "Here art thou!"
>
> The question and the cry "Oh, where?" melt into tears of a thousand streams and deluge the world with the flood of the assurance "I am!"
>
> (10)

"The traveller has to knock at every alien door," the poet writes. Then in the next poem, he laments that the divine cannot be asked to cross his humble threshold: "the lamp has not been lit and I cannot ask him into my house" (11). Yet again, in section 24, the speaker is a traveler, this time worn and impoverished. He begs, "From the traveller, whose sack of provisions is empty before the voyage is ended, whose garment is torn and dust-laden, whose strength is exhausted, remove shame and poverty, and renew his life like a flower under the cover of thy kindly night" (19–20). In other poems (for example, section 49), the master, the divine, comes to stand at the poet's "cottage door," poised on the threshold as the poet sings (42); in the course of the poems, the cottage is transformed into a temple as its inhabitant longs for *darshan,* a glimpse of the divine.

Ultimately, the seeker claims that in a vision of the divine there is no final alienation. The unhomely, the fear that there may be no hospitality, the alienation of living between "worlds"—either cosmic or cultural—is allayed through the metaphors of hospitality and friendship. Section 63 renders these tropes explicit:

> Thou hast made me known to friends whom I knew not. Thou hast given me seats in homes not my own. Thou hast brought the distant near and made a brother of the stranger.
>
> I am uneasy at heart when I have to leave my accustomed shelter; I forget that there abides the old in the new, and that there also thou abidest.
>
> Through birth and death, in this world or in others, wherever thou leadest me it is thou, the same, the one companion of my endless life who ever linkest my heart with bonds of joy to the unfamiliar.
>
> When one knows thee, then alien there is none, then no door is shut. Oh, grant me my prayer that I may never lose the bliss of the touch of the one in the play of the many.
>
> (58–59)

The final poem of *Gitanjali* exemplifies the poet's success in self-translation as it echoes and approximates the repetitions of the original. The final poem strikes a note that hovers somewhere in the air between Bengal and London, evoking its religious origins in *bhakti* and in Vaishnava poetry even as it presents, through the medium of prose poem translation, the speaker's unhomeliness:

> In one salutation to thee, my God, let all my sense spread out and touch this world at thy feet.
>
> Like a rain-cloud of July hung low with its burden of unshed showers let all my mind bend down at thy door in one salutation to thee.
>
> Let all my songs gather together their diverse strains into a single current and flow to a sea of silence in one salutation to thee.
>
> Like a flock of homesick cranes flying night and day back to their mountain nests let all my life take its voyage to its eternal home in one salutation to thee.
>
> (94)

Like Sarojini's birds of time, which also appeared in London in 1912, Tagore's poems, his "homesick cranes," seek a place both in and beyond the metropole. For Rabindranath, that place is the liminal one between heaven and earth, between the plains of Bengal and a mountain fastness. But this liminal space of a transformed bardic poetry is by no means the only one the poet claimed.

Like Sarojini Naidu and Manmohan Ghose, Rabindranath Tagore established relations of affection, affiliation, and hospitality with English poets and artists: most importantly, for Tagore, with William Rothenstein. For each of these poets, affiliation was not a simple matter, and *hospes* and *hostes*—as in the case of Tagore and Pound—were potentially interchangeable.

Tagore's initial reception in London exemplifies the limits of the discourse of authenticity, its potential for imprisoning poets and their poetry and for rendering illegible the simultaneous uncontemporaneities of modernisms. Or, as Rabindranath's unheroic modernist barrister put it in his satire on the literary competitions, "down with the witchery of rhythmic fetters!" The discourses of authenticity would reduce Rabindranath in Euro-American eyes to bard or guru and Sarojini to a bird; they rendered Manmohan a "denationalized" ghost of his guru brother. Yet each of these poets achieved a shadowed mutuality with poets in the metropole. The long history of English poets in India lamenting their exile ends with Indian poets in London making unhomely music.

EPILOGUE

> So, at sixteen years and nine months, but looking four or five years older, and adorned with real whiskers which the scandalised Mother abolished within one hour of beholding, I found myself at Bombay where I was born, moving among sights and smells that made me deliver in the vernacular sentences whose meaning I knew not. Other Indian-born boys have told me how the same thing happened to them.
>
> There were yet three or four days' rail to Lahore, where my people lived. After these, my English years fell away, nor ever, I think, came back in full strength.
>
> —Rudyard Kipling, *Something of Myself*

> We had a profusely decorated volume of Moore's Irish Melodies: and often have I listened to the enraptured recitation of these by Akshay Babu. The poems combined with the pictorial designs to conjure up for me a dream picture of the Ireland of old. I had not then actually heard the original tunes, but had sung these Irish Melodies to myself to the accompaniment of the harps in the pictures. I longed to hear the real tunes. . . . Some longings unfortunately do get fulfilled in this life, and die in the process. When I went to England I did hear some of the Irish Melodies sung, and learnt them too, but that put an end to my keenness to learn more. They were simple, mournful and sweet, but they somehow did not fit in with the silent melody of the harp which filled the halls of the Old Ireland of my dreams. When I came back home I sung the Irish melodies I had learnt to my people. "What is the matter with Rabi's voice?" they exclaimed. "How funny and foreign it sounds!"
>
> —Rabindranath Tagore, *My Reminiscences*

The images of Rabindranath Tagore singing the *Irish Melodies* to his astonished family and of the young Kipling able to speak a language he could not understand measure forms of unhomeliness that persisted over the long nineteenth century and were expressed with particular intensity in poetry. For poetry—its mix of classical and vernacular languages, its demands on choice of diction, and its formal and metrical constraints—requires of its writer a very high degree of attention to language. Through the constraints of poetic repertoire, cultural contradictions and political uncontemporaneities are magnified. "What is wrong with Rabi's voice?" his family asked. Moore's melodies sounded more jarring to the physical than to the metaphorical ear. "What are the words coming out of my mouth?" Kipling wondered. In the years after his return to India, he cast about through every sort of language available to him, short of classical allusions. A poet's cadences and vocabulary are often made in the linguistic sources of early childhood, and Kipling had to go in search of them. In the 1880s, both Kipling and Tagore engaged these incongruities, often in a comic or satirical vein.

I end this volume with a brief excursion through satire and parody, genres (little addressed elsewhere in the book) that were coeval with the birth of "serious" English language verse in India. A poem by Tagore from his 1890 volume, *Mānasī*, never before translated, provides the context for saying *ave atque vale* to this volume and to Kipling—who along with Tagore represented Indian English poetry to American and British readers for most of the twentieth century.[1]

Both Tagore's poem, "Baṅga Vīr" (Bengali Heroism), and Kipling's early poetry written in India bring us back to the oldest topos of English language verse in India, the hapless griffin. The griffin (that is, the young man in a foreign place embarking on, or attempting to embark on, a career) provided occasions for a long tradition of Anglo-Indian satire. Because much of this study is concerned with juvenilia—the poetry of the very young, among them Mary Carshore, Mary Leslie, H. L. V. Derozio, Kasiprasad Ghosh, Michael Madhusudan Dutt, and Toru Dutt, and even the youthful efforts of David Lester Richardson—it seems right to conclude with the young. Kipling, arriving in India at sixteen, inhabited the place of the griffin; the older Tagore upended the topos, satirizing griffinism in reverse. Tagore's satires reflect a mature reflection on the young, but the productions of Kipling's maturity lie beyond my scope here. In the works of Kipling and Tagore at the end of the nineteenth century, we find parodies of griffins and, in Kipling's case, a griffin's parodies.[2]

Even the dictionary indulges in satire when it comes to griffins. "Griffin" is defined in *Hobson-Jobson* (Yule, Burnell, and Crooke) with tongue in cheek: "One newly arrived in India, and unaccustomed to Indian ways and peculiarities; a Johnny Newcome. . . . Prof. Skeat (ibid. si. 504) quoting from *Piers Plowman*, ed. *Wright*, p. 96, '*Gryffyn* the Walshe,' shows that *Griffin* was an early name for a Welshman, apparently a corruption of *Griffith*. The word may have been used abroad to designate a raw Welshman, and thus acquired its present sense." The raw recruit, the young "writer" or employee of the East India Company, was already the butt of satire by the time the first company officials got their boots dry. The griffin was an aspirant to fortune, a mark for loan sharks, and a reluctant student. And, as *Hobson-Jobson* reminded readers, he might have been only a peripheral "Englishman" at that. The secondary (or original) meanings of griffin as noted in the *Oxford English Dictionary* are apt as well: a mythological bird, now represented by the griffin vulture, or, alternatively, a signal among players in betting or gambling.

Gambling vultures, peripheral "Englishmen": these are fair enough representations of imperial excess. Tagore's griffin-babus, like their counterparts the Anglo-griffins, imbibe the historical and orientalist learning expected of English youth, and like the griffins in British satire, their lives, too, devolve into a game of chance.

By the time of Tagore's poem, the satiric griffin was at least three generations old. One of the earliest and perhaps most amusing examples, *The Grand Master; or, Adventures of Qui Hi in Hindostan: A Hudibrastic Poem in Eight Cantos,* by the anonymous poet "Quiz," recounted multiple misadventures of a young English writer who was early in debt, late to rise, sloth of study, and a suitable mark for unscrupulous British expatriates and Indian moneylenders. Quiz gave no quarter to English pretension. In 1816, he imagined sending Lady Justice out to India to engage the satirist's task:

> Let her expose the asses' ears,
> Of all the group—Judges or Peers;
> Let her, in just consideration,
> Alter the people's situation;
> Let her examine, and she'll find,
> That certain people are inclin'd
> To give rewards where *none*[3] are due,
> Unto a servile, stupid crew
>
> (60)

Lady Justice would find, as Quiz does, that young writers on the civilian side moved too quickly toward too much cash, while young subalterns on the military side had more cash in the silver buttons of their uniforms than in their pockets. Once thoroughly in debt, Quiz's griffin lives mostly to eat, drink, and gamble:

> The billiard-table's now resorted;
> A palanquin and horse is sported;—
> To be like others, is the fashion,
> Qui Hi determin'd is to *dash on,*
> Never reflecting that too soon
> His borrowed money will be gone
>
> (52)

Quiz's subalterns and young writers soon find, like John Leyden in his "Ode to an Indian Gold Coin," that they have sacrificed too much for a metal matched only by their jaundiced faces. In the case of Qui Hi, the griffin is partially redeemed. Quiz's satire nonetheless has much in common with Tagore's ironies, and Qui Hi's companions are predecessors, too, of Kipling's civil servants, sent up in *Departmental Ditties.*

Quiz's *Qui Hi* was followed by many other satires on griffins, including James Atkinson's *City of Palaces* (1824), Pips's *Lyrics and Lays* (1867), Aliph Cheem's *Lays of Ind* (1871; numerous later editions), and J.A.N.'s *Soldierin'* (1899).[4] I suspect that both Tagore and Kipling were acquainted with such verse. Of course, Tagore—unlike Kipling—had many Bengali satires upon which to draw as well. As Anuradha Roy demonstrates,

Tagore joined writers from Hemchandra Bandyopadhyay to Bankimchandra Chattopadhyay to Rajanikanata Sen in "laughing [his] way out of the prison of colonialism."[5] It is fitting, after the sometimes ponderous seriousness of English language poetics and the aesthetic nationalisms of the late century, to end in a tone that Leyden, Atkinson, and Quiz might recognize—even if they would not fully share the sentiments expressed.

I TURN FIRST to Tagore's "Baṅga Vīr," verse made in a polyglot enterprise, where words get away from, turn round on, and are turned by their makers in a fashion that suggests the slippages, gaps, awkwardnesses, and felicities of conflicting identities and multiple linguistic registers. Such play—and such irony as Tagore's—surely constitutes one of the pleasures of poetry. Poetry and pleasure, after all, are intimates, speaking to each other in the familiar *du* or *tu* or *tumi,* a grammatical form that modern English lacks.

The familiar word in Tagore's satire, the polyglot vernacular, is a sharp rapier indeed. Tagore gives no quarter in his pastiche of youthful nationalist attitudes and European historical narratives. Colonialism and armchair nationalism, the poet implies, form a prison from which only laughter and movement can free one. Tagore's "Baṅga Vīr," or "Bengali Heroism," mocks English history, Englishness, and English/Bangla code switching all at once.

I reproduce "Bengali Heroism" here with deepest thanks to the translator, S., on whose learned annotations I also rely:

Bhulu Bābu sits in the next room
reciting loudly multiplication tables.
History books in our laps
        backs propped against a chair
we two brothers are happily settled
on the floor, kerosene lamp flickering,
just as we finished chapter three—
        My elder brother is MA, I BA.

The amount of oil that burns is the amount I read,
and that many ideas fill my head.
How was it brave Cromwell managed
        to lop off the King's head?
It was as easy as when as a boy I used a long stick
to knock down ripe mangoes into ever-growing piles—
with that same delight now does curiosity grow
        bit by bit with each turn of the page.

Some lose their heads to religion,
some heads roll for the welfare of others,

some heads are simply severed on battle fields—
it's all written in the books.
My head is safely ensconced against the chair;
the more my eyes take in these tales
the more inclined I am to read—
my what one can learn from reading!

Sitting near the window, I have been reading about those
who forgot the world in their search for knowledge,
I have committed to memory precisely when they died
in what month, on what day.
Those committed to strict discipline of law,
those who undertook the rigors of fasting,
those who have accepted the thorns of tribulation—
I have preserved their tales in my notebook.

I listen to big speeches, so I speak big,
I collect big books and read,
in this way do I gradually grow big—
who can keep me in check?
Ensconced in my chair all day long,
I read and read and memorize;
sometimes my head aches, or my head spins,
realizing I might go crazy.

In what way are we inferior to the English?
That we are lesser—what a terrible misconception—
in form and shape, in attitude and behavior,
only in these trivial ways do we differ.
Whatever they write, we commit in full to memory,
those very same things we then rewrite in Bāṅglā;
in so many ways do we plagiarize our teachers,
only with the pen does our grief disappear.

The enlightened ancients have called us noble, *ārya,*
so everyone who heeds that has given up work;
calling ourselves important, we have maintained that position,
as we lie in our ease and comfort.
Manu was certainly most spiritually accomplished,[6]
so we too—that we've clearly affirmed;
should anyone suggest otherwise, to them we cry shame, fie!
so we curse them and touch our sacred thread.

To those who wish to suggest we are not brave,
we make obeisance and bow deeply, yet
our ancient forebears cut down their enemies with sharp arrows
        before the very eyes of Veda Vyāsa.[7]
But now, nothing more is needed than
to gather twelve or thirteen people in a group
only to carry on, to rant and rave—
        this has become our preferred habit.

Unhusked rice and rice boiled with green banana
mixed together on a banana leaf plate,
eating only small handfuls while the stomach practices restraint,
        the sages undertook their ascetic penance.
Even though we have a table set,
we breathlessly escape college for the hotel,
but we still evoke the brilliant power, *tejas,* of a brahmin
        by reading Manu in translation.

Ancient Hindu digests and Islamic rituals of chicken slaughter—
in these two great studies everyone engages,
especially we three brothers
        Nimāi, Nepāl, and Bhuto.
Into the ears of our unlettered country folk
we spin the top of our brilliant learning,
with long-winded speeches and burning newspapers—
        for which we've learned a thousand excuses.

When we discuss what really happened
at Marathon and Thermopylae
the blood in our veins instantly boils,
        as quickly as a wick of dried jute flames.
Those benighted masses who read nothing at all
can they even fathom the ashes of this discussion?
They can only gape and yawn—
        it tears my heart apart.

They could have read from beginning to end
the biography of Garibaldi[8]—
I can't imagine what else they might have done
        as they reclined against their stools.
They could have written poetically rhymed verse,
might have learned to talk about a thing or two,

then newspapers may have survived for a while—
and the country might well have developed.

They did not learn to savor literature,
they did not touch the faintest ideas of history,
they didn't even memorize
the date of Washington's birth.
Not the first thing did these folk understand
of Mazzini's activities, such innovative genius[9]—
alas, how unlettered is our unfortunate country,
may you hide your face in shame.

Look as I set up my cot to stand guard,
and bring a book of history from the library,
as much as I read, I compose even more,
ever increasing the eloquence of my language.
When my soul flares with fever, I fan myself,
and feel lightheaded with pure inspiration—
regardless of what might be, I harbor some small hope
to save our homeland.

Come on, let's read about the battle of Naseby[10]—
alas, beloved Cromwell, you are immortal!
Stop here, my back is aching—
I'm losing my concentration.
Where did the maidservant go? Bring my sago snacks!
Oh, oh come, come in Nanibābu—
Pick up the cards and let's play a game of *grābu*—
I'll pay you back for yesterday.[11]

(21 *Jyaiṣṭha* [May–June] 1888, *Rabīndra-racanāvalī*, 1:312–15)

To behead a king, the Bengali "hero" says, was as easy as knocking mangoes from the trees or turning the page of history.

The speaker's miscellaneous information is at once the material for a government examination and, ironically, a recapitulation of the elements that had constituted the nationalist fervor and revolutionary language of Young Bengal. Our hero finds in the English republic and in the Risorgimento the models of Indian nationalism—as Derozio did. He evokes Marathon and Thermopylae—as Derozio, like Byron before him, also did. He memorizes the date of Washington's birth for an examination, not for the revolution. It must have given Tagore, the barrister manqué, particular delight that his heroic speaker reduces the law to Hindu digests and to Muslim rituals for chicken slaughter. So much for the *Laws of Manu.* So much, indeed, for their famous translator, Sir William Jones. So much for the various legal edifices built or supposedly built upon them. To this mishmash of information is added the Aryan heritage argument (put forward in the late nineteenth century by Hindu nationalists and Max Müller alike) which our hero says has provided those claiming an ancient and noble Indian heritage the best excuse for taking their ease.

All these notions of law, identity, and national culture come down to the speaker's assertions that he and his brothers are *only* inferior to the English "in form and shape, in attitude and behavior, / only in these trivial ways do we differ." These delicious ironies do double duty. They satirize the whole panoply of "Western" history and orientalist scholarship, yet by the backdoor they reintroduce the very discourses of liberty that have provided the speaker with such superficial sustenance. The discourses of liberty, in a reductio ad absurdum, come down to success in the examinations for the Indian Civil Service. And all this miscellaneous learning is reduced to a game of chance. The Bengali hero is, in short, not much of a Roundhead. And he behaves like a Cavalier.

The ironies inhabited by Tagore's babu-griffin or griffin-babu go all the way down. Would one wish, after all, to be a Roundhead? Or a Cavalier? An Aryan Brahmin Cavalier? An ascetic Roundhead, both Puritan and regicide, advocate of liberty and theocratic dictator? "Alas, beloved Cromwell, you are immortal." Is our heroic speaker, our griffin-babu, ironizing others or himself?

The poet inhabits a location outside and above the study room, outside the dim lights of the griffin-babu's kerosene lamp. In contrast, the sixteen-year-old Indian-born griffin with whiskers, Rudyard Kipling, was not above the fray, but, as a cub reporter, immersed in it. In his years as a newspaperman in India, Kipling wrote a Christmas annual with his family (*Quartette,* 1885), and numerous poems—occasional, satiric, and serious—in addition to a double handful of fine stories. In the same year that Tagore published *Mānasī,* the United States Book Company issued its own enlarged edition of Rudyard Kipling's *Departmental Ditties, Barrack Room Ballads, and Other Verses* (1890). This collection famously satirized society in India, especially Anglo-Indian society, though Kipling also took shots at the Bengali babu. In contrast to Tagore's sophisticated ironies, Kipling's verse paints Anglo-India with broad satiric strokes.

Taken together with his other early poems, Kipling's verse evidences the radically conflicted understanding of empire that gave rise at the end of his time in India to the subtle ironies of *Plain Tales from the Hills.* Andrew Rutherford argues that Kipling "ended his apprenticeship" in 1899 with "The Ballad of East and West," but despite their apprentice-like quality he singles out for praise the wit of many of the *Departmental Ditties* and the *Ballads* (1). Such early poems, in Rutherford's view, are "far more accomplished" than their predecessor, *Lays of Ind.* Rutherford acknowledges, though, that the early poetry simplifies too much: "Notwithstanding his occasional revulsion from Anglo India . . . there was a thin division between distilling shared experience and values in his verse and acting as a mouthpiece for the lowest common denominator of Anglo-Indian prejudice" (17). It is not far off the mark to think of Kipling at this point as a griffin, albeit a hardworking and debt-free version of the tribe who, unlike the typical British griffin or Tagore's griffin-babu, did not aspire to government office.

At their best—racism and misogyny aside—Kipling's Indian poems cast a critical eye on the powerful and a sympathetic one on the ordinary soldier or peasant.[12] "What the People Said" is promissory of Kipling's later elegiac poems for empire (such as "Recessional"), "celebrating" as it does the queen's Diamond Jubilee—but from the point of view of an Indian farmer, in whose vision history only brings conquerors who in turn are conquered:

> Mogul, Mahratta, and Mlech from the North,
> And the White Queen over the Seas—
> God raiseth them up and driveth them forth
> As the dust of the ploughshare flies in the breeze
>
> (*Departmental Ditties* [1890], 204)

Here the ordinary peasant is given a voice, though not perhaps a voice the poet truly understood; but clearly Kipling attempts to cast the pageantry of empire in a satiric light. In addition to attempting to see empire from the "peasant's" point of view, Kipling in his most popular early poems ("The Sons of the Widow," "Tommy," and "Danny Deever," for example) takes up the position of the common soldier. This stance comes later than the poems Rutherford edits in *Early Verse*—once Kipling, in London, comes to see the working classes at play in London music halls.

The juvenilia (all of Kipling's poems before the *Barrack-Room Ballads*) largely consist of imitations, parodies, and satires, some of which misfire. At their worst, they reduce rather than refract or satirize the tropes of English language Indian verse and orientalist poetics. For example, the "other verses" of Kipling's 1890 volume include "Certain Maxims of Hafiz," which, despite Kipling's admiration for Muslim culture, ring especially hollow, as "Hafiz" is reduced to Kipling's griffinish maxims on griffins. Take maxims 8 and 9:

> VIII
> Seek not for favor of women. So shall you find it indeed.
> Does not the boar break cover just when you're lighting a weed?
> IX
> If He play, being young and unskillful, for shekels of silver and gold,
> Take His money, my son, praising Allah. The kid was ordained to be sold.
>
> (Departmental Ditties [1890], 187)

Kipling's maxims measure both continuity and difference, for the griffins of an earlier age (deserving objects of satire though they were) at least ostensibly read Hāfiz in the original language.[13]

A poem such as "The Masque of Plenty" is both more successful and more sardonic than the takeoff on Hāfiz, for it has a political point—a critique of the government's inadequate attempt to come to terms with the famine of the 1880s. Kipling prefaces the poem by saying that the government "being minded to discover the economic condition of their lands, sent a Committee to inquire into it; and saw that it was good" (140). The matter of inquiry is famine, and the government listens only to what it wishes to hear. In a takeoff on Shelley, the poet recounts the "triumphal return to Simla of the Investigators, attired after the manner of Dionysus, leading a pet-tiger cub in wreaths of rhubarb leaves, symbolical of India under medical treatment" (140). The committee choruses, "We have paid a particular visit to the affluent children of men." Then, in a mix of Indian and English words, they dance to their own particular tune,

> Oh, the *dom* and the *mag* and the *thakur* and the *thag*,
> And the *nat* and the *brinjaree*,
> And the *bunnia* and the *ryot* are as happy and quiet
> And as plump as they can be!
>
> (141)

Forthwith a hired band salutes them:

> God bless the Squire
> And all his rich relations
> Who teach us poor people
> We eat our proper rations
>
> (142)

The poem concludes by sending up viceroys in succession and all their various statistics, which have done little to nothing to alleviate drought, suffering, and starvation.

In these poems and in the satires labeled as *Departmental Ditties*, Kipling creates a kind of charivari of verse forms, in imitation and mockery of his predecessors. The pointed satire and the in-jokes of many of Kipling's early parodies (published in *Echoes*, 1884) and the pronounced Anglo-Indian flavor of *Departmental Ditties* mean that these poems are seldom anthologized. Understanding their frames of reference requires a considerable knowledge of British poetry and of daily Anglo-Indian life and a fair dose of *Hobson-Jobson* into the bargain. Kipling's multiple poetic registers (and his use of Anglo-Indian argot) render concrete in poetic terms his sense of speaking a language he does not quite understand.

On occasion, Kipling also echoes the poetic traditions of orientalist learning and descriptions of Indian flora and fauna. "Christmas in India" and "In Springtime" evoke the sentiments and settings of earlier Anglo-Indian verse.[14] Very occasionally he echoes the poetry of exile, though he admits in his autobiography *Something of Myself* that his English years never "came back in full strength."[15] Such a moment of experiencing or at least writing about the drama of exile occurs when Kipling imitates Browning's line "Oh, to be in England, now that April's there." In the short, serious lyric titled "In Springtime," the poet evokes the same bird that Indian English poets had made their nightingale. The koil (known to other poets as the *coil* or *kokila*) sings to him of his own ennui:

> I am sick of endless sunshine, sick of blossom-burdened bough.
> Give me back the leafless woodlands where the winds of Springtime range—
> Give me back one day in England, for it's Spring in England now!
>
> (*Departmental Ditties,* [1890] 243)

Here Kipling takes up the time-honored trope that poets at least since Heber and Roberts had exploited. Though it is certain that Kipling sometimes longed for England, it is equally true that, like many of the poets I discuss in this volume, he felt at home in India or nowhere. This complication is reflected in the syntactic inversions that end "In Springtime." Like Manmohan Ghose, Kipling experiences "exile" as a kind of double cross:

> But the garland of the sacrifice this wealth of rose and peach is;
> Ah! *köil,* little *köil,* singing on the *siris* bough,
> In my ears the knell of exile your ceaseless bell-like speech is—
> Can *you* tell me aught of England or of Spring in England now?
>
> (244)

Kipling, just past griffinhood, is perhaps himself the little köil.

Certainly, when he arrived back in London after seven years in India, Kipling experienced exile from the other direction; he found the metropole, too, unhomely. The sentiment is expressed in the counter poem to "In Springtime." "In Partibus" begins with more than ennui—with disgust:

> The 'buses run to Battersea,
> The 'buses run to Bow
> The buses run to Westbourne Grove
> And Nottinghill also;
> But I am sick of London town
> From Shepherd's Bush to Bow.
>
> . . . .
>
> Earth holds not horror like to this
> In any land displayed,
> From Suez unto Sandy Hook,
> From Calais to Port Said;

And 'twas to hide their heathendom
The beastly fog was made.[16]

Thus for the young Kipling—the griffin growing to maturity, the cub reporter become a confident "man of letters" (however little he might have liked that term)—parody, satire, and imitation provide a polyglot workshop. The syntax of exile meets the multifarious diction of a poet-in-the-making. Like Tagore's griffin-babus, Kipling as Anglo-griffin wants to take a long stick to history. He may not go for the king's head, but he certainly decapitates some mangoes.

I HAVE ARGUED in these chapters that the homely and the unhomely, friendship and shadowed mutuality, the interplay of multiple classical languages and vernaculars, and the material constraints of publishing shaped what could be said in English language poems and established the conditions of their legibility. The creation of English language poetry in India had a broad and lasting effect in Indian literary culture and in British poetry and European modernism. The story of this verse is a tale of arranged marriage among cultures. For the progeny of these combinations, for William Jones and Derozio, for Kipling and Tagore, there was no simple recourse to the imagined purity of a mother tongue. Such poetry could be thought of as language in its travels.

IN HIS LECTURES in China in 1924, Rabindranath spoke of his poetic career as his "vagabondage" (*Talks in China,* 19). His passionate defense of language learning—that one must "woo a language" to understand its poetry—was delivered in English and translated into Chinese. As he elaborated his metaphor to encourage the study of Bangla outside Bengal, he defended learning multiple languages as a necessity of art. "Languages are jealous," Rabindranath told his listeners. "They do not give up their best treasures to those who try to deal with them through an intermediary belonging to an alien rival. You have to court them in person and dance attendance on them. Poems are not like gold or other substantial things that are transferable. You cannot receive the smiles and glances of your sweetheart through an attorney, however diligent and dutiful he may be" (21). Translation is impossible; translation is vital. In Rabindranath's ideal, great poetry is local, yet great poetry transcends the local. The poets I study here often found themselves courting another language, whether it was English, Hindi, Bangla, Persian, or Sanskrit.

I conclude with two aphorisms from Tagore's vagabondage, from his bilingual work *Lekhan* (1926), first published in Hungary in the poet's handwriting. This slim volume contains short poems in English and in Bangla, some evidently translations of the other and some with no translation. Many of these small poems were written by the poet during his travels in China and Japan, where he composed them on fans or on pieces of silk.

White and pink oleanders meet
and make merry in different dialects.

✡

Emancipation from the bondage of the soil
is no freedom for the tree.

(*English Writings*, 578, 596)

Pleasure, anger, loneliness, love, religious despair, delight in the natural world, sociality, political fervor, great and little learning, translations among multiple languages: all these elements constitute the rich and sometimes odd world of English language poetry in India during the long nineteenth century. If I am inordinately lucky, and you, gentle reader, have accompanied me to the end of my story about these poems, it is my hope that we may, on various continents and in various places, make merry in different dialects.

Little Switzerland, North Carolina
March 21, 2009

NOTES

Introduction

1. See W. W. Tulloch, "Biographical Sketch of the Author," in Leyden, *Scenes of Infancy.*

2. John Malcolm, "To the Editor of the Bombay Courier," quoted in Walter Scott, "Supplementary Memoir," which introduces Leyden, *Poems and Ballads,* xli.

3. Shaw's *Printing in Calcutta* is an invaluable resource from which we can extrapolate the importance of institutions of literary sociality, including, for example, the Masons and the Highland Society, whose *Rules* and membership list were published in 1788 in, not one, but two editions (Shaw, *Printing in Calcutta,* 120).

4. Tracy Davis, "Sonic Repertoire," Conference Paper. North American Victorian Studies Association, Yale University, November 2008.

5. On hospitality see Benhabib, *Another Cosmopolitanism,* 156; Derrida, *Monolingualism of the Other,* 14–25.

6. Leyden, *Poems and Ballads,* 313. In a letter to his friend Ballantyne written in 1805 and subsequently reproduced in Walter Scott's memoir of Leyden, the poet distinguished between those among the British in India whom he admired, whom he characterized as committed to good government and administration, and those "who would sell their own honour or their country's credit to the highest bidder without a shadow of a scruple" ("Memoir of the Author," in Leyden, *Poems and Ballads,* 50).

Chapter 1: Contact Poetics in Eighteenth-Century Calcutta

1. Sir William Jones to George John Spencer, August 23, 1787, *Letters,* 2:755. The poets alluded to are Vālmic (Vālmīki), author of a famous *Rāmāyaṇa;* Vyāsa (traditionally named as the author or source of the *Mahābhārata*), and Kālidāsa (widely acknowledged as among the greatest of Sanskrit poets, whose *Śakuntalā* Jones translated in 1789).

2. Schwab, *Oriental Renaissance,* 58–59; see also the whole of Schwab's chapter 3, "Europe Learns Sanskrit," 51–80. Wordsworth's formulation comes in the preface to the second edition of *Lyrical Ballads* (*Poems,* 1:867–96).

3. For a discussion of Jones's poetic and religious views, see Drew, *India and the Romantic Imagination;* Priestman, *Romantic Atheism;* and Cannon, *Life and Mind of Oriental Jones.*

4. Horsford's fellowship at St. John's, Oxford (1768–71), overlapped with Jones's time as a fellow of University College (1766–83). Details of Horsford's life can be gleaned from the *Oxford Dictionary of National Biography* and, for his military career, from Stubbs, *History.*

Poems in Three Parts is cataloged in Worldcat and in the Eighteenth-Century Collections Online database as written by three authors: Sir William Jones, John Hawkesworth, and John Horsford. This attribution, however, is misleading, for part one, as I detail below, consists of facing page translations into English of Jones's Latin poems by an author writing after Jones's death; the author of the translations is anonymous, but his style is coherent with Horsford's as is the esteem in which the translator holds Sir William. The second section of the volume is attributed by bibliographers to Hawkesworth, but I can find no warrant for this claim, and indeed the poem "Literary Characteristicks of the Most Distinguished Members of the Asiatic Society" was published under a different pseudonym, "John Collegins Esq.," in the *Asiatic Annual Register, 1801* (London, 1802): 118. The conclusion of the poem includes a paean to the Howrah Orphanage, from which the author claims to have taken two daughters, a claim identical to that made by J— H— [John Horsford] in the third section of *Poems in Three Parts*, which is signed with his own initials. Internal evidence, then, these examples among others, makes for a strong claim that Horsford was the author of all three parts of this volume, modestly saving the expanded collection of his own verse for the end of the volume.

5. Obviously the notion of culture, let alone "English language literary culture," is subject to critique; I do not intend to hypostasize the notion of culture as a singular, uncontested entity, as my point is precisely the opposite. Any singular equation of language with identity or of identity with culture can be dismantled in numerous ways: linguistic (see Kachru, *The Other Tongue* and Myers-Scotton, *Contact Linguistics*) or philosophical (see Derrida, *Monolingualism of the Other*).

6. The data are based on the house tax in Calcutta, as reported in S. N. Mukherjee, "Class, Caste and Politics, 1814–38," in Leach and Mukherjee, *Elites in South Asia*, 37. "Mugs" is a term referring to the natives of Arakan, particularly the area bordering Bengal. "Mug," according to *Hobson-Jobson*, referred particularly to a native of Chittagong (now in Bangladesh, but formerly an independent kingdom at one time and under the influence of Burma at others). *Hobson-Jobson*, edited by Henry Yule, A. C. Burnell, and William Crooke, is subtitled *A Glossary of Colloquial Anglo-Indian Words and Phrases*. It provides a kind of *Oxford English Dictionary* for English usage in India through the nineteenth century—hence it is indispensable.

7. Bayly's description of Hindustani (roughly Hindi/Urdu) is helpful here; he uses the term *Urdu* to represent "the more refined and Persianised form of the common north Indian language Hindustani" (*Empire and Information*, 193); Bayly more or less follows the late eighteenth-century scholar Sirajuddin Ali Arzu, who proposed a typology of languages that ran from "pure Sanskrit, through popular and regional variations of Hindustani to Urdu, which incorporated many loan words from Persian and Arabic. His emphasis on the unity of languages reflected the view of the Sanskrit grammarians and also affirmed the linguistic unity of the north Indian ecumene. What emerged was a kind of register of language types which were appropriate to different conditions. . . . But the abiding impression is of linguistic plurality running through the whole society and an easier adaptation to circumstances in both spoken and written speech" (193). The more Persianized the language, the more likely it was to be written in Arabic script; the more Sanskritized the language; the more likely it was to be written in devanagari.

8. The best known of these schoolmasters were David Hare, a Scottish free-thinking watchmaker, who started a school before 1818 in Calcutta, and David Drummond, who a generation later was the first headmaster of Hindu College. Also important were schools set up by the Society for the Promotion of Christian Knowledge in the eighteenth century, including that of John Frederic Kiernander, a Swedish minister and teacher of Latin, who preached in Calcutta in the 1760s in German, Portuguese, and English to congregations of those nationalities, plus Malays, Wadugas, Bengali Hindus, and Muslims. Kiernander's school, which included English education and other practical subjects, was established for the destitute children of Europeans. A similar school had operated from the 1730s in the buildings of the Scottish church at Calcutta. See Wilkinson, *Sketches of Christianity*, 1–3.

9. "The Threshold of Interpretation" is itself the paratext, that is to say, the subtitle, of Genette's volume.

10. Genette concludes *Paratexts* by admitting that he has not dealt with illustration, translation, or serial publication—all of which can also function as paratexts. Here I treat both illustration and translation, as both were crucial to the paratextual situation in India.

11. In the following account I rely heavily on Shaw, *Printing in Calcutta,* especially 1–41; on his essay "Printing at Mangalore and Tellicherry"; and on Bayly, "Indian Ecumene."

12. A survey of the *Calcutta Gazette* from 1780 through 1790 reveals the contours of this literary culture. The *Gazette* advertised new books arrived from Britain at Calcutta booksellers; it reveals as well the importance to social life of the theatre and of various friendly societies. On theatre, see Suresh Ghosh, *Social Condition,* 134–35. Subscribers' lists of books of poetry in the period indicate the importance of book circulation among army officers and private circulating libraries. On the Masons, see Shaw's description of *The Oriental Masonic Muse* (Calcutta, 1791), which listed nine lodges in Calcutta, one in Serampore (up the Hooghly from the city, a Danish settlement that was also the home of various British missionaries), two in Madras, and three in Bombay. See Shaw, *Printing in Calcutta,* 183.

13. *Calcutta Chronicle and General Advertiser* 3, no. 135; *India Gazette* 10, no. 509.

14. In *Music of the Raj,* Ian Woodfield discusses a similar strategy among musicians—the subscription concert—and documents the difficulties of making a living through subscription concerts in late eighteenth-century Calcutta. In 1792, the *Asiatick Miscellany* advised London readers that previous volumes of the *Miscellany* (1785, 1786) were priced in Calcutta at one gold mohur each, equivalent to one pound sterling seven shillings, a not inconsiderable investment but the going rate in the late eighteenth century. In contrast, the volume of extracts from the two volumes of the *Miscellany* was priced at three shillings in London by John Murray in 1792.

15. Jones, for example, wrote to Charles Wilkins, the pioneering Sanskrit scholar, on February 27, 1789, "The ships of this season will carry home seven hundred copies of our first volume of Transactions; and the second will be ready, I hope, next year: but unless the impression should be sold in London, Harington and Morris (who print the book at their hazard) will be losers, and we must dissolve the Society" (*Letters,* 2:827–28).

16. Population estimates are necessarily inexact, particularly as the category "European" could be, to say the least, somewhat flexible. See Bayly, *Indian Society,* 71.

17. George Addison, editor, *The Moofussil Magazine,* no. 2, pp. 19–20, British Library Mss. Eur C 268.

18. Anonymous editor's preface to Addison, *Indian Reminiscences,* x.

19. See the Indian letters of William Jones, which indicate a vigorous network of book borrowing by post and in person; the process continued in the next generation, as Emma Roberts indicated in her *Scenes and Characteristics of Hindostan.* The importance of such exchanges of books and music is also confirmed by the memoirs cited in Raza, *In Their Own Words.*

20. I have combined Shaw's separate categories for registers, government publications, and regulations; have combined the various useful subjects that he lists separately; and have combined translations from Persian and Sanskrit (as well as religion, music, and artworks) into single, rather than separate categories. For a more detailed breakdown, see Shaw, *Printing in Calcutta,* 41, and the entire volume for a complete listing of items printed.

21. P. H. Matthews, *Concise Oxford Dictionary of Linguistics.* Oxford University Press, 2007. Oxford Reference Online. Oxford University Press.

22. Here we should think of domination in the Gramscian sense of hegemony, with the recognition that no hegemony is ever complete and with the corollary understanding that power relations were complex both between colonizer and colonized and among the colonized. Such relations had attendant ramifications for language learning and use.

23. Shaw quotes Hadjee Mustapha, "a French-born Muslim convert, translator of the *Seir Mutaqherin*," as commenting in a letter appended on the likelihood of Francis Gladwin finding an audience for his English/Persian dictionary: "From Mr. Gladwin's *Vocabulary* . . . you must exclude four-fifths of the common herd of readers; you must exclude women; and all those who have neither inclination to, nor an insight in, oriental learning . . . if then so very small a work has produced so large a sum, it was because the author's reputation, as an author and a man of letters, is formed, known, and established; whereas no one knows anything of me. Secondly because he is an Englishman, a man high in station; and of course has many friends: whereas I am next to nobody, and my station is immediately after nothing" (Shaw, *Printing in Calcutta*, 23, 26). Mustapha had composed his own English/Persian dictionary but could not afford to publish it.

24. In his memoir of Jones, Lord Teignmouth translates and transcribes two brief poems, one in Sanskrit and one in Arabic, addressed to Jones by two of his pandits. There is no evidence that they had enough English or sufficient interest to write English verse as well; their verses arose from the poetic traditions with which they were most familiar, which they could assume would be more meaningful to Jones than any they might make in vernacular verse. See Jones, *Collected Works*, 2:307–8; see also Rocher, "Weaving Knowledge."

25. See Myers-Scotton, *Contact Linguistics*. Jones's work in comparative religion, astronomy, and botany argues for the fact that he was highly self-conscious about his place as a translator of knowledge. Perhaps the most important indication of this open-mindedness was his willingness to acknowledge Nadia as the third university at which he had studied, after Oxford and the Inns of Court—third in the chronology of his life but not in its importance. As he wrote to Earl Spencer, his former pupil, on August 21, 1787, "*Navadwipa*, or *Nuddea*, as Rennel writes it," is the "celebrated University of the *Brahmans*" and "the third University of which I have been a member; and there I finish my education" (Jones, *Letters*, 2:754).

26. Michael Franklin makes a similar point in contrasting Jones with Nathaniel Brassey Halhed; Halhed, despite publishing the first Bengali grammar, displayed "a distrust of the vernacular . . . and a refusal to tolerate a developing and dynamic Indian society" (Franklin, "Cultural Possession," 18).

27. Jones not only remade vernacular English but also translated Persian poetry into French, thus broadening his reach. Jones's English translations, including the version of Jayadéva's *Gítagóvinda*, were quickly translated into German and had a dramatic impact on Schelling, Herder, Novalis, and Schlegel; Goethe was struck by the initial version published in the third volume of *Asiatick Researches* (see Schwab, *Oriental Renaissance*, 206).

28. Michael J. Franklin, "Jones, Sir William (1746–1794)," in Matthew and Harrison, *Oxford Dictionary of National Biography*, http://www.oxforddnb.com/view/article/15105 (accessed April 18, 2010). See the memoir by John Shore, Lord Teignmouth, that prefaces Jones, *Collected Works*; see also Jones, *Letters*; and Priestman, *Romantic Atheism*.

29. Jones, *Collected Works*, 2:503. Jones probably alludes to John Gay's "Fable X," "The Elephant and the Bookseller," which in turn alludes to Pliny's tale of an elephant reading Greek. Gay's fable begins,

> The man who, with undaunted toils,
> Sails unknown seas to unknown soils,
> With various wonders feasts his sight:
> What stranger wonders does he write!
> We read, and in description view
> Creatures which Adam never knew:
> For, when we risk no contradiction,

It prompts the tongue to deal in fiction.
Those things that startle me or you,
I grant are strange; yet may be true.
Who doubts that elephants are found
For science and for sense renowned?
Borri records their strength of parts,
Extent of thought, and skill in arts;
How they perform the law's decrees,
And save the state the hangman's fees;
And how by travel understand
The language of another land.
Let those, who question this report,
To Pliny's ancient page resort;
How learn'd was that sagacious breed!
Who now (like them) the Greek can read!

(Gay, *Poetical Works*)

30. As Franklin notes with respect to the hymns, Jones declared in his letters (2:777) that he commonly had ten or twenty copies printed of everything he composed and that these copies were, in Jones's view, to be considered as manuscripts. See Franklin, *Sir William Jones*, 406n, on "Hymn to Náráyena" and its "proof" version.

31. I am assuming here that the first Calcutta edition of this poem appeared with Jones's supervision as a proof edition, much as the hymns did. That the poem would have been published in Calcutta in 1784 without his permission is highly unlikely, though it was issued anonymously both there and in the *Asiatick Miscellany*, where Jones did allow his name to be printed with the hymns, probably on account of their more serious tone.

32. The ages of the cosmos in the *Purāṇas* can be summarized thus: "At the end of each aeon *(kalpa)*, the universe is destroyed by fire to remain submerged in the cosmic waters while Brahmā sleeps, until the time when all is to be created anew. Each *kalpa* consists of four ages *(yugas)*, named after four throws of the dice: the first, the Kṛta Age, is the best (often it is called the Satya Age, the Age of Truth); it is followed by the Tretā Age, the Dvāpara Age, and finally the Kali Age, the present age, when virtue is at its lowest ebb and the human life-span is the shortest" (Doniger, *Hindu Myths*, 43).

33. Jones's "Mr. Bogle" refers to a treatise on Tibetan polyandry by George Bogle, the first British person to establish diplomatic relations with Tibet. Bogle hailed from Glasgow, where his father was a tobacco lord. His two older brothers established plantations in Virginia and Grenada, and he wrote extensively about his adventures and about Tibetan culture, including the essay in *Philosophical Transactions* referenced by Jones.

34. Of course, there is also the possibility that Jones is obliquely referencing the anonymous satires about Joseph Banks himself, whose sexual exploits in Tahiti became the subject of verse satires such as *The Historic Epistle from Omiah to the Queen of Otaheite; Being His Remarks on the English Nation* (London, 1775); Pamela Cheek quotes this poem, which describes Banks as a guide for a Tahitian visitor to England's sexual favors and botanical curiosities:

. . . O'er verdant plains my steps *Opane* [Banks] leads,
To trace the organs of a sex in weeds;
And bids like him the world for monsters roam,
Yet finds none stranger than are here at home.

(Cheek, 143)

In my quotations from Jones and references to his poems, I follow his transliterations, which, as in the case of *Camdew,* shift from work to work. There was at this time, of course, no standard transliteration for Sanskrit.

35. See Jones's letter to Johnson, December 15, 1783, *Letters,* 2:624.

36. Damodara's work was composed in 1625, and Harivallabha's Hindi translation was made within the next twenty years. Falk and Archer, *Indian Miniatures.*

37. http://rpo.library.utoronto.ca/poem/889.html.

38. Jones alludes to the famous pilgrimage site in Allahabad, which marks the confluence of these rivers and is perhaps the most sacred site for bathing in India; hundreds of thousands of pilgrims flock to Allahabad every twelve years in the Kumbh Melā.

39. For placing Jones as a Christian of deist leanings in the context of late eighteenth-century freethinking, see Priestman, *Romantic Atheism.*

40. The *Oxford Dictionary of National Biography* records this episode and also the names of Horsford's Indian "bibi," Sahib Jaun, with whom he is supposed to have had several children. H. M. Chichester, "Horsford, Sir John (1751–1817)," rev. Enid M. Fuhr, in Matthew and Harrison, *Oxford Dictionary of National Biography,* http://www.oxforddnb.com/view/article/13817 (accessed April 24, 2010).

41. As indicated in "Ode to My Infant Daughter Eliza Howrah," Horsford might have adopted an Anglo-Indian orphan from the Howrah orphanage or placed his biological daughter for some reason in the orphan school; his obituaries report that Horsford died unmarried. In his poems, he addresses the biracial children in the Howrah orphanage as "my auburn beauties" and counsels young British men in India to marry them. Though he hopes nobler bards will sing their praises, he dedicates "The Art of Living in India" finally to the young women of the orphanage:

> Ye shapely Nymphs, who form my pleasing theme!
> Ye, born where Ganga rolls her hallow'd stream,
> Accept the numbers, written with spirit free,
> I love your India and your India me!
>
> (*Poems in Three Parts,* 119)

The *DNB* records Horsford as having three sons and three daughters (including Eliza) with "his Indian partner, Sahib Jaun." One could conjecture, however, that Eliza might either have spent some time in the Howrah orphanage—hence her middle name—or was, if she was not adopted, then named after the town. The Howrah orphanage was specifically intended to care for the biracial children of British soldiers; officers traditionally took responsibility for ensuring care for the orphaned children of members of their companies and sometimes oversaw the marriage within their units of girls who had been reared in the Howrah institution. Children of the military unit were, by custom, generally considered its responsibility, and officers collected a fee from the soldiers as a cooperative insurance pool to benefit orphaned children.

42. Compare Jones's "Perfido ridens Erycina vultu" with Horace:

> sive tu mavis, Erycina ridens,
> quam Iocus circum volat et Cupido;
> sive neglectum genuse et nepotes
> respicis, auctor
>
> (Horace, *Odes* 1.2.33–36)

The Loeb translation reads "or thou, if thou will rather, blithe goddess of Erix, about whom hover Mirth and Desire; or thou, author, if thou regardest the neglected race of thy descendants"

(8–9). The second half of Jones's Latin version of Sappho also echoes Catullus, 50 and 51, Virgil's bucolics, and Propertius.

43. Horsford refers to a note stating that "this poem ['Literary Characteristicks of the Most Distinguished Members of the Asiatic Society, 1799'] was written about the period of the conquest of Mysore" (*Poems in Three Parts*, 53).

44. Merry took his pseudonym from the Accademia della Crusca, founded in Florence in 1582 to purify the Tuscan language; no doubt Merry was bowing to the Tuscan academicians' admiration for Petrarch and Boccaccio.

45. Anna Matilda's phrase "hapless Verse" echoes the end of Della Crusca's "To Anna Matilda":

> But should, with Anna's Verse, his hapless Rhime,
> In future meet th'impartial eye of Time,
> Say, that thy wretched victim long endur'd,
> Pains which are seldom felt, and never cur'd!
> Say 'midst the lassitude of hopes o'erthrown,
> MATILDA's strain could comfort him alone.
> Yet was the veil mysterious ne'er remov'd,
> From him th'admiring, and from her the lov'd,
> And no kind intercourse the Song repaid,
> But each to each remain'd—a Shadow and a Shade.
>
> (Merry, *British Album*, 1:100)

46. Ovid, "Oenone Paride," *Heroides*, line 53.

47. An anonymous translation of the text of the Heroides (The Epistles) is available at http://www.perseus.tufts.edu/hopper/text?doc=Perseus%3atext%3a1999.02.0085, line 149.

Chapter 2: Bards and Sybils

1. Rosemary Cargill Raza, "Roberts, Emma (1791–1840)." *Oxford Dictionary of National Biography*, Oxford University Press, September 2004; online ed., Jan 2008 [http://www.oxforddnb.com/view/article/23747, accessed 15 March 2009].

2. Rosinka Chaudhuri includes as appendixes to her edition of Derozio's poems a series of letters published by Derozio in the *India Gazette* and by one Robert McNaghten in *John Bull.* This "huge row," as Chaudhuri appropriately calls it, was occasioned by McNaghten's attempt to get Derozio to pay postage for and sell additional copies of "a lady's book." The poet apparently complied with this request but was not paid, and when these circumstances were made public McNaghten challenged Derozio, who said he was forbidden by his friends from dueling with one who was not a gentleman. The connection between Robert McNaghten and "Mr Jerdan" (the editor of an English newspaper that published Letitia Landon), the assumption by him that Derozio would take an interest in this "lady's book," and his name all suggest that Derozio's assailant was Emma Roberts's brother-in-law, Robert Adair McNaghten, though Chaudhuri does not draw this connection. See Chaudhuri, *Derozio, Poet of India*, 322–41.

3. Roberts wrote on many topics in addition to Indian ones, including an edition of a cookbook for John Murray, numerous essays, and a first book telling the history of the houses of York and Lancaster.

4. Derozio's poems (including those on Tasso) give evidence of his continuing interest in Italian poetry, as does his pseudonym Leporello, taken from Mozart's *Don Giovanni*, which, as Chaudhuri points out, he may or may not have known directly but which would have attracted him as a parallel to Byron's *Don Juan.* On Leporello, see Chaudhuri, *Derozio, Poet of India*, 272–75.

5. See Rocher, "Sanskrit for Civil Servants."

6. The orientalist footnote, as deployed by Roberts, may have influenced Landon's later practice.

7. See Rogers, *Modern Scottish Minstrel,* 3:34.

8. Chaudhuri makes a good case in *Derozio, Poet of India* (389) that this review was probably written by Grant.

9. The typographer also used this wingding to separate poems in order to save paper; subsequent poems, but not "The Harp of India," were set as running text rather than each poem beginning on a new page.

10. Partly, of course, Derozio is evoking the music of Thomas Moore, who in turn is evoking a lost bardic music. A good example of the music Derozio imitates is the second stanza of Moore's famous lyric "The Harp That Once Through Tara's Halls":

> No more to chiefs and ladies bright
> The harp of Tara swells;
> The chord alone, that breaks at night
> Its tale of ruin tells.
> Thus Freedom now so seldom wakes,
> The only throb she gives,
> Is when some heart indignant breaks,
> To show that still she lives.
>
> (Moore, 131)

11. For a discussion of the East Indian community, see Marshall, "British Society in India," and Hawes, *Poor Relations.*

12. I owe this reading to Roger Gilbert.

13. The Calcutta edition included, under "Dramatic Sketches and Tales," five long poems, mostly on Italian subjects, including a long closet drama, "Geraldi Sforza," and a long poem, "The Florentines."

14. Chaudhuri notes that Derozio's poems "The Ruins of the Rajmahal" and "The Fakeer of Jungheera" were "evidently inspired by the depictions of these 'picturesque' spots" by William Hodges and by William and Thomas Daniell, among others (*Derozio, Poet of India,* lxxi).

15. See Archer, *Early Views of India.*

16. See Archer, *Early Views of India,* especially the preface (7–9) and the chapter titled "Publication and Influence" (219–33).

17. See *The Poetess Archive,* edited by Laura Mandell.

18. Major, *Pious Flames,* 204. Major's book is the most useful recent treatment of the topic, building on the work of Lata Mani, Vasudha Dalmia-Luderitz, and others, along with significant research in the English language periodicals of nineteenth-century India.

Chapter 3: Books, Reading, and the Profession of Letters

1. David Lester Richardson, "The Warrior's Farewell to the Family Bard," *Oriental Herald* (London) no. 9, (September, 1824): 22. The poet had just returned from India, where no doubt he was acquainted with the journal's editor, James Silk Buckingham, whose strong criticism of the East India Company's government in his newspaper had led to his recent deportation from India. Indeed, D.L.R. had contributed to Buckingham's *Calcutta Journal* in 1820 at the tender age of nineteen. He published his *Miscellaneous Poems* in 1822, the year before Buckingham had to

pack his bags. When the two found themselves in London in the 1820s, they evidently renewed their association.

2. Khan, *Bengali Book,* 1:82.

3. See Khan, *Bengali Book,* Volume 1; Bayly, "Indian Ecumene"; Shaw, "Printing at Mangalore"; and Diehl, *Printers and Printing.*

4. Srinivas Aravamudan notes that even in the late twentieth century, while India had the third largest total number of fluent English speakers worldwide, that number remained at about 3–5 percent of the total population, though the percentage of the population with passive comprehension, as in the nineteenth century, was considerably higher. This makes English an "acrolect," or elite language, but one that became a "lingua franca with considerable cosmopolitan appeal" and created the circumstance in which India continues to be a major creator of English language books, now the third largest number of English language books after the United States and Great Britain (*Guru English,* 3–5).

5. *India Gazette,* August 5, 1822, 1–2.

6. Moitra, *History of Indian Journalism,* 91. Rangaswami Parthasarathy argues that there was substantial cooperation and engagement in a mutual enterprise between much of the English language press and the press in Indian languages before 1857 and shows that Charles Metcalfe in the 1830s was largely responsible for relaxing the government restrictions on the press that were epitomized by the deportation of Buckingham. The jingoist behavior of the English language press in 1857, however, drove a wedge between the vernacular and the English press. See Parthasarathy, *Journalism in India,* 38–39.

7. Thomas Noon Talfourd's copyright bill did not become law in Britain until 1842.

8. *Calcutta Journal,* August 12, 1819, quoting the *Belfast Newsletter* of March 5.

9. This traditional form of annual holiday publishing continues even today; for the Durga puja holidays (in October), both the *Statesman* and the *Telegraph,* the two English language newspapers in Calcutta, publish a literary annual as a supplement to the papers' usual offerings. These annuals offer a forum for reviews and English language literature as well as an opportunity to sell additional advertising.

10. Other offerings included Fisher's *Drawing Room Scrap-Book* for 1833 by L.E.L., *Friendship's Offering,* Falstaff's *Comic Offering, Hood's Comic Annual* for 1830, Heath's *Picturesque Annual, The Juvenile Keepsake, The Keepsake, The Literary Souvenir, The Landscape Annual, The Oriental Annual, The Missionary Annual, The Orient Pearl, The Talisman, The Remembrancer,* and *The Young Lady's Book,* to name only some of the most significant.

11. Anonymous review of *Bengal Annual* in *Calcutta Literary Gazette,* January 1, 1833, 11.

12. See, for example, Ledbetter, "Begemmed and BeAmuletted."

13. Purchasers of books before the 1840s, when print remained relatively expensive, sometimes clubbed together in addition to sharing books. Subscribers' lists from volumes of poetry published in the 1820s and 1830s show that regimental book clubs were already common, and these continued their function even past the point when subscription publishing was on the decline. Such clubs allowed soldiers (one imagines officers much more often than enlisted men) to pool their resources in purchasing books. Several such clubs, for example, are listed among the subscribers to Emma Roberts's *Oriental Scenes.*

14. Priya Joshi cites James Long's midcentury survey of Indian reading habits to argue that though "native females" made up a very small number of the literate population, less than 1 percent even in 1881, that many more were read to by others (*In Another Country,* 41). Joshi further discusses book prices, which, as in Britain, declined toward midcentury and were further reduced by such efforts as John Murray's Colonial and Home Library, which ran from 1843 through 1849 (92–94). As Joshi notes, such reductions in price and multiplication of volumes

applied as well to the vernacular press in Bengal, as indicated by James Long's *Returns Relating to Publications in the Bengali Language, Selections from the Records of the Bengal Government* (1859).

15. Partha Mitter discusses the Lyceum and the Mechanics Institute in *Art and Nationalism* (30–31). Madhusudan Dutt's letters indicate that he and other young men of Hindu College regularly patronized the MI, as they called it.

16. Kaye, "English Literature in India," 204.

17. The Dr. Grant who authored this essay is likely to have been John Peter Grant, son of John Peter Grant (1774–1848), who was no relation to the John Grant who was the Calcutta editor and friend of Derozio's and Richardson's. John Peter Grant the younger was secretary to Macaulay's Indian Law Commission and from 1848 was secretary to the government of Bengal; his father (of the same name) was a judge in Bombay and then Calcutta and died in 1848 en route to Britain.

18. Grant, review of *Literary Leaves, Literary Chit-Chat,* and *Notices of the British Poets,* in *Calcutta Review* 10 (1848): 28, 57.

19. Chaudhuri also cites in this connection Madhusudan Dutt's farce, *Eki ki boley sabhyata?* [Is this your civilization?] (*Derozio, Poet of India,* lxi). For orthodox reactions to Westernization, see Dalmia, *Nationalization of Hindu Traditions.*

20. T. W. Smyth's *Ella, or A Tale of the Waldensian Martyrs* included a poem in memory of Derozio, lamenting his death as a national loss.

21. Smyth's book of poems is bound with Henry Page's *The Land of Poesy* in a volume now held by the Carey Library, Serampore. I am grateful to the librarians for access to their collections.

22. Page, *Land of Poesy,* 7.

23. See A. Leslie, *Memoirs and Remains.*

24. For an account of Richardson's career, see S. C. Sanial, "Captain David Lester Richardson"; for the controversy that led to Richardson's forced resignation in 1849 from his second term as the principal of Hindu College, see Mukhopadhyay, *Hindu College,* 56–58 and 116–21. For reasons that are not quite clear, Richardson fell afoul of John Drinkwater Bethune (an evangelical divine who was then president of the Council of Education); John Peter Grant was then secretary to the Council of Bengal and accepted Richardson's resignation. The historian of Hindu College also conjectures that Richardson had somehow offended another Calcutta divine, Alexander Duff, the minister of the Scottish Free Church.

25. See Sanial, "Captain David Lester Richardson." Richardson appears to have been relatively depressed at various times in his life, and his putative misdeeds may have resulted from nothing more problematic than absenteeism. That he threatened Bethune with a libel suit, however, suggests that other rumors circulated, however little they might have been based in fact.

26. Viswanathan discusses other elements of the missionary/government differences over education—particularly with respect to caste segregation, with upper-caste Hindus attending institutions such as Hindu College while lower-caste boys attended missionary schools. She quotes the Baptist missionary John Marshman's sarcastic remark, "I am not certain that a man's being able to read Milton and Shakespeare, or understand Dr Johnson, would make him less susceptible of the honour of being a Brahmin" (*Masks of Conquest,* 152).

27. A brief list of colleges (advanced secondary and/or higher education institutions) in Bengal, mostly in and around Calcutta, founded in the first half of the century is instructive; in addition to Hindu College, Drummond's Academy, and other eighteenth-century institutions, we find more than half a dozen significant private institutions: Serampore College (1818), Bishop's College (1822), Doveton College (1823), the Free Church Institution (1830), La Martiniere (1836), St. Paul's School (1845), Krishnaghur College (1845), Hooghly College (1836), and Dacca College (1841), not to mention Calcutta University a bit later (1857).

28. "Reports of the Examination Questions and Answers of the Students of the Hindu College and the Free Church Institution," *Calcutta Review* 5 (1846): xxiii–l.

29. Richardson spelled Ghosh's name Ghose; both transliterations are "correct," but I follow the spelling chosen by Kasiprasad Ghosh on the title page of his volume of verse, *The Sháïr and Other Poems* (1830).

30. Parker, "Young India: A Bengal Eclogue," in *Bole Ponjis,* 1:223–28.

31. Chaudhuri, *Gentlemen Poets,* 24–25.

32. Parker's later political views, if somewhat incoherent, included fierce opposition to the abolition of the East India Company in 1858 following the rebellion, an opposition he predicated on the British government's failures in Ireland and on the folly of evangelicals in India. Parker sarcastically dedicated a collection of "sermons" (that is, essays), titled *Short Sermons on Indian Texts, Concerning the Empire of the Middle Classes,* to "that devout, earnest, and conscientious body of Englishmen, whose fervent zeal for Conversion has clearly helped to create a fearful Mutiny, and will probably excite a National Rebellion in India" (n.p.). Parker represents a skepticism about empire, particularly its religious justification; he reminds his readers that the Hindu who has no desire to convert Christians to his religion can only believe that evangelism "proceeds from motives which have for their aim and end the advancement of our own worldly interests" (*Short Sermons,* 17). Parker clearly shares such skepticism.

33. "The Draught of Immortality," the title poem of his early first volume, is a long paraphrase of the famous churning of the ocean from the *Mahābhārata,* an episode more ably translated by Horace Hayman Wilson.

34. In *Literary Recreations,* Richardson laments the separation from children as "the stroke that goes most directly to the heart. It is not the mere absence alone that constitutes the better trial, but a consciousness of the vast, intervening distance. The parent and the child are divided from each other by a world of waters. They live in different spheres" (34).

35. R., "Written on Leaving England for India," *Oriental Herald* 7, no. 22 (1825): 21.

36. Richardson's correspondence with Hunt mostly dates from his home leave in 1844–45. In these letters, he offers a friendly notice of a book by Hunt in the *Jersey Times,* which he was editing during his leave, and he asks for Hunt's help in finding employment in Britain. Though he has strong letters of recommendation from Lord Auckland, the former governor-general, and others, he declares that they have no power to help him, and he, unsuccessfully, throws himself on Hunt's influence. At the end of his leave, Richardson returned to India, where shortly after, his son (who had come out to India in the army) died suddenly, to his great grief. Richardson was appointed headmaster of Hindu College but then dismissed, possibly owing to religious differences with the evangelicals, who were then in the ascendant in Bengal. Madhusudan Dutt was a student during this time; he declared to his friend that he did not wish to attend classes unless Richardson was reinstated. The students were forbidden to offer a testimonial to Richardson upon his dismissal. See correspondence with Hunt, British Library 38110. For the controversy over Richardson's dismissal, see Mukhopadhyay, *Hindu College,* 56–122.

37. Richardson took this epigraph from Thomas Cowper's "To the Rev. W. Cawthorne Unwin" and used it to introduce his *Sonnets and Miscellaneous Poems* (1822).

38. Sanial ("Captain David Lester Richardson," 74–75) provides evidence from Richardson's students that he emphasized teaching Shakespeare and Pope, varied by Young's *Night Thoughts* and either *Paradise Lost* or *Childe Harold's Pilgrimage.* But he greatly admired Wordsworth, who was important to the informal curriculum. See discussion of Madhusudan Dutt in chapter 4.

Chapter 4: Sighing, or Not, for Albion

1. Quoted in Sanial, "Captain David Lester Richardson," 75.

2. Chaudhuri is the best interpreter of Ghosh's work, though I would disagree that his poetry, except in a limited sense, foreshadowed a "secular consciousness." See Chaudhuri, *Gentlemen Poets.*

3. This account is necessarily schematic. The discourses of feminization became acute in the criticism of Wordsworth by 1812 and widespread thereafter, but the eighteenth-century poetic tradition, even with a patronage poetic economy, already brought with it a highly masculinized critical language. One need only think of Pope's "Epistle to a Lady" or the satirical treatment of Ambrose Phillips's domestic praise of his patron's children; Phillips became the original Namby Pamby, infantilized and feminized through the language of the nursery. See below for the reception of Kasiprasad Ghosh, who was told not to imitate namby-pamby poets. The success of the literary annuals, mostly edited by women, in the late 1820s and 1830s heightened this gendered critical discourse.

4. See Bandyopadhyay, *Samvadpatre Sekaler Katha,* 29–30.

5. Even David Lester Richardson, as we have seen, acting successfully in the colonial capital but unsuccessfully in the metropole, found himself taken in London for a mimic man, a minority, the invisible. On his "home leave" in Britain in the 1840s, he wound up editing a newspaper on the Isle of Jersey, hardly in the thick of things despite all his correspondence promising to puff Leigh Hunt's new book. At home (that is in India), conversely, he created the ultimate disciplinary institution for a poet—the poetic canon. Perhaps one could argue that his poetry would have benefited from an ability to bring more clearly to the text the recognition that he was regarded as a minority in Britain; a larger measure of poetic recalcitrance (as in his rewriting of Wordsworth's Westminster Bridge sonnet) might have served D.L.R. well.

6. Derozio dedicated a poem to Parker, a sonnet in which he praises Parker's "delicious minstrelsy" (*Derozio, Poet of India,* 264). Both Derozio and Kasiprasad dedicated work to Horace Hayman Wilson: Derozio commended his second volume of verse to Wilson, and Kasiprasad dedicated to Wilson another canto of "The Sháïr." Kasiprasad intended Emma Roberts to write his biography, though there is no indication that she ever completed it (see Chaudhuri, *Gentlemen Poets,* 63). Parker, in turn, wrote for Buckingham's newspaper before the latter was deported. See Moitra, *History of Indian Journalism,* 67.

7. The widow, one presumes, is about to undergo the ritual cutting of her hair following her husband's death.

8. While these debts to and revisions of orientalist poetics and bardic nationalism are obvious, the tropes of the poems themselves indicate Ghosh's broader debts to late eighteenth-century and early nineteenth-century British poetry. The volume is prefaced with an epigraph from Byron; a long poem titled "Haunt of the Muses" is prefaced by an epigraph from Akenside's "Pleasures of the Imagination." The title poem has, as Chaudhuri notes, substantial debts to English poetry written in India (*Gentlemen Poets,* 68). I believe it also presents the title character as yet another version of Letitia Landon's doomed poet; the Sháïr, grief-stricken at the loss of his love, ends his life by throwing himself—Sappho- and L.E.L.-like—off a cliff. Here the links both to L.E.L. and to her admirer Derozio are significant.

9. In his biography of the poet in the *Oriental Annual* (1835), Hobart Cauntor speaks of Kasiprasad as being of "Brahminical descent": "his ancestors were distinguished by holding high and responsible appointments under the native rules of Bengal. Since the occupation of this vast province by the British, they have held a rank equally high as private members of their community" (250–51). I think it highly likely, given that Kayasthas are often considered by caste to overlap with Brahmins, that Kasiprasad was educated in Sanskrit before his matriculation at age fourteen at Hindu College. At any rate, his connection to Horace Hayman Wilson over his years at the college argues for his interest in Sanskrit learning, as does his subsequent support of Hindu religious conservatism. See Ahmed, *Social Ideas,* 197.

10. It is important to see that Kasiprasad's claim to "native" knowledge is a claim to a place in a scholarly tradition; if in his notes he performs the role of "native informant," it is only to

establish a kind of pedagogical or scholarly authority. He is thus not only poet but also pandit—categories fundamentally inseparable, in any case, in Sanskrit as opposed to European learning.

11. The footnotes (which are among the paratexts of The Sháïr), like the doubling or trebling of "the poet" in the title poem, have the effect of iterated explanation. Although they are a tic of orientalist poetics, the notes in this volume reframe the European in the Indian context, the Indian in the European context. One of the most extensive footnotes, directly related to "The Sháïr" and its bardic heroes, comes in the lyric titled "The Viná; or the Indian Lute." This poem is dated 1828 and I suspect was originally intended to preface the volume (and perhaps to reprise and revise Derozio's prefatory poems). But it is not a particularly strong poem and instead was printed in the penultimate position in the volume. It does provide, however, a gloss on the bardic claims of "The Sháïr," particularly because it has itself a gloss. The title of the poem is followed by an asterisk directing the reader to a footnote that reads as follows:

> The Viná or Indian Lute is a fretted instrument of the guitar kind, usually having seven wires or strings and a large gourd at each end of the finger board; the extent of the instrument is two octaves; it is supposed to be the invention of NAREDA (the greatest of celestial saints and the son of BRAHMA) and has many varieties, enumerated according to the number of strings, &c *Am. Co.—Mr. Wilson's Sanscrit Dictionary.* Page 841. For a more particular account of this instrument, see Asiatic Researches Vol. 1. Page 295.

The poem, with another kind of iteration, reprises the tropes of bardic nationalism:

> Lute of my country! why doest thou remain
> Unstrung, neglected, desolate, and bound
> With envious Time's and Ignorance's chain?
>
> (185)

Kasiprasad, of course, goes on to predict that the vina, lute, or harp will be revived and become "the joy of bards again," and he begs to number himself among the bards (186).

12. The structure of the poem, with its interpolated lyrics and reference to the harp, may owe a good deal to Landon, in poetic sequences such as "The Golden Violet."

13. The words in brackets were found in a copy of *The Sháïr* in the Michigan State University Library; no provenance for the volume is indicated in it, but the hand clearly is a nineteenth-century one, and the writing suggests that the alterations were made by a friend or perhaps even by the author himself. Although the volume does contain an errata list, it is for the poems only. This suggests that the proof copy of the poetry but not the preface was read by someone assisting the poet; my conjecture, given the dedication and their relationship, is that the reader, if not of this copy at least of the proof pages of poetry, was Horace Hayman Wilson—but this is only conjecture, and the reader might very well have been someone else.

14. Kasiprasad may also owe something to John Keble's famous volume *The Christian Year* and to Reginald Heber's hymns, which were similarly adapted to the liturgical cycle.

15. In the biographical letter he provided to Richardson, which was published in the *Calcutta Literary Gazette,* Kasiprasad speaks of being recommended to read "Carey's Prosody," probably John Carey's *Practical English Prosody* (1827) or perhaps an earlier book on Latin prosody; however, Kasiprasad said that it could not be found in Calcutta. Upon failing to find that work, Kasiprasad noted, "I returned to Murray's Prosody, and Lord Kames's Elements of Criticism from which I derived all my first knowledge of English versification. I then commenced reading the best

poets in a regular and measured tone, which soon accustomed my ears to English rhythm. I then re-wrote my first piece, and showed it again to Mr. Halifax [a teacher at Hindu College], who approved of it" (*Calcutta Literary Gazette,* November 1, 1834, 278). Probably Kasiprasad was referring to Lindley Murray's *Abridgment of Murray's English Grammar, with an Appendix, Containing Exercises in Orthography, in Parsing, in Punctuation, and in Prosody,* published in various editions in the period.

16. Ghose may have been inspired by Byron's versification in "The Destruction of Sennacherib."

17. Chaudhuri quotes the *Athenaeum* and other reviews (*Gentlemen Poets,* 78). See also Richardson, preface to *Bengal Annual* (1833).

18. Anonymous review of Ghosh's *Sháïr, Asiatic Journal and Monthly Register for British and Foreign India, China and Australasia,* n.s. 5, no. 18 (May–August 1831): 105.

19. See Bandyopadhyay, *Samvadpatre Sekaler Katha,* 57, quoting the February 27, 1830, edition of the *Samachar Chandrika.*

20. For orthodox Hindus, to go over the black water, necessarily involved losing caste; even for those with reformist notions, it was often thought right for men returning from abroad to engage in rituals of purification (Murshid, *Heart of a Rebel Poet,* 15).

21. Madhusudan did consider becoming a missionary when he arrived at Bishop's College, particularly after the death of a friend who had intended a missionary career. Madhusudan was the only student not of East Indian or European parentage at the college and one of the few not studying for holy orders; clearly, he never followed through on a missionary or clerical vocation. Given what appears to have been his alcoholism (his biographers do not have a precise sense of the progression of this disease) or at least his rebellious temperament, that he would have been found fit for this vocation is doubtful. So I would attribute his continuing interest in Hebrew on his arrival at Madras to his admiration for Milton and his sense of the poet's role, more than to any intention of pursuing a clerical path. See Murshid's biographical accounts in *Heart of a Rebel Poet* and *Lured by Hope.*

22. See Roessel, *In Byron's Shadow,* 55.

23. Though Madhusudan claimed in a letter to Bysack that he had married a woman of "English parentage," Murshid points out that while her father was certainly British, a gunner in the East India Company's army, her mother, Catherine Dyson, "was born in Nagpur in India and was described as an Indo-Briton in the marriage document" (*Heart of a Rebel Poet,* 62–63).

24. Canto 2, note q in Dutt, *Captive Ladie,* 61.

25. Stewart and Dimock point out in "Kṛttibāsa's Apophatic Critique" that Madhusudan would have been most familiar with Kṛttibāsa's Bengali *Rāmāyaṇa,* not Vālmīki's version, and that Kṛttibāsa's version is quite subversive in comparison, his attitude toward Ram being much less sympathetic than Vālmīki's (243–64).

26. Radice, "Reflections on Clinton B. Seely's Translation."

27. Except where noted, all quotations from Carshore's *Songs of the East* are taken from the first edition, 1855.

28. At this period and throughout the century, officials traveling on business stayed at dak bungalows (designed to serve the postal service) along frequently traveled roads and slept in large tents in other locations. Mrs. V. and her husband evidently stayed in such a tent, and this probably reflects the fact that with several living children Carshore had no room to house official visitors.

Chapter 5: From Christian Piety to Cosmopolitan Nationalisms

1. The date of "An Evening Walk" is somewhat uncertain. I follow here George Smith's suggestion in his *Bishop Heber,* 196.

2. My view of poetic—as opposed to polemical and oratorical—dogmatism is necessarily an overgeneralization, meant to capture the growing importance of evangelical, and especially Calvinist, Christianity by the middle of the century. Heber's poetic fame in the context of Christian missions rests on a poem he wrote before leaving England: "From Greenland's Icy Mountains." The poem (which became a staple missionary hymn) was sung "on the occasion of his preaching a sermon for the Church Missionary Society in April 1820"; the famous first stanza reads thus:

From Greenland's icy mountains,
  From India's coral strand,
Where Afric's sunny fountains
  Roll down their golden sand;
From many an ancient river,
  From many a palmy plain,
They call us to deliver
  Their land from error's chain.

(*Poems*, 139)

3. Govin, Hur, and Greece used these spellings (rather than their given names, Govind, Hari, and Girish) in their English language writing. Toru used the shortened form of Torulata. Here I follow their English language practice.

4. The Dutts' epigraph is taken from Leigh Hunt's "Thought or Two on Reading Pomfret's," which reads, in part,

  I have been reading Pomfret's "Choice" this spring,
A pretty kind of—sort of—kind of thing,
Not much a verse, and poem none at all,
Yet, as they say, extremely natural.
And yet I know not. There's an art in pies,
In raising crusts as well as galleries;
And he's the poet, more or less, who knows
The charm that hallows the least truth from prose,
And dresses it in its mild singing clothes.
Not oaks alone are trees, nor roses flowers;
Much humble wealth makes rich this world of ours.

(*Poetical Works*, 144)

5. The nature of the Dutts' social circle, or at least that of the women, who of course had no professional life, is indicated in Toru Dutt's late letter to Mary Martin, a letter that also indicates how Toru's family thought, even toward the very end of her short life, about emigrating. Of the coming hot weather, Toru wrote, "Everybody seems to be going away from Calcutta; Dr. Cayley is going in April; Dr. Smith is going too; the Rev. Mr. Macdonald is gone, Mr. Clifford is gone, all the Missionaries and their families seem to be going, and last, we too perhaps. If we go to England first, and stay in London or Hastings, or anywhere else, you must come and be the first to welcome us; you will come, will you not?" (March 5, 1877; *Life and Letters*, 272–73).

6. Of course, what can be said in a poem and what can be experienced in life are quite different; Toru Dutt's letters provide ample testimony that Govin and his family delighted in the Bengal countryside, especially their country house at Baugmaree. Harihar Das provides a picture of the house in *Life and Letters* (150), and Toru's letters frequently refer to her happiness there and to her mother's family visiting there as well.

7. Harihar Das indicates that the family was baptized at Christ Church, Cornwallis Square, in 1862 (*Life and Letters,* 10). This was commonly known as the Scottish Church. In 1862, Toru Dutt would have been six years old. Das does not discuss the doctrinal differences of Christian sects.

8. Patrick Brantlinger discusses the coupling of sati and the *rath yatra* at the Jagganath temple as the motifs most common to missionary discourse; the journals of the evangelical clergymen and self-defined missionary Henry Martyn are a fine example, for Martyn confirms his horror at Hinduism by describing both in the opening passages of a journal obviously intended for later publication. See Brantlinger, *Rule of Darkness,* 86; and Sargent, *Memoir of Henry Martyn,* 177, 184.

9. Wine is not typically offered in a puja except in Tantric rituals, in which it functions as one of the five transgressive substances. Milk is a more common offering. Whether the poet alludes to such transgressive offerings or is moving by association to Christian sacrifices is unclear.

10. In addition to historical and economic writing and a history of Bengali literature (1895), Romesh was to publish translations from the *Mahābhārata* (1899) and the *Rāmāyaṇa* (1899).

11. Shoshee Chunder Dutt's "Lays of Ancient Greece" might be read as containing contradictions similar to those in his ballads. In the "Lays" he takes up the position of female speakers to lament the conquest of Troy. The conquering Greeks, then, are spoken against by a voice of double submission—a female, Trojan voice. Whereas Macaulay in *Lays of Ancient Rome* developed an implicit variation on the comparison of the Roman and British empires, Shoshee's poems move the center of emotional gravity from conquerors to conquered. His historical writing makes perfectly clear that, despite his love of things English and his Christianity, he viewed the British tenure of India as a matter of conquest, a conquest not easily maintained and "at all times more or less inexcusable" (*Historical Studies and Recreations,* 143). Although Shoshee views British government as on the whole just—citing its courts, education, social practices, and commitment to good order rather than the "anarchy and confusion" under the Afghans, Mughals, and Marathas—he is under no illusion that the people generally will submit to government by "strangers" without the conviction that those strangers wield superior power. In *Historical Studies and Recreations,* he argues that the entirely misguided and disastrous Afghan wars had reduced Britain's power, reputation, and ability to govern the rest of India:

> The first result of the Afghan war was the contumacy of the Ameers of Scinde, a kind of feudal lords who occupied the lower delta of the Indus. They were easily conquered and their country taken—an arrangement which Sir Charles Napier, who recommended and gave effect to it, could only defend "as a very advantageous, useful, and humane piece of rascality." The next affair was more complicated—namely, the quarrel with the Sikhs. They attacked British territory, and were repelled and their power overthrown,—but after such hard fighting as had not been witnessed in India since the days of Lake and Wellesley. We cannot help stating it, but it is a fact, that this semi-barbarous people fought more heroically for their homesteads than did the French against the Germans in the last war between them.
>
> These victories went a great way in reimpressing on the native mind the invincibility of the British arms. But, as we have said already, that end has not yet been fully attained. The annexation of Oude on the mere pretext of misgovernment was sufficient to lead to the Sepoy War, the Sepoy having imbibed the notion that, if he only resisted as the Afghans did, the English would disappear. The suppression of the revolt has quieted men's minds for the

> time, but it takes a much longer time to re-establish a good name than to lose it, and it cannot yet be said that the English are so much feared in India now as they used to be; and this is the real source of their weakness in the land. (243)

12. Toru Dutt described the family fascination with Milton and recollected that she and her siblings had memorized the first book and part of the second book of *Paradise Lost* (H. Das, *Life and Letters*, 18).

13. Tricia Lootens suggests a resemblance of Shoshee's poem to Elizabeth Barrett Browning's "Dead Pan" (private communication). Barrett Browning evokes the Greek pantheon in much the same way that Shoshee Chunder Dutt evokes the Hindu pantheon—Barrett Browning refuses to lament (even as she does lament) the death of "gods bereavèd, gods belated."

14. Evans and Hooper, *Welshman in India*, 126, 218. Andrew Leslie wrote the memoir of H. E. Page, probably the father of the poet whose work is described in chapter 3; the memoir includes poems by H. E. Page's son and daughter (a not uncommon practice—the memoir of Mary Carshore, preceding the second edition of her poems, likewise includes a poem by Carshore's sister).

15. Mary Leslie's missionary writings include *The Dawn of Light* and *Eastern Blossoms*, the former being a novelist account of the "zenana missions," which were intended to educate (and with luck to convert) Indian women. The American Methodist missionary James Mills Thoburn wrote that Mary Leslie became active with the Methodists at least by 1874–75 and was deeply relieved by the notion that she could experience divine grace in this life (in contrast to Calvinist doctrine). He recorded that she was

> the daughter and granddaughter of a Baptist missionary, a gifted writer and devoted worker in her Master's vineyard. This Baptist Phoebe threw herself heartily into our work, and proved so successful in training new converts that I formally appointed her a class-leader, and in this capacity she rendered us most efficient service. At the close of every quarter she would present one or more probationers as suitable persons for admission into full membership, and always seemed as glad to see them admitted as if they were becoming Baptists. I was well aware that I was doing a very irregular thing in appointing this Baptist lady to fill the position of a Methodist class-leader, but it was one of those acts of audacious irregularity which God seemed in a special manner to approve, and which during the four years that she filled this office, we never had the slightest reason to regret. (*My Missionary Apprenticeship*, 344)

Thus, the spiritual suffering expressed in *Heart Echoes* may have found some resolution in Mary Leslie's move from a Calvinist to an Arminian theology.

16. In an undated letter to Mary Martin, probably written in July 1876, Toru reprises and excerpts at Martin's request the various reviews of *A Sheaf*, and she concludes by saying, "I am adding some more translations to the Sheaf and revising it, in case there should be a second edition; for Mr. Knight, the bookseller, told us the Sheaf was in great demand, and that he had received several orders" (Dutt, *Life and Letters*, 178). How far Toru proceeded on these intentions is unknown, but she clearly at least wished to further a second edition of this project. For more details about Toru's last writings, see H. Das, *Life and Letters*.

17. For Toru's and Clarisse Bader's touching correspondence, see Dutt, *Life and Letters*, 44–50, 353–55.

18. Toru Dutt wrote to Mary Martin, "Have you read any of Mrs. Barrett Browning's pieces. I like her poetry very much. There are some verses of hers called the *Wine of Cypress*,

addressed to H. S. Boyd, who used to teach her Greek. When I am reading Sanskrit, some of these verses occur to me malgré moi. The Sanskrit is as old and as grand a language as the Greek" (March 13, 1876; Dutt, *Life and Letters,* 133). Of Mme. Ackermann, she wrote in the notes to *A Sheaf,* "The scenes of her principal stories are laid in India, and she says in one of her poems,

> L'Inde me plait, non pas que j'aie encore
> De mes yeux vu ce rivage enchanteur ;
> Mais on sait lire, et me'me, sauf erreur,
> On a du lieu de'chiffre' maint auteur.
>
> Ind pleases me, not that I've seen as yet
> With my own eyes, its shores renowned in story,
> But I can read, appreciate, and have met
> Its bards in spirit, with their brows of glory."
>
> (210)

19. Here Govin parted company with his cousin Shoshee Chunder, who showed himself to have a quite conservative view of women's education in *Historical Studies and Recreations* (126–40). Govin, I would argue, could be characterized, if somewhat anachronistically, as a feminist—his daughters would have been among the few women in Britain and virtually the only ones in India of their generation to have access to higher education.

20. The Christian Book and Tract Society published *The Blood of Jesus,* in a Bengali translation by Toru's mother, Kshetramoni. See H. Das, *Life and Letters,* 7.

21. Keats, of course, had lost a brother to tuberculosis by the time he wrote his ode.

22. Lootens and Talookdar both point to the importance of Toru's notes; in particular, Lootens shows how they function in Toru's triangulation of Bengal, Britain, and France. (I am indebted here to Lootens's and Talookdar's sophisticated readings of these notes.) Talookdar argues that Toru's notes constitute a serious work of scholarship, and Lootens concurs. She quotes Talookdar's exclamation, "Shades of Sainte-Beuve, Taine, Arnold, Saintsbury, Gosse! How you must have trembled for the safety of your laurels" (from *Poetry of Toru Dutt,* 10–11); Lootens adds that they might have trembled for the safety of their home ground, for Dutt was after reshaping the mental geography of English language literature in Britain and India (see especially Lootens, "Bengal, Britain, France," 581–82).

23. Here I echo also the fine work of Alpana Sharma, who argues for Toru Dutt as a product of an "in-between position"; Sharma writes that Toru's position is "risk-ridden" and "in-between," a "productive space in the newly emerging international arena of modern textual production and reception" ("In-Between Modernity," 99).

24. See Lootens, "Bengal, Britain, France," 585n19.

25. Toru Dutt wrote to Mary Martin, with tongue firmly in cheek, after quoting from various reviews of *A Sheaf:* "You see I have become quite a public character like L. E. L. or Mrs. Hemans!" (n.d. [probably July 1876]; *Life and Letters,* 178). Her previous letter asked Martin whether she had seen "Hugo's grand speech in the French Assembly for the release of the French communists" (June 29, 1876; *Life and Letters,* 174). Though the poetess was not supposed to be disdainful, nevertheless Toru could have found plenty of that sentiment and a precursor for her own political engagement in the work of Barrett Browning and even in L.E.L.—that is, in the L.E.L. of the sarcastic footnote.

26. Toru Dutt would have been well aware of late eighteenth- and early nineteenth-century republicanism in Bengal, given her essay on Derozio published in the *Bengal Magazine* (December 1874).

27. Sharma, "In-Between Modernity," 106. In this essay, previously published in a briefer version under the name Alpana Sharma Knippling, the author argues persuasively that Toru Dutt was both rejected and claimed on nationalist grounds. Citing various contemporary reviews and more recent criticism, Sharma shows that "if Toru's French-to-English poetry did not find altogether safe harbor on English soil (deemed not English enough), her Sanskrit-to-English verses did not meet with unanimous success in India either (they were not Indian enough). Thus, some felt that the 'plaintive cadence' and 'natural charm' of the original Sanskrit was lost in English" (106).

28. Shoshee Chunder Dutt was Govin's first cousin and thus Toru's first cousin once removed; her letters do not indicate that Govin and Shoshee shared the same closeness as the brothers Govin and Girish did. I use the term *uncle* in the Bengali sense here.

29. See, for example, M. Mukherjee, *Perishable Empire*, 95.

30. See especially Lootens, "Alien Homelands," and Sharma, "In-Between Modernity."

31. Meenakshi Mukherjee and Lootens both note that Toru reads Savitri against the grain, making her agency and her independence central (Lootens, "Bengal, Britain, France"). It may be a bit farfetched also to read Toru's Uma against Tennyson's Lady of the Lake—for here the mystic arm carries not a sword but a flower, and perhaps a flower emblematic of India or Bengal, at least, as the poet conceives it.

32. Lootens makes a similar point in "Alien Homelands": "The title already raises the question 'Who are "we"'?" (300). Here and in the reading of the poem's allusions to Wordsworth, I follow Lootens's very useful argument, though perhaps I grant other contexts of allusion slightly more weight than she does.

33. The seasonal allusions connect, biographically, to the fact that Toru's family spent the hot months (at least March usually through June) at their country house in Baugmaree outside Calcutta, returning to the city during the monsoon when the Baugmaree house became unhealthy, presumably because of damp and mosquitoes. In her letters to Mary Martin, Toru records her delight in snow and Mary's dislike of it. In "Alien Homelands," Lootens remarks on the sudden, and even shocking, appearance of the baboon.

34. Perhaps the casuarina here also exists intertexually with Coleridge's lime tree in "This Lime Tree Bower My Prison," where the landscape becomes more dear to him for the sake of his companion, Charles Lamb.

35. Inderpal Grewal has a fine reading of this passage. She argues that though English education left "some Indians nostalgic for England," in this poem Indian landscape also becomes "an element for nostalgia. Under colonialism, this nostalgia enables a feeling of loss for an Indian landscape and nature that was being appreciated with the Romantic aesthetic. Thus the Casuarina tree can become a reminder of the lost past under colonialism, a reading that explains why this poem has been so popular since it was written and why it became a staple in anthologies of Indian poetry after independence" (*Home and Harem*, 175–76). While I agree strongly with this reading, it is important too to note that Toru continued up until her death to long to travel to England—not for nostalgic reasons so much as for the freedom, intellectual stimulation, and companionship she experienced there—and that Indian readers in part continue to relate strongly to this poem for the same reason that students continue to respond to Keats: genuine pathos brilliantly expressed. It is also quite possible that the poem has since Toru's death accumulated a patina of postcolonial nationalist nostalgia, the leftover formation of colonial nostalgia. For Toru's longing to travel to England, see the letters of 1876 to Mary Martin (Dutt, *Life and Letters*). Lootens's reading of this passage emphasizes also the eeriness of the Wordsworthian original, in which the trees of Borrowdale are so ancient that they are pre-English or, in a manner of speaking, un-English—in their ancient eeriness, they emphasize that

Borrowdale is somehow not quite England; Lootens argues that Baugmaree is for Toru Dutt perhaps analogous to a "more abstract concept of India" ("Alien Homelands," 304). I would argue that the tree/garden is also liminal in being outside of Calcutta society, somewhat distant from the center of British colonial government, and, in its enclosure, in a measure protected from the necessary social tensions occasioned by the Dutts' conversion.

36. Lootens discusses the *fain* rhyme and its connection to English bardic tradition ("Alien Homelands," 305).

Chapter 6: Cosmopolitanism, Nationalism, and Aestheticism in Fin-de-Siècle London

1. This "fictive ethnicity" functions as the overarching concept also gestured toward by Meenakshi Mukherjee in her discussion of Sarojini Naidu, who she argues was pushed to write a poetry asserting a pan-Indian identity.

2. The posthumous reception of Toru Dutt, and the many recountings by later critics of her relationship to her mother's oral storytelling and recitation, makes this point quite literally. Lootens (in "Alien Homelands") and H. Das, for example, both recount this story as told by Edmund Gosse in his preface to Toru's *Ancient Ballads and Legends.*

3. See Binyon, "Introduction," *Songs of Love and Death.*

4. Sarojini Naidu, letter to Arthur Symons, quoted in the introduction to *The Golden Threshold,* 19.

5. Beginning in the early nineteenth century, the various affiliations that came under the Brahmo name espoused, among other ideas, religious rationalism, the education of women, and other reforms. In the wake of Rammohun Roy's intellectual leadership, Brahmo institutions emphasized a vision of Hinduism that most critics recognize as influenced by monotheism and Protestant Christianity, particularly by Unitarian principles. Caste was critiqued, and traditional ritual was to a significant extent deemphasized in favor of a blend of ethical thought based on the Upanishads, the Vedas, and Christianity. Very much in the Enlightenment rationalist tradition, Rammohun took education as central to his mission, and his great respect for and attachment to the view of civil liberties that had developed in the French and American revolutions underpinned a basic Brahmo orientation toward science, modernity, and democracy that lasted well into the twentieth century and had significant impact on nationalist leaders, including Sarojini Naidu.

6. Binyon, "Introduction."

7. Binyon invited into print his cousin, Stephen Phillips, who by then was an actor with a traveling company and aspiring playwright, and his Oxford friend Arthur Cripps. Cripps was later to be revered by the people of Mashonaland (South Africa), to whose land rights and material well-being he dedicated himself, first as an Anglican missionary and then as an independent one.

8. Binyon, "Introduction"; Lotika Ghose reports that Ghose experienced an equal feeling of estrangement in India, for Manmohan reported to Binyon in 1916 that, while nursing his very ill wife, he experienced "utter friendlessness" (quoted in Lotika Ghose, introduction to *Collected Poems,* 3:viii).

9. Ghose's great worry at the time was, in fact, not about leaving his Indian home but that he might have to return to an India that could only be a home in memory or imagination. His preference was to seek London employment in the Civil Service or the British Museum (Hatcher, *Laurence Binyon,* 57).

10. Quoted in Lotika Ghose, introduction to *Collected Poems,* 2:viii.

11. Binyon, "Introduction," xx; see also Gandhi, *Affective Communities,* chapter 6.

12. Review of *Primavera* in *Athenaeum,* June 11, 1890, 796.

13. Wilde, review of *Primavera* in *Pall Mall Gazette,* May 24, 1890, 546; reprinted in Wilde, *Reviews.*

14. Leela Gandhi reads Wilde's response within the parameters of her discussion of affiliation, or "affective community," and sees Ghose and Wilde as both closer friends and more united in an anti-imperialist project than I do. She argues that Wilde celebrated "Ghose's estranging aestheticism as a counter to the homogenizing violence of empire" (*Affective Communities,* 170). Though I share her broader view that imperial/colonial relations need to be reconceived, in the place of Wilde's rather more ambiguous position, I would put Binyon's efforts to support his friend's poetry—both in its production and in its publication.

15. The paradox of not owning one's own language, of not having one's "own" language, is the central concern in Derrida's *Monolingualism of the Other.*

16. It is probable that Binyon also facilitated Ghose's acquaintance with members of the Rhymers' Club, including Lionel Johnson, whom Binyon knew at Oxford (Hatcher, *Laurence Binyon,* 23).

17. In a letter from Ernest Dowson to Victor Plarr, Dowson lists Ghose as a probable but not yet definite contributor to the first *Book of the Rhymers' Club.* He asterisks Ghose's name along with those of several others who have not yet definitely committed and assures Plarr that "the expense will be very small, as it will be distributed amongst all in proportion to the pages given to each; and in view of their number, and the fact that the maximum of space allowed to any Rhymer is 6 pieces: it could not very well be any thing than inconsiderable; profits of course, if any, on the same scale." Quoted in Alford, *Rhymers' Club,* 24.

18. Ghose, *Songs of Love and Death,* 30. In stanza 3, I have substituted *makes* for *takes,* which appears to be a misprint.

19. Selma was the Palace of the Fingallians in James Macpherson's *Poems of Ossian,* and Morven the name of Fingal's kingdom. Arnold thus conflates Ossian, the Celtic, and the Indo-European racial and linguistic roots of English verse. Arnold, *On the Study,* 116.

20. Aravinda (Aurobindo) did write a verse drama on Perseus, however, after his return to India; it was transformed into a play for the Calcutta stage in 1906, about the same time he was engaged in running his political, or "terrorist," cell from the Ghoses' garden house. See Aravamudan, *Guru English,* 97.

21. "Can It Be?" "The Rider on the White Horse," "Lines" ("Ah, why so solemn, Memory?"), and "The Lonely Road" are particularly effective. The latter, for example, ends this way:

> You, of song-birds the sweetest,
>   Filled the thickets with singing,
> And still the sweet notes ringing
>   As every moment back
> Would bring the voice I lack.
>   Sweet notes! of all sounds now
> The mournfullest that thou,
>   Echo, repeatest.
>
> The world to silence hollow
>   Empty of you is grown,
> Since the silver is flown
>   Of your fresh voice. Yet all
> Of you is musical.
>   Is it only fancy's ear

Catches the sound? I hear
  And long to follow.

(Ghose, *Songs of Love and Death,* 104)

22. Mukherjee, in arguing that Gosse's advice to Naidu made her into a "mockingbird," details the late twentieth-century Indian responses to Naidu's poetry, including readings of "The Palanquin Bearers," and discusses such poetry's "reactionary ideology" and problematic language:

> Apart from the obvious fact that Sarojini's poem presupposes the elegance and grace of a nawabi lifestyle, eliding the factor of labour that goes into its maintenance, there is the additional difficulty of making barefoot Indian load-bearers, be they from Bengal or Hyderabad—sing in the cadence of Georgian or Edwardian English. It is worth speculating how much Sarojini's choice of language, and consequently of audience, determined her aesthetic and ideological position, poem after poem conjuring up romantic and colourful moments in a resplendent pageantry, intended presumably to 'introduce' readers like Edmund Gosse to a 'voluptuous and unfamiliar' territory. (*Perishable Empire,* 104)

23. One wonders whether, having invoked Wordsworth at the beginning of this passage, Sarojini was alluding to Wordsworth's description of Chatterton, in "Resolution and Independence": that "marvelous boy / Who perished in his pride" (*Poems,* 1:553).

24. This reading of Sarojini in London accords with Makarand Paranjape's evaluation of her importance in the Indian Nationalist movement years later. Her career, he observes, is an

> intriguing paradox. She was one of those great people whose greatness is most difficult to identify and substantiate. . . . I would attempt to solve the riddle of the greatness of Sarojini by suggesting that she was a minor figure in a major mode. In other words, though whatever she did was not necessarily profound or significant in itself, it was nevertheless performed on a scale which was truly extraordinary and central to the formation of the Indian nation. . . . Her unusual energy contributed to an extraordinary public presence, which was both dynamic and catalytic. (*Selected Poetry and Prose,* 2–3)

25. Beckson, *Arthur Symons: A Life,* 3. Beckson argues that Symons's devout upbringing contributed to his sense of the "double life"; Sarojini's father, like Symons's, seems to have over valued the other-worldly.

26. In the manuscript, Naidu has struck through the word *best* with a single line, betraying a possible tension between England as the "land she loved best" or the land "she loved next to India."

27. Pollock, *Language of the Gods.*

28. Symons's parents were both of old Cornish families. In a letter to Edward Hutton, he wrote that his ancestors dated back to the "William Fitz Simon of Almedroc, who received lands from King John. He died in 1216" (Beckson, *Arthur Symons: A Life,* 4). In a poem on a similar theme, "Bone by Bone," Symons declares,

Bone by bone, blood by blood,
I am a Cornish man,

And by God's throne, by the Holy Rood,
The wild blood that in me ran
Was the blood of my father's and my mother's
And that since the world began.

(Beckson, *Arthur Symons: A Life*, 4)

29. "Alul," in Paranjape, "Introduction," *Sarojini Naidu: Selected Poetry and Prose* (9).

30. See Symons, *Symbolist Movement in Literature*, 6–7.

31. See Thornton and Small, eds., *Book of the Rhymers' Club;* and Symons, preface to *Images of Good and Evil*, n.p.

32. "The Temple" begins with an epigraph, not from Fitzgerald but from Tagore (in English).

33. Meenakshi Mukherjee points out in *The Perishable Empire* (112) that Naidu's *Broken Wing* created something of a scandal on its publication.

34. See also Somjit Dutt, "Foreign Shine and Assumed Gestures," especially the examples from *Gitanjali*, which indicate what was lost in translation.

35. Two decades earlier, Rothenstein had been part of a cosmopolitan group of young artists in Paris and had become a friend or acquaintance of James, Whistler, Sargent, and Wilde, along with Degas, Rodin, and the ailing Verlaine; he was a prominent member of the New English Art Club and an early proponent of the work of Augustus John and William Orpen. See Lago, *Imperfect Encounter;* and Rothenstein, *Men and Memories.*

36. Fry, *The Nation*, June 10, 1911; quoted in Speaight, *William Rothenstein*, 248.

37. According to Mary Lago, "Yeats wrote an effusive introduction that exaggerated Tagore's standing in India, for in fact he was then virtually unknown outside of Bengal. Even there he belonged to a circle of scholarly individuals whom many regarded as rarefied, not to say dangerous, intellectuals. Yeats's impression of Tagore came not only from their meeting at Rothenstein's but from several Bengalis whom he met in London, who were thrilled that their countryman got such English notice and were eager to confirm Yeats's romantic impressions of poet and poems" (*India's Prisoner*, 73).

38. *New York Times Book Review*, March 5, 1916, 76.

39. I have discovered no other volume of contemporary English verse published in Britain with an Indian language title before *Gitanjali*.

40. See Pound, "Rabindranath Tagore." Pound's example of Tagore's precision, however, would have amused a native speaker, for he describes how a friend had been singing and translating a poem in which the word *scarf* might have been used but which, in fact, included a more precise noun; my sense from Pound's description is that the word Tagore had used was *anchal*, which is simply the part of the sari that is draped over one's shoulder—it is as though Pound had lauded, as especially precise, an English poet's use of the word *pocket*.

41. Pound's remarks on Tagore's religion are highly curious as he says the following: "If we take these poems as an expression of Bhuddistic [*sic*] thought, it is quite certain that they will change the prevailing conception of Bhuddism [*sic*] among us. For we usually consider it a sort of ultimate negation, while these poems are full of light. . . . They are far closer in temperament to what we are usually led to call Taoism." The implication is that neither Pound nor the editors of the *Fortnightly Review* could distinguish between Tagore's loose Brahmo spirituality and other forms of "Asian" religions. All Asian religions, one must conclude, are versions of the same. Pound, "Rabindranath Tagore," 571.

42. See the discussion of the textual transmission in S. Das, *English Writings*.

43. Ironically, even as he was unfairly rejecting Tagore, it was Sarojini Naidu, on her extended visit to London, who introduced Pound to Mary Fenellosa and paved the way for

Pound's famous essays on ideogram and his volume *Cathay.* See Hakutani, *Modernity.* Pound's criticism of Tagore lamented his continuing to write in English and particularly referenced the translations of Kabir: "I am glad Tagore hasn't gone to pot personally," he wrote Alice Corbin Henderson on February 9, 1917; "His work has and Yeats says he will no longer stand criticism, and that he has taken to composing in English, which will destroy all the advantage he had in using familiar idiom, and also lead him to only thought that will fit into such English as he knows. The descent from Yeats to Evelyn Underhill, was *facilis,* like the more famous descensus. Poor Rabby." Pound, *Letters,* 186–87.

44. Among those engaging in this innovation as if it were translation were Amy Lowell, Alice Corbin Henderson (Harriet Monroe's coeditor at *Poetry*), John Gould Fletcher, Ezra Pound, and earlier, in France, Judith Gautier's Chinese translations, *Le livre de jade,* Allen Upward's "Scented Leaves—From a Chinese Jar" (which appeared in *Poetry* in 1913), and even Pierre Louÿs' *Les chansons de Bilitis* (presented as translations from the Greek). In *Invisible Fences,* Steven Monte cites several of these examples to argue that primitivism and exoticism, including real and pseudo-translation, were at the basis of *vers libre* and especially prose poem innovations from the 1860s on. See especially chapter 2.

45. In a review of Tagore's *Nationalism* (London: Macmillan and Company, 1917), the reviewer, M. J., argues,

> Sir Rabindranath Tagore is a Chrysostom, and his book, which is chiefly concerned with political theory, is a prose poem. Especially beautiful are the passages describing the secular life of India under her rulers and conquerors. . . . But with these earlier conquerors he has no concern; his book is an arraignment of the Western state organised for power. He causes his readers some discomfort by his peculiar use of the word 'nation' for 'state,' and we have constantly to translate 'nation' by 'state' before it is possible to get at Sir Rabindranath's meaning of the state organised for power. India's most intimate experience is with the British nation, and "as far as government by the nation (i.e. by the organised state) goes, there are reasons to believe that this is one of the best." But the aspect of any one of the western states organised for power is anathema to him, driving as it does its tentacles of machinery deep into the soil; and to him therefore what he calls nationalism is "a crude epidemic of evil." Like Ruskin, he passes judgment upon our commercialism, with its barbarity of ugly ornament, and the standards of value of the western industrial state and its mechanical progress in which "the civilization of humanity has lost its path in the Wilderness of Machinery." "The nation has thriven long upon mutilated humanity. Suddenly, all its mechanism going mad, it has begun the dance of the Furies, shattering its own limbs, scattering them into dust. It is the fifth act of the tragedy of the unreal." He hopes, it would seem, for a Utopia such as Samuel Butler's, where men have destroyed the machine they had made. (*International Journal of Ethics* [28 (1918): 439–40])

46. To make this point clear for English language readers, I quote below three versions of Tagore's famous poem *Ei korech bhalo,* which appeared as poem 91 of Tagore's Bangla volume *Gitanjali;* first I give the transliterated Bangla, which provides a glimpse of the formal qualities of the verse (rhythm and rhyme); second, Tagore's self-translation, which appeared in his volume *Lover's Gift and Crossing;* and third, a literal rendering by Sanjukta Dasgupta.

Ei korech bhalo, nithur
ei korecho bhalo
emni kore hridoye mor
tibro dahan jalo
amar e dhoop na porale
gondho kichui nahi dhale
amar e deep na jalale
jakhan thakey achetane
e chitto amar
aghat se je parash tabo
sei to purashkar
andhakare mohe laje
chokhe tomai dekhi na je
bajre tolo agoon korey
ama jato kalo

(transliteration of poem 91 of Tagore's original *Gitanjali*)

> Thou hast done well, my lover, thou hast done well to send me thy fire of pain.
> For my incense never yields its perfume till it burns, and my lamp is blind till it is lighted.
> When my mind is numb its torpor must be stricken by thy love's lightning; and the very darkness that blots my world burns like a torch when set afire by thy thunder.
>
> (poem 6, *Lover's Gift and Crossing*, 84)

> This is the best, o cruel one; this is the best you've done. Carry on. Ignite an intense agony in my heart. If my incense hadn't burnt, there would have been no fragrance. If my lamp had not been lit, there would have been no light. When my soul is in oblivion, pain is like an awakening touch from you. That's my prayer. In the darkness of illusion and shame, my eyes are unable to see you. Ignite with lightning all that is dark in me. (literal translation of poem 91 from Tagore's Bangla volume, *Gitanjali*, by Sanjukta Dasgupta)

Obviously, the meaning of the last lines was lost in translation, as were the complex aural effects of the original. Many sung versions of this poem are readily available, and they also provide a useful counterpoint to the poet's self-translation.

47. This judgment is echoed by biographers and critics. As S. K. Das observes in his introduction to Tagore's *English Writings*, Tagore's poems, for the most part, by the 1990s had still not found the translations they deserve; I would argue that this is partly because he had become both the revered teacher, as Gandhi called him, and a Bengali cultural icon. Even now, we have the "mystical" Tagore but not the satirical Tagore translated into English. The notion that translations need "authorization," implicit or explicit, has been a barrier as well to fine translation—perhaps the expiration of copyright is allowing younger translators to have a fresh look at Tagore's poems and songs.

48. The text of a lecture, "Tagore's Gifts to English" (sponsored by the English-Speaking Union and the Royal Commonwealth Society), by William Radice can be found at http://www.williamradice.com/, under "Recent Events," March 22, 2006.

Epilogue

1. As Krishna Dutta and Andrew Robinson describe the writing of *Mānasī*, Tagore

> went to Ghazipur, famed for its roses, and here he lived the poetic life, shut in with flowery thickets. Here he wrote most of *Manasi*, the book with which his genius definitely attains maturity, both in power over rhythm and thought. The verse is compact. After this, when he searches for form, it is not because he is not form's master. He experiments to enlarge the range of his instrument and not because he fumbles with it within its present range. There are poems in *Manasi—The Mind's Embodiment,* or *Expression*—which explain why the Ghazipur sojourn finished. There is the group of poems which savagely satirise his countrymen, the "rice-eating, milk-drinking tribe of Bengalis." From his rose-bowers, the poet was watching with the angriest scorn the bigotry and brag and variegated folly of the Neo-Hindu movement. One of the poems, *Dharma-Prachdr—Preaching of Religion*—is at once a lofty and generous tribute to a Salvationist missionary who was brutally assaulted, and a scorching arraignment of his assailants. Other poems pour the fiercest contempt on the "Aryan" boasting which arrogated to the Bengalis of the present all the virtues, real and imaginary, of the Indian heroic age, while it left them complacent regarding the cruelties sanctioned by social rules. Other poems, again, make a frontal attack on those social rules, and especially on the abominations of child-marriage of girls. It is no wonder that a poet so militant amid his roses should have soon sallied out from their shelter. *Manasi* shows, too, the virile influence of Browning, who had succeeded Shelley as the chief English influence on the poet. (*Rabindranath Tagore,* 19)

2. Kipling's still earlier poems, his schoolboy verses, were published without his permission by his parents, at least according to the recollection of his sister, who claimed that Kipling knew nothing of these publication plans and was much put out (see Rutherford, *Early Verse,* 11).

3. Quiz appended a note here: "Every one knows about the annual distribution of gold medals, and *thousands* of rupees, at Calcutta *college*!!! while the distributor, and, of course, *judge,* cannot understand a syllable that is *said;* but concludes, that the youth who *talks most* is most learned."

4. Toru Dutt commended Aliph Cheem's (that is, Walter Yeldham's) satires to her friend Mary Martin: "Have you seen a book of verses titled Lays of Ind by Aliph Cheem? It is rather an amusing collection of vers de societé, chiefly on Indian subjects. The writer is an officer of the 18th Hussars and shows considerable talent. Papa was much amused with the book" (November 13, 1876; *Life and Letters,* 238).

5. Roy, *Nationalism as Poetic Discourse,* 90.

6. Manu is the putative author of the first *Dharma Śāstras,* legal texts of classical India. (S.)

7. Veda Vyāsa was the ancient seer reputedly responsible for writing the *Mahābhārata* and all of the *purāṇas.* (S.)

8. Giuseppe Garibaldi (1807–82), known as the "Hero of Two Worlds," was, as a member of the Carabinieri, an Italian military and political figure. Eventually exiled to Uruguay, he fought in the civil war there, only to return to Italy as commander in the conflicts of the Risorgimento. (S.) Mazzini (see below) and Garibaldi were heroes for Young Bengal some two generations before Tagore.

9. Giuseppe Mazzini (1805–72), like Garibaldi an Italian political figure and member of the Carabinieri, was instrumental in the creation of the modern Italian state. (S.)

10. The battle of Naseby was the first battle of the English Civil War in 1645, in which Charles I was defeated by Sir Thomas Fairfax and Oliver Cromwell. (S.)

11. The original poem appears in Tagore, *Rabīndra-racanāvalī,* 1:312–15). The translator wrote to me on January 29, 2009:

> It was indeed my pleasure to translate aforementioned poem by Sri Rabindranath Tagore, though he was not yet Sir when it was composed. After reading the poem, you can well see why I felt compelled to translate the work in its entirety, etc., in which I paid special attention to every single word, phrase, idiom, and the general tenor thereof, taking pains to capture some of the curiosities of native speech. In only four places were lines transposed, simply to make the English more readable since Bangla uses a dastardly correlative construction (which thing . . . that thing . . .), which makes for ever-so-tiresome reading in English; in each case the transposition was of but two contiguous lines. As was his wont, Mr. Tagore, most inconveniently for the translator, has established double-entendres by several techniques, some of which were captured in the translation, some of which were not, for instance, the verse in which he sets up the cot to stand guard, the *cauki* (=carpoy) he erects is also the root for *caukidārs* or watchmen, who are notorious for sleeping. Technically the "to stand guard" is implied in his setting up the cot, which a native speaker who was awake would undoubtedly catch. Mr. Cromwell's line in the last stanza presented a special problem to the translator who, at 5:45 a.m. was in no condition to wrestle therewith. However, after a refreshing slumber of some five hours, he has this to say about the line, which reads in transliteration: *āhā, krameyel, tumii amara!,* but which would be pronounced: *āhā, Cromwell, tumi-i awmor.* The current translation, alas, is insufficient to the cause. The additional *ikṣāra* (*i*) at the end of *tumi* is emphatic, which indicates "especially" you, or "only" you; the use of *tumi* for "you" is a familiar term which places the writer, in this case the young man reading the history book, on an even par, exactly the same social station as Mr. Cromwell, *tumi* being used by adults only among the closest of friends and members of family. And of course *amara,* is redolent of the French *amour,* a deliciously felicitous touch to the final stanza. The use of measures throughout presented their own special problems to the translator, but the poet insinuated a deliberate symmetry of quantities, for instance numbers of pages measured in time spent reading measured in the oil consumed, etc., or the ease with which heads were piled up like so many mangoes knocked off the tree, ripe and ready to fall. And in the fifth stanza, the use of "big" was the same word throughout, hence the apparently uninspired translation of *baḍo* (pronounced "*boro*")—the translator is most annoyed with Mr. Tagore for that nasty twist, because to be faithful is to leave the impression that the translator is himself of limited facility. As one might well imagine, the use of *baḍo* is of course a slap at the *bhadralok,* who to the illiterate masses are sometimes referred to as *baḍolok,* though that term *per se* does not find a specific residence in that stanza, but whose absence *ipso facto* renders it all the more powerful, *inter alia, über alles,* and *etc.* It should also be noted that *baḍo* is used intermittently throughout said poem to same effect, though the translator, labor though he might, was unable satisfactorily to incorporate the same word so frequently, violating as it does his sense and sensibility, with many apologies to the reading public. You have rightly surmised the choice of Manu, first translated by Sir William Jones, who can still be found today guarding the right (southern) transom of St. Paul's in London, appropriately toga-clad, holding in his hand that famous tome,

inscribed upon which is the single word "Manu" in the native *nāgari* script. In the final stanza, sago is *sāgu,* rhyming of course with Nānibābu and *grābu,* and which is normally fried into a small pancake accompanied by fish, for which Bengalis especially have a predilection and the English do not; alas no fishes swam through the murky waters of that last stanza, so the allusion to the fish-eating Bang must go unaddressed. The title of the poem, alas, must be left perforce to its own devices.

From this insufficient exposition on the craft of his poetry, we might comfortably conclude that Mr. Tagore was in this particular case one particularly witty poseur.

Yours most sincerely, etc.,

S.

12. I concur with Rutherford's argument that in the later years in India, prose fiction engaged Kipling's "creative talents more deeply and continuously" than poetry (*Rutherford, Early Verse,* 21–22).

13. One wonders whether Kipling's "Certain Maxims" gave Pound (in a peculiar echo) the title "Certain Poems of Kabir," poems for which Tagore was undoubtedly a more important influence; however that may be, clearly Kipling mocks Hāfiz (and griffins) with abandon.

14. As Bart Moore-Gilbert has argued in detail in *Kipling and "Orientalism,"* Kipling's work evidences his acquaintance with Anglo-Indian writing, particularly fiction and comic poetry from the latter part of the century, though Moore-Gilbert also shows the persistence of the tropes of exile in Kipling's fiction.

15. Kipling, *Something of Myself,* 39. Chapter 3, "Seven Years' Hard," begins with an epigraph from Browning's "Fra Lippo Lippi" and provides the epigraph to my epilogue.

16. "In Partibus" was, not surprisingly, omitted from the "Definitive Edition" of Kipling's verse (Doubleday, 1940). It originally appeared in the *Lahore Civil and Military Gazette* in 1889 and was reprinted in *Turnovers from "The Civil and Military Gazette": 1888–90* (Lahore: Civil and Military Gazette Press, 1890), 8:104–5. It was again reprinted in *Abaft the Funnel.* New York: B. W. Dodge, 1909 (213–17). For bibliographical details, see E. W. Martindell, *Bibliography of the Works.*

BIBLIOGRAPHY

Nineteenth-Century Periodicals Consulted

Ackermann's Forget-Me-Not
Amulet
Asiatic Journal and Monthly Register [Parbury's]
Asiatic Mirror
Asiatic Researches
Athenaeum
Baptist Magazine
Belfast Newsletter
Bengal Annual
Bengal Hurkaru
Bengali Press (Samchar Chandrika)
Bengal Magazine
Biblical Annual
Bijou
Botanic Annual
Calcutta Chronicle and General Advertiser
Calcutta Gazette
Calcutta Journal
Calcutta Literary Gazette
Calcutta Morning Post
Calcutta Review
Christmas Box
Comic Offering
Court Journal
Delhi Gazette
Falstaff's Comic Offering
Fisher's Drawing Room Scrap-Book
Friend, The
Friendship's Offering
Government Gazette (Calcutta)
Heath's Picturesque Annual
Hindu Intelligencer
Hood's Comic Annual for 1830
India Gazette
John Bull
Juvenile Forget-Me-Not
Juvenile Keepsake

Keepsake, The
Landscape Annual
Literary Souvenir
Literary Gazette (London)
Literary Gazette (Madras)
Missionary Annual
Oracle
Oriental Annual
Oriental Herald
Orient Pearl
Parbury's Asiatic Journal and Monthly Register
Quarterly Oriental Magazine
Talisman
World, The
Young Lady's Book

Other Works

Adams, Matthew. "Furnishing the Colonial Mind: Book Ownership in British India, 1780–1850." Conference Paper. http://www.ehs.org.uk/ehs/conference2006/Assets/VFAdams.doc.

Addison, George Augustus. *Indian Reminiscences; or, The Bengal Moofussul Miscellany.* London: E. Bull, 1837.

———. *Moofussil Magazine,* nos. 1–6 (1811). British Library Mss. Eur C 268.

———. *Original Familiar Correspondence between Residents in India, Including Sketches of Java.* Edinburgh: W. W. Blackwood, 1846.

Ahmed, A. J. Salahuddin. *Social Ideas and Social Change in Bengal, 1818–1835.* Calcutta: Papyrus, 2003.

Alford, Norman. *The Rhymers' Club: Poets of the Tragic Generation.* New York: St. Martin's Press, 1994.

Anderson, Amanda. *The Powers of Distance: Cosmopolitanism and the Cultivation of Detachment.* Princeton: Princeton University Press, 2001.

Anna Maria [pseud.]. *The Poems of Anna Maria.* Calcutta: Thomson and Ferris, 1793.

Anonymous. *India: A Poem, in Three Cantos, by a Young Civilian of Bengal.* London: Priestley, 1834.

———. *The Oriental Masonic Muse: Containing a Collection of Songs, Odes, Anthems, an Oratorio, Prologues, Epilogues, and Toasts.* 1791. Calcutta: Joseph Cooper, 1891.

Appiah, Anthony. *Cosmopolitanism: Ethics in a World of Strangers.* New York: W. W. Norton, 2006.

Aravamudan, Srinivas. *Guru English: South Asian Religion in a Cosmopolitan Language.* Princeton: Princeton University Press, 2006.

———. *Tropicopolitans: Colonialism and Agency, 1688–1804.* Durham, NC: Duke University Press, 1999.

Archer, Mildred. *Early Views of India: The Picturesque Journeys of Thomas and William Daniell, 1786–1794; The Complete Aquatints.* New York: Thames and Hudson, 1980.

Arnold, David. *The Tropics and the Traveling Gaze: India, Landscape, and Science, 1800–1856.* Culture, Place, and Nature. Seattle: University of Washington Press, 2006.

Arnold, Matthew. *On the Study of Celtic Literature; and On Translating Homer.* London: Macmillan, 1899.

Arts Council of Great Britain. *Indian Paintings and Drawings from Sir William Rothenstein's Collection.* London: Arts Council of Great Britain, 1947.

Atkinson, James. *The City of Palaces, a Fragment; and Other Poems.* Calcutta: Government Gazette Press, 1824.

———. Translator. *The Sháh Námeh* by Firdausī. Oriental Translation Fund 22. London: Oriental Translation Fund of Great Britain and Ireland, 1832.

Bandyopadhyay, Brajendranath, ed. *Samvadpatre Sekaler Katha* [Contemporary Accounts from Newspapers], vol. 1, *1818–1830*. Kolkata: Bangiya Sahity Parisat, 1377 B.E. [1970 C.E.].

Bassnett, Susan, and Harish Trivedi, eds. *Post-Colonial Translation: Theory and Practice.* London: Routledge, 1999.

Bayly, C. A. *Empire and Information: Intelligence Gathering and Social Communication in India, 1780–1879.* Cambridge Studies in Indian History and Society 1. Cambridge: Cambridge University Press, 1996.

———. "The Indian Ecumene: An Indigenous Public Sphere." In *The Book History Reader,* edited by Alistair McCleery and David Finkelstein, 174–88. London: Routledge, 2002.

———. *Indian Society and the Making of the British Empire.* Cambridge: Cambridge University Press, 1987.

Beckson, Karl. *Arthur Symons: A Life.* Oxford, UK: Clarendon Press, 1987.

Benhabib, Seyla. *Another Cosmopolitanism.* Edited by Robert Post. Oxford: Oxford University Press, 2006.

Bhabha, Homi. *The Location of Culture.* London: Routledge, 1994.

———. "Untimely Ends." *Artforum International* 42 (2004): 19–20.

Bhattacharya, Malini, and Anasuya Ghosh, eds. *Romanticism in Bengal, 1881–1922: An Anthology of Articles from Bangla.* Calcutta: Papyrus, 2003.

Bhattacharya, Tithi. *The Sentinels of Culture: Class, Education, and the Colonial Intellectual in Bengal (1848–85).* New Delhi: Oxford University Press, 2005.

———. "A World of Learning: The Material Culture of Education and Class in Nineteenth-Century Bengal." In *Beyond Representation,* edited by Crispin Bates, 177–209. New Delhi: Oxford University Press, 2006.

Binyon, Laurence. *The Burning of the Leaves, and Other Poems.* London: Macmillan, 1944.

———. *Collected Poems of Laurence Binyon.* London: Macmillan, 1931.

———. "The Garden of Criticism." In *Echoes from the Oxford Magazine,* 3rd ed., 88–90. London: Henry Frowde, 1890.

———. Introduction to *Songs of Love and Death,* by Manmohan Ghose. Oxford, UK: Basil Blackwell, 1926.

———. *Koya San: Four Poems from Japan.* London: Red Lion Press, 1932.

———. *Selected Poems.* New York: Macmillan, 1922.

Binyon, Laurence, Arthur Shearly Cripps, Manmohan Ghose, and Stephen Phillips. *Primavera: Poems, by Four Authors.* Oxford, UK: Blackwell, 1890.

Boehmer, Elleke, ed. *Empire Writing: An Anthology of Colonial Literature, 1870–1918.* Oxford: Oxford University Press, 1998.

Bogle, George, Thomas Manning, and Clements Robert Markham. *Narratives of the Mission of George Bogle to Tibet, and of the Journey of Thomas Manning to Lhasa.* Edited by Clements Robert Markham. London: Trübner, 1876.

Booth, Howard J., and Nigel Rigby, eds. *Modernism and Empire.* Manchester: Manchester University Press, 2000.

Brantlinger, Patrick. *Rule of Darkness: British Literature and Imperialism, 1830–1914.* Ithaca, NY: Cornell University Press, 1988.

Breckenridge, Carol Appadurai. *Cosmopolitanism.* Durham, NC: Society for Transnational Cultural Studies by Duke University Press, 2000.

Breckenridge, Carol A., and Peter van der Veer, eds. *Orientalism and the Postcolonial Predicament: Perspectives on South Asia.* Philadelphia: University of Pennsylvania Press, 1993.

Burrage, Henry S. *Baptist Hymn Writers and Their Hymns.* Portland, ME: Brown, Thurston, 1888.

Byron, George Gordon, Lord Byron. *The Complete Poetical Works.* Edited by Jerome McGann and Barry Weller. New York: Oxford University Press, 1980.

Cannon, Garland. Introduction to *The Collected Works of Sir William Jones.* 13 vols. 1807. Edited by Garland Cannon. Facsimile reprint, New York: New York University Press, 1993.

———. *The Life and Mind of Oriental Jones: Sir William Jones, the Father of Modern Linguistics.* Cambridge: Cambridge University Press, 1990.

Cannon, Garland, and Kevin R. Brine, eds. *Objects of Enquiry: The Life, Contributions, and Influences of Sir William Jones, 1746–1794.* New York: New York University Press, 1995.

Carlyle, Thomas. *The Collected Works of Thomas Carlyle.* London: Chapman and Hall, 1858.

Carshore, Mary. *Songs of the East, by Mrs. W. S. Carshore.* Calcutta: D'Rozario and Co., Tank Square, 1855. 2nd ed., Calcutta: Englishman Press, 1871.

Catalogue of an Exhibition of the Collection of Paintings and Drawings of the Late Sir William Rothenstein (1872–1945). Leicester Galleries, London, June [15 to] July [11], 1946. [London]: E. Brown and Phillips, 1946.

Catullus, Gaius Valerius. *Catullus, Tibullus and Pervigilium Veneris.* Translated by Francis Warre Cornish, J. P. Postgate, and J. W. Mackail. The Loeb Classical Library. Cambridge, MA: Harvard University Press, 1962.

Chakrabarty, Dipesh. *Provincializing Europe: Postcolonial Thought and Historical Difference.* Princeton: Princeton University Press, 2000.

Chakravarty, Gautam. *The Indian Mutiny and the British Imagination.* Cambridge: Cambridge University Press, 2005.

Chatterjee, Partha. *The Nation and Its Fragments: Colonial and Postcolonial Histories.* Princeton: Princeton University Press, 1993.

———, ed. *Texts of Power: Emerging Disciplines in Colonial Bengal.* Calcutta: SAMYA, 1996.

Chattopadhyaya, Gautam. *Bengal, Early Nineteenth Century: Selected Documents.* Calcutta: Research India Publications, 1978.

Chaudhery, Sumita Mitra. "William Butler Yeats and Rabindranath Tagore: A Comparative Study." Ph.D. dissertation, University of Michigan, 1973.

Chaudhuri, Rosinka, ed. *Derozio, Poet of India: The Definitive Edition.* New Delhi: Oxford University Press, 2008.

———. *Gentlemen Poets of Colonial Bengal.* Calcutta: Seagull, 2002.

———. "An Ideology of Indianness: The Construction of Colonial/Communal Stereotypes in the Poems of Henry Derozio." *Studies in History,* n.s., 20, no. 2 (2004): 167–87.

Cheek, Pamela. *Sexual Antipodes: Enlightenment, Globalization, and the Placing of Sex.* Palo Alto, CA: Stanford University Press, 2003.

Cook, S. B. *Imperial Affinities: Nineteenth Century Analogies and Exchanges between India and Ireland.* New Delhi: Sage Publications, 1993.

Cousins, James H. "The Poetry of Sarojini Naidu: A Critical Appreciation." *Modern Review* 22 (October 1917): 410–16.

Cowper, William. *The Poems of William Cowper.* London: J. Limbird, 1824.

Dalmia, Vasudha. *The Nationalization of Hindu Traditions: Bhāratendu Hariśchandra and Nineteenth-century Banaras.* New Delhi: Oxford University Press, 1999.

Daniell, Thomas, and William Daniell. *Oriental Scenery: One Hundred and Fifty Views of the Architecture, Antiquities, and Landscape Scenery of Hindoostan.* London: Thomas and William Daniell, 1816.

Daniell, William. *A Voyage Round the North and North-West Coast of Scotland, and the Adjacent Islands: With a Series of Views, Illustrative of Their Character and Most Prominent Features.* London: W. Lewis, 1820.

Darnton, Robert. "Literary Surveillance in the British Raj: The Contradictions of Liberal Imperialism." *Book History* 2 (2005): 133–76.

Das, Harihar. *Life and Letters of Toru Dutt.* Foreword by H. A. L. Fisher. London: Oxford University Press, 1921.

Das, Sisir Kumar, ed. *The English Writings of Rabindranath Tagore,* vol. 1, *Poems.* New Delhi: Sahitya Akademi, 1994.

———. *A History of Indian Literature, 1800–1910: Western Impact: Indian Response.* New Delhi: Sahitya Akademi, 1991.

———. *A History of Indian Literature, 1911–1956: Struggle for Freedom: Triumph and Tragedy.* New Delhi: Sahitya Akademi, 1995.

Das Gupta, Arun Chandra. *The Story of the* Calcutta Gazette. Calcutta: Publication Branch, West Bengal Government Press, 1957.

Datta, Kitty Scoular. "Iskandar, Alexander: Oriental Geography and Romantic Poetry." In *Reorienting Orientalism,* edited by Chandreyee Niyogi, 35–64. New Delhi: Sage, 2006.

De Almeida, Hermione. *Indian Renaissance: British Romantic Art and the Prospect of India.* Burlington, VT: Ashgate, 2005.

Deb Roy, Rama. "Glimpses of the History of Calcutta, 1600–1800." *Annales de Démographie Historique* (1988): 243–57.

Derozio, Henry. *Derozio, Poet of India: The Definitive Edition.* Edited by Rosinka Chaudhuri. New Delhi: Oxford University Press, 2008.

———. *Fakeer of Jungheera, a Metrical Tale; and Other Poems.* Calcutta: Samuel Smith, 1828.

———. *Poems.* Calcutta: Baptist Mission Press, 1827.

———. *Song of the Stormy Petrel: Complete Works of Henry Louis Vivian Derozio.* Edited by Abrilal Mukhopadhya and the Derozio Commemoration Committee. Calcutta: Progressive Publishers, 2001.

Derrida, Jacques. *The Monolingualism of the Other: The Prosthesis of Origin.* Stanford: Stanford University Press, 1998.

———. *Of Hospitality.* Translated by Rachel Bowlby. Palo Alto, CA: Stanford University Press, 2000.

———. *On Cosmopolitanism and Forgiveness.* Translated by Mark Dooley and Michael Hughes; preface by Simon Critchley and Richard Kearney. London: Routledge, 2001.

De Souza, Eunice. *Early Indian Poetry in English: An Anthology, 1829–1947.* New Delhi: Oxford University Press, 2005.

Diehl, Katherine Smith. *Printers and Printing in the East Indies to 1850.* New Rochelle, NY: Aristide D. Carazas, 1988.

Doniger, Wendy. *Hindu Myths: A Sourcebook.* Harmondsworth, UK: Penguin, 1975.

Drew, John. *India and the Romantic Imagination.* Delhi: Oxford University Press, 1987.

Duff, Alexander. *India, and India Missions.* Edinburgh: John Johnstone, 1839.

Duff, James Cuninghame Grant. *A History of the Mahrattas.* London: Oxford University Press, 1921.

Dunn, Theodore Douglas. *The Bengali Book of English Verse.* Calcutta: Longmans, Green, 1918.

———. *Poets of John Company.* Calcutta: Thacker, Spink and Co., 1921.

Dutt, Govin Chunder, Greece [Girish] Chunder Dutt, Hur Chunder Dutt, and Omesh Chunder Dutt. *The Dutt Family Album.* London: Longmans, Green, 1870.

Dutt, Greece [Girish] C. *Cherry Blossoms.* London: T. Fisher Unwin, 1887.

———. *Cherry Stones.* Calcutta: P. S. D'Rozario, 1881.

Dutt [Datta], Michael Madhusudan. *The Captive Ladie (An Indian Tale), in Two Cantos.* Madras: Advertiser Press, 1849.

———. *The Heart of a Rebel Poet: Letters of Michael Madhusudan Dutt.* Edited by Ghulam Murshid. New Delhi: Oxford University Press, 2004.

———. *Madhusūdana racanābalī.* Edited with a biography and introductory essays by Kṣetra Gupta. Calcutta: Sāhitya Saṁsada, 1965.

———. *The Slaying of Meghanada: A Ramayana from Colonial Bengal.* Translated by Clinton B. Seely. New York: Oxford University Press, 2004.

Dutt, Romesh Chunder. *The Literature of Bengal: A Biographical and Critical History from the Earliest Times, Closing with a Review of Intellectual Progress under British Rule in India.* Calcutta: Thacker, Spink and Co., 1895.

———. *Mahabharata: The Epic of Ancient India.* Temple Classics. London: J. M. Dent, 1899.

———. *Ramayana: The Epic of Rama, Prince of India, Condensed into English Verse.* Temple Classics. London: J. M. Dent, 1899.

Dutt, Shoshee Chunder. *Historical Studies and Recreations.* London: Trübner, 1879.

———. *Miscellaneous Verses.* Calcutta: Sanders, Cones, and Co., 1848.

———. *A Vision of Sumeru, and Other Poems.* Calcutta: Thacker, Spink, and Co., 1878.

Dutt, Somjit. "A Foreign Shine and Assumed Gestures: The Ersatz Tagore of the West." *Parabaas.* http://www.parabaas.com/rabindranath/articles/pSomjit1.html.

Dutt, Toru. *Ancient Ballads and Legends of Hindustan.* London: Kegan Paul, Trench and Co., 1882.

———. *Le journal de Mlle. d'Arvers, nouvelle écrite en Français.* Edited by Clarisse Bader. Paris: Didier, 1879.

———. *Life and Letters of Toru Dutt.* Edited by Harihar Das. London: Oxford University Press, 1921.

———. *A Sheaf Gleaned in French Fields.* Bhowanipore: Saptahik Sambad Press, 1876.

———. *Toru Dutt: Collected Prose and Poetry.* Edited by Chandani Lokugé. New Delhi: Oxford University Press, 2006.

———. *Toru Dutt's Bianca; or, The Young Spanish Maiden: The First Novel by an Indian Woman.* Edited by Subhendu Mund. New Delhi: Prachi Prakashan, 2001.

Dutta, Krishna, and Andrew Robinson. Introduction to *Selected Letters of Rabindranath Tagore,* edited by Krishna Dutta and Andrew Robinson. Cambridge: Cambridge University Press, 1997.

———. *Rabindranath Tagore: The Myriad-Minded Man.* New York: St. Martin's Press, 1995.

Elliot, Robert, and Emma Roberts. *Views in India, China, and on the Shores of the Red Sea.* London: H. Fisher, R. Fisher, and P. Jackson, 1835

Elphinstone, Mountstuart, and Edward Byles Cowell. *The History of India: The Hindu and Mahometan Periods.* London: Murray, 1889.

Evans, Thomas, and David Hooper. *A Welshman in India: A Record of the Life of Thomas Evans, Missionary.* London: Clarke, 1908.

Falk, Toby, and Mildred Archer. *Indian Miniatures in the India Office Library.* London: Sotheby Parke Bernet, 1981.

Feldman, Paula R. *British Women Poets of the Romantic Era: An Anthology.* Baltimore, MD: Johns Hopkins University Press, 1997.

Finneran, Richard J., George Mills Harper, and William M. Murphy, eds. *Letters to W. B. Yeats,* vol. 1. New York: Columbia University Press, 1977.

Firdausī. *The Sháh Námeh.* Translated by James Atkinson. Oriental Translation Fund 22. London: Oriental Translation Fund of Great Britain and Ireland, 1832.

Fletcher, Ian, and John Stokes, eds. *The Book of the Rhymers' Club and the Second Book of the Rhymers' Club.* Reprint. New York: Garland Publishing, 1977.

Franklin, Michael J. "Cultural Possession, Imperial Control, and Comparative Religion: The Calcutta Perspectives of Sir William Jones and Nathaniel Brasey Halhed." *Yearbook of English Studies* 32 (2002): 1–18.

———, ed. *Sir William Jones: Selected Poetical and Prose Works.* Cardiff: University of Wales Press, 1995.

Fraser, Robert. *Book History through Postcolonial Eyes: Rewriting the Script.* London: Routledge, 2008.

Gandhi, Leela. *Affective Communities: Anticolonial Thought, Fin-De-Siècle Radicalism and the Politics of Friendship.* Durham, NC: Duke University Press, 2006.

Gay, John. *The Poetical Works of John Gay, Including His Fables, In three volumes, With the life of the author, From the Royal Quarto Edition of 1720,* vol. 1. Edinburgh, 1777. *Eighteenth Century Collections Online.*

Genette, Gérard. *Paratexts: Thresholds of Interpretation.* Foreword by Richard Macksey. Literature, Culture, Theory 20. Cambridge: Cambridge University Press, 1997.

Ghose, Aurobindo. *The Future Poetry.* Pondicherry: Sri Aurobindo Ashram, 1953.

Ghose, Benoy, ed. *Selections from English Periodicals of 19th Century Bengal,* vol. 1, *1815–33—Calcutta Monthly Journal; John Bull; India Gazette; Bengal Hurkaru; Reformer.* Calcutta: Papyrus, 1978.

Ghose, Lotika. Introductions to *Collected Poems of Manmohan Ghose.* Edited by Lotika Ghose. 4 vols. Calcutta: University of Calcutta, 1970.

Ghose, Manmohan. *Collected Poems of Manmohan Ghose.* Edited by Lotika Ghose. 4 vols. Calcutta: University of Calcutta, 1970.

———. *Love-Songs and Elegies.* Elkin Mathews' Shilling Garland no. 9. London: Elkin Mathews, 1898.

———. *Songs of Love and Death.* Oxford, UK: Basil Blackwell, 1926.

Ghose, Manmohan, Laurence Binyon, Arthur Shearly Cripps, and Stephen Phillips. *Primavera: Poems, by Four Authors.* Oxford, UK: Blackwell, 1890.

Ghosh, Anindita. "Identities Made in Print: Literary Bengali and Its 'Others,' c. 1800–1905." In *Beyond Representation,* edited by Crispin Bates, 210–31. New Delhi: Oxford University Press, 2006.

———. *Power in Print: Popular Publishing and the Politics of Language and Culture in a Colonial Society, 1778–1905.* New Delhi: Oxford University Press, 2006.

Ghosh, Durba. *Sex and the Family in Colonial India: The Making of Empire.* Cambridge: Cambridge University Press, 2006.

Ghosh, Kasiprasad. *The Sháïr and Other Poems.* Calcutta: Scott, 1830.

Ghosh, Suresh Chandra. *The Social Condition of the British Community in Bengal, 1757–1800.* Leiden: E. J. Brill, 1970.

Gokak, Vinayak Krishna, ed. *The Golden Treasury of Indo-Anglian Poetry.* New Delhi: Sahitya Akademi, 2001.

Gosse, Edmund. Introduction to *The Bird of Time: Songs of Life, Death and the Spring,* by Sarojini Naidu. New York: John Lane, 1912.

———. Memoir. In *Ancient Ballads and Legends of Hindustan,* by Toru Dutt. London: Kegan Paul, Trench and Co., 1882.

Grant, John. Review of *Literary Leaves, Literary Chit-Chat,* and *Notices of the British Poets. Calcutta Review* 10 (1848): 28, 57.

Grewal, Inderpal. *Home and Harem: Nation, Gender, Empire, and the Cultures of Travel.* Post-Contemporary Interventions. Durham, NC: Duke University Press, 1996.

Hakutani, Yoshinibu. *Modernity in East-West Literary Criticism.* Madison, NJ: Fairleigh Dickinson University Press, 2001.

Halhed, Nathaniel Brassey. *A Grammar of the Bengal Language, 1778.* Menston, UK: Scolar Press, 1969.

Hatcher, John. *Laurence Binyon: Poet, Scholar of East and West.* Oxford, UK: Clarendon Press, 1995.

Hawes, Christopher J. *Poor Relations: The Making of a Eurasian Community in British India, 1773–1833.* Surrey, UK: Curzon Press, 1996.

Heber, Reginald. *Poems.* Hingham, UK: C. and E. B. Gill, 1830.

Horace. *The Odes and Epodes.* Translated by C. E. Bennett. Loeb Classical Library. London: Heinemann, 1939.

Horsford, Sir John. *A Collection of Poems Written in the East Indies, with Miscellaneous Remarks on Real Life, by J.—H.—.* Calcutta: Joseph Cooper, Telegraph Press, 1797.

———. *Poems in Three Parts.* Calcutta: Thomas Hollingbery, Hircarrah Press, 1800.

Horwitz, Henry. "The Disadvantaged in Early Modern Britain." *Historical Journal* 35 (1992): 233–38.

Hugo, Victor. *Les châtiments: L'année terrible.* Paris: E. Flammarion, 1913.

Hunt, Leigh. *The Poetical Works of Leigh Hunt, Containing Many Pieces Now First Collected.* London: Edward Moxon, 1849.

Hurwitz, Harold M. "Ezra Pound and Rabindranath Tagore." *American Literature* 36 (1964): 53–64.

Irigaray, Luce. *This Sex Which Is Not One.* Translated by Catherine Porter with Carolyn Burke. Ithaca, NY: Cornell University Press, 1985.

Jones, Steven E., ed. *The Satiric Eye: Forms of Satire in the Romantic Period.* New York: Palgrave Macmillan, 2003.

Jones, William. *The Collected Works of Sir William Jones.*13 vols. 1807. Edited by Garland Cannon. Facsimile reprint, New York: New York University Press, 1993.

———. *A Discourse on the Institution of a Society for Enquiring into the History, Civil and Natural, the Antiquities, Arts, Sciences, and Literature of Asia, Delivered at Calcutta, January 15th, 1784; A Charge to the Grand Jury at Calcutta, December 4th, 1783; and a Hymn to Camdeo, Translated from the Hindu to Persian, and from the Persian into English.* London: T. Payne and Son, 1784.

———. *The Letters of Sir William Jones.* Edited by Garland Hampton Cannon. Oxford, UK: Clarendon Press, 1970.

———. *Sir William Jones: A Reader.* Edited by Satya S. Pachori; foreword by Rosane Rocher; preface by Peter H. Salus. Delhi: Oxford University Press, 1993.

———. *Sir William Jones: Selected Poetical and Prose Works.* Edited by Michael J. Franklin. Cardiff: University of Wales Press, 1995.

———. *The Works: In Thirteen Volumes.* Edited by John Shore, Lord Teignmouth. London: Stockdale, 1807.

Joshi, Priya. *In Another Country: Colonialism, Culture, and the English Novel in India.* New York: Columbia University Press, 2002.

Kachru, Braj B. *The Indianization of English: The English Language in India.* Delhi: Oxford University Press, 1983.

———. *The Other Tongue: English across Cultures.* Urbana: University of Illinois Press, 1982.

Kālidāsa. *The Mégha Dúta; or, Cloud Messenger: A Poem, in the Sanscrit Language.* Translated by Horace Hayman Wilson. London: Black, Parry, and Co., 1814.

Kapur, Geeta. *When was Modernism: Essays on Contemporary Cultural Practice in India.* New Delhi: Tulika, 2000.

Kaul, Raj Kumar. *Studies in William Jones: An Interpreter of Oriental Literature.* Shimla, Himachal Pradesh: Indian Institute of Advanced Study, 1995.

Kaul, Suvir. *Poems of Nation, Anthems of Empire: English Verse in the Long Eighteenth Century.* Charlottesville: University Press of Virginia, 2000.

Kaye, John. "English Literature in India." *Calcutta Review* 5 (1846): 202–20.

Keble, John. *The Christian Year: Thoughts in Verse for the Sundays and Holydays throughout the Year.* London: Bickers and Son, 1875.

Kejariwal, O. P. *The Asiatic Society of Bengal and the Discovery of India's Past, 1784–1838.* New Delhi: Oxford University Press, 1988.

Khan, Mofakhkhar Hussain. *The Bengali Book: History of Printing and Bookmaking, 1667–1866.* 2 vols. Dhaka, Bangladesh: Bangla Academy, 1999–2001.
King, Bruce. *Modern Indian Poetry in English.* New Delhi: Oxford University Press, 2002.
Kipling, Rudyard. *Abaft the Funnel.* New York: B. W. Dodge, 1909.
———. *Barrack-Room Ballads and Verses.* New York: M. F. Mansfield and Co., 1898.
———. *Departmental Ditties, Barrack-Room Ballads, and Other Verses.* New York: United States Book Company, 1890.
———. *Early Verse by Rudyard Kipling, 1879–1889: Unpublished, Uncollected, and Rarely Collected Poems.* Edited by Andrew Rutherford. Oxford, UK: Clarendon Press, 1986.
———. *Something of Myself.* London: Macmillan, 1937.
[Kipling, Rudyard, Alice MacDonald Kipling, Alice Kipling and John Lockwood Kipling.] *Quartette: The Christmas Annual of the Civil and Military Gazette by Four Anglo-Indian Writers.* Lahore: Civil and Military Gazette, 1885.
Kundu, Kayan, Sakti Bhattacharaya, and Kalyan Sircar. *Rabindranath and the British Press, 1912–1941.* London: Tagore Center, 1990.
Lago, Mary, ed. *Imperfect Encounter: Letters of William Rothenstein and Rabindranath Tagore, 1911–1941.* Cambridge, MA: Harvard University Press, 1972.
———. *India's Prisoner: A Biography of Edward John Thompson, 1886–1946.* Columbia: University of Missouri Press, 2001.
———. "Tagore in Translation: A Case Study in Literary Exchange." *Books Abroad* 46 (1972): 416–21.
Landon, Letitia Elizabeth. *Fisher's Drawing Room Scrap-Book, 1834, with Poetical Illustrations.* London: Fisher, Son, and Jackson, 1834.
Leach, Edmund Ronald, and S. N. Mukherjee. *Elites in South Asia.* Cambridge, UK: Cambridge University Press, 1970.
Ledbetter, Kathryn. "'Begemmed and BeAmuletted': Tennyson and Those 'Vapid' Gift Books." *Victorian Poetry* 32 (1996): 235–45.
Leslie, A. [Andrew]. *Memoirs and Remains of the Late Captain H. E. Page of the Service of the Hon. East Indian Company; and Fort-Adjutant at Monghyr.* 2nd ed. Calcutta: Baptist Mission Press, 1840.
Leslie, Mary E. *A Child of the Day: A Brief Memorial of Mrs. H. C. Mukerji.* Calcutta: Baptist Mission, 1882.
———. *Dawn of Light: A Story of the Zenana Mission.* London: John Snow, 1868.
———. *Eastern Blossoms: Sketches of Native Christian Life in India.* London: John Snow, 1875.
———. *Heart Echoes from the East; or, Sacred Lyrics and Sonnets.* London: James Nisbet, 1861.
———. *Ina, and Other Poems.* Calcutta: W. Newman, 1856.
———. *Sorrows, Aspirations, and Legends from India.* London: John Snow, 1858.
Leyden, John. *Poems and Ballads.* Introduction ["Supplementary Memoir"] by Walter Scott. Kelso, Scotland: J. and J. H. Rutherfurd, 1858.
———. *Scenes of Infancy, Descriptive of Teviotdale.* Edinburgh: J. Ballantyne for T. N. Longman and O. Rees, 1803.
Lokugé, Chandani, ed. *Toru Dutt: Collected Prose and Poetry.* New Delhi: Oxford University Press, 2006.
Lootens, Tricia. "Alien Homelands: Rudyard Kipling, Toru Dutt, and the Poetry of Empire." In *The Fin-de-Siècle Poem,* edited by Joseph Bristow, 285–310. Athens: Ohio University Press, 2005.
———. "Bengal, Britain, France: The Locations and Translations of Toru Dutt." *Victorian Literature and Culture* 34 (2006): 573–90.
Macaulay, Thomas Babington. *Lord Macaulay's Essays and Lays of Ancient Rome.* London: Longmans, Green and Co., 1885.

———. "Minute on Indian Education." In *Selections from Educational Records, Part I (1781–1839)*, 107–17, edited by H. Sharp. Calcutta: Superintendent, Government Printing, 1920.

Madge, Elliot Walter. *Henry Derozio: The Eurasian Poet and Reformer.* Calcutta: Naya Prokas, 1982.

Major, Andrea. *Pious Flames: European Encounters with Satī, 1500–1830.* New Delhi: Oxford University Press, 2006.

Mandell, Laura, ed. *The Poetess Archive.* http://unixgen.muohio.edu/~poetess/index.html.

Marshall, P. J. *Bengal: The British Bridgehead; Eastern India, 1740–1828.* New Cambridge History of India. Cambridge: Cambridge University Press, 1987.

———. "British Society in India under the East India Company." *Modern Asian Studies* 31 (1997): 89–108.

———. "The White Town of Calcutta under the Rule of the East India Company." *Modern Asian Studies* 34 (2000): 307–31.

Martindell, E. W. [Ernest Walter.] *A Bibliography of the Works of Rudyard Kipling (1881–1921).* London: The Bookman's Journal, 1922.

Marx, Edward. *The Idea of a Colony: Cross-Culturalism in Modern Poetry.* Toronto: University of Toronto Press, 2004.

———. "Sarojini Naidu: The Nightingale as Nationalist." *Journal of Commonwealth Literature* 31 (1996): 45–62.

McBratney, John. *Imperial Subjects, Imperial Space: Rudyard Kipling's Fiction of the Native-Born.* Columbus: Ohio State University Press, 2002.

McGann, Jerome J. *The Poetics of Sensibility: A Revolution in Literary Style.* New York: Clarendon Press, 1996.

McGuire, John. *The Making of a Colonial Mind: A Quantitative Study of the Bhadralok in Calcutta, 1857–1885.* Australian National University Monographs on South Asia 10. Canberra: Australian National University Press, 1983.

Mehrotra, Arvind Krishna, ed. *An Illustrated History of Indian Literature in English.* New Delhi: Permanent Black, 2003.

Merry, Robert [Della Crusca], Hannah Cowley, Miles Peter Andrews, Benedict, and Jerningham. *The British Album.* Boston: Belknap and Hall, 1793.

Mitchell, Lisa. "Parallel Languages, Parallel Cultures: Language as a New Foundation for the Reorganisation of Knowledge and Practice in Southern India." *Indian Economic and Social History Review* 42 (2005): 445–67.

Mitchell, W. J. T. "Imperial Landscape." In *Landscape and Power.* Edited by W. J. T. Mitchell, 5–34. 2nd ed. Chicago: University of Chicago Press, 2002.

Mitter, Partha. *Art and Nationalism in Colonial India, 1850–1922: Occidental Orientations.* New York: Cambridge University Press, 1994.

Moitra, Mohit. *A History of Indian Journalism.* Calcutta: National Book Agency, 1969.

Monte, Steven. *Invisible Fences: Prose Poetry as a Genre in French and American Literature.* Lincoln: University of Nebraska Press, 2000.

Moore, Thomas. *The Poetical Works of Thomas Moore.* Edited by Charles Kent. London: G. Routledge, 1883.

Moore-Gilbert, B. J. *Kipling and "Orientalism."* New York: St. Martin's Press, 1986.

Mukherjee, Meenakshi. *The Perishable Empire: Essays on Indian Writing in English.* New Delhi: Oxford University Press, 2000.

Mukherjee, Soumyendra Nathy. *Sir William Jones: A Study in Eighteenth-Century British Attitudes to India.* London: Cambridge University Press, 1968.

Mukhopadhya, Abirlal, and the Derozio Commemoration Committee, eds. *Song of the Stormy Petrel: Complete Works of Henry Louis Vivian Derozio.* Calcutta: Progressive Publishers, 2001.

Mukhopadhyay, Pratap. *Hindu College: Presidency College*. Kolkata: Nivedita Mukhopadhyay, 1993.

Munro, John. "The Poet and the Nightingale: Some Unpublished Letters from Sarojini Naidu to Arthur Symons." *Calcutta Review*, series 4, vol. 1 (1969): 135–46.

Murshid, Ghulam, ed. *The Heart of a Rebel Poet: Letters of Michael Madhusudan Dutt.* New Delhi: Oxford University Press, 2004.

———. *Lured by Hope: A Biography of Michael Madhusudan Dutt.* New Delhi: Oxford University Press, 2003.

Myers-Scotton, Carol. *Contact Linguistics: Bilingual Encounters and Grammatical Outcomes.* Oxford: Oxford University Press, 2002.

Naidu, Sarojini. *The Bird of Time: Songs of Life, Death and the Spring.* Introduction by Edmund Gosse. New York: John Lane; London: William Heinemann, 1912.

———. *The Broken Wing: Songs of Love, Death and Destiny, 1915–1916.* New York: John Lane, 1917.

———. *The Golden Threshold.* Introduction by Arthur Symons. London: W. Heinemann, 1905.

———. *Sarojini Naidu: Selected Letters, 1890s to 1940s.* Edited by Makarand Paranjape. New Delhi: Kali for Women, 1996.

———. *Sarojini Naidu: Selected Poetry and Prose.* Edited by Makarand Paranjape. New Delhi: Indus, 1993.

———. *The Sceptred Flute: Songs of India.* New York: Dodd, Mead, 1928.

———. "Sunalini: A Passage from Her Life." Manuscript. Eur 95. British Library.

Naik, M. K. *Perspectives on Indian Poetry in English.* New Delhi: Abhinav Publications, 1984.

Nair, P. Thankappan. *A History of the Calcutta Press.* Calcutta: Firma KLM, 1987.

Nugent, Maria. *A Journal of the Year 1811 till the Year 1815, Including a Voyage to and Residence in India.* 2 vols. London: T. and W. Boone, 1839.

Oaten, Edward Farley. *A Sketch of Anglo-Indian Literature.* London: Kegan Paul, Trench, Trübner, 1908.

Ogborn, Miles. *Indian Ink: Script and Print in the Making of the English East India Company.* Chicago: University of Chicago Press, 2007.

Ovid. *The Epistles.* Edited and translated by R. Ehwald. http://www.perseus.tufts.edu/cgi-bin/ptext?doc=Perseus%3Atext%3A1999.02.0085.

Page, Henry. *The Land of Poesy.* Calcutta: Baptist Mission Press, 1842.

Paranjape, Makarand. Introduction to *Sarojini Naidu: Selected Letters, 1890s to 1940s.* Edited by Makarand Paranjape. New Delhi: Kali for Women, 1996.

———. Introduction to *Sarojini Naidu: Selected Poetry and Prose.* Edited by Makarand Paranjape. New Delhi: Indus, 1993.

Parker, Henry Meredith. *Bole Ponjis, Containing The Tale of the Buccaneer; A Bottle of Red Ink; The Decline and Fall of Ghosts; and Other Ingredients.* 2 vols. London: W. Thacker, 1851.

———. *The Draught of Immortality and Other Poems: With Cromwell, a Dramatic Sketch.* London: J. M. Richardson, 1827.

———. *Short Sermons on Indian Texts, Concerning the Empire of the Middle Classes.* London: W. Thacker, 1858.

Parthasarathy, Rangaswami. *Journalism in India: From the Earliest Times to the Present Day.* New Delhi: Sterling Publishers, 1989.

Pascoe, Judith. *Romantic Theatricality: Gender, Poetry, and Spectatorship.* Ithaca, NY: Cornell University Press, 1997.

Paterson, John David. *Odes to the Rágas and Other Poems.* Calcutta: 1818.

Phillips, Natalie A. "Claiming Her Own Context(s): Strategic Singularity in the Poetry of Toru Dutt." *Nineteenth-Century Gender Studies* 3, no. 3 (Winter 2007). http://ncgsjournal.com/issue33/Phillips.htm.

Piozzi, Hester Lynch, Bertie Greatheed, Robert Merry, and William Parsons. *The Florence Miscellany.* Florence, Italy: G. Cam, 1785.

Pollock, Sheldon. "Cosmopolitan and Vernacular in History." *Public Culture* 12 (2000): 591–625.

———. *The Language of the Gods in the World of Men: Sanskrit, Culture, and Power in Premodern India.* Berkeley: University of California Press, 2006.

———, ed. *Literary Cultures in History: Reconstructions from South Asia.* Berkeley: University of California Press, 2003.

Pope, Alexander. *The Complete Poetical Works of Pope.* Edited by Henry Walcott Boynton. Boston: Houghton Mifflin, 1931.

Pound, Ezra. *The Cantos of Ezra Pound.* London: Faber, 1987.

———. "Jodindranath Mawhwor's Occupation." *Little Review* (May 1917): 12–18.

———. *Letters of Ezra Pound to Alice Corbin Henderson.* Edited by Ira Nadel. Austin: University of Texas Press, 1993.

———. *Pound/The Little Review: The Letters of Ezra Pound to Margaret Anderson; The Little Review Correspondence.* Edited by Thomas L. Scott and Melvin J. Friedman. New York: New Directions, 1988.

———. "Rabindranath Tagore." *Fortnightly Review* 93 (March 1913): 571–79.

———. "Troubadours: Their Sorts and Conditions." *Quarterly Review* (London) 219 (October 1913): 426–40.

Pound, Ezra, and Kali Mohan Ghose, trans. "Certain Poems of Kabir." *Modern Review* (Calcutta) 13 (June 1913): 611–13.

Powers, Harold. "Illustrated Inventories of Indian Ragamala Painting." *Journal of the American Oriental Society* 100 (1980): 473–93.

Pratt, Mary Louise. *Imperial Eyes: Travel Writing and Transculturation.* London: Routledge, 1992.

Priestman, Martin. *Romantic Atheism: Poetry and Freethought, 1780–1830.* Cambridge: Cambridge University Press, 1999.

Quiz [pseud., William Combe?]. *The Grand Master; or, Adventures of Qui Hi in Hindostan: A Hudibrastic Poem in Eight Cantos by Quiz.* London: Thomas Tegg, 1816.

Radice, William. "Reflections on Clinton B. Seely's Translation of *Meghanad-Badh Kabya.*" *Parabaas.* http://www.parabaas.com/translation/database/reviews/radice_meghanad.html.

———. "Tagore's Gifts to English," text of a lecture to the English Speaking Union. http://www.williamradice.com/.

Ray, Amit. *Negotiating the Modern: Orientalism and Indianness in the Anglophone World.* Literary Criticism and Cultural Theory. New York: Routledge, 2007.

Raychaudhuri, Tapan. *Europe Reconsidered: Perceptions of the West in Nineteenth-Century Bengal.* New Delhi: Oxford University Press, 2002.

Raza, Rosemary Cargill. *In Their Own Words: British Women Writers and India, 1740–1857.* New Delhi: Oxford University Press, 2006.

"Reports of the Examination Questions and Answers of the Students of the Hindu College and the Free Church Institution." *Calcutta Review* 5 (1846): xxiii–l.

Richardson, David Lester. *Literary Chit-Chat, with Miscellaneous Poems and an Appendix of Prose Papers.* London: J. Madden; Calcutta: P. S. D'Rozario, 1848.

———. *Literary Leaves; or, Prose and Verse.* Calcutta: Samuel Smith and Co., 1836.

———. *Literary Recreations; or, Essays, Criticisms and Poems: Chiefly Written in India.* London: W. Thacker and Co., 1852.

———. *Selections from the British Poets from the Time of Chaucer to the Present Day.* Calcutta: Baptist Mission Press, Circular Road, 1840.

———. *Sonnets and Miscellaneous Poems, Partly Written in India.* Vol 4. Cabinet Edition of British Poets. London: Henry G. Bohn, 1851.

Richman, Paula. *Many Rāmāyaṇas: The Diversity of a Narrative Tradition in South Asia.* Berkeley: University of California Press, 1991.

Roberts, Emma. *The East India Voyager; or, Ten Minutes Advice to the Outward Bound.* London: J. Madden, 1839.

———, ed. *A New System of Domestic Cookery.* 66th ed. London: John Murray, 1842.

———. *Notes of an Overland Journey through France and Egypt to Bombay.* London: Wm. H. Allen, 1841.

———. *Oriental Scenes, Dramatic Sketches and Tales.* Calcutta: N. Grant, 1830. 2nd ed. published as *Oriental Scenes, Sketches and Tales.* London: Edward Bull, 1832.

———. *Scenes and Characteristics of Hindostan, with Sketches of Anglo-Indian Society.* 3 vols. 1st ed. London: W. H. Allen, 1835.

Rocher, Rosane. *Orientalism, Poetry, and the Millennium: The Checkered Life of Nathaniel Brassey Halhed, 1751–1830.* Columbia, MO: South Asia Books, 1983.

———. "Sanskrit for Civil Servants, 1806–1818." *Journal of the American Oriental Society* 122 (2002): 381–90.

———. "Weaving Knowledge: Sir William Jones and Indian Pandits." In *Objects of Enquiry: The Life, Contributions, and Influences of Sir William Jones, 1746–1794,* edited by Garland Cannon and Kevin R. Brine, 51–82. New York: New York University Press, 1995.

Rodensky, Lisa, ed. *Decadent Poetry from Wilde to Naidu.* London: Penguin Classics, 2006.

Roessel, David Ernest. *In Byron's Shadow: Modern Greece in the English and American Imagination.* New York: Oxford University Press, 2002.

Rogers, Charles. *The Modern Scottish Minstrel; or, The Songs of Scotland of the Past Century.* 3 vols. Edinburgh: Ballantyne, 1856.

Roselli, John. *Lord William Bentinck: Making of a Liberal Imperialist.* London: Chatto and Windus for Sussex University Press, 1974.

Rothenstein, William. *Men and Memories: Recollections, 1872–1938.* Edited by Mary Lago. Columbia: University of Missouri Press, 1978.

Roy, Anuradha. *Nationalism as Poetic Discourse in Nineteenth Century Bengal.* Calcutta: Papyrus, 2003.

Rutherford, Andrew, ed. *Early Verse by Rudyard Kipling, 1879–1889: Unpublished, Uncollected, and Rarely Collected Poems.* Oxford, UK: Clarendon Press, 1986.

Said, Edward W. *Culture and Imperialism.* New York: Knopf, 1993.

———. *Orientalism.* New York: Pantheon Books, 1978.

———. *The World, the Text, and the Critic.* Cambridge, MA: Harvard University Press, 1983.

Sanial, S. C. "Captain David Lester Richardson." *Calcutta Review* 123 (1906): 70–89.

Sanyal, Ram Copal. *Reminiscences and Anecdotes of Great Men of India, Both Official and Non-official, for the Last One Hundred Years.* Calcutta, 1894.

Sargent, John. *Memoir of the Rev. Henry Martyn, B.D.: Late Fellow of St. John's College, Cambridge, and Chaplain to the Hon. East India Company.* London: J. Hatchard, 1819.

Sarkar, Sumit. *A Critique of Colonial India.* Calcutta: Papyrus, 2000.

———. *Writing Social History.* New Delhi: Oxford University Press, 1999.

Sarma, M. N., and V. A. Shahane, eds. *The Flute and the Drum: Studies in Sarojini Naidu's Poetry and Politics.* Hyderabad, Andhra Pradesh: Osmania University, 1980

Schwab, Raymond. *The Oriental Renaissance: Europe's Rediscovery of India and the East, 1680–1880.* Translated by Gene Patterson-Black and Victor Reinking; foreword by Edward W. Said. New York: Columbia University Press, 1984.

Scott, Walter. *Minstrelsy of the Scottish Border: Consisting of Historical and Romantic Ballads, Collected in the Southern Counties of Scotland; with a Few of Modern Date, Founded upon Local Tradition.* 2 vols. London: James Ballantyne, 1802.

Seely, Clinton B. Introduction to *The Slaying of Meghanada: A Ramayana from Colonial Bengal,* by Michael Madhusudan Dutt, 3–67. Translated by Clinton B. Seely. New York: Oxford University Press, 2004.

Sen, Krishna, and Tapati Gupta, eds. *Colonial and Post Colonial Perspectives: Context Text Intertext.* Kolkata: Dasgupta, 2007.

Sen, Kshiti Mohan. "In Remembrance of Kali Mohan Ghosh." *Visha Bharate Newsletter,* April 1971, 298–300.

Sen, Nabaneeta. "The 'Foreign Reincarnation' of Rabindranath Tagore." *Journal of Asian Studies* 25 (1966): 275–86.

Sen, Sudipta. *Distant Sovereignty: National Imperialism and the Origins of British India.* New York: Routledge, 2002.

Sengupta, Anjali. *Cameos of Twelve European Women in India, 1757–1857.* Calcutta: Ṛddhi-India, 1984.

Sharma, Alpana. "In-Between Modernity: Toru Dutt (1856–1877) from a Postcolonial Perspective." In *Women's Experience of Modernity, 1875–1945,* edited by Ann L. Ardis and Leslie W. Lewis, 97–110. Baltimore, MD: Johns Hopkins University Press, 2003.

Shaw, Graham W. "Printing at Mangalore and Tellicherry by the Basel Mission." *Libri* 27, no. 2 (June 1977): 154–64.

———. *Printing in Calcutta to 1800: A Description and Checklist of Printing in Late 18th-Century Calcutta.* London: Bibliographical Society, 1976.

Sinclair, May. "The 'Gitanjali'; or, Song-Offerings of Rabindranath Tagore." *North American Review* 197 (May 1913): 659–76.

Smith, George. *Bishop Heber, Poet and Chief Missionary to the East, Second Lord Bishop of Calcutta, 1783–1826.* London: J. Murray, 1895.

Smyth, T. W. *Ella, or A Tale of the Waldensian Martyrs; and Other Poems.* Calcutta: Calcutta Schoolbook Society Press, 1843.

Speaight, Robert. *William Rothenstein: The Portrait of an Artist in His Time.* London: Eyre and Spottiswoode, 1962.

Staves, Susan. *Married Women's Separate Property in England, 1660–1833.* Cambridge, MA: Harvard University Press, 1993.

Stewart, Tony K., and Edward C. Dimock. "Kṛttibāsa's Apophatic Critique of Rāma's Kingship." In *Questioning Rāmāyaṇas: A South Asian Tradition,* edited by Paula Richman, 243–64. Berkeley: University of California Press, 2001.

Stubbs, Francis W. *History of the Organization, Equipment, and War Services of the Regiment of Bengal Artillery: Compiled from Published Works, Official Records, and Various Private Sources.* London: Henry S. King and Co., 1877.

Symons, Arthur. *Arthur Symons: Selected Letters, 1880–1935.* Edited by Karl Beckson and John Murchison Munro. Basingstoke, UK: Macmillan, 1989.

———. *Images of Good and Evil, 1899.* Poole, UK: Woodstock Books, 1996.

———. *The Memoirs of Arthur Symons: Life and Art in the 1890s.* Edited by Karl Beckson. University Park: Pennsylvania State University Press, 1977.

———. *Silhouettes, 1896, and London Nights, 1897.* Oxford, UK: Woodstock Books, 1993.

———. *The Symbolist Movement in Literature.* London: W. Heinemann, 1899.

Tagore, Rabindranath. "Baṅga Vīr." In *Mānasī* in *Rabīndra-racanāvalī.* 1:312-15. Dhaka, Bangladesh: Aitihya [registered English name: Oitijjhya], 2004.

———. *The English Writings of Rabindranath Tagore,* vol. 1, *Poems.* Edited by Sisir Kumar Das. New Delhi: Sahitya Akademi, 1994.

———. *Gitanjali (Song Offerings)*. Introduction by W. B. Yeats. London: Macmillan, 1913.
———. *The Home and the World.* Translated by Surendranath Tagore; introduction by Anita Desai. London: Penguin Books, 1985.
———. *The Lover of God.* Translated by Tony K. Stewart and Chase Twichell. Port Townsend, WA: Copper Canyon Press, 2003.
———. *Lover's Gift and Crossing.* London: Macmillan, 1918.
———. *My Reminiscences.* New York: Macmillan, 1917.
———. *Particles, Jottings, Sparks: The Collected Brief Poems of Rabindranath Tagore.* Translated by William Radice. New Delhi: Harper Collins Publishers India, 2000.
———. *Selected Letters of Rabindranath Tagore.* Edited by Krishna Dutta and Andrew Robinson. Cambridge: Cambridge University Press, 1997.
———. *Selected Writing on Literature and Language.* Edited by Sukanta Chaudhuri. New Delhi: Oxford University Press, 2001.
———. *Talks in China.* New Delhi: Rupa, 2002.
Talookdar, Byram. *The Poetry of Toru Dutt.* Bombay: Longmans Green, 1936.
Teignmouth, John Shore. *Memoirs of the Life, Writings, and Correspondence of Sir William Jones.* Edited by Samuel Charles Wilks. London: J. W. Parker, 1835.
Tennyson, Alfred Tennyson. *The Poems of Tennyson.* Edited by Christopher B. Ricks. Berkeley: University of California Press, 1987.
Thoburn, J. M. *My Missionary Apprenticeship.* New York: Phillips and Hunt, 1887.
Thornton, R. K. R., and Ian Small, eds. *The Book of the Rhymers' Club and the Second Book of the Rhymers' Club.* Oxford, UK: Woodstock Books, 1993.
Tod, James. *Annals and Antiquities of Rajasthan, or the Central and Western Rajput States of India, by Lieut. Col. James Tod.* Edited by William Crooke. 3 vols. London: Oxford University Press, 1920.
Topham, Edward, and Della Crusca. *The British Album, Containing the Poems of Della Crusca, [Robert Merry], Anna Matilda, Benedict, the Bard, Etc. . . . Which Were Originally Published under the Title of* The Poetry of the World. Dublin: Bernard Dornin, 1790.
Trench, Richard Chenevix. *Sabbation; Honor Neale; and Other Poems.* London: Edward Moxon, 1838.
Trumpener, Katie. *Bardic Nationalism: The Romantic Novel and the British Empire.* Princeton: Princeton University Press, 1997.
Van Remoortel, M. "The Secret Life of the Della Cruscan Sonnet: William Gifford's Baviad and Maeviad." *Modern Language Review* 102 (2001): 311–25.
Viswanathan, Gauri. *Masks of Conquest: Literary Study and British Rule in India.* New York: Columbia University Press, 1989.
Von Schlegel, August Wilhelm. *Lectures on Dramatic Art and Literature.* Translated and edited by John Black and A. J. W. Morrison. London: G. Bell and Sons, 1886.
Walkowitz, Rebecca L. *Cosmopolitan Style: Modernism beyond the Nation.* New York: Columbia University Press, 2006.
Webster, Tony. "An Early Global Business in a Colonial Context: The Strategies, Management, and Failure of John Palmer and Company of Calcutta, 1780–1830." *Enterprise and Society* 6 (2005): 98–133.
Wilde, Oscar. *Reviews.* London: Methuen, 1908.
Wilkinson, M. *Sketches of Christianity in North India.* London: Seeley, Burnside and Seeley, 1844.
Williams, Patrick. "'Simultaneous Uncontemporaneities': Theorising Modernism and Empire." In *Modernism and Empire.* Edited by Howard J. Booth and Nigel Rigby, 13–38. Manchester, UK: Manchester University Press, 2000.
Wilson, Horace Hayman. *Select Specimens of the Theatre of the Hindus.* Calcutta: V. Holcroft, 1826.
Winford, Donald. *An Introduction to Contact Linguistics.* Malden, MA: Blackwell Publishers, 2003.

Woodfield, Ian. *Music of the Raj: A Social and Economic History of Music in Late Eighteenth-Century Anglo-Indian Society.* New York: Oxford University Press, 2000.

Wordsworth, William. *The Poems.* Edited by John O. Hayden. 2 vols. New Haven, CT: Yale University Press, 1977.

Yeats, W. B. Introduction to Rabindranath Tagore, *Gitanjali (Song Offerings).* London: Macmillan, 1913.

Yule, Henry, A. C. Burnell, and William Crooke. *Hobson-Jobson: A Glossary of Colloquial Anglo-Indian Words and Phrases, and of Kindred Terms, Etymological, Historical, Geographical and Discursive.* Delhi: Munshiram Manoharlal, 1968.

INDEX